Family, Law, and Community

Family, Law, and Community

Supporting the Covenant

MARGARET F. BRINIG

THE UNIVERSITY OF CHICAGO PRESS CHICAGO AND LONDON

MARGARET F. BRINIG is the Fritz Duda Family Chair in Law and Associate Dean for Faculty Research at the University of Notre Dame. She is the author of *From Contract to Covenant: Beyond the Law and Economics of the Family*, as well as more than seventy articles and book chapters.

The University of Chicago Press, Chicago 60637
The University of Chicago Press, Ltd., London

Printed in the United States of America

19 18 17 16 15 14 13 12 11 10   1 2 3 4 5

ISBN-13: 978-0-226-07499-3 (cloth)
ISBN-10: 0-226-07499-4 (cloth)

Library of Congress Cataloging-in-Publication Data

Brinig, Margaret F.
Family, law, and community : supporting the covenant / Margaret F. Brinig.
p. cm.
Includes index.
ISBN-13: 978-0-226-07499-3 (cloth : alk. paper)
ISBN-10: 0-226-07499-4 (cloth : alk. paper) 1. Families—United States. 2. Family policy—United States. 3. Domestic relations—United States. I. Title.
KF505.Z9B755 2010
306.850973—dc22

2009033286

♾ The paper used in this publication meets the minimum requirements of the American National Standard for Information Sciences—Permanence of Paper for Printed Library Materials, ANSI Z39.48-1992.

IN MEMORY OF STEVEN L. NOCK (1950–2008),
COAUTHOR, CONSULTANT EXTRAORDINAIRE, AND FRIEND,
AND WITH GRATITUDE TO HIS WIFE AND PARTNER IN LIFE,
DAPHNE G. SPAIN

Contents

Acknowledgments

My colleagues and friends Nicole Stelle Garnett, Notre Dame Law School, and Don Browning, University of Chicago Divinity School, have my sincere appreciation for reading the whole manuscript (some chapters more than once) and offering terrific suggestions and encouragement.

For having read at least one chapter, I would like to thank Ann Astell, Notre Dame Department of Theology; Claire Huntington, Colorado Law School; Elizabeth Marquardt, Institute for American Values; and Viviana Zelizer, Princeton University Department of Sociology.

The University of Notre Dame Law School granted me a research leave during which I was able to produce the original draft of this book. During the summer of 2006, Steven Nock and I were supported in part by a research grant from the Center for Research on Unlimited Love, now located at Case Western Reserve University. I also thank the University of Iowa and the University of Notre Dame for summer and travel support that led to the publication of many of the underlying pieces.

I also thank again all the editors of and referees for various publications where work has appeared over the last ten years that led me to write this volume. I owe debts as well to my coauthors, who, apart from Steven L. Nock, to whom this book is dedicated, are Douglas W. Allen, Simon Fraser University Department of Economics, and Frank Buckley, George Mason University Law School. This work has been presented in part at numerous workshops, conferences, and classes devoted to law and economics and family law around North America and Europe. I give my thanks to all who read the papers and gave me helpful feedback and who would be too numerous to list here. Any attempt to do so would probably inadvertently leave someone out. The same is true of my students, who consistently let me know when I'm too far off base.

For their able research assistance, especially for tedious data work, I am grateful to Francis Budde, Jaclyn Sexton, and Shanin Wilson from Notre Dame Law School, and Nathan Brandenburg, Jamil Gill, and Nicholas Keppel, then students at the University of Iowa, College of Law. Two wonderful administrative assistants, Andrew T. Mason and Layla Krog, were particularly masterful with the tables and figures. At the University of Iowa, Kati Jumper provided years of cheerful and competent assistance.

I also acknowledge the helpful suggestions of three anonymous referees and the patient and able editorial assistance from David Pervin of the University of Chicago Press.

My love and thanks, for all they teach me and for their willingness to put up with their idiosyncratic and occasionally distracted mother, to Mary, Wendy, Katie, Jill, and especially Brian.

Introduction

On New Year's Eve of 2007, my middle daughter married on a beach on the island of Maui. This occasion would not be noteworthy outside the bride's and groom's groups of acquaintances except, perhaps, for some words the officiating clergyman included at the couple's request. The twenty-some of us who witnessed the ceremony (in dressy clothes and bare feet) vowed to support the new spouses in their marriage. Did our promises or the help we may give over time change the nature of the marriage, as opposed to simply adding participation (and noise) to the ceremony? Will the fact that this was a "destination wedding" only a small number could afford make a difference in the long run? That is, does being surrounded by a large community of family and friends matter? Does it matter who attends? That is, is it important, outside following social convention, to have parents and other kin at one's wedding?

This book will discuss the interplay of norms and families from a number of perspectives. It will tie theoretical and empirical observations to subjects of current law reform as varied as cohabitation, custody, grandparent visitation, payment for household work, and domestic violence. Relevant norms and what is called social capital affect family members' relationships with each other, that is, within the family community. They also govern the way outside communities interact with families, and social capital built within the family influences commercial and public relationships that do not directly involve families at all. Law reform, even from the best of intentions, often misfires because norms and the impact of social capital are not considered.

My book *From Contract to Covenant: Beyond the Law and Economics of the Family* argued that family relationships can be distinguished from commercial contracts in several ways and that these distinguishing features fit more closely with a covenant paradigm than with contract analogies. The three characteristic traits mentioned in the introduction are permanence, unconditional love, and community involvement.

After its brief appearance in the introduction, the idea of community largely disappears from this earlier work except for the discussion of the legal requisites for entry to and exit from families in several chapters. Since completing the book, my writing agenda has substantially focused on the intersection of norms and family law and thus with the community part of the model. Perhaps because of the nature of the subject, I have been working on parts of this project with a family demographer, Steven Nock of the University of Virginia. This project will consequently have a more law and socioeconomics feel than did the first one.

One way I conceive of this book is in terms of types of capital, an economic concept for a produced asset that itself is used to produce wealth. The most obvious of these types is financial or physical capital like tools, noted as one of the factors of production by economists dating from Adam Smith.[1] During the twentieth century, Gary Becker and others of the Chicago School added to this the idea of human capital, mostly education and training, that makes labor more productive in the use of other factors.[2] More recently, social scientists have theorized that social capital, about which much of this book deals, itself enhances human capital.[3] Social capital is described in terms of networks and trust (social relationships) that enhance efficiency by reducing transaction costs. This book will try to make the case for the way social capital is built in and defines families.

The first part of the book, called Norms, Families and Communities, will relate the development of community recognition (trust) to the permanence and unconditional love discussed in *From Contract to Covenant*, which postulates that unconditional love becomes rational only when relationships lose their exchange quality. The first requisite, therefore, is permanence (or at least a long-run time horizon as opposed to a short one). When permanence and unconditional love are both found in relationships, communities trust that they will perform desired functions of promoting intimacy and allowing children to flourish. When trust disappears in marriage, spouses are likely to seek divorce. The spouse filing usually receives custody and with custody continues to have the community's trust. The noncustodial parent loses trust (now in two ways, from both the spouse and the community) and is likely to be depressed and to return to an exchange-based interaction with children. These themes of attaining outside trust and, therefore, normative status because the relationships generate internal trust, one of the manifestations of social capital, will be treated with examples from cohabitation, covenant marriage, interracial relationships (marriage and adoption), and child custody.

The second part of the book, called The Boundaries of Family Communities, deals with family law and the limits of community. How does community "shore up" relationships? What happens if there are too many rights accorded to individual family members? What happens if the family boundaries become more porous? The law and economics paradigms employed in this section will be Michael Heller's "tragedy of the anticommons" as well as Fred McChesney, Jon Macey, and Henry Butler's work on corporate stakeholders. This portion discusses how communities strengthen the family, but how giving people outside the immediate family "stakes" in family decision making weakens the family's ability to function effectively. It further develops the concepts of trust and social capital as applied to family life.

The third part, called Families, Mimetics, and Community, considers the question of whether families in fact are "little commonwealths." In other words, do families (small societies) function like larger communities? Chapter 5 begins with a discussion of what families with children try to maximize, concluding that trust and the ability to love unconditionally are at least as important as wealth accumulation and human capital. The chapter then turns to the ways this social capital is transmitted in families (through imitative behavior, or mimetics), dealing with the old nature/nurture debate and the role of peers. The final substantive chapter takes theories typically used to describe society- or economy-level behavior and applies these to families. Larger societies typically embrace something like "patriotism" or "nationalism" that celebrates membership. "Family name" may resemble nationalism. Members of some families may treat outsiders the same way Americans treat immigrants (if not hostilely, then with suspicion). The equivalent of nationalism in families may typically be a source of stability but may be a problem in "blended" or "reconstituted" families on remarriage or adoption. To the extent that related family members seem dissimilar, or alien, they may be singled out for different treatment. In particular, the chapter will consider whether family violence follows the scapegoating pattern found in real societies like Salem, Massachusetts, or Hitler's Germany, or, perhaps, the more allegorical ones like the prophet Jonah's Nineveh or the mythological Oedipus's Athens. Does the change in spouses' feelings toward each other follow a similar progression? Practically speaking, certain patterns may predict the change in families from unconditional love to the comparisons and jealousy that precede family dysfunction, including not only violence but also dissolution. Assuming these predictive patterns, should legal or other steps be taken to prevent or halt the progression? What about patterns that predict good outcomes, like altruism in children? Topics in this part include marriages in distress, family violence, elder abuse, religion and fertility, and unconditional love.

Each of these parts will have applications to law as well as to social science. The first part's discussion of trust has direct relevance for the design of child custody rules (toward a standard replicating existing parental patterns and away from equal custody preferences) and kinship care, and for a preference for marriage as opposed to cohabitation (and perhaps an argument for civil union recognition). The second part suggests an alternative rationale for doctrines of parental autonomy, including the 2000 *Troxel* decision. With *Elk Grove v. Newdow*, we can explore not only why the federal courts shouldn't be involved in most family disputes but also how the presumption that parents act in their kids' best interests may be rebutted in divorce situations. In several places in the book, we discuss the difficult problems created by the poignant case of a Down syndrome child called *In re Phillip B.* The last chapter deals with mandatory domestic violence arrest policies, the federal Adoption and Safe Families Act, and various divorce reform strategies.

Law and economics scholars generally approach the concepts treated in this volume through their discussions of social norms, primarily using signaling and the self-enforcing mechanism of esteem (from self and others). While this book is generally consistent with this approach and builds upon it, the reader will see some differences. The literature of social norms generally presupposes a market and ideas of exchange, which may not translate well into family relationships. Further, in a very large proportion of families, there will always be children who are third parties affected by whatever adults do. Sometimes, in the language of contract law, children are direct beneficiaries of their parents' agreements, but many times they are important incidental beneficiaries who do not have the power themselves to enforce them. Sometimes, because of the importance of families to society, outsiders will seek to influence family law. For example, when an

Iowa judge allowed a same-sex couple to dissolve their relationship (even though Iowa did not then recognize same-sex marriage or civil union and had legislation saying they did not need to recognize such relationships), a group of third parties, including a state congressman and religious organizations, sought to challenge the judge's act.[4] That is, family decisions have third-party effects not only on children but also on society at large. Children are beneficiaries of what their parents do because they imitate their parents and because of intergenerational transfer (which also occurs, of course, with financial capital and, perhaps, through assortative mating, human capital).

To return to the themes discussed in my earlier book, families differ from other relationships because they are more permanent and because society directly invests in them. There is also a role, as there may not be in commercial relationships, for mediating institutions such as voluntary associations. Religious organizations in particular have always been associated with families and apparently continue to play a big role. Religious schools seem to support better outcomes, especially for those living in the inner city.

PART I

Norms, Families, and Community

CHAPTER ONE

The Relationship between Trust and Community Recognition

This chapter begins the search for the links between family and community and will then move to the roles of trust and norms in human motivation in chapter 2. In particular, I will make the case here for why particular institutions, marriage and legal parenthood, have been accorded special status, and why others that seem factually close—cohabitation, step-parenting, and kinship care—have not. In economic terms, marriage and adoption (or legal parenthood) send strong signals both to the participants in them and to those on the outside looking at them. I will also provide theoretical evidence for maintaining the distinction, except perhaps for special subgroups in the community, and will further describe how the strong societal consensus surrounding these institutions may change and what role laws may play as opposed to social developments.

Legal communities recognize certain family relationships, accord them status, and privilege them above others. Recognizing someone as married or a legal parent, especially a custodial parent, serves as shorthand for automatic ascription of bundles of legal rights and duties as well as access to numerous financial rewards. Understandably, people who are unable to fit into a legal status but who undertake its obligations or pay its costs desire these rights and rewards. Increasingly, people who seem to functionally match marriage or parenthood claim the benefits, if not the obligations and costs as well.

From both a legal and a public policy standpoint, the question is whether maintaining the distinctions and reserving benefits only for those who are married or who are legal parents makes sense. Some Western societies have recently abolished many of the distinctions between marriage and cohabitation (same sex or different sex). Some communities, even within the United States, have advocated much more fluid and less legal roles for parenting (inside and outside marriage). Lawyers ask whether there is a "rational basis" for classifications when such important rights and benefits are at stake. Similarly, policymakers ask whether the laws are punitive, mean spirited, or simply archaic. The initial question is whether there really is something unique about marriage or being a legal parent. Admittedly the inquiry is somewhat circular (and therefore difficult to prove empirically), since in the United States there are currently strong distinctions between married and unmarried, legal parent and not. In the terminology I will use here, our society trusts that spouses and parents will generally fulfill their functions well and much more reliably than the alternative. In other words, we assume that there is a difference between formal and informal relationships and base our norms upon it.

From the Perspective of the Adults Involved, Cohabitation Does Not Equal Marriage

Earlier public reports on cohabitation have focused on the question of whether cohabitation before marriage increases or decreases the divorce rate.[1] Increasingly, however, cohabitation is being proposed not as a testing ground for marriage but as a functional substitute for it. The trend in family law as well as in scholarship in Europe and Canada is to treat married and cohabiting couples similarly, or even identically.[2] In Britain, the Social Attitudes Survey released in January 2008 found that two-thirds of the British felt there was no real difference socially between cohabitation and marriage.[3] In France, the National Institute for Statistics and Economic Studies (INSEE) reported that in 2007, more than 50% of French births occurred outside marriage.[4] In the United States, the American Law Institute (ALI) recently proposed that, at least when it comes to the law of dissolution, couples who have been living together for a substantial period of time should be treated the same as married couples.[5] The ALI recommendations particularly carry intellectual weight, given they are the product of ten years of study by one of the most influential, and mainstream, voices on legal reform.

These legal and intellectual trends no doubt reflect in part the increasing prevalence of cohabiting couples, including those with children. The best evidence (from the 2000 Census) indicates that 41.3% of opposite-sex cohabiting couples have a biological or unrelated child under 18 living with them, not much lower than the 45.6% of married couples who do.[6] Births to cohabiting women in the United States now account for 40% of all births to unmarried women.[7]

Law and public policy could actively support any movement toward cohabitation by removing barriers to it. These might include laws against fornication,[8] sodomy,[9] or cohabitation[10] and proscribing remaining legal differences in children's treatment based on their parent's marital state.[11]

Courts and legislatures in some jurisdictions have taken more affirmative actions to institutionalize and support cohabitation, including establishing legal principles of "nondiscrimination" between married and cohabiting couples and equalizing government benefits for formal and informal unions.[12] Government could remove barriers to cohabitation for single mothers such as "man-in-the-house" welfare rules.[13]

As mentioned in the introduction, the most radical view, espoused by some academics, would abolish marriage as a legal institution (although it could, of course, remain a religious practice).[14] In this view, the law should treat all family forms the same. The move toward recognizing same-sex marriage in Massachusetts has created surprising support for this view from some advocates of the traditional legal definition of marriage. Thus, law professors Douglas Kmiec and Mark Scarberry of Pepperdine University recently urged that Massachusetts "temporarily get out of the new marriage business entirely," rather than offer same-sex couples marriage licenses.[15]

The above is rhetoric, or rhetoric translated into policy. We are left with several questions: What does the weight of social science evidence have to say about whether cohabitation is the functional equivalent of marriage? From a law and economics perspective, are there mechanisms through which formal recognition of a relationship as a marriage may boost well-being? What are the likely consequences of blurring the legal distinction between formal and informal unions, as the ALI proposes?

As a preview of what is to come, there seem to be too many problems with cohabitation defined as an alternative to marriage to believe that law and social policy should actively support this emerging family form, though persuasive arguments can be made for regularizing same-sex relationships.[16] However, the weight of social science evidence on marriage and cohabitation suggests that law and public policy might well distinguish between cohabitation as a prelude to marriage (or a courtship strategy) and cohabitation as an alternative to marriage. The evidence points to many fewer problems with the former than the latter.

The fuzzy signal of cohabitation

Modern couples carry many hopes for the informal relationship. When they move in together, they may be holding a number of different expectations (and may differ even between themselves about the meaning of this step). Part of the reason I argue for restraint in supporting cohabiting relationships when marriage is possible stems simply from this lack of individual and social meaning. In economic terms, the signal is a fuzzy one for both the couple and those outside. Because we as a society mean different things by cohabiting, there can be no community support through ritual.[17] Moving itself has no ritual. We may buy pizzas for the friends who help us move, and we are undoubtedly stressed and anxious, but moving residences happens too frequently, particularly for young adults, to be an occasion for ritual. Nor does moving in with a sexual partner constitute a ritual-producing event, because it, too, has many meanings.[18] Thus, as sociologist Steven Nock puts it, "Cohabitation is an incomplete institution. No matter how widespread the practice, nonmarital unions are not yet governed by strong consensual norms or formal laws."[19] Couples may not even see the importance of the step they take in moving in together. One or both members of a cohabiting couple may even cohabit (rather than marry) in order to side step difficult disagreements about the meaning and future of their relationship.

One of the results of all this uncertainty is what economists call dilution of the marriage signal. British economist Robert Rowthorn argues that "marriage is like a professional qualification, whose value as a signal depends crucially on its reputation. . . . Committed couples and society at large have a common interest in discouraging modifications to the marriage contract or forms of behavior that undermine the reputation of marriage."[20] By this, he means that marriage now serves as an important signal that a person is committed. Without knowing more about a person, marriage gives outsiders and particularly government agencies a basis for choosing between two otherwise like couples. This signal or shorthand would disappear, with its associated efficiencies, were marriage to lose its unique screening quality.

The lack of common definition of the term, either culturally or empirically, also makes study of cohabitation difficult. How does one phrase a survey question that would get at the complexity of informal intimate unions (especially since perceptions may change with time even for an individual couple)? Some individuals who live together undoubtedly see cohabitation as an alternative to marriage (perhaps because they cannot marry or do not see the need for marrying or see an overwhelming dark side to the institution of marriage itself). In some couples, one or both partners may see cohabitation as a prelude to marriage. One or both may wish to cohabit simply because it is a convenient way to live until the wedding or because, like the transition from dating to going steady to engagement, living together seems another stage in a deepening relationship.[21] Finally, a person may cohabit to test the relationship: Can I live with this partner without squabbling about cleanliness or sharing household chores?[22] Will we still find each other sexually attractive lounging in threadbare gym clothes? Can we really spend all our leisure time together without being bored with one another?

Revisiting signaling, esteem, and trust

Earlier in this chapter, I indicated that some of the distinctions between marriage and cohabitation or adoption, stepparenting, and foster care might be analyzed in terms of signaling. In fact, substantial law and economics work on the family has used these terms. Eric Posner, in particular, uses a general theory of signaling to explain the powerful influence of social norms.[23] Posner postulates that people dealing with others—whether in terms of purely social relationships or more intimate ones—are looking, in a world of imperfect information, for "good types," people who will cooperate over the long term and who have, as economists put it, low discount rates.[24] When people are willing to marry, they signal that they are excluding others and are willing to make significant investments in the other.[25] Posner also indicates that while society will heavily regulate marriage at its beginning and at its end, social norms will largely govern conduct during the interim,[26] which, in his opinion, will consist of a series of exchanges.[27] If one spouse fails to perform satisfactorily, the other will retaliate or at least note dissatisfaction.

Posner's signaling model has been taken up in the context of antenuptial (or premarital) agreements by Heather Mahar.[28] Mahar surveyed numerous adults in various cities and asked them whether they had asked, or would ask in the future, a spouse to sign an antenuptial agreement, which she defined, leaving out distribution at death, as governing assets upon dissolution. Very few of her subjects (but more law students) indicated they would.[29] When queried about their reasons for not using the strategy, most indicated a mistaken certainty that their marriage would last (which Mahar says leads to an underestimation of the value of the agreement) or worried that it would signal they feared their relationship was likely to end. While Mahar may be right in important ways, an antenuptial agreement may do more than signal uncertainty about marriage. My position is that the contracting regime itself establishes an exchange framework, or series of trades, that is likely to work against a successful marriage.

Robert Ellickson addresses this problem with exchange relationships in his article "Unpacking the Household."[30] Ellickson claims people live with intimates in order to facilitate informal coordination and reduce transaction costs (the costs of making and enforcing contracts). They are apt to rely on consensus, "which signals that participants are intimate and trustworthy" and on their own rules as opposed to those set by the outside.[31] The norms they create are those that arise out of patterns of gift exchange, not contract. Ellickson notes that an intimate relationship cannot succeed if it is based upon a tit-for-tat exchange, and "temporary imbalances of trade are likely to arise,"[32] while each keeps a rough mental account of where things stand.[33] The parties will need to engage in an informal give-and-take for the relationship to prosper over time and therefore, if they trust each other, will be more likely to keep things informal (to reduce costs). "[R]eciprocated acts of cooperation" will themselves "generate pleasure."[34] Unlike contracts, gift exchange can be kept money free, signaling mutual feelings of intimacy and trust and thus enhancing prospects for future cooperative interactions.[35] As Ellickson notes in a footnote,[36] there may be a biological basis for trust and for trusting behavior.[37] In the footnote, Ellickson makes the point that oxytocin, a pleasurable hormone, is released when experimental subjects played in a way that demonstrated trust in the other human player. These findings suggest not only that we are "hardwired" to want to trust but also that trusting behavior is individual based, that is, it fits the rational choice model that characterizes law and economics that will concern us in the next chapter.

This theme of norms fitting models of individual choice is taken up by Richard McAdams, in his paper on the origins and development of norms. McAdams proposes that norms develop because of the desire people "have for respect or prestige, that is, for the relative esteem of others."[38] Law, he claims, can influence norms, because it "expresses normative principles and symbolizes societal values."[39] In other words, it provides what he calls a "focal point" for norm development.[40]

The individual signal one gives can go further than to the other marriage partner, as McAdams's emphasis on the need for publicity of the new norm suggests. For example, entering into a covenant marriage may act as a potent signal of the spouses' belief in God and marriage and intent to serve as a public example of the sanctity of marriage.[41] This might be simply because the couple brings public figures—typically religious leaders—into their marriage. But further, according to a survey, the couples in covenant marriages thought carefully about the signals they were sending, not only to their partners, but also to the wider society. The researchers note, "These couples see their covenant marriage as a public signal that sets them apart from couples who lack a sanctified understanding of commitment to marriage and God." In McAdams's terminology, they can gain elevated esteem (become "heroes") by incurring greater-than-average costs.[42] Thus, norms can come from people in the community one does not even know.

Is Cohabitation the Functional Equivalent of Marriage? Evidence from the Social Sciences

Although I mentioned that collecting evidence on cohabitation is difficult because of its many meanings, we do know some empirical facts about cohabiting couples as a result of research conducted since the mid-1980s. First, there are growing proportions of cohabiting couples, particularly among African Americans and Hispanics.[43] Second, the relationships themselves last a shorter time than marriage, even if there are children.[44] Third, cohabitation followed by marriage (particularly when the couple cohabits without being engaged) leads to less-stable marriages than marriages not preceded by living together.[45] Fourth, cohabiting couples experience a larger incidence of domestic violence than do married couples.[46] The U.S. Justice Department reports that "those who never married became violent crime victims at more than four times the rate of married persons."[47] Compared to married couples of the same duration (i.e., couples who have been together for the same length of time), those in informal (cohabiting) unions are less committed to their partnership (they see fewer costs should the relationship end) and report poorer-quality relationships with one another and with parents.[48]

Scholars debate whether to view such findings as healthy adaptations to the constantly changing institution of marriage[49] or a sign of social decline and growing impermanence in the intimate lives of children and adults.[50] However, there is little disagreement that cohabitation is still an informal union ungoverned by strong cultural beliefs and presumptions. As such, it is not a social institution, but marriage is. In sharp contrast to cohabitation, marriage is surrounded by legal, social, and cultural beliefs about the broad contours of the relationship. This is the defining difference between legal marriage and informal cohabitation.[51] Thus, not only do scholars have difficulty pinning down the meaning of cohabitation, but (often) so do cohabiters themselves.[52] From Posner's signaling standpoint, the signal that one is a "good type" (having a low discount rate) comes from marriage, not cohabitation, perhaps because of this fuzziness.[53]

The cohabiting relationship itself is qualitatively different from marriage. (This may be for some couples exactly what they wanted—an alternative to marriage.) Couples who cohabit, though they may boast of the strength of their love, as an old song tells us,[54] express less interdependence than typical married couples do. The strong health effects seen by married couples—especially by men, though by women too—are not as pronounced.[55] Sex is reportedly not as good, on average.[56] Fathers are less likely to stay involved with their children, or to support them.[57]

While I suspect that many of these undesirable features are not just "selection effects" but (at least in part) come from cohabitation itself, proving this thesis is definitively difficult. To begin with, studies in the United States simply have not collected the right data. Further, causation is difficult to establish empirically.[58] For example, did a particular couple cohabit (and then separate) because they were less dependent on each other, or did the smaller degree of interdependence cause the instability (or both)? Or did the cohabitation produce some other effects that led to unhappiness, but in a case where divorce would have been practical only if the couple were not dependent?

Because the meaning of cohabitation is difficult to establish and the consequences of cohabitation for adults difficult to prove, whether or not the movement toward cohabitation deserves social (and monetary) support has been the subject of considerable debate.[59] Whatever the consequences for adults, however, the effects of a lack of legal status may be felt most keenly by the children of cohabitants.

Any policy dealing with cohabitation will also be affected by wealth effects. That is, though the two groups are converging, cohabitation still occurs much more among the poor and especially people of color. One of the haunting claims of each poor, unmarried mother in Edin and Kefalas's *Promises I Can Keep*[60] is that at least she can guarantee she will love her child, even though she cannot promise to make a lifelong commitment to a mate. The authors write:

> While the poor women we interviewed saw marriage as a luxury, something they aspired to but feared they might never achieve, they judged children to be a necessity, an absolutely essential part of a young women's life, the chief source of identity and meaning.[61]

That love, each young mother says, will be a sustaining gift benefiting both her and the child. "Poor women realize that marriage is fragile, and so they make their primary emotional investments in their relationships with their children, which are not subject to the threats that so often destroy relationships between men and women."[62] Similarly, in work done by sociologists McLanahan and Sandefur to counteract the claim that it was not single parenting that made children's prospects dim but poverty, sociologists have found that many of the bad effects of single parenting "go away" when income is taken into account.[63]

So, is love the answer here for children, is it income, or is it something else? Does a legal marriage even matter, at least insofar as children's welfare is concerned, or will cohabitation suffice?[64] Does it matter for all groups equally, and if some do equally well (or poorly) with or without marriage, should we still support marriage?

Not surprisingly, love, measured in terms of parental warmth, is critically important to children's psychological well-being. The data supporting my position comes from the Child Development Supplement to the University of Michigan's Panel Survey of Income Dynamics (CDS). This sample contains nearly 2,700 children in a nationally representative sample. Love (again, referred to as warmth) continues to remain important both in terms of impact and statistical significance though other variables are added (see figs. 1.1–3; a list of the variables appears in table 1.2). Income, measured in terms of total family income divided by the census needs standard for a family of that size, initially seems important to child well-being (on measures of depression, acting out, self-esteem, and self-efficacy). However, for problem behaviors, income's significance typically entirely disappears once family structure and particularly legal status like marriage and adoption come into play. This is not true for all subgroups

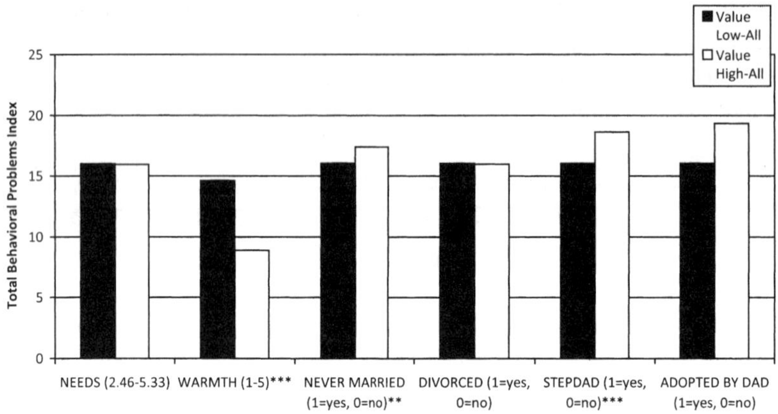

FIGURE 1.1 Total behavior problems. ** $p < .01$; *** $p < .001$. (From Margaret F. Brinig and Steven L. Nock, "Legal Status and Effects on Children." *University of Saint Thomas Law Journal* 5, no. 2, 2008.)

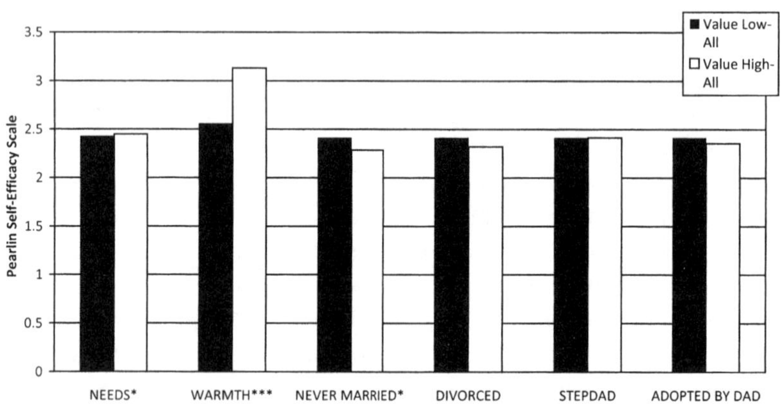

FIGURE 1.2 Self-efficacy. * $p < .05$; *** $p < .001$. (From Margaret F. Brinig and Steven L. Nock, "Legal Status and Effects on Children." *University of Saint Thomas Law Journal* 5, no. 2, 2008.)

FIGURE 1.3 Self-esteem. * $p < .05$; ** $p < .01$; *** $p < .001$. (From Margaret F. Brinig and Steven L. Nock, "Legal Status and Effects on Children." *University of Saint Thomas Law Journal* 5, no. 2, 2008.)

in the sample. For African American children, who make up 14.6% of the children in the CDS sample, income retains its importance and legal status makes little difference. The details of these results are reported elsewhere.[65]

"'Tis better to have loved and lost / Than never to have loved at all," wrote Tennyson,[66] and, from the children's perspective and controlling for other things, it seems better for parents to have married even if the marriage does not work out. Children as a whole do better if they are in two-parent married homes but are worse off in homes where their mothers never married, even in cases where the mother married, divorced, remarried, and was widowed, a tragic set of circumstances that is clearly not stable. Similarly, children do better where their fathers are living in the home but less well with stepparents unless the stepparents adopt them. For the entire group, children who live with relatives (let alone foster parents) do less well than those who are adopted by third parties.

These rather dramatic findings suggest that law and public policy (as an instrument of law) should encourage and support marriage, particularly marriages that last, since divorce does play a negative role as well. They also suggest supporting adoption in preference to foster care and that having a male father figure does not substitute for a child's "real" father. Law can encourage official family relationships in part merely by leaving well enough alone—by *not* adopting domestic partnership laws that equate unmarried, cohabiting couples with those that are married, and by *not* getting rid of special "privileges" enjoyed by the married when academics clamor that such benefits are not fair. Law ought also to make premarriage counseling and skill building more attractive and affordable, as some states have done through lower license costs or subsidizing premarital couples programs. Laws might make some sort of real counseling effort requisite to divorces on no-fault grounds, as the covenant marriage movement suggests.[67] Laws can be written to require mutual consent for divorce or, better, to increase waiting periods on the birth of children, so that the waiting period for no-fault separation divorce lengthens. I will argue later that while marriage by itself may not typically be worthy of lengthy waiting periods before divorce, marriage with children is "real marriage," as C. S. Lewis reportedly put it in the movie *Shadowlands*, which portrayed his life and his two marriages to his wife Joy, one technical and one "in the sight of God and everybody."

The income-is-more-important-than-status idea: The push to delegalize marriage

Much academic argument for eliminating marriage as a status begins with the observation that family forms have changed,[68] or that the married household with minor children no longer comprises even half of American households (see table 1.1). Because the majority of Americans no longer live as married couples with children, it is unfair and "punitive" to privilege marriage, according to these writers.[69] They strenuously argue that this holds true for African American families, who are unfairly singled out, scrutinized, and penalized when neglect or abuse is shown, when, they say, the real problem is poverty.[70]

Martha Fineman reasons that the basic unit of society revolves around dependent people and the derivative dependence of those who care for them. According to her, then, a couple's perhaps fleeting or violence-plagued romantic attachment should not be the basis for assigning lifetime support or the concomitant emotional relationship to a biological parent of the resulting child (or, indirectly, the romantic partner).[71] This obligation should be met by the wider community.[72]

Furthermore, feminist scholars challenge marriage itself as a patriarchal and hierarchical institution.[73] Nancy Polikoff, in her gentler version of the argument, notes that the institution of marriage has not only ancient but also religious roots that should be respected, but as a separate tradition without state involvement. On the other hand, cohabiting couples are much more egalitarian and substantially likely to feature those with similar earnings in the labor force (or in which women earn more than their mates).[74]

Academics claim the real problems for families that become entwined with the public welfare system are poverty and racism, not marriage. Social policy critic Dorothy Roberts notes that while the African American family is critically important, it is not typically a marital family.[75] Similarly, she writes that adoption should not be promoted at the expense of protecting the biological family, including the extended family.[76]

Thus, as noted in the introduction, the idea that differentiated marriage should be confined to religious institutions, that marriage should no longer be a status, and that private relationships should be treated alike by the state, holds sway.[77] The Law Commission of Canada[78] suggested that Canadian "[g]overnments have taken important steps forward in recent years by extending rights and obligations to persons who are living in non-marital relationships, whether same-sex or opposite sex. But this extension of rights and obligations has maintained the legal focus on conjugal relationships. A more principled and comprehensive approach is needed to encompass the full range of Canadians' close personal adult relationships." This report culminated in the extension of full benefits to cohabiting couples (of whatever gender composition) in C-23 and the redefinition of marriage in C-38 (which received royal assent on July 20, 2005, to include same-sex couples).[79]

In this chapter, I am not examining evidence or writing primarily about the very unusual families that figure prominently in the work of scholars such as Robin Wilson[80] or Dorothy Roberts.[81] That is, I am not writing about families where the public welfare system may intervene because of abuse and neglect, subjects addressed in the last chapter of this book. I cannot say much about these children here because they are not in the datasets I analyzed, which were limited to the 95% of children who are living with their mothers (except in the case of two parent adoption). Nothing in the CDS addresses extensive interaction with social services in any event.[82]

A competing idea: The formal family makes a difference

In contrast to suggestions for the decoupling of marriage and its legal effects, I argue here that marriage and legal parenting matter, not only for the adults involved, but also for their children, especially. While I would

TABLE 1.1 **Selected Household and Family Characteristics of Married-Couple and Unmarried-Partner Households, 2000**

Area	Percentage of householders female		Percent of households with children under 18 years							
				Unmarried-partner households						
				Opposite-sex partners		Male partners		Female partners		
	Married-couple households	Opposite-sex unmarried-partner households	Married-couple households	Own children	Own and/or unrelated children	Own children	Own and/or unrelated children	Own children	Own and/or unrelated children
United States	12.9	46.4	45.6	38.9	43.1	21.8	22.3	32.7	34.3
Region									
Northeast	15.4	48.4	45.2	37.4	40.9	21.3	21.7	31.2	32.6
Midwest	11.1	45.8	45.1	38.7	43.9	22.3	22.9	32.8	34.7
South	12.6	46.7	44.4	39.7	44.0	22.1	23.9	34.4	36.1
West	13.4	45.0	48.5	39.2	42.7	20.6	21.1	31.5	33.1
State									
Alabama	11.7	48.2	43.1	41.6	46.1	27.8	28.3	36.8	38.1
Alaska	15.0	43.8	54.4	40.6	45.1	36.2	37.1	37.0	38.6
Arizona	12.7	44.6	43.5	40.5	44.3	22.5	23.0	33.1	35.0
Arkansas	9.9	44.4	41.9	41.8	47.6	26.1	26.7	36.2	38.2
California	14.0	45.3	50.9	41.4	44.4	19.6	20.2	32.8	34.3
Colorado	13.8	45.7	47.2	31.3	34.6	19.9	20.5	26.1	27.8
Connecticut	17.2	50.7	45.4	35.6	38.7	21.9	22.2	30.2	31.6
Delaware	14.5	48.6	42.8	39.9	44.1	18.4	18.9	29.4	31.8
District of Columbia	24.9	56.6	36.6	31.8	32.8	4.8	5.0	23.4	24.5
Florida	14.4	46.5	38.1	35.5	39.2	17.4	17.8	29.3	31.0
Georgia	14.1	48.9	47.3	42.2	46.1	21.1	21.6	34.4	36.2
Hawaii	13.9	45.2	44.8	35.8	39.0	20.7	21.3	30.6	32.6
Idaho	10.0	42.3	47.8	37.6	43.0	30.3	30.8	35.7	37.9
Illinois	11.9	46.2	47.3	38.3	42.5	23.5	24.0	35.6	37.0
Indiana	10.3	44.0	44.4	40.5	47.0	22.8	23.5	33.6	36.3
Iowa	10.0	44.6	43.4	37.5	43.0	24.9	25.4	33.8	35.5
Kansas	10.1	44.8	45.9	39.1	44.1	28.3	29.0	36.5	38.1

Kentucky	11.4	46.1	43.7	40.1	46.0	23.5	24.4	33.0	34.9
Louisiana	12.1	47.7	46.2	44.4	48.5	25.9	26.3	38.5	39.8
Maine	15.1	45.2	41.4	35.7	40.9	18.7	19.0	25.2	27.1
Maryland	15.0	49.5	46.4	38.1	42.1	23.3	24.0	31.7	33.3
Massachusetts	16.6	49.8	45.8	32.8	35.9	18.1	18.6	27.7	29.0
Michigan	11.3	46.9	44.8	40.1	45.3	22.8	23.6	33.2	35.3
Minnesota	11.4	45.7	46.9	35.4	40.2	17.2	17.9	26.8	28.5
Mississippi	12.2	48.9	45.0	49.2	53.4	30.7	31.1	42.0	43.8
Missouri	10.3	45.5	43.6	39.9	45.7	20.9	21.5	31.7	33.7
Montana	11.7	44.0	42.9	35.1	39.3	28.7	29.6	34.2	35.5
Nebraska	9.8	44.6	45.9	36.4	41.5	24.7	25.7	32.7	34.4
Nevada	13.9	41.9	44.5	36.1	40.2	24.7	25.3	35.4	37.5
New Hampshire	15.3	43.7	45.9	33.0	38.1	22.3	22.9	27.2	29.0
New Jersey	14.7	48.0	47.4	38.1	40.9	25.4	25.8	33.6	34.7
New Mexico	12.0	44.2	46.1	48.4	51.7	27.4	27.9	31.0	32.2
New York	17.5	50.1	46.4	39.2	42.2	21.3	21.7	33.1	34.3
North Carolina	12.3	46.1	43.0	38.4	42.9	25.2	25.9	33.3	34.7
North Dakota	8.8	43.0	45.1	36.9	41.5	21.4	21.7	34.4	34.7
Ohio	12.4	46.9	43.6	40.2	45.3	20.9	21.6	31.8	34.0
Oklahoma	10.6	45.1	43.4	42.1	47.2	26.7	27.3	35.0	36.9
Oregon	13.7	45.6	42.8	33.9	38.4	18.9	19.5	26.3	28.1
Pennsylvania	11.6	45.6	42.3	38.5	42.8	20.9	21.3	31.5	33.2
Rhode Island	16.6	50.4	43.6	37.1	40.1	20.5	20.6	27.3	28.6
South Carolina	14.2	47.8	42.6	41.9	45.7	26.8	27.2	37.1	38.8
South Dakota	9.9	44.2	45.2	42.1	47.4	33.2	33.9	41.4	42.3
Tennessee	11.3	46.3	42.5	39.1	44.3	23.9	24.7	33.4	35.4
Texas	11.5	45.2	50.2	42.9	46.8	26.7	27.3	39.2	40.9
Utah	8.9	41.9	55.5	42.2	47.2	29.7	30.2	40.6	42.3
Vermont	16.5	46.2	44.2	33.8	38.3	19.9	20.6	26.7	28.9
Virginia	12.6	46.5	45.3	35.0	39.6	19.8	20.3	31.2	32.7
Washington	13.3	45.9	45.8	35.1	39.7	18.1	18.6	26.7	28.2
West Virginia	9.9	43.7	39.5	40.2	45.6	27.6	27.9	34.9	36.4
Wisconsin	10.5	45.4	44.5	34.9	40.5	21.7	22.4	30.6	32.4
Wyoming	10.9	41.2	44.3	36.0	41.8	28.2	29.9	35.7	37.5
Puerto Rico	14.1	54.4	49.4	56.5	56.7	39.2	39.2	42.2	42.5

Source: U.S. Census Bureau, Census 2000, *Married-Couple and Unmarried-Partner Households:* 2000, *Census* 2000 *Special Reports* (http://www.census.gov/prod/2003pubs/censr-5.pdf). For information on confidentiality protection, nonsampling errors, and definitions, see http://www.census.gov/prod/cen2000/doc/sf1.pdf.

certainly be pleased if childhood poverty could be greatly reduced and if basic living conditions for Americans could be improved, it seems more practical to legally protect and strengthen marriage and the rights and obligations that come with legal parenting. While the effects for the majority of children do not hold true equally for some racial subgroups, I do not believe that these differences (since they do not run counter to what we find for most children) suggest abolition of the status effects for all.

I am convinced that the children ought to do better when parents have legal responsibility for each other and all the other benefits and obligations of marriage. In one sense, this is an extension of a simple economic argument dealing with the permanence of the relationship. People, in this case the parents, are more apt to behave strategically (that is, look out for their own short-term interests) when they know the relationship is about to end. This concept is carefully discussed in Eric Posner's *Law and Social Norms*[83] and in Richard McAdams's "The Origin, Development, and Regulation of Norms."[84] In game theory terms, this is referred to as the "last period problem."[85] When parents know they are in a long-term relationship (lasting "until death do us part" or at least until the age of emancipation), they have incentives to make specific investments in the relationship and in the other party to it. Additionally, though I understand this reasoning is somewhat circular, legal recognition provides a signal for the provision of all kinds of outside support for the family, whether by government, by extended family, or by other affinity groups. With minimal selfish behavior, the great investments and the outside support, families ought to thrive, and these benefits should and do accrue to children as well as adults.

Norms, Biology, and Fatherhood: Stepparents and Cohabiting Partners

We have discussed spouse substitutes and turn now to two fairly common types of father substitutes—stepparents or mothers' cohabiting partners. The strong norms involving husbands and fathers do not reach these other males living in the household. In fact, like the cohabitation discussed earlier, stepparenting provides a case of an "incomplete institution."[86] There is again confusion about terminology. How should a child refer to a stepparent?[87] When there is no commonly understood terminology, sociologists maintain there are no societal norms.[88] In his seminal piece, Cherlin notes that most family life is carried out as "habitualized action" accepted as typical by all members. For example, parents know how harshly to discipline their children and children learn from them and their friends "which parental rules are fair and which to protest." Choices are narrowed, there are fewer decisions that will cause disagreements, and the family will be able to maintain unity without difficulty. Habitualization is often absent from stepparent families, so there is more opportunity for disagreements and divisions among family members and more strain after divorce.[89] Most states also have not included stepfamilies within incest prohibitions despite the fact that it may be a problem in at least some of these households.[90] Yet if 77% of divorced women with a child remarry within ten years,[91] living in a stepparent family is hardly a rare phenomenon.

What is the norm for stepfathers? For evolutionary reasons, parent substitutes might be expected to see the children of their spouse as competing with them for the mother's time and affection.[92] Stepfathers might be seen as competing more directly with adolescent males for the "head of the house" function, particularly if the household had been fatherless for some time before they came along, or with daughters' close mother-daughter relationships.[93] More obviously, when these males had children of their own with the women in question, they would naturally favor their own biological children.[94] For the small number inclined to sexual relations with the young, daughters might become targets for abuse by stepparents or their mother's boyfriends.[95] Despite strong social conventions (norms) that pull us against such instinctive or "natural" behavior (such as revulsion against child abuse and incest),[96] some evidence points disturbingly toward each of these observations.[97]

The norm for stepfathers, and particularly for cohabitants, is not strong enough to either move most to behave just like biological fathers or prevent larger percentages of abusive relationships than among biological parents.[98] Of course, this phenomenon may also be seen as the absence of the normal protective role biology plays in parenting. As anthropologist Sarah Hrdy notes in her book *Mother Nature*,[99] among dads with poor impulse control and an annoying child, a biological link may keep the male from harming the child where an unrelated male with the same poor control will lack such constraints. Even for the vast majority of stepparents who do not abuse, a host of competing factors, some driven by law, make fatherlike relationships difficult to construct and maintain. Because of the lack of norms, stepparenting is "one of the most difficult of all human assignments."[100]

Many very good men will respect the relationships children have with their biological parents.[101] In fact, where visitation or shared custody is ordered, they will need to help the mothers conform to the schedule. However, many states will not make it an obligation to support the nonbiological children who live with them (particularly if the relationship with the children's mother ends), in part because the obligation to provide support is tied in a complex way to the visitation. Particularly if the men have experienced stepparenting relationships before, they may realize that the statistics for breakup are far higher than those for second unions without children.[102] Though, as with first marriages, people will discount this information; for a stepparent, believing that there is no chance of a breakup will then fly in the face of their own experience rather than just common knowledge.[103] As with cohabitation, the more tentative nature of the relationship (even without the pull of the biological father) will make solidifying stepparenting more difficult. And, as with adoption of unrelated children from foster care, the stepparent is also handicapped by dealing with children who have been emotionally formed in a different setting,[104] which may have been an unhappy one that most often ended by divorce, itself a traumatic event from the child's perspective.[105] From a psychological point of view, too, the thoughtful stepparent may be living in a quandary, and in some respects like a foster parent. The child will become attached in any event if the stepparent shows affection, and it may be hard to let this happen knowing that the relationship is tentative, possibly short-lived. From the stepfather's perspective, the child must always be a reminder of the previous relationship—that it existed for some time, was sexual, and left lasting markers.

The high breakup statistics for remarriages with stepchildren do not seem to be because of lesser selectivity, or because of the increased complexity of the adult-adult relationships involved, or even because of problems like substance abuse that might make stable marriages difficult.[106] The problem seems to be the presence of stepchildren,[107] whom Becker, Landes, and Michael[108] called "negative capital" in remarriages.[109]In the early 1980s, couples with stepchildren were more than twice as likely to end their marriages in divorce.[110] A double remarriage (where both parties had previously divorced) with stepchildren was even more likely to end in divorce, at nearly three times the rate of first marriages. This effect is not modified by the addition of joint children (though more than half will have additional children during the first eighteen months of the remarriage).[111] Having children does not destabilize remarrying couples who do not bring stepchildren into the marriage, but the combination of their own children with stepchildren increases positive attitudes toward divorce.[112] On every dimension of attitude toward children and family (and away from divorce), those with stepchildren were less positive.[113] They report problems with the children, less satisfaction with their relationship to their spouse, and a negative effect from their marriage. About 16% report that "if they had it to do all over again, they would not have married at all."[114]

And if the remarriage does dissolve, what are the standards for the relationship then? Does the stepparenting even extend beyond the length of the remarriage? We have no readily agreed upon terms to refer to such people, and the vagueness of the relationship itself is likely to be parallel to the vagueness and ambiguity of role expectations. White notes that in stepfamilies broken by divorce, 57% of the children never see their stepparents and 57% never talk to them.[115] She maintains that when the marriage ends, the relationship falters or dies.[116] Yet these relationships can be very significant to the children involved.[117] Despite the fragility of stepparenting relationships, many states, in a desire to keep children off public support, require stepparents to provide support of the children living with them if the children would otherwise go on welfare.[118] However, unless the stepparent is barred from making such an argument (called estoppel), the duty in most states, by case or statutory law, ends with the marriage.[119]

Once children are born to the "blended family," the web of relationships becomes still more complex. Demographer Jan Bartlema notes that confusion among the kinship networks "leaves the individual free to fill in the nature and degree of affinity of such relationships according to his or her own needs and preferences."[120] Those who wish to have a child to cement their new relationship are likely to find that it makes things worse for the children. Susan Stewart, using the two waves of the National Survey of Families and Households (NSFH), found that birth of a child increased parental involvement 17% of the time, made no difference 34% of the time, and decreased it nearly 50% of the time between the two waves of the study.[121] This was because the childbearing lessened parental involvement with existing children. As Elizabeth Marquardt writes, "However blended our parents might have felt or hoped to become in their new marriages, as children we have always had two families, quite often with members who did not even know each other. After a divorce and remarriage, our reality was *divided*, not blended.[122]

What is the economic model for remarriage?

One way to look at stepfamilies would be, again, to analyze them like cohabitation, as relationships that are more diffuse and that bear the hallmarks of impermanence, that is, as more like exchange relationships. Demographer Lynn White writes, "[t]he structural weakness of the stepfamily implies that stepfamilies will be less able to maintain and enforce obligations to one another. They may be more apt to operate as a voluntary group, characterized by demands for immediate as opposed to diffuse reciprocity and more dependent on affect. They will be weaker support mechanisms than biological families."[123]

As an alternative to this exchange model, a group of seemingly unrelated relational contracting cases has features like those present in blended families and presents instead a picture of disrupted networks. The similarities are the existence of a prior long-term involvement depending upon a personal relationship between two contracting parties; a change of person on one side, so that the original relationship is disturbed; and an attempt by the replacement party to renege on, strictly enforce, or otherwise modify the deal that was dependent upon the original relationship. What the courts do when confronted with such commercial problems is (again, for a variety of reasons, since different legal rules are implicated) stress the importance of the original relationship. The value of the relationship does not seem to be in the signals sent, or even in "reputation effects" involved, but rather in its intrinsic social utility.

The oldest of these cases involves an attempted assignment of a requirements contract between an ice producer and a local ice cream processing plant.[124] Terminal Freezing (the ice company) extended credit to W. C. Frederick and over the six years of their relationship knew about how much ice would be needed per week. When Frederick attempted to assign its contract to Crane Ice Cream, a regional company (with more substantial ability to pay for the ice), Terminal refused. The court disallowed the assignment, holding:

> The appellee [Terminal] would here be obliged not only to perform the subsequent stipulations of the contract for the benefit of a stranger and in conformity with his will but also to accept the performance of the stranger in place of that

of the assignor with whom it contracted, and upon whose personal integrity, capacity, and management in the course of a particular business he must be assumed to have relied by reason of the very nature of the provisions of the contract and of the circumstances of the contracting parties.[125]

That is, the ice plant would have to accept an entirely new arrangement with a party it did not know, with needs more difficult to anticipate. Because it was new and trust hadn't been established, although the ice cream manufacturer would be likely to pay, there would be nothing to prevent arbitrage in the ice market (that is, buying of huge quantities when the contract price was lower than the market price, for use elsewhere).

A second case involves the familiar Burger King restaurant chain, but in the days of its infancy.[126] James McLamore, the president of Burger King, went to Cornell University with Carl Ferris, the principal of Family Dining. When Burger King contemplated expanding beyond Florida, McLamore induced Ferris to open a series of restaurants in two counties outside Philadelphia in an exclusive dealing arrangement that was to last for ninety years, so long as Ferris opened a restaurant a year for ten years. Although the dates were relaxed for various reasons (some delay on each side plus some events beyond either party's control), Ferris did open nine very successful restaurants in the first nine years. By that time, McLamore was no longer running Burger King. His successor was eager to allow other franchisees into the territory and tried to deny Ferris the opportunity to open the last restaurant or to enjoy the remaining years of the exclusive dealing arrangement. While Friendly Dining had not breached the contract, Burger King was technically correct that it had not complied with a condition precedent to its maintaining exclusive dealership privileges. Still, using the legal doctrine of forfeiture, the court denied any relief to Burger King other than damages (coming from any loss of franchise fees based on the delayed openings). Friendly Dining therefore retained the exclusive dealership, in large part because of the relationship of McLamore and Ferris.

A third case involves the sale of a wholesale liquor distributorship that had handled Seagram's products for many years. One of the owners, Harold Lee, had an even longer relationship with the distillery since he had worked for them for several years prior to purchasing the distributorship.[127] By the time the deal went through, different people at Seagram's were handling the transaction and declined to honor the verbal agreement between Seagram's Jack Yogman and Lee to find another distributorship for Lee's sons to run. Although normally such an unwritten "side deal" would have foundered on the shoals of the legal doctrine called the parol evidence rule, in this case the court found "it is significant that there was a close relationship of confidence and friendship over many years between two old men, Harold Lee and Yogman, whose authority to bind Seagram has not been questioned. It would not be surprising that a handshake for the benefit of Harold's sons would have been thought sufficient."[128] Again, a relationship of trust developed over years of business transactions required the court to go beyond strict enforcement of a contract.

Finally, *Nanakuli Paving and Rock v. Shell Oil*,[129] in several casebooks because it sits at the extreme end of the contract interpretation/trade usage rule spectrum, involves yet another of these cases where the ongoing relationship gives the court pause. At issue was a long-term supply contract between a supplier of asphalt and a large paver in Hawaii, where nearly all of the contracts were with the government, so that cost increases could not be passed along to consumers. Although the contract provided for no price protection, Shell's executives had allowed Nanakuli to maintain the lower original contract prices for existing contracts over the last ten years. Again, by the time Shell sought enforcement of the original price, the cast of characters with whom Nanakuli was dealing had changed. The court maintains, in allowing Nanakuli to use the lower price:[130]

> Common sense argues, however, that long-term associates whose success has been mutually dependent are more likely to deal in friendly terms than to seek instant confrontation at each misunderstanding. Shell and Nanakuli had acted as partners on Oahu, and thus Smith was used to dealing cooperatively with Shell. He testified that this was his personal style and that of Nanakuli. "(J)ust in our nature of business. If you go around demanding things, you won't have an amicable relationship. It is not our company policy and not my personal policy."

Yet again, the court involved allowed the ongoing relationship to trump the ordinary contract rule.

Stepfamilies are in some respects like the replacement contracts in the four cases discussed above. A stranger (typically a stepfather) ends up dealing with a complex parent-child relationship that has existed for many years, in some instances replacing someone who had a personal relationship (typically the biological father) with the child. All the cues, all the history (good and bad), are lost. The stepfather may forge a healthy relationship but may also become emotionally estranged from the stepchild (or disengaged),[131] and the family is likely to be troubled.[132] Society doesn't trust stepparents to do the same job as biological parents. Consequently, stepparents are not treated the same in terms of either rights or responsibilities. Statutes such as those requiring support, even as a backup to biological parents' duties, mix signals and probably are not appropriate. Stepchildren, even in the comparatively rare circumstance where biological noncustodial parents are completely absent (or even unknown), will be better served by adoption and assumption of full responsibility by the stepparent.

Sociologist Nan Lin[133] provides a more formal explanation for the distinction I am trying to draw between exchange and social relationships (the ones with norms). Lin distinguishes between the economists' use of reputation (investment in information or signaling), quality, discipline, and commitment, which might all reduce moral hazard or transaction costs (the costs of contract making and enforcement). Without an appreciation of its social nature, Lin writes that social exchange is reduced to an unobservable notion used to account for unexpected economic phenomena such as market failure.[134] Here Lin's theoretical idea receives some support from experiments conducted by sociologist Peter Kollock, who finds more trusting and committed behavior in cases with much uncertainty about outcome.[135] Lin understands reputation as a network asset, built on the processes of transactions and creditor-debtor relations and on the acts of recognition and dissemination in social networks. Social norms reinforce the legitimacy of certain actors who claim their resources and positions and, at the same time, offer incentives for further social exchanges and unequal transactions among actors, enhancing their social capital. The social network also enhances the group or collective reputation and, thus solidarity and the building of public capital.

Is Living with Kin the Same as Adoption?

In some communities, where long-term care by extended families is common, the kin relationship has a fixed meaning to be distinguished from the "fuzzy" meaning given to cohabitation. In others, where there is no such extended family tradition, kinship care has been rare historically and remains uncommon except where mandated by state practice. Without an accepted meaning, the community is apt to treat kin caregivers like foster parents (who are understood to be in an ambiguous status, half parents and half state agents, and to be transitory by legal definition). These intuitions are confirmed by empirical research.

In a study reported in the *Family Law Quarterly*,[136] Steven Nock and I found that foster care does not compare favorably with adoption for any children, regardless of race. Adopted children of any race, perform about as well as children remaining with biological families. As shown in tables appearing later in this chapter, there are very small effects associated with adoption, most notably for Native Americans and children of "other" races. Overall, however, adoption has very small, and generally insignificant, effects in our analyses. But foster children do worse on both internal (depression and expectation of early death) and external (substance abuse and juvenile delinquency) problem measures. Kinship care, likewise, is generally associated with considerably higher depression, delinquency, and drug use. The differences between living with at least one biological parent and living in foster or kinship care are statistically significant and the coefficients are large. Interestingly, the negative effects associated with kinship care are found for children of all racial groups *except* African American. For most groups, then, kinship care resembles foster care. For African American children, however, kinship care resembles living with one's biological or adoptive parent.[137]

In order to see why this might be so, it is necessary, as it was with cohabitation, to lay out the parameters for the academic and policy debate surrounding out-of-home placement. Beginning in the mid-1970s, family intervention decisions moved from a rather quick and streamlined separation of children from biological parents with an eye toward swift adoption to a much slower and more process-oriented focus with twin goals of rehabilitating troubled parents and reunifying families.[138] For a number of reasons, including the growing number of fragile families and the increasing cost (with slim returns) of providing family stabilizing services, the emphasis shifted again in the mid-1990s.[139] Since then the child's safety has taken precedence over family preservation.[140] Congress has gone so far as to threaten transfer payment funding for states that do not improve their record of adoptions from foster care.[141]

The poor and those advocating for them and minority groups, including Dorothy Roberts,[142] who, as you will remember, also suggested removing status from marriage, see this changing policy toward quick removals and termination of parental rights as yet another encumbrance on disadvantaged groups. She writes that at a time when public assistance payments are shrinking, impermanent financial problems may cause indigent parents to permanently lose their children.[143]

Since about the same time as the family preservation movement reached its apex, a small, vocal, focused, and deeply interested group, the National Association of Black Social Workers (NABSW), has virtually closed off one method of getting children out of foster care.[144] In 1972 (and continuing to the end of the twentieth century), the group's official position was that transracial adoption was to be a very last resort for children of color.[145] Black children raised in primarily middle-class white families would not develop the coping skills necessary to live as independent adults in a racist society.[146] Further, white parents raising them could not adequately pass along black culture.[147] This concern raised a specter of cultural genocide,[148] at least on a small scale. The NABSW's position became practice in all relevant states and legislation in a few.[149] The number of transracial adoptions dropped precipitously in the 1970s[150] and until quite recently remained low,[151] despite the growing percentage of minority children in foster care.

When the NABSW articulated its position, it promulgated an alternative: so-called kinship care. Kinship care, which will be described in a moment, remains the out-of-home placement option of choice for many children in many states. As the name implies, kinship care involves living with relatives in a situation ranging from completely informal sharing of care to permanent and somewhat supervised arrangements.[152] Unlike adoption, with kinship care, the ties to the birth family need not be severed, and some birth parents continue to visit and have close relationships with the children in question.[153] Further, the kin caregivers receive subsidies paid to foster parents (almost always substantially higher than public assistance and ongoing rather than temporary).[154] Even though since 1996, Congress has forbidden explicit racial matching in child custody placement and adoption,[155] an exception has been made for kinship care,[156] which is recognized as a viable permanent alternative for children (though not one preferred to reunification or adoption).[157] Studies of kinship care were mandated by federal statute[158] but are consistently descriptive: Who are the children in kinship care and who are their caregivers?[159] How long do children remain in kinship care? How often are they returned to biological parents and how often are the children adopted? When comparisons are made, they are made between third-party (unrelated) foster care and kinship care. They consistently report that although kinship care providers do not seek services as frequently as do third-party foster parents (and hence the program is somewhat less expensive),[160] children in kinship care do about as well as do children in other foster care settings.[161] The caregivers are reportedly older, more apt to be working, and less apt to be affluent than their third-party counterparts. They, and therefore the children they care for, are much more likely to be African American than are third-party foster parents or the pool of foster children in general.[162] The next section contributes an empirical comparison between kinship care families and others from the perspective of children's welfare.

The empirical conclusion: Kinship care is like foster care for whites and adoption for blacks

In data from the National Longitudinal Study of Adolescent Health (Add Health), conducted at the Carolina Population Center at the University of North Carolina,[163] many of the African American children who were in foster care, like at least half of them in the general population, were being cared for by kin (see the three bold rows in table 1.2).[164] This was a school-based study of children in grades 7–12 first administered in 1994–95, involving enough children (over 15,000) that there were significant numbers of children in the various living arrangements of interest. That is, there were 403 children of all races adopted by both parents, 61 living with foster parents, and 472 living with either an aunt or grandmother they thought of as their mother—the group we defined as living in kinship care.

Steven Nock and I began by compare kinship care, adoption, and foster care for all children. We focused on four indicators of well-being that form the columns of table 1.3.[165] First, we used a standard nineteen-item depression scale (mean = 13.4, s.d. = 5.9; Depression). Second, we assessed monthly use of cigarettes, alcohol, and marijuana by counting the number of times in the past month the child estimated he/she had used each. Our measure, called Drug Use in table 1.3, simply adds monthly use of these

TABLE 1.2 **Effects of Children's Legal Relationship to Parents**

All mothers	Depression	Drug use	Delinquency	Morbidity
Variable	R^2 = 0.047** (N = 15,315)	R^2 = 0.071** (N = 15,024)	R^2 = 0.031** (N = 15,177)	R^2 = 0.038** (N = 15,271)
Constant	6.645 (1.197)**	−2.113 (0.710)**	8.262 (1.378)**	0.0068 (0.030)*
Child lives with mother only	0.621 (0.177)**	0.531 (0.102)**	0.670 (0.204)**	0.008 (0.004) ns

TABLE 1.2 *(continued)*

All mothers	Depression	Drug use	Delinquency	Morbidity
Child lives with dad only	1.305 (4.137) ns	2.615 (2.357) ns	1.343 (4.759) ns	0.009 (0.105) ns
Child's age	0.417 (0.029)**	0.342 (0.016)**	0.065 (0.033)*	0.006 (0.001)**
Child's sex 1 = m, 2 = f	1.224 (0.095)**	−0.215 (0.055)**	−1.869 (0.110)**	−0.002 (0.002) ns
Household income (000)	−003 (0.001)**	−0.0008 (0.001) ns	0.0005 (0.001) ns	−0.00008 (0.0001)*
Mother's age	−0.018 (0.008)*	−0.013 (0.005)*	−0.024 (0.010)*	0.0001 (0.0001) ns
Mother never married	1.005 (1.045) ns	−0.364 (0.630) ns	−0.249 (1.213) ns	0.015 (0.027) ns
Mother is married	0.541 (1.038) ns	−0.175 (0.621) ns	−0.478 (1.194) ns	0.006 (0.026) ns
Mother is widowed	0.752 (1.069) ns	−0.082 (0.638) ns	−0.185 (1.231) ns	0.017 (0.027) ns
Mother divorced-separated	0.697 (1.042) ns	−0.147 (0.623) ns	0.088 (1.199) ns	0.012 (0.026) ns
Mother ever divorced?	0.313 (0.131)**	0.302 (0.075)**	0.187 (0.152) ns	−0.001 (0.003) ns
Mother's years of schooling	−0.172 (0.021)**	−0.037 (0.012)**	−0.020 (0.025) ns	−0.005 (0.001)**
Mother is Hispanic	1.613 (0.932) ns	−0.076 (0.538) ns	2.223 (1.027)*	0.041 (0.024)
Mother is black	−0.113 (0.359) ns	−0.890 (0.208)**	−0.803 (0.415)*	0.018 (0.009)*
Mother is Asian	0.865 (0.433)*	−0.334 (0.247) ns	−0.025 (0.497) ns	0.001 (0.011) ns
Mother is Native American	0.371 (0.478) ns	−0.563 (0.278)*	0.712 (0.551) ns	0.031 (0.012)*
Mother is other race	0.502 (0.261)*	−0.451 (0.150)**	−0.212 (0.302) ns	0.009 (0.007) ns
Child in kincare	**1.257** **(0.355)****	**0.460** **(0.205)***	**1.631** **(0.409)****	**0.013** **(0.009) ns**
Child adopted	**0.732** **(0.263)***	**0.010** **(0.150) ns**	**0.597** **(0.303)***	**0.011** **(0.007) ns**
Child fostered	**3.244** **(0.916)****	**1.164** **(0.524)***	**2.175** **(1.066)***	**0.069** **(0.030)***
Child Hispanic	0.378 (1.763) ns	−1.004 (0.962) ns	1.998 (1.942) ns	−0.002 (0.043) ns
Child black	0.807 (0.361)*	−0.712 (0.210)**	0.365 (0.418) ns	0.024 (0.009)*
Child Asian	0.493 (0.446) ns	−0.683 (0.255)*	0.318 (0.511) ns	0.022 (0.011)*
Child Native American	0.891 (0.428)*	.0001 (0.246) ns	2.055 (0.499)**	0.050 (0.011)**
Child other race	0.344 (0.226) ns	−0.628 (0.130)**	1.311 (0.261)**	0.024 (0.006)**

Source: From Margaret F. Brinig and Steven L. Nock, "How Much Does Legal Status Matter? Adoptions by Kin Caregivers." *Family Law Quarterly* 36, no. 3, 2002.

* $p < 0.05$

** $p < 0.01$

ns = Not statistically significantly different from zero

various substances (mean = 1.55, s.d = 3.45). Third, we computed an index of juvenile delinquency developed by the researchers who designed the survey (Juvenile Delinquency). This consisted of fifteen questions, each asking the adolescent how often he/she had committed a particular act in the past year (mean = 5.22, s.d = 6.83). Finally, Morbidity combined two questions designed to gauge a young person's fatalism—the adolescent's estimate of his or her chances of living to 35 or being killed by age 21.

Table 1.3 reports the results of multiple regressions designed to investigate the differences among adopted, kinship-care, and foster children while holding constant aspects of the child's living arrangement (dad only, mom only), age, race, sex, and mother's marital status, education, income, race, and divorce history. Admittedly, there are probably many other differences between adopted and fostered children, though these seem adequate to capture the most obvious and important.

Each child who mentioned that he/she shared a residence with an adult variously referred to as mother, mom, father, dad, or any other designation implied that a parent was included in these equations. We then determined the relationship between the child and the adult(s) mentioned. Children who mentioned no biological, foster, or adopted parent were asked if anyone in the household acted in that role. Grandparents and aunts were the overwhelming choices in such circumstances. We have designated all 472 such situations as kinship care.

Though there are many factors that have consequences for the outcomes we studied, only one appears strongly related to all four—whether the child is fostered. Kinship care is also negatively related to three of the four outcomes. Consider the coefficient for depression for Child Fostered in column 1 of table 1.2, near the bottom of the table. This value (3.244) implies that children who are identical on all elements in this table except that one is in foster care and the other lives with at least one biological parent differ by about 3.24 points, on average, in depression (with the fostered child more depressed). Given the standard deviation for this variable (5.97), the effect is actually rather large—more than half a standard deviation in magnitude. Foster children, in short, are considerably more depressed, even when matched on a wide range of racial, socioeconomic, and household characteristics. In a similar pattern, fostered children also display greater use of drugs, higher rates of delinquency, and a firmer conviction that they will not live to adulthood.

Children in kinship care also appear more depressed, more likely to use drugs, and more likely to engage in delinquent behaviors, though these

TABLE 1.3 **Effects of Adoption, Foster Placement, and Kinship Care by Race**

Effect by race	Depression	Drug use (#/month)	Juvenile delinquency	Perceived chance of dying
Adopted child				
White	0.466 ns	−0.013 ns	0.640 ns	0.012 ns
Black	1.434 ns	−0.163 ns	0.671 ns	0.003 ns
Asian	2.874*	−0.578 ns	0.660 ns	−0.005 ns
Native American	N/A	2.217*	0.252 ns	N/A
Other race	0.625 ns	2.095*	0.616 ns	0.021 ns
Fostered child				
White	0.196 ns	2.884**	−0.682 ns	0.011 ns
Black	5.251**	−0.578 ns	0.086 ns	0.107*
Asian	5.585 ns	N/A	5.682**	0.363*
Native American	N/A	−2.034 ns	3.214 ns	N/A
Other race	6.461*	2.055 ns	6.500*	0.024 ns
Kincare child				
White	1.464*	0.467 ns	2.340**	0.017 ns
Black	0.164 ns	−0.097 ns	0.247 ns	−0.011 ns
Asian	3.092 ns	1.488*	4.003*	0.102*
Native American	N/A	1.315 ns	5.474*	N/A
Other race	3.236*	0.327 ns	2.128 ns	0.017 ns
R^2/N				
White	0.042**/9,905	0.057**/9,745	0.032**/9,825	0.023**/9,882
Black	0.048**/3,135	0.035**/3,045	0.028**/3,090	0.019**/3,113
Asian	0.068**/793	0.050**/781	0.086**/794	0.049**/797
Native American	0.075 ns/253	0.144**/248	0.106*/248	N/A
Other race	0.062**/1,213	0.056**/1,188	0.043**/1,203	0.036*/1,213

Source: From Margaret F. Brinig and Steven L. Nock, "How Much Does Legal Status Matter? Adoptions by Kin Caregivers." *Family Law Quarterly* 36, no. 3, 2002.

Note: All equations control for household structure, child's gender, household income, mother's age, mother's current and previous marital status, mother's education, and mother's race.

* $p < 0.05$

** $p < 0.01$

ns = Not statistically significantly different from zero

N/A = Insufficient number of cases or insignificant equation

effects are only a third to half the magnitude of those found for foster care. As we will show, the effects associated with kinship care also vary by race. To investigate the potentially differing consequences of foster care, kinship care, and adoption by race, we performed analysis designed to isolate the effects separately for each of the major racial groupings available. We produced equations similar to those in table 1.3 for children of each racial group separately. The results of these twenty equations (four outcomes times five racial groups) clearly illustrate the differing responses of children of various races to adoption, foster care, and kinship care. These results are shown in table 1.3.

The first value in table 1.3 (0.466) indicates that white children in an adopted home score only .466 points higher on the measure of depression than do comparable white children living with at least one biological parent. (All comparisons use living with a biological parent as the comparison reference.) This value (.466) is annotated with an "ns" to indicate that the effect found is *not* statistically significant. Essentially, this means that the statistical evidence is inadequate to conclude that white adopted children differ from white children living with at least one biological parent on this measure of depression. And, in general, the results of this table replicate those of table 1.2 in showing trivial and generally nonsignificant effects of adoption for children of various races. This is not surprising since many children will be adopted shortly after birth, unlike most children in either foster care or kinship care. The only significant effects of adoption are those for Native Americans and children of other races in regard to minimally higher drug use.

Foster placement, however, is associated with a number of significant effects, all of which are negative. For example, black children and children of other races who are in foster placement are notably more depressed than comparable children are. Asian and Other race children in foster homes are more likely to be involved in various types of delinquency. Black and Asian foster children are also more likely to think they will die (or be killed) young.

The results for kinship care show clearly that white and other race children in such situations are more depressed. Asian children in kinship care admit to more drug use. White, Asian, and Native American children in kinship care engage in more delinquent behavior, and Asian children in kinship care are more fatalistic. In short, kinship care is associated with at least some significant negative effects for all but African American children.

The statistical technique that we applied attempts to make children identical in all ways except their foster, adopted, or kinship-care status. That foster care (and to a lesser extent kinship care) have such consistent and negative effects even after the imposition of such controls suggests that there is a story to be told about the lives of children in these living arrangements that may explain their diminished expectations, higher depression, and other negative experiences. Part of that explanation, in all likelihood, is the distinction among the statuses as they are incorporated into our cultural belief systems. Quite simply, adoption is a recognized and understood social (and legal) status. Foster care and, especially, kinship care are much less so.

When asked whether they would adopt the children in their care, kin caregivers are reluctant for at least two reasons: First, they do not want to insult the child's parents or otherwise interfere with ongoing family relationships.[166] Second, they maintain that they cannot afford adoption.[167]

Kinship care remains, and from an empirical standpoint should remain, an approved method for dealing with African American children who are free for adoption. Our results suggest that black children do no worse (or better) in kinship care than when adopted, at least on our limited range of outcomes, even when this is decidedly not the case for children of other races. The caregivers in kinship care, often not wealthy people, are better off financially because they continue to receive foster care subsidies[168] that evaporate, at least in some states,[169] upon the child's adoption. The caregivers are also not put in the difficult position of having to cut ties with their relatives who are the child's biological parents (usually their daughter or sister). From the agency's perspective, there is a permanent solution for the child. Funding for social services depends on caseload, and these children cost less even though they remain on the caseload. In addition, kinship care meets the concerns of the NASBW because kin will also likely be black.

At the outset of this section, I outlined why adoptive and original families might be virtually identical for particular children, or groups of them. For most Americans, living in a legally recognized family is critically important. Like marriage, it signals to the outside world that you belong and are loved. Marriage or adoption means that the family relationship is permanent and, relatedly, that there is no ambiguity about the status, as there is with cohabitation, stepparenting, and foster care.

The "legally recognized relationship" may also signal something else, in addition to removing ambiguity. It may mean that the parties to the relationship have, even aside from law, support from the community and especially close friends and families. If this is true, it undermines arguments for recognizing socially unrecognized relationships. Even if the relationships were to become legally recognized, they would not necessarily function the way the lawmakers would hope. That is, if the law precedes social acceptance of a particular relationship, especially acceptance by close friends and family, the legal status alone—even with the public benefits and obligations that flow from it—would not be enough to overcome the strong societal distrust. As a society, we would be resorting to individual compensatory actions to protect the person disadvantaged, should such a relationship fail, rather than creating an expectation, supported by a requirement of a legal action for termination, that the relationship is permanent. If for constitutional or simple fairness reasons a particular legal status must be accorded some family type, as, for example, interracial or same-sex marriage, it would be important to see how other institutions fill in for the support the family and close community provides. This will help make the default expectation of permanence a reality.

The Dominance of Social Reality Over Legal Status: Marriage Recognition

Social reality thus dominates legal recognition, though arguably legal recognition may eventually change the social perception by, in McAdams's terminology, creating a focal point, signaling a new social norm.[170] One way we can look at how this works is through the lens of interstate marriage recognition. We begin with the classic case of *In re May's Estate*,[171] involving a contest between heirs of Fannie May: her surviving "husband" and three of their children versus the other three. Sam May and the first group of children were attempting to establish the validity of a thirty-two-year marriage that he and Fannie had celebrated in a religious ceremony in Rhode Island. The other three children claimed the status never existed because Sam was Fannie's uncle, and such marriages were prohibited by the law of New York, where the Mays always lived and where the case was heard. In fact, Sam and Fannie had travelled to Rhode Island for the express purpose of being married there, since this was one of two states that had an exception from the general consanguinity rule for persons of the Jewish faith, married in that tradition, who were uncle and niece. Since there was no New York statute expressly forbidding people from doing precisely what Sam and Fannie had done, the court upheld the marriage. The interesting part of the opinion, from our point of view, is the following conclusion:

> such marriage, solemnized, as it was, in accord with the ritual of the Jewish faith in a State whose legislative body has declared such a marriage to be 'good and valid in law,' *was not offensive to the public sense of morality to a degree regarded generally with abhorrence* and thus was not within the inhibitions of natural law.[172]

For our purposes, the interesting feature is the celebration in a state recognizing the validity of the marriage that was not grossly offensive to the public sense of morality in the state of New York. This case can be contrasted with another case from virtually the same time period, a predecessor of the famous *Loving v. Virginia*[173] case that overruled it. In *Naim v. Naim*,[174] Virginia residents travelled to North Carolina to avoid the prohibition in their home state of interracial marriages. Shortly afterward, Mrs. Naim, who was Caucasian, sought and received an annulment of the marriage with Mr. Naim, who was Chinese. This time there was a statute expressly making marriages void when people went out of state to evade Virginia law. In language that today would certainly be found offensive and inflammatory, and quoting from still more racist language, the Virginia court found that its public policy was offended by the marriage in question:

> We are unable to read in the Fourteenth Amendment to the Constitution, or in any other provision of that great document, any words or any intendment which prohibit the State from enacting legislation to preserve the racial integrity of its citizens, or which denies the power of the State to regulate the marriage relation so that it shall not have a mongrel breed of citizens.[175]

What do these two cases from more than half a century ago have to add to the discussion? The rule is that except where the Constitution requires otherwise, as the court found in *Loving*, states will defer to their own strong public policy rather than recognize relationships given the legal status of marriage elsewhere. Why? Perhaps because marriages (and the children emanating from them) critically need community support and approval. Marriages are not simply a matter of Rhode Island's or North Carolina's concern, as the states where the marriages were celebrated, but are matters of concern for the states where the couples will actually live.

Recent studies of covenant marriage couples in Louisiana have found, not only that they are more religious (which would certainly be expected) and have lower divorce rates (not surprising, given the more stringent divorce grounds and counseling requirements that do not apply to standard marriage), but also that they have more approval from their parents, siblings, in-laws, and friends than do standard married couples.[176] This approval of their close network was significantly different between the two groups both when they announced their marriage plans and some years after they married. In fact, significantly more people (an average of 178) showed up at the covenant marriage ceremonies than for the standard marriages (an average of 109).[177] What does this mean? When times are rough for these couples, as they will occasionally undoubtedly be, they have many more people to turn to for advice, steadying, and tangible support in addition to the counseling resource provided by the premarital counseling requirement. Here a legal change, for this relatively small group of people, is adding to what is already strong social, if not societal, support.

Of course, the oldest indication of family support is the arranged marriage. In many parts of the world, families are involved with marriages from the very beginning, as Posner notes.[178] Families can overcome the information barriers that couples "in love" without much foresight may possess, and that we will encounter presently. Parents can also provide day-to-day support in trouble, and their involvement in choosing the family and indicating support may cement their tendency to do this.[179] Because I introduced my daughter Katie to my former student Steve, I may well feel more connected to their marriage, described in the introduction, than to the marriages of my other children.

On the negative side, lack of family support can significantly affect marital problems. While *Loving* happily has removed any legal barriers to interracial marriage, the law has apparently moved beyond some families' private social acceptance. In her dissertation research on interracial marriages, demographer Rose Kreider examined black-white couples and found that they had nearly twice the likelihood of divorcing as did homogenous couples of either race.[180] Controlling for other variables that typically predict divorce, if the respondent saw her mother infrequently, the chance of dissolution between waves of the survey increased by 8%. This lack of parental support might be mitigated by support from the community. Thus, if the husband attended religious services frequently, dissolution occurred only about two-thirds as often and at the same rate as for other black marriages.[181]

A case much like *Naim* and *Estate of May* on a currently divisive issue is *Chambers v. Ormiston*.[182] Both members of a same-sex couple were residents of Rhode Island who in 2004 went to marry in Massachusetts, where they were married in a civil ceremony according to Massachusetts law. Though Massachusetts does not ordinarily marry nondomiciliaries, that state had determined that Rhode Island and New York had no public policy against such marriages. After returning together to Rhode Island

and living together as a couple, both wanted a divorce. The majority of the Rhode Island Supreme Court found that the divorce court had no jurisdiction since the word "marriage" in the statute giving jurisdiction would only have contemplated marriages between a man and a woman in 1961, when the statute was enacted. Two justices dissented, finding that the parties could have gotten annulment relief in that court (so that not granting them a divorce was incongruous), and that in any event under principles of comity (and much as in *Estate of May*), same-sex marriages were not "strongly against the public policy" of Rhode Island.[183] This also seems to be the direction New York is taking.[184]

Is this public policy against same-sex marriage likely to change? The answer is complicated and mixed. As previously mentioned, the rules have changed in Canada already, and marriage between any two consenting adults is now legal. A story that fits better with the development of a public policy shift comes, however, from South Africa. Law professor Ryan Goodman surveyed many young and old citizens of that country before and after the Constitutional Court struck down criminal sanctions against sodomy.[185] What he found was that the criminal statutes, though never enforced, provided a mechanism that permitted other South Africans (and even the gays and lesbians themselves) to view their conduct as wrong. In other words, it provided an excuse for others to discriminate and for the gays and lesbians to feel disadvantaged. Once the legislation was lifted, attitudes by both the majority and minority groups changed perceptively, so that gays and lesbians were not discriminated against and felt freer to think positively about themselves. After publication of his article, same-sex marriage was eventually legalized.[186] As McAdams would say, law operated as a signal of consensus.[187]

For the United States, the question is whether that same progression and change in public policy will follow (or has already followed) the abolition of laws criminalizing sodomy that took place in *Lawrence v. Texas*.[188] Both the case itself and the earlier Vermont decision requiring that state to enact civil union legislation note that the underlying issue is about community recognition of the relationship. Thus, the majority opinion in *Lawrence* notes:

> When sexuality finds overt expression in intimate conduct with another person, the conduct can be but one element in a personal bond that is more enduring. The statutes do seek to control a personal relationship that, whether or not

> entitled for formal recognition in the law, is within the liberty of persons to choose without being punished as criminals.[189]

In the Vermont civil union case, *Baker v. Nelson*,[190] the court was perhaps even more explicit:

> The State's interest in extending official recognition and legal protection to the professed commitment of two individuals to a lasting relationship of mutual affection is predicated on the belief that legal support of a couple's commitment provides stability for the individuals, their family, and the broader community. Although plaintiffs' interest in seeking state recognition and protection of their mutual commitment may—in view of divorce statistics—represent "the triumph of hope over experience," the essential aspect of their claim is simply and fundamentally for inclusion in the family of state-sanctioned human relations.[191]

Thus being able to engage in a "state-sanctioned human" relationship is essential to being a full member of the community. In the recent California Supreme Court opinion striking down that state's statutory limitation of marriage to different-sex couples only, the court also mentions the benefit of external network support. The court notes the "opportunity to become a part of one's partner's family, providing a wider and often critical network of economic and emotional security."[192]

Extrapolating from the work of Richard McAdams on the origin of norms indicates that the criminal sodomy statute itself may have provided a focal point for the creation of norms that work against the gay and lesbian community. In order to maintain status with and retain esteem from one's group, it is important to follow group behavior in discriminating against members of the "out" group, in this case gays and lesbians. Removal of the statute may indicate that the focal point is inappropriate or even that it is not recognized by the majority of the community.

Many empirical questions remain but cannot really be answered without careful longitudinal studies. To the extent that constitutional provisions or recognition as full members of the community requires same-sex marriage immediately, these studies will probably follow rather than precede acceptance of same-sex marriage. The results might suggest that appropriate distinctions aren't between same- versus different-sex marriage, but between all childless couples and those with children. Among the most important are whether the norms developed for marriage work with legally recognized same-sex couples, and, if they do not, whether the difference is significant enough to cause concern.[193] The most critical questions would not seem to revolve around the division of labor (which, you'll recall, did not predict stable marriages) but more crucially around the duration and stability of the relationship and whether the partners or spouses invest heavily in the relationship or each other. Further, the well-being of children needs to be examined. Does it matter whether their parents live as married, as domestic partners, or in civil unions? Does it matter, for happiness or the indices of good citizenship, whether both genders play a role in upbringing? For community norms not to lag too far behind legal preference for the relationship, answers to these questions should be sought through carefully designed studies done by people without stakes in any particular outcome.[194]

Norms, Community, and Children

Earlier in this chapter I noted that the arguably gloomy effects of parents' failing to marry or failing to adopt kin did not seem to affect African American children significantly, though most other children were affected. Why not? Here we have a large group of people for whom legal status is no longer providing the kind of support it does everyone else. Although African American families are faced with a host of problems related to poverty, the children for the most part exhibit relatively few psychological or behavioral problems. In fact, controlling for income, they exhibit less anxiety and depression,[195] lower incidents of behavioral problems,[196] and significantly higher self-esteem[197] than do white children.

Steven Nock and I have postulated two accounts for this seeming resiliency. Stemming at least from before the book *It Takes a Village*,[198] the folk wisdom has been that the extended family is critically important for African American children. In the important Supreme Court case of *Moore v. City of East Cleveland*,[199] Justices Brennan and Marshall, in their opinion concurring with the decision to invalidate an ordinance that defined "single family" in terms of the nuclear family, wrote:

> The "extended" form is especially familiar among black families. We may suppose that this reflects the truism that black citizens, like generations of white immigrants before them, have been victims of economic and other disadvantages that would worsen if they were compelled to abandon extended, for nuclear, living patterns. Even in husband and wife households, 13% of black families

> compared with 3% of white families include relatives under 18 years old, in addition to the couple's own children. In black households whose head is an elderly woman, as in this case, the contrast is even more striking: 48% of such black households, compared with 10% of counterpart white households, include related minor children not offspring of the head of the household.[200]

The implication of the extended family model is that in cases where the African American parents had not married, but grandmothers provided help, children would do better. However, the ties with extended family seem to be weaker for African Americans than for others.[201] Some very contemporary pieces on the complex families with several different fathers for children of a single mother (or a father who has children through several different mothers) suggest that the extended family ties are less strong in such families.[202] Even when this complexity does not occur, the kin that might otherwise help may not be able to provide as much support (as, statistically, they do not), because they are so financially stressed. This point may explain why income is so strongly related to African American children's welfare, a point I will make several times in the chapters that follow.

An alternative explanation that also fits what we know about African American families is that it is not primarily the help of grandparents that signals family resources, but support from another mediating institution, in this case religion. It is self-identified as the heart of the black community[203] and as an important source of social cohesion.[204] That is, mothers who receive help from their church communities (and/or perhaps from prayer) might do better in difficult circumstances. Of course, both explanations might be true, but some empirical investigation would help.

While America is unique in its religiosity compared to other industrialized nations,[205] African Americans are still more religious. While the average church attendance in 1998 was 3.51 for white Americans on a scale from 0 to 8 (or a little less than once a month), the average black American attended 4.18 times, or between once and twice a month.[206] Religion might be providing the same sort of social support that marriage does for most Americans.

Using the Panel Survey of Income Dynamics (PSID) and its Child Development Supplement (CDS), I was able to track whether aid given (in terms of hours of help) by grandmothers to children's mothers when the children were small affected children as they became young people.[207] Because the help given occurred before the behavior measured in the CDS, there is

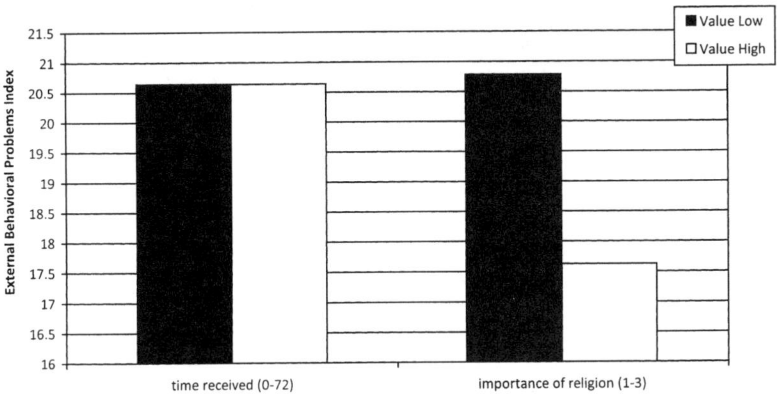

FIGURE 1.4 External behavioral problems with relative effects of grandmother time and importance of religion to mothers. (Based on the PSID and CDS public use data set, 1997 and 2002. Data available from the author.)

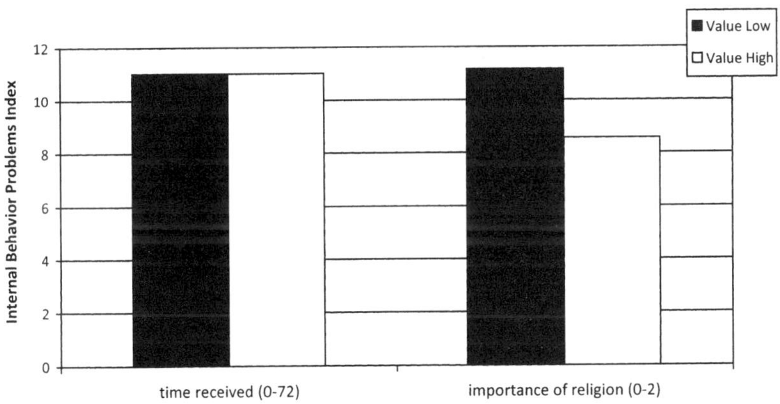

FIGURE 1.5 Internal behavioral problems in black children with relative effects of grandmother time and importance of religion to mothers. (Based on the PSID and CDS public use data set, 1997 and 2002. Data available from the author.)

some evidence not only of the intergenerational effects but also of causal direction. In 1987, the mothers of the children studied in the CDS were asked how many hours of help they received from their own parents who lived outside the family unit. I restricted the original sample of 392 black children to include children born in 1987 or before (and who therefore were at least 15 in 2002) whose mothers answered the question. This left 195 children. In 2002, their mothers were also asked how religious they considered themselves, apart from attending services. Results of regression equations appear in figures 1.4 and 1.5. The bottom line is that the mother's religiosity, not the help from relatives, seems most important to child well-being, holding everything else constant, as in table 3.1.[208]

It is possible that other mediating institutions work in the same way to help support the African American family. I am currently exploring the effect of religiously affiliated schools, not on the individual children[209] but on the neighborhoods surrounding them. The preliminary findings are that the closing of such schools in Chicago, even controlling for other demographic factors, is strongly associated with a decline of social cohesion in their neighborhoods. I hope to eventually isolate the effect of black families' association with the military or with local political organizing, either of which might also provide alternative, external support.

What We Can Take at This Stage

In order for relationships to gain state recognition, they should have a track record that promises certain rewards: stability and the ability to trust in the relationship and to invest in children. In a somewhat circular reasoning, states have acknowledged that relationships begun elsewhere will be recognized if they are not grossly against public policy. Based on the cases, it is not a big stretch to rephrase the rule in positive terms: they will be recognized if they conform to certain norms and expectations.

In addition, recognition of the relationship should not dilute the usual signal the status provides. Signaling behavior, as discussed earlier in this chapter, is clearly important in understanding when relationships will be recognized and when they will not. When a type of relationship gives off a fuzzy or unclear signal, it will not be capable of receiving community support. But whether the signal is of one's "good type" marked by low discount rates, as Eric Posner claims, or something more about the relationship itself, rather than the individuals that comprise it, remains to be seen. We have touched on the role of networks in establishing and maintaining family institutions, but these important binding third-party effects will be described more fully in succeeding chapters.

We can also take some lessons for public policy. Governments should not rush to legalize or create status (without constitutional reasons for doing so, as some courts have found for same-sex couples) for relationships before these relationships are likely to have societal support. Assuming that it is the just thing to do before society has changed its norms, it will be important to provide or find substitutes for the kind of support that communities generally provide marriage and parenting. These probably cannot be created by mere funding, as studies from cohabitants in Sweden and Canada have shown that subsidies did not stabilize cohabiting families but may have decreased religiosity,[210] but, as seems to be the case for interracial marriages, will have to come from the mediating institutions—religious organizations, schools, family, voluntary associations, and even, perhaps, corporations.[211]

Gill and Lundsgaarde[212] postulate that religious organizations (firms) will offer a variety of tangible services designated to build trust among the community of potential followers, encourage participation in the organization, and capture revenue. Trust is needed for the religious because religion, like marriage, is essentially a "credence good,"[213] meaning that it cannot be verified before one gets involved. To the extent that people on the margin (in Gill and Lundsgaarde's terms, for whom religion is highly priced and inelastic) can get the services, such as education or financial support, more cheaply because they are provided by the government, church attendance should decline as a gradual, generational matter.[214] This hypothesis depends on the idea that some people have highly elastic preferences for spiritual goods contingent upon social services, meaning, in lay terms, that people will move quickly to a less costly option. To the extent that religiosity is negatively associated with welfare spending, kinship care, which privately done does not often involve state subsidy,[215] may also be associated with religiosity. We will shortly take up the interrelated roles of both networking and other mediating institutions like religiosity.

CHAPTER TWO

Norms within Families, or the Family Community

Chapter 1 concluded as it began, with a reminder that families gain community trust and recognition if they are seen as stable and capable of generating trust among family members. Obviously, trust is being used for both within-family relationships and relationships between family members and outsiders. This chapter will focus on the building of trust between members of the family: how this is achieved and just what it means. This chapter also begins with the work done by eminent law and economics scholars to explain how social norms work in families and households. But after this beginning, the chapter turns to the scholarship from other disciplines—psychology, political science, and sociology—that describes networks of trust, called social capital, primarily in larger units than the family. My contribution is to take the larger social capital theory and move it back into the family sphere, where it, like the other forms of capital, financial and human, helps families produce the "goods" of intimacy and flourishing. Love and trust are not only part of what might be called the family's production function, helping the couple or parents to succeed, but also part of the constituent individuals' utility function. They are qualities that make families more "efficient" as societal building blocks and also constitute intangible "goods"[1] that make a part of what economists call utility. That is, among other things, we look for greater quantities of love and trust when we make choices in our rational self-interest.

Having read Eric Posner's *Law and Social Norms*[2] or Robert Ellickson's "Unpacking the Household,"[3] we might expect that relationships between husbands and wives would be characterized by an exchange of gifts, whether immediately reciprocated (which seems to be Posner's position) or reciprocated in a more leisurely fashion (as Ellickson supposes). However, it turns out that neither model precisely describes what happens in families, at least if we consider the social science evidence, because neither is complete. The legal economists are right that norms of marriage do serve as guides to behavior, and people on the outside will become involved to enforce them informally, as Posner[4] and Richard McAdams[5] would assume. As we saw in the relational contracting cases presented in the last chapter, the outsiders may furnish advice, support, or criticism, but neither they nor an aggrieved spouse will generally resort to law except in the most egregious cases (for example, when one has abused the other or a child or when the marriage has become so intolerable that exit through divorce becomes the salient remedy).

One limitation of the law and economics model is that tit-for-tat exchange, which characterizes much of the nonfamily contracting, corporate, and even political worlds, is only characteristic of marriages in what game theorists call the "last period." In the marriage context, the last period would arise when couples are moving toward divorce. At that point, they may only be looking out for themselves (and secondarily for children if they have them). Instead, in a well-functioning marriage, couples tend to function "outside time."[6] Contrary to what Ellickson proposes,[7] they do not keep even rough track of who owes what to whom. Although it is clear that most American marriages no longer represent the highly specialized marriages that Gary Becker wrote about in the 1970s[8] (and that probably did characterize many middle-class marriages in the mid-twentieth century), there does not seem to be a very good economic model for the modern marriage.[9] Becker supposed that under the economic principle of comparative advantage, it would be most efficient for wives to specialize in "household production" since they bore children and might need to nurse those children when small, and that their husbands should specialize in "market production" even if both could have done either job well outside of marriage. In a large percentage of current marriages, both spouses work outside the home. As eminent sociologists Goldschneider and Waite wrote in the early 1990s:

> We have suggested that such families have the potential to solve critical problems facing families today. But what do we really know about them? What effects

does this pioneer family form have on marriages and families and on the men, women, and children who live in them? Are more egalitarian and sharing families possible? This is largely uncharted territory.[10]

Sociologist Peter Kollock argues that trusting and committed relationships, as opposed to more contractual exchanges, are particularly likely to flourish in conditions in which, like marriage, there is a lot of uncertainty.[11]

Trying to develop a model of modern marriages, Steven Nock and I explored questions about the division of labor and its effect on marital dissolution using the first two waves of the NSFH, a large nationally representative survey compiled at the University of Wisconsin.[12] Table 2.1 shows the actual division of labor on various household tasks, as well as how we characterized these as either "men's" or "women's" work. Our (or at least my) original prediction was that as wives worked more hours in the labor force, their husbands would increasingly pick up the slack so that the division of labor would be fair. In fact, even holding constant the hours of paid labor-force work, wives do more housework and work more total hours.[13]

Nock and I reached three main conclusions. First, it mattered whether the work done was "men's" or "women's." Increased hours devoted by either spouse to "men's" work in 1987–88 meant less likelihood of divorce or separation between the two waves of the survey. Increased hours devoted

TABLE 2.1 **Average Hours Spent on Household Tasks by Husbands and Wives**

Household tasks	Husbands	Wives	N	Sig. t
1) Preparing meals	2.05	9.75	4377	.001*
2) Washing dishes	1.76	6.07	4377	.001*
3) Cleaning house	1.59	8.13	4379	.001*
4) Outdoor tasks	4.96	1.81	4380	.001*
5) Shopping	1.39	2.81	4380	.001*
6) Washing, ironing	0.57	4.29	4379	.001*
7) Paying bills	1.36	1.60	4378	.001*
8) Auto maintenance	1.84	0.18	4379	.001*
9) Driving others	1.15	1.39	4372	.001*
Male tasks (4+8)	6.80	1.99	4375	.001*
Female tasks (1+2+3+5+6+7+9)	9.87	33.98	4381	.001*

Source: From Steven L. Nock and Margaret F. Brinig, "Weak Men and Disorderly Women: Divorce and the Division of Labor." In *The Law and Economics of Marriage and Divorce*, edited by Antony W. Dnes and Robert Rowthorn. Cambridge: Cambridge University Press, 2002.

* Paired samples t-test (2-tailed) is significant at $p < 0.001$

by either spouse to "women's" work, on the other hand, meant a less stable marriage during the same period (see table 2.2). This is all interesting and presents important public policy implications but is rather beside my point here.

Our second, more pertinent, finding was that perceived fairness did not seem to be the main indicator of stability. If the spouses answered that the division of labor in the household and workplace was "fair to both of us," there was a *higher* chance of divorce than the average (see table 2.3). The lowest risks of divorce (in the upper right cells) occurred when the husband saw the arrangement as very unfair to his wife, and she agreed that the paid work arrangement was unfair but thought the household arrangement was about right or that he did too much. But any time the husband thought the arrangement was unfair to his wife, the chances for divorce were *less* than the average. (The worst possible marriages, in the lower left cells, understandably, occurred when both spouses thought things were unfair to themselves.)

The third pertinent finding, reported in another paper,[14] was that couples who didn't keep precise track—who answered "don't know" or left the questions blank, had a significantly lower rate of dissolution than those who answered the questions. This finding is consistent with what Yoram Ben-Porath mentioned in his 1985 paper on families and firms: spouses just do not keep track in good marriages, for "there is no running quid pro quo" and "large outstanding balances are tolerated."[15]

The second and third findings, combined, cast doubt on Posner's suggestion that marriages—at least successful ones—may be tit-for-tat exchanges. As I will show later, it is precisely when spouses start to keep internal balance sheets that their marriage is in trouble. Both Nock and I have written about couples we knew who had kept track of arguments they'd had, chores each of them had done (or failed to do), and so forth. My contribution was a doomed couple I'd visited for dinner one night during law school who had a calendar posted in their kitchen with heart stickers appearing every so often. When I innocently inquired what the stickers were for (guessing that they weren't showing administration of heartworm medicine since they had no pet), the wife replied that they identified the days on which they'd made love. Couples who are keeping score have relationships characterized by "inherently dynamic emotional states."[16]

There may be a biological reason, as there was for gift giving, why such couples fly apart after several years of marriage. Anthropologist Helen Fisher supposes that when the hormones (pheromones) that initially attract

TABLE 2.2 **Cox Regressions Predicting Marital Disruption**

Variable	Model 1		Model 2		Model 3		Model 4	
	B	Risk	B	Risk	B	Risk	B	Risk
I. Control variables								
Cohabited	1.7717	5.8808**	1.6776	5.3528**	1.6677	5.2998**	1.6651	5.2863**
Number of children	−.6076	.5447**	−.6187	.5387**	−.6291	.5331**	−.6475	.5234**
Husband's wages	−.0019	.9981	−.0047	.9953	−.0046	.9954	−.0050	.9951
Wife's wages	−.0101	.9899	−.0130	.9870	−.0108	.9893	−.0103	.9898
Husband black	.4167	1.5169*	.3728	1.4519*	.3759	1.4562*	.4213	1.5239*
Husband Hispanic	.3080	1.3607	.2441	1.2765	.2716	1.3120	.3054	1.3572
Husband Asian	.3517	1.4215	.2471	1.2804	.2455	1.2783	.2506	1.2848
Husband American Indian	.5910	1.8058	.4515	1.5707	.3698	1.4475	.3338	1.3962
Different races	.0184	1.0186	.0492	1.0505	.0402	1.0410	.0396	1.0404
Husband's education	.0017	1.0017	−.0141	.9860	−.0164	.9837	−.0219	.9783
Wife's education	.0017	1.0017	−.0083	.9918	−.0154	.9847	−.0142	.9859
Husband age marriage	.0002	1.0002	.0041	1.0041	.0039	1.0039	.0055	1.0055
Wife age marriage	−.0757	.9271**	−.0689	.9334**	−.0700	.9324**	−.0745	.9282**
Husband parents divorced	.6762	1.9665**	.6231	1.8648**	.5941	1.8115**	.5326	1.7033**
Wife parents divorced	.6771	1.9681**	.6203	1.8594**	.6096	1.8396**	.6080	1.8368**
II. Division of labor								
Husband hours paid work			.0154	1.0155**	.0154	1.0155**	.0090	1.0091
Wife hours paid work			.0019	1.0020	.0015	1.0015	.0360	1.0367*
Husband hours male tasks			−.0244	.9759**	−.0253	.9750**	−.0926	.9115
Husband hours female tasks			.0133	1.0134**	.0150	1.0151**	.1142	1.1210*
Wife hours male tasks			−.0417	.9592*	−.0386	.9621*	−.2882	.7496*
Wife hours female tasks			.0065	1.0065*	.0066	1.0066*	.0497	1.0509**

III. Sense of fairness						
Husband household			−.1558	.8557	.1775	1.1942
Wife household			−.2478	.7805**	−.4391	.6446*
Husband paid work			−.3753	.6871**	−.6066	.5452*
Wife paid work			−.0176	.9825	.7369	2.0895**
IV. Fairness-Hours Interaction						
Husband fairness paid X hours male tasks					.0201	1.0203
Husband fairness paid X hours female tasks					−.0218	.9784
Husband fairness household X hours paid					−.0054	.9946
Wife fairness paid X hours male tasks					.0884	1.0925*
Wife fairness paid X Hours female tasks					−.0141	.9860**
Wife fairness household X hours paid					.0092	1.0093*
Husband fair household X hours male tasks					.0029	1.0029
Husband fair household X hours female tasks					−.0117	.9883*
Wife fair household X hours male tasks					−.0079	.9922
Wife fair household X hours in female tasks					−.0002	.9997
Husband fair paid X hours paid work					.0083	1.0084
Wife fair paid X hours paid work					−.0199	.9803**
N	2,858					
−2LL	778.310					
Change (−2LL)	443.766**	44.070**	20.076**		24.066**	

Source: From Steven L. Nock and Margaret F. Brinig, "Weak Men and Disorderly Women: Divorce and the Division of Labor." In *The Law and Economics of Marriage and Divorce*, edited by Antony W. Dnes and Robert Rowthorn. Cambridge: Cambridge University Press, 2002.

* $p < 0.05$

** $p < 0.01$ for coefficient or −2LL change over prior model

TABLE 2.3 **Combined Effects of Interactions of Fairness and Hours of Work on Risk of Marital Disruption**

	Husband's sense of fairness about paid work								
	Very unfair to me			Fair to both			Very unfair to her		
	Husband fairness about household work			Husband fairness about household work			Husband fairness about household work		
Wife's sense of fairness about paid work	Very Unfair to Me	Fair to Both	Very Unfair to Her	Very Unfair to Me	Fair to Both	Very Unfair to Her	Very Unfair to Me	Fair to Both	Very Unfair to Her
Very unfair to me									
Wife fairness household work									
Very unfair to me	4.43	3.10	2.17	2.06	1.44	1.01	.96	.67	.47
Fair to both	2.55	1.79	1.25	1.19	.83	.58	.55	.22	.16
Very unfair to him	1.47	1.03	.72	.68	.48	.34	.32	.22	.16
Fair to both									
Wife fairness household work									
Very unfair to me	8.48	5.93	4.15	3.94	2.76	1.93	1.83	1.28	.90
Fair to both	8.48	3.42	2.39	2.27	1.59	1.11	1.06	.74	.52
Very unfair to him	2.82	1.97	1.38	1.31	.92	.64	.61	.82	.30
Very unfair to him									
Wife fairness household work									
Very unfair to me	16.22	11.35	7.95	7.54	5.28	3.69	3.51	2.45	1.72
Fair to both	9.35	6.55	4.58	4.35	3.04	2.13	2.02	1.42	.99
Very unfair to him	5.39	3.77	2.64	2.51	1.75	1.23	1.17	.82	.59

Source: From Steven L. Nock and Margaret F. Brinig, "Weak Men and Disorderly Women: Divorce and the Division of Labor." In *The Law and Economics of Marriage and Divorce*, edited by Antony W. Dnes and Robert Rowthorn. Cambridge: Cambridge University Press, 2002.

sexual partners and cause sexual passion wear off, they are typically replaced by those that characterize affection (endorphins). If a new child comes along, the relationship will likely endure.[17] Otherwise, one or both of the partners may stray, causing what she calls the "four-year itch."

Whatever the reason, as Ira Ellman suggests, couples don't think of their relationship in contract terms.[18] The successful intimate relationship, he says, is reciprocal but not contractual. "Relationships are themselves the source of legal duties, without the need for any assistance from contract."[19] As Steven Nock wrote, marriages "are experienced mainly in the future and in the past," unlike contracts, which "embody a temporal association that views the future as predicated on the present."[20] Moreover, and despite our notions that this ought not to be so,[21] the legal duties stemming from marriage are gendered. Nock continues, "Marriage is the primary locale in which gender is experienced because it is where our sexual lives are realized."[22] The combination of suspended time and gender results in what Nock refers to elsewhere as turn-taking behavior.[23]

Saul Levmore[24] suggests that legal actors will use property rules (requiring exit before accounting) rather than liability rules (allowing suits while the relationship continues) when it is too difficult to value the contributions of each during an ongoing relationship. In the difficult cases in both corporations and families, though the parties can exit from the relationship, they cannot demand even an accounting while it continues. But more than this, not only would ongoing "valuation" require neutrals to make difficult valuations, but also such valuation in itself is apt to destroy the relationship. This may be an argument against allowing tort actions to be brought in ongoing marriages, or disallowing other actions that would require the court to breach family autonomy (both liability rule-type solutions). In our studies of household work, remember, we were surprised to find that the marriages in which spouses were unable or unwilling to list how many hours they or their partners spent doing various household tasks were more stable than those who made a list.

How Do Gender Differences Manifest in Marriage?

We have already seen that men and women both see arrangements of household labor as fair (or at least accept them) even when women do the majority of the housework and work more total hours. We have also seen some evidence that rigid or self-conscious contract frameworks, even when self-imposed, tend to predict marital instability rather than more stable marriages. The questions remain of where this role specialization comes from—biology, ingrained preferences from socialization, economic gains from specialization, social norms, or law—and whether role specialization is a good thing for society, children, couples, and individual adults or whether it can or should be changed by law. It is clear from the evidence that families continue to be highly gendered. Gender equality is one of the major concerns of Linda McClain's recent book on marriages,[25] and I am quite persuaded by her suggestion that any laws or policy that obstruct or unduly burden equality have no place in modern society. But overcoming biology, if that is the source of the distinction, will likely take more than a few generations.

Anthropologists, and those relying upon them, note that in prehistoric society where large numbers of children were important to maintain subsistence, women would need to bear and nurse children while men maintained their hunting or agricultural pursuits. While they were tending children, as Becker notes in his "Theory of Marriage,"[26] it would be more efficient for these women to watch other children and perform other household tasks. From an evolutionary standpoint, the families in which this specialization occurred would have been more likely to survive into reproductive years and produce their own children.

Becker also relies on the fact that each of us is taught (largely in the family, but also in school) to carry on particular roles.[27] Boys are taught to be tough and, from a very tender age, are more likely to think about justice than be sensitive to relationships and context.[28] At some point, those of us who are now adults *prefer*, for the most part, to act in fundamental ways as everyone expects us to.[29] And clearly, as we have already seen, social norms have a major role to play.

Academics seem agreed that whatever their precise origins, the differences in male and female functions in the household are ancient, persistent, and very slow to change. However, there is some evidence that women work fewer hours on housework than they did a few generations ago and men work slightly more when their partners are employed outside the home. Men also do more child care than their parents did.[30] One of the current disputes is whether this pattern, which tends to result in women's lifetime earnings being lower than men's even with equal education and training, needs to be changed through interventions in the workplace[31] or through family law.[32]

Gender, Norms, and Parenting

A key debate that plays out in same-sex marriage discussions as well as those dealing with custody in (heterosexual) divorce is whether fathers and mothers play different roles in parenting. The answer, according to most available evidence, which comes from different-sex couples, is that they do.[33] Let me be quick to note that I am not arguing here that either fathers or mothers are irreplaceable in child rearing (though on the whole stepparents do not seem to do as good a job as biological parents).[34] Further, emotional closeness of children to nonresidential fathers is important to their well-being.[35]

Children are important to fathers too—men are "supposed" to be providers, procreators, and protectors.[36] When men cannot fulfill these normative roles, they may become depressed,[37] may become violent,[38] or may seek another family.[39] They also may carry out seemingly endless lawsuits against the custodians of their children.[40]

Men also play more with their children, and even earn more,[41] when they have sons.[42] Families with sons are more apt to be stable—parents who know they are having sons are more likely to marry,[43] and families with sons are less likely to separate or divorce.[44] This may be because both mothers and fathers express concerns that divorce may more negatively impact boys than girls.[45] Women will be more secure about their marriages when they have sons[46] (with reason, apparently) but will not change their parenting quantity or their money-earning capacity based upon the gender of their offspring.[47] According to my own research based on reported relocation cases, noncustodial fathers will be more apt to try to block custodial mothers' moves out of the area if sons are involved; noncustodial mothers will file suit regardless of the gender of the children.[48] These gender differences in parenting undoubtedly affect not only the wealth of boys as opposed to girls but also the way children receive their most important cues about gender.

Though they do not spend more when they have daughters than when they have sons, women do spend more on *children* if they have the money to do so than their husbands.[49] One comparative and qualitative paper concluding that inequalities in marriage are the result of bargaining was published by Bina Agarwal of the University of Delhi.[50] Agarwal, writing from a feminist economics perspective, begins with the assertion that the endowments that govern bargaining are socially rather than biologically constructed. She claims that although biology may have originally been important, the changes in technology that allow women to work at almost any job should have rendered these gender distinctions obsolete, and that there is too much variation among cultures to support such a universal assumption. Agarwal concludes that inequality need not be built into families to keep them stable (an assumption contradicting Steven Nock's more recent empirical work on spouses who earn nearly comparable salaries).[51] She further maintains that it is incorrect to assume a unitary model—that is, bargaining is done over all matters simultaneously. Instead, it occurs over a subset of issues at a time. Like other economists studying bargaining, she assumes that a woman's bargaining power within the household critically depends upon her power (particularly market power) outside it as well as social norms and the perception others hold of this outside power.[52] Gendered norms, she maintains, "set the stage for the form that bargaining can take, even within the marketplace."[53] In the rural Indian families she studies, she notes that any incorrect perceptions women might have of what might be most beneficial for them are limited by the power they actually have to effect change: they may be acting out of self-interest over the long run rather than simply because they are more altruistic than the men in their families.[54]

Sociologists Sayer and Bianchi[55] perhaps make some of the same points, though they are working with quantitative data (the NSFH). They, too, find that women's outside opportunities make a difference in their relationships. But what labor-force opportunities do is make it possible for women in emotionally unsatisfying marriages to exit from them. And the reason they leave is that women, unlike men, benefit from good marriages but not from emotionally unsatisfying ones. While men benefit in numerous ways from even the most unhappy marriage,[56] women, if they have the financial ability to leave and if they are not constrained by religion or concerned for the children, will exit.[57] As I will show presently, it is women who primarily file for divorce.[58] Nock postulates that women exit because their husbands are unlikely to recognize the greater efforts expanded by the wives, either by the husbands doing additional housework or expressing gratitude.[59]

To reach this conclusion, Nock relies on data from the 1999 March Demographic Supplement of the Current Population Survey (which included approximately 50,000 U.S. households with more than 19,000 married couples) as well as the NSFH (which included nearly 3,600 married couples). About 22% of these featured couples with each contributing at least 40% to family income (those he calls the marriages of equally dependent spouses, or MEDS). Nock measured the commitment of each of these spouses in terms of "a subjective assessment of the likely consequences for ending the relationship."[60] What he found was that as wives became less dependent upon their husbands' income, in other words, when they became MEDS because of increases in their own earnings, they became less committed to their marriages.[61] There was no corresponding effect for husbands. Equally dependent spouses have higher chances (57% higher) of divorce, related most closely to the hours wives commit to working for that nearly equal income.[62] Nock found for those MEDS marriages that ended by divorce, it was the wife who wanted divorce more than the husband (and the chances were more than two and a half times as high as they would have been if they were more dependent on their husbands).[63]

Like the caregiving of children, caregiving of parents has a gendered pattern. Daughters are more likely than sons to provide care to the elderly,[64] and this is especially true for biological parents.[65] It is even true when there are sons who could provide the care.[66] This means that for many women, there may be a period when they are caring for their own children as well as their parents.[67] For the very old parents, this competing set of demands on the women poses a risk, albeit a small one, of elder abuse,[68] a phenomenon we will discuss at greater length in chapter 6. Perhaps because of the strong lobbies by groups like the AARP, states have recently enacted statutes mandating financial provision for elderly but destitute parents, since, for most of us, the inclination will be to spend money on our minor children first.[69]

So given all this gloomy gender news, what makes marriage good for so many people (especially women)? After the pheromones and heightened sexual passion die down, we saw that anthropologist Fisher maintains that what the body produces instead is endorphins, which produce a feeling of contentment and affection.[70] But if it is biological, that help should be there for every couple, not simply those who survive the "itch." What I have been characterizing as a primary value in these longer-running marriages is trust. We have already encountered trust in the recognition that the division of household labor isn't precisely equal and in what Nock called the living in the past and future. Another and related value, again supported by extra-familial norms, is the overcoming of either selfishness or its less active counterpart, shirking.

In his chapter on marriage, Eric Posner writes that the outside community guards against married couples' shirking or deviating too far from the marital norm by means of community enforcements (for example, in the ancient practice of charivari, noisy community members gathered around the house of a newly wedded couple, particularly when the marriage was socially questionable).[71] He reasons that people are trying to signal to others in the community that they are of the "good type" that can be trusted (in his terminology, have low discount rates) and therefore will engage in punishing others who violate social norms. He maintains that this should be easier in homogeneous communities, and some research on family violence indicates that this is so.[72] Both he[73] and Richard McAdams[74] also mention the conforming tendency of gossip.

Exogenous social norms can certainly help with minimizing both selfishness and shirking—by convincing us to look at the long run, providing us with examples of successful couples (which may be one reason why the divorce rate is lower in communities that haven't seen lots of divorces), or pointing out our own imperfections or fault in a particular misunderstanding. Sometimes community members can even pitch in to help when we are just worn out from trying to do too much. Husbands can adjust their behavior to recognize a new norm for their contributions to marriage, and probably slowly are, as Nock notes in the MEDS piece, but wives probably need to make some normative adjustments as well as we transition to an age when most spouses work outside the home. At this moment of nonequilibrium, married women's labor-force roles have dramatically changed (and the household roles have changed some) while men's labor-force roles have not (and the household roles have changed only a little).

One last point about housework returns to our earlier discussion of when law can usefully precede norms. Before the reunification of Germany, East Germany by legislation attempted to set a norm, to be enforced by outsiders at work and in the neighborhood, of equal participation in household work by husbands and wives.[75] Since both men and women were supposed to work in the socialist economy,[76] this law must have been seen as only fair (as it was, indeed, by one later commentator trying to urge the solution for the reunified Germany).[77] However, what happened? Men did not pick up a larger share of the housework, though women in fact did work outside the home at rates approaching 91%.[78] The divorce rate soared compared to the rate of the historically very similar West Germany.[79] Why? As Inga Markovits reflected, it was because of the "total disregard of economic and social realities,"[80] that is, norms. In her view, socialist legislators enacted a radical marriage philosophy that was not backed by the "customs and morals of the vast majority of a largely agrarian population." Interestingly, once the "two Germanys" reunified, the country settled on the former

West German policy favoring individual decisions about labor allocations in the family and a social norm keeping most women with small children at home. Compared to the United States, which has never had a formal law dealing with responsibility for household labor, far fewer women in the unified Germany now work (despite the vast number previously working in East Germany): 65% of working-aged women were employed in the United States in 1997 compared to 54% in Germany. The difference was still more dramatic with married women with preschool children, of whom 60% were employed in the United States compared to 46% in Germany.[81] By 2001, the rates had crept up to 71% for the United States and 65.2% for Germany, but though the two countries are converging, the German rate remains far lower than it was in socialist East Germany twenty years earlier.[82]

How External Norms Affect Internal Behavior

Another possibility besides equal division of labor during marriage would be to allow explicit payment by a working spouse for homemaking services. This possibility was first raised in the logic behind the famous palimony, or support of a former cohabitant, case of *Marvin v. Marvin*.[83] In *Marvin*, the California Supreme Court declared that a disadvantaged cohabitant might recover damages when the relationship dissolved. The *Marvin* court employed a variety of legal theories including express and implied contract. Not only has the case influenced our thinking about cohabitation, but it has also indelibly affected marriage.[84] The undisputed good coming from the case, from a feminist point of view at least, is that *Marvin* recognizes the value that women confer on men and family. At the same time *Marvin* was being argued and written, a number of legislatures were enacting property distribution statutes.[85] Many of these first-generation statutes explicitly recognized spouses' nonfinancial contributions to the family as well as their financial contributions.[86] As will be shown shortly, the question is whether the way that revelation has played out (only at dissolution, instead of more pervasively) poses a problem for marriage. If compensation is made pervasively and does not require periodic cost accounting, it should not destabilize marriage. That is the benefit of the fifty-fifty sharing assumptions that have been in place in community property regimes governing intact marriages for some years.[87] The important insight is that household work needs to be dignified and the property/support thus gained treated as *earned*, not as a gift or handout.[88] In dissolution cases, household work needs to be treated as contributing not only to financial assets but also to future earnings generally.[89] The investment made in the other's future earning capacity is not necessarily tied to the contributing spouse's earning potential. That is, to some extent, though the career sacrifice of the homemaker may be quite different, the employed spouse will gain the same whether the homemaker has given up a legal, secretarial, or nurse's aide career.[90] This point is missed by the ALI *Principles*, which allow permanent compensation to reduce loss and equalize income but not rise to the level of the gain to the other spouse.[91] In other words, a spouse's sacrifice for the benefit of the marriage is recognized, but only to replace what she might have made otherwise. Her contributions during the marriage are not treated as investments in the career of the other spouse, even if they contributed vitally to a very successful career. (She would then receive a share of the tangible property accumulated but not a share of future earnings.)

But to keep from destabilizing marriage and reducing marital behavior to the series of exchanges we have criticized earlier in the context of cohabitation, the contributions of what Nock discusses in terms of marital-specific capital[92] must be realized during ongoing marriages as well. This concern might argue for something like the taxation solution proposed by Nancy Staudt.[93] Such a "carrot" or reward approach, as opposed to arguing for equal division of assets upon divorce, might also include the moribund "comparable worth" compensation for traditionally female occupations that require as much training or education as traditionally male "comparables." It might suggest direct compensation from the employer who, as in the case of the university president, requires significant service by the key employee's spouse.[94] For recipients of government benefits, it suggests treating all caretakers as being as dependent upon external wage supports as their charges.[95] Another positive step may be marriage education, which focuses on communication skills learned prior to marriage and reinforced throughout it.[96] Of course, though this tactic seems to help reduce divorce, it may not promote equality of power during marriage. And, as Katharine Bartlett observed, that continues to be the central problem for family law.[97]

Another way of looking at social norms is to realize that they are soft boundaries around some institutional arrangement.[98] They are called soft because, unlike laws or even contracts, they are enforced informally and are flexible. A norm is a norm only because most people conform most of the time. This means that, to some extent, people involved in "domestic relations" set their own norms. Thus some parents may be strict while others are permissive; some couples may share household tasks evenly while others allocate them according to traditional gender roles. Elizabeth and Robert Scott[99] argue that many marital norms are of this negotiated variety and the wide subject matter allowed by the Uniform Premarital Agreement Act[100] bears this out. While still conforming to parental norms of support, discipline, and so forth, some parents interpret these to call for greater, and some for lesser, strictness. In another example, covenant marriage couples in Louisiana, even controlling for differences at the time of marriage, were far more likely to become *more* committed to an idea of lifetime marriage and to a more traditional division of labor between husband and wife than those choosing standard marriage.[101] Nock and his coauthors describe the difference as follows:

> We describe the difference as institutionalization of the marriage. Covenant couples describe their marriages as involving three parties: the husband, the wife, and the marriage itself. For covenant couples, the marriage warrants consideration apart from the individualistic concerns of either partner. In regard to some matters, covenant couples appear to defer to the interests of their marriage even when the individual concerns of the partners may appear to conflict. And this orientation to married life, we argue, helps resolve the customary problems faced by newly married couples in regard to fairness and equity.[102]

On the other extreme, the concept of parties setting their own terms, like writing their own vows as my daughter and her husband did in the Hawaiian wedding, seems to fit well with the libertarian view of the world as well as the related sixties idea that marriage should be a unique and individualistic experience. And, as we have seen, neither idea (inventing one's own norms, or having a marriage that is a completely individualistic experience) works. Social norms may be interpreted, or even ignored, but individuals cannot totally create them. When couples or parents waive what we might call status requirements or do not enforce contractual duties owed by others, we may also think of Stewart Macaulay's famous article about commercial actors who view lawsuits as threatening to their long-term relationships and violative of good-faith norms.[103] According to Macaulay, business people simply ignore breaches of quantity, payment, or delivery date and adjust terms to meet the others' current needs and the well-being of the long-term relationship. Remember, in this vein, the *Nanakuli Paving* case discussed in the previous chapter in which a contracting party said, in essence, that "demanding things" just wasn't done.[104] Married couples who are able to renegotiate the day-to-day terms of their union are more likely to weather the crises of life stages and persist as a lasting and stable couple.[105]

As Goethe put it, "The human condition is compounded of so much joy and so much sorrow that it is impossible to reckon how much a husband owes a wife or a wife a husband. It is an infinite debt; it can be paid only in eternity."[106] Couples do better when they adjust their situations, as opposed to the very rules of the game, as they go along. But no couple may go it alone, that is, live entirely outside external marital norms, without paying a heavy price. Married couples who try to invent their own norms resemble unmarried couples who live together. Cohabiting couples may have everything else that married couples have, but, as we have seen, they surely do not have strong norms to define their relationship. Cohabiters must invent their own customs and standards. They cannot rely on any social script to help them organize and arrange their lives together. Thus, we have seen that the lack of social norms partially explains the poorer quality of cohabiting relationships and the very short duration of most such unions.[107] And, as we have explored, many of the same features seem to mark stepparents' relationships, although in the stepfamilies there are additional complications of trying to merge two different "worlds," as Elizabeth Marquardt calls them.[108] Blended families might learn from the business literature that suggests that for many failed corporate mergers the problem is that the entities' cultures cannot be reconciled.[109]

While in some cases norms present a set of general guidelines within which the couple can vary their own relationship, there remain some components at the core of families that cannot be varied or waived. Parents cannot marry off their children at young ages or have sexual relations with them or contract out of the duty to support or care for them. Spouses cannot agree, in a legally binding way, to five-year marriages with the option to renew or to divorce only for fault grounds or to not hold each other responsible for support during marriage. There are, in short, limits to the soft boundaries of norms—and law often defines these.

For example, Iowa, in its premarital agreement act formulation, disallows future waivers of support even for times after the marriage has ended.[110] Many family norms, then, are set externally by the state. These will tend to be the legal expressions of the values promoted by families—unconditional giving and permanence.[111] But here I want to stress other kinds of external norms that govern matters like housework.

Both husband and wife have as part of their goals (conscious or not) the desire to demonstrate that they are "not weird" (that is, they may seek to be within the standard variance from norms). Arlie Hochschild pointed out that although the company she studied had rather generous provisions for flextime and family leave, many mothers and nearly all fathers were unwilling to take advantage of these programs. To quote one father who is obviously conflicted about his work and family obligations,

> I'm a closet workaholic. There are times my wife has to jolt me back into family life. The last hour at work I get nervous that I've stayed at work too long. Going home in the car, I worry she'll be in a bad mood. My family comes first, but sometimes I ask myself, do I really need to be home? Or is this a passing thing? If I don't get home for an hour, is Tamara going to die? No, probably not. But if I don't meet this deadline at work, maybe the consequences will be severe.[112]

This book proposes that when the community sets a clear set of norms for a relationship, it tends to strengthen and reward the new institution through a grant of autonomy. To the extent the relationship is "normal" or "not weird" in this sense, the community trusts its members to perform the functions of marriage or parenting and, as the next chapters suggest, allows them to vary as they will within the guidelines set by the norms. The external trust and the consequent autonomy that result fill us with a deep sense of well-being.

In order to test the impact of cultural environment (or social norms) upon attitude formation that might affect marriage and divorce, Steven Nock and I ran special estimates called Cox proportional hazards model regressions estimating factors increasing or decreasing the probability of divorce or separation. We again used the NSFH[113] and limited the sample to couples in first marriages only. We held constant almost all known predictors of divorce (age at first marriage, education, income, race, whether parents had divorced, etc.). We added the statewide percentage of adults who were divorced, separated, or never married in the state of residence and at the time the respondent was sixteen. The purpose in this analysis was to estimate the influence of the prevailing living arrangements in the state a person lived in (at age sixteen) on the chances that he or she would eventually divorce. These results are shown in table 2.4.

TABLE 2.4 **Odds of Divorce as a Function of Marital Status of the Population in the State and Year the Respondent was 16**

Variable name	B	SE	t-stat	Sig.	Exp. B
Cohabited before marriage	0.333	0.131	2.539	0.011	1.395
Number of children	−0.489	0.06	8.14	0	0.613
Husband's wages	0	0	3.609	0	1
Wife's wages	0	0	2.364	0.018	1
Husband is Black	0.426	0.186	2.291	0.022	1.531
Husband is Hispanic	−0.343	0.258	1.329	0.184	0.709
Husband is Asian	−0.438	0.73	0.6	0.548	0.645
Husband is American Indian	−0.088	0.561	0.158	0.875	0.918
Spouses are of the same race	−0.012	0.079	0.144	0.884	0.989
Wife's highest level of education	−0.006	0.03	0.1844	0.853	0.994
Husband's parents divorced	−0.113	0.154	0.7294	0.466	0.894
Wife's parents divorced	0.549	0.136	4.0212	0	1.731
Husband's age when married	0.017	0.11	1.537	0.124	1.017
Wife's age when married	0.19	0.018	10.37	0	1.209
Percentage divorced in state where respondent lived at 16	0.984	0.059	16.725	0	2.675
Percentage separated in state where respondent lived at 16	0.415	0.092	4.499	0	1.514
Percentage never married in state where respondent lived at 16	−0.012	0.014	2.083	0.037	0.972

Source: From Margaret F. Brinig and Steven L. Nock, "'I Only Want Trust': Norms, Trust, and Autonomy." *Journal of Socio-Economics* 32, 2003.

The last three lines of this table show that the current prevalence of divorce and separation and their prevalence for the state where the respondent lived at age sixteen both significantly predict the respondent's divorce. Consider the coefficient for the percentage divorced of .984. This can be translated into the odds of divorce, as shown in the last column of the table. The relevant statistic (2.675) indicates that each additional percentage of the state population that is divorced is associated with almost 2.7 times the risks of divorce for an individual. More generally, an increase in divorce and separation percentages increases the odds of divorce, while an increase in the percentage who never married lowers the odds of divorce. Growing up in a state with a high percentage of divorced adults is associated with higher chances of divorce when an individual becomes an adult. In similar work, John Johnson and Christopher Mazingo[114] estimated the chances of becoming divorced in a particular state (as a function of the divorce regime in place). They used this probability to estimate education (finding lower education for girls but not boys) and marriage (predicting delay in marriage).

What Happens to Trust on Divorce?

Although we will discuss the precise mechanism by which a less-than-happy marriage heads for divorce later in this chapter, it is clear that while some unhappy families divorce, some do not.[115] Children seem to do relatively better even when the marriage is unhappy, so long as it is stable and not accompanied by high conflict.[116] Women, again, gain few of the benefits of marriage unless the union is a happy one. So let us assume for the present discussion that the wife no longer trusts her husband to fulfill his part of the bargain, so that the marriage no longer works for her.

As we have seen, norms in families, at least in the sociological sense of community expectations of family patterns, seem to involve at least two important characteristics: the permanence of the relationship and the unconditional love within it. The normative expectation of permanence and unconditional love is the basis for collective trust that the relationship will function in its prescribed way. For couples, that means that others will trust that they will pursue intimacy in socially recognized (i.e., normative) ways.[117] For parents, that means trusting that they will provide an environment within which children can flourish. In return for conforming to community norms, people in relationships are given various legal and other supports that further encourage and promote the relationship.[118]

It should be clear that families differ in important ways from commercial interactions—intimacy and flourishing are rather unusual "goods" for the participants to maximize. Elizabeth and Robert Scott's point is that strong norms (expectations) exist about the ongoing family and for parents. To the extent that people conform to those norms, they are trusted as reliable and dependable members of a collective. To the extent that they do not, they lose that trust and will pay a price. One criterion for being trusted (by the larger community) is open and conspicuous conformity—as shown by a stable, permanent parent-child union. Steven Nock and I believe that norms and trust affect the formation of marriage, the conduct of married people, and their relative happiness following divorce. In "I Only Want Trust,"[119] we began with the last of these time periods and worked backward to the first.

A question we focused on in that paper involves what happens when someone who was in a legal family no longer is, or no longer is in the fullest sense. The particular individuals we considered were noncustodial fathers, though we could perhaps envision similar outcomes for noncustodial mothers, birth parents following adoption, or any parents once their children are emancipated.[120] We attempted to demonstrate that losing the community trust and recognition that a custodial parent possesses causes a significant (in both statistical and practical terms) amount of depression in divorced men. So one important lesson we have learned is that factors that affect emotional states, like depression, matter to social policy as much as do factors that affect people's behavior, like filing for divorce, seeking custody, or considering financial costs and benefits.

A second empirical observation is at least suggestive of what happens when the law tries to put a "fix" on a problem that is perhaps intractable. Many of these noncustodial divorced fathers have for the last twenty years or so been denoted "joint legal custodians."[121] Part of the project was to determine whether that title, which was seemingly a low-cost solution to the problem of pleasing both the parents at the time of divorce, moderated the otherwise unhappy effects of loss of custodial status. Various studies have shown that joint legal custody has marginal effects on child support receipt[122] or visitation.[123] If it is not a better status for the child, does it at least benefit the noncustodial parent?

Marriages are viewed as good when the spouses trust each other. They founder when trust is no longer there. If a wife loses trust in her husband (usually if she no longer believes he is acting unselfishly), quite often she files for divorce. In fact, as we have seen, her satisfaction with the relationship is significant in predicting divorce, while his is not. Though she loses financially by divorcing, she keeps (if she has custody) not simply an asset, though this is important too, but the third-party trust and autonomy that go with being a custodial parent (married or single). Her former spouse gains financially but, arguably, will be depressed by his loss of custody far more than by his simple loss of marital status.

This sense of loss occurs because, at a basic level, norms, including custody norms, function to give the person conforming to them a sense of identity as a member of a group of like-minded people. Thus, the young law associate knows, not only what he or she is to wear to work, but also how much firm service or pro bono work is expected, how many billable hours must be completed, and what image he or she is expected to project to the client, other firms, and the world in general.[124] Firm identity or trade name may become shorthand for reliable performance.

We have already seen that these principles work in families too. At a basic level again, family arrangements are scripted—there are norms concerning how one is to behave in his or her family roles. Cultural beliefs provide guidance about how one should behave as a husband (some collection of characteristics that includes protector and good provider), a wife (some bundle of characteristics plus nurturer and emotional supporter), or a child (some group of traits including good ambassador of family well-being). These norms are part of the institutions of marriage and parenting. If we do not follow the script, we may well be uncomfortable and almost certainly will suffer loss of esteem. We care about our families' reputation with outsiders, punish those who fail to live up to our expectations, and sometimes expel them from the community.

Conformity to social norms (social control) undoubtedly produces consistent personal orientations and reactions (self-control). That is, what was once seen as obedience to a social script evolves into a personal attribute—something that is simply seen as normal and taken for granted. Deep inside us we also check to some extent what we feel—whether we feel maternal or paternal toward our newborn, whether we feel good about how our home looks when guests arrive, whether we feel guilty if we are not caring for aging parents. In this way, on an individual level the norms become part of our utility functions. We are more content if we reside safely within the script constructed for us by these outside norms. Collectively, those who share common norms and who interact with one another come to share the trust that springs from that sharing. This is, of course, social capital.[125]

To understand how loss of custody interacts with norms, we need to look at several other family related norms questions. The first of these, which we might call "personal trust," relates most closely to the relationship quality women consider most important in a marriage. The second, the institutional trust issues (including prestige, esteem, and honor) involved with loss of custody at divorce, suggests that men are more influenced by community norms than relationship issues, but that those trust-related community judgments affect them deeply. We have already considered the broader social norms relating to marriage and divorce and how these influence the behavior of individual men and women.

Family law and family policy, of course, involve all three sets of trust-and-norms questions, which not only exist independently but also interact. Outside influences, primarily the change in women's labor-force participation, have destabilized family dynamics. Of course, divorce also affects labor-force participation.[126] As we consider new or revised family laws, we simply must consider the various ways norms operate within families.

Personal trust: An empirical view of the wife's perspective on divorce

In Connecticut, in 1995, wives filed almost exactly two-thirds of the divorce petitions (.669). In marriages where there were children, though these break up less often, wives filed more than seven out of ten (.713). In the vast majority of cases, who filed (husband or wife) was identical to who received custody (see table 2.5).[127]

We might describe this custody-related filing behavior as taking valuable assets from the marriage. However, it may be that in a mediocre marriage, the wife (who may in fact be working more hours and not being appreciated) may have less to lose by divorcing than does her husband. Having custody of children reflects a profound societal trust in our ability as parents,[128] a trust that results in the granting of autonomy that the Su-

TABLE 2.5 **Logit Regression Results, Women as Petitioners, 1995**

Variable	All states	Three states	Virginia	Oregon
Age variables				
Wife's age at marriage	0.0177	0.0147	0.0137	0.0151
	(5.3177)[b]	(4.4380)[b]	(3.050)[b]	(1.7962)[a]
Husband's age at marriage	−0.0173	−0.0151	−0.0155	−0.0254
	(5.4535)[b]	(4.7868)[b]	(3.5972)[b]	(3.1825)[b]
Wife's age times years of marriage	−0.0019 (7.0133)[b]	−0.0019 (6.563)[b]	−0.0017 (4.7080)[b]	−0.0020 (2.4841)[b]
Husband's age times years of marriage	0.0025 (9.2940)[b]	0.0024 (8.5562)[b]	0.0020 (5.6911)[b]	0.0028 (3.4308)[b]
Years married	−0.0384	−0.0343	−0.0243	−0.0381
	(6.1570)[b]	(5.2958)[b]	(2.8242)[b]	(2.0923)[b]
Child variable				
Number of children Under 18	−0.0565 (5.366)[b]	−0.0621 (5.7659)[b]	0.0001 (0.000)	−0.0386 (0.9881)
Number of children awarded to husband	−0.5454 (30.6433)[b]	−0.5371 (28.9189)[b]	−0.6859 (10.3143)[b]	−0.7673 (12.7164)[b]
Number of children awarded to wife	0.4780 (34.89)[b]	0.4884 (33.9654)[b]	0.3334 (6.0704)[b]	0.5149 (11.9904)[b]
Number of children awarded joint custody	0.1307 (9.0465)[b]	0.1252 (8.1261)[b]	−0.1461 (2.5093)[b]	0.0205 (0.4382)
Human capital variable				
Relative education	−0.0815	−0.0865	−0.076	−0.2173
	(33.7153)[b]	(33.5112)[b]	(27.8460)[b]	(14.5573)[b]
Wife's education	0.0030	0.0025	0.0064	−0.0207
	(1.2081)	(1.0099)	(2.3483)[b]	(1.3342)
Wife is white		0.2021	0.1709	0.1906
		(6.8051)[b]	(4.9084)[b]	(1.7263)[a]
Husband's number of marriages	0.0281 (1.4670)		−0.004 (0.1466)	0.0930 (2.0662)[b]
Wife's number of marriages	−0.0562 (3.0718)[b]		−0.0515 (1.9912)[b]	0.0420 (0.9975)

TABLE 2.5 *(continued)*

Variable	All states	Three states	Virginia	Oregon
Aggregate variables				
State is no-fault	0.1277	0.0889		
	(3.0988)[b]	(1.7251)[a]		
Divorce rate	0.0075	0.0062	0.0349	−0.0250
	(1.0376)	(0.8243)	(2.5123)[b]	(2.5814)[b]
Poverty rate	0.0000	0.0000	0.0068	0.0000
	(3.3326)[b]	(3.3486)[b]	(3.0375)[b]	(0.6678)
Population density	−0.0000	−0.0000	−0.0000	0.0003
	(4.0029)[b]	(2.7098)[b]	(4.0073)[b]	(2.1023)[b]
Per capita personal income			0.0000	
			(2.9165)[b]	
Filing/initiating				
Length of separation				−0.0380
				(3.0067)[b]
Bad marriage				
Grounds of cruelty			1.5604	
			(5.9783)[b]	
Constant	0.4213	0.2182	−0.0209	0.9688
	(6.0238)[b]	(2.8502)[b]	(0.1631)	(3.7144)[b]
Correct estimations	66.43	66.46	64.91	71.181
N	46,547	43,329	26,067	7,234

Source: From Margaret F. Brinig and Douglas W. Allen, "'These Boots Are Made for Walking': Why Most Divorce Filers Are Women." *American Law and Economics Review* 2, no. 1, 2000.
[a] Significant to 0.1 level. T-statistics in parentheses.
[b] Significant to 0.05 level. T-statistics in parentheses.
All states = Connecticut, Virginia, Oregon, and Montana
Three states = Connecticut, Virginia, and Oregon

preme Court calls a fundamental liberty interest, "the fundamental right of parents to make decisions concerning the care, custody, and control of their children."[129] The noncustodial parent possesses far less autonomy and trust. Not only does he (or she) lose time with beloved children, but also the societal certification as the parent with whom it is in the children's best interest to live.[130] There is a norm, a gendered script for parents who live with their children. There is none for noncustodial parents. As one embittered father noted, "the autonomy [power] over their children's contact with the father, often in tandem with revenge for real or perceived misdeeds, is one of the few compensating or 'positive' emotions they [custodial mothers] may be experiencing at this time [divorce]."[131] Pediatrician Robert Fay goes on, "He is expected to visit, not parent," and notes that too often he is expected to seek new relationships rather than persist in the old ones.

Others have observed that custody issues—and changes in custody laws—have taken over "gender wars,"[132] particularly those involved with divorce.[133] Further, men who have lost custody appear to be more bitter about this type of loss than they would be about the loss of even a very valuable financial asset. They use terms like "being in jail," "left in a lurch, unhappy and extremely uncomfortable," and "despair and sadness."[134]

Even at the end of a marriage, the courts therefore face special problems. Where there are minor children, much of the valuation made by courts is not financial but is emotional: how good a parent are you? It is predictive as well, for the court must look at what has occurred in the past to place the child in an environment for the future.[135] Even where the determination is purely financial (how much marital property each spouse gets), the case may involve even more difficult worth/valuation problems than those of commercial partnership, because sorting out contributions to a marriage gets the court very involved with issues of quality rather than quantity.[136]

Once a woman feels that her husband is not emotionally supporting her, the marriage becomes less stable and divorce or separation far more likely. As we have seen, demographers have shown recently that though the emotional quality of marriage influences the changes of divorce for women, it does not seem to for men.[137] Women may simply be more sensitive than men to the emotional quality of their relationships. Whatever the reason, the finding correlates with findings of other social scientists: men "profit" in many ways from any marriage, regardless of quality, and women "profit" in terms of health, longevity, and mental health only when the marriage goes well.[138]

If a marriage is essentially a "love it or leave it" relationship, what is parenting? Is it appropriate, because of the societal trust that custodial parenting confers, to allow a spouse's judgment about the quality of the marriage relationship, however righteous, to trigger the personal "accounting" and societal judgment about parenting that custody litigation requires? My own strong preference in the custody area matches the collective proposal of the ALI: first allow the parents to make their own "parenting plan," and only if they cannot reach agreement, have the court replicate, or "approximate," the way they allocated child care during the relationship.[139]

Institutional trust: An empirical look at the husband's view

DATA AND METHODS. To discover how custody norms operate, Steven Nock and I analyzed the NSFH, a nationally representative household sample of those 18 and over, which was first administered in 1987–88 and included personal interviews with 13,007 respondents. In 1992–93, 10,003 of these individuals were reinterviewed. The sample includes a main cross section of 9,637 households plus an oversampling of blacks, Puerto Ricans, Mexican Americans, single-parent families, families with stepchildren, cohabiting couples, and recently married persons. In all analyses reported here, suitable weights were applied as required for such samples. One adult per household was randomly selected as the primary respondent, and spouses and cohabiting partners completed a self-administered questionnaire (with more limited coverage of topics). Several portions of the main interview were self-administered to facilitate the collection of sensitive information and to ease the flow of the interview.

The respondents to this survey provided a great deal of demographic information (the more normal fodder for economists). They were also asked, in both waves and among numerous other inquiries, a series of questions that make up a brief, simple depression scale (the Centers for Epidemiological Studies Depression Scale [CESD]) drawn from a well-known and validated measure used in the diagnosis and treatment of psychological disorders. Briefly, each respondent was asked the following: *On how many days during the past week did you . . . ?* This was followed by questions related to the twelve symptoms of depression, such as the following: *Have you felt bothered by things that usually don't bother you? Have you not felt like eating? Have you felt that you could not shake off the blues even with help from your family or friends? Have you felt lonely?*[140] Answers to these questions ranged from "none" to "7 days in the past week." The possible range of the scale, therefore, is zero (none on all twelve items) to 84 (7 days last week on all 12 items). In the present analysis, for example, the average for married respondents (on the first interview) was 13 while it was 17 for divorced respondents. That is, divorced men were more likely to be depressed than married men were. The CESD is a widely used measure of depression.[141] In clinical and diagnostic settings, the scale has thresholds to indicate a (clinical) risk of depression. Nock's and my concern in the piece was analytical rather than clinical. We studied only whether this indicator of symptoms of depression changed when divorce and associated events occurred.

The regression analyses that follow are based on both waves of interviews. The same men were analyzed to determine how much (and in which direction) their scores on the depression scale changed. The method used was essentially the same as calculating the difference between scores in each wave (so the question was whether the difference in Depression Score wave 2 – Depression Score wave 1 was influenced by the difference in Divorced wave 2 – Divorced wave 1). Since there are statistical reasons to avoid using actual "change scores" as dependent variables in regression,[142] we relied on a slightly different technique (technically known as "static score change model" regressions). The results may be understood to show the influence of change in some causal (independent) variable on the amount of change in the depression score between waves.[143]

The analysis sought to isolate some of the effects of divorce, loss of custody (separation from the child) and legal loss of custody, from other factors that also might affect depression. Thus we controlled for depression in the first period (1987–88), income (and change in income), education, race, remarriage, or loss of a spouse through death.

The sample analyzed includes all men, married or single at the time of the initial interview, who also completed interviews in the second wave. This allowed us to compare the effects of changing marital status over time (getting divorced, remarried, etc.), as well as the custody change of interest to us.

FINDINGS. Having a legal agreement or order giving custody to the other parent, while maintaining that you are "fit," impliedly means that you are less trustworthy than the other is in the normative sense. We argue that this is so because the universal standard for awarding custody is the "best interests of the child." An award of custody to the wife means that as far as the child's welfare is concerned, placement with her is preferable. (See table 2.6 for a complete list of variables, plus our results.)

The coefficient for loss of custody (4.256) is not only statistically significant ($p < .01$) but also has one of the largest standardized (beta) coefficients in the equation. In practical terms, loss of custody through a legal agreement or decision increases depression by about 4 points, or one-quarter of a standard deviation, on average. This is even taking into account the greater depression following marriage. For comparison, consider the coefficient of being separated from his child in the line above. The coefficient is not statistically significant ($p < .901$) and is 25 times smaller than that for the legal loss.[144] We could not, of course, be certain that it was not the fathers' depression that caused the loss of custody (though fathers in intact marriages are, generally speaking, less depressed). Since so many of the noncustodial fathers are more depressed following loss of custody than they were earlier, this direction of causation seems unlikely.

TABLE 2.6 **Risk of Men's Depression as a Result of Changes In Children's Living Arrangements, Comparisons Based on Time 1 (1988) and Time 2 (1993) (Responses Men Only)**

Model	B	Std. error	Beta	t	Sig.
Constant	13.403			14.117	0.000
Married since Time 1 (1988)?	−1.760	1.743	−0.016	−1.009	0.313
Remarried since Time 1?	−2.341	2.608	−0.018	−0.897	0.370
Divorced since Time 1?	1.298	1.799	0.016	0.722	0.471
Widowed since Time 1?	1.733	2.732	0.010	0.634	0.526
Education (years)	−0.123	0.058	−0.035	−2.106	0.035
Respondent is black (1=yes/0=no)	4.753	0.967	0.081	4.914	0.000
Respondent is Hispanic	1.919	1.377	0.023	1.394	0.163
Respondent is Asian	−2.519	3.747	−0.011	−0.672	0.501
Respondent is Am. Indian	0.181	5.196	0.001	0.035	0.972
R has biological minor children now living elsewhere who were living with R at Time 1 (1=y, 0=n)	0.189	1.516	0.002	0.125	0.901
R has legal agreement granting custody of children to other parent? (1=yes, 0=no, not applicable)	4.256	1.541	0.050	2.761	0.006
R Income-Time 1 ($1,000s)	−0.027	0.016	−0.033	−1.744	0.081
R Income-Time 2	−0.042	0.001	−0.071	−2.708	0.002
Depression-Time 1	0.240	0.018	0.221	13.487	0.000

Source: From Margaret F. Brinig and Steven L. Nock, "'I Only Want Trust': Norms, Trust, and Autonomy." *Journal of Socio-Economics* 32, 2003.
Note: CEDS2 is a brief version of the "Centers for Epidemiological Studies Depression Scale." Averages for married respondents were 13.0843; divorced was 18.07; separated was 22.73. Respondents are compared to those who never married.

The overall explanatory power of the equation ($R^2 = .083$) is modest and suggests that change in the depression scale between waves was possibly caused by additional systematic factors not included in the model. We could not identify such factors, however, using analyses of residuals.

Incidentally, we would have predicted a similar increase in depression for women who lose custody. Unfortunately, in the NSFH sample there were so few of them (10) that results are not statistically significant. It may also be that the results simply cannot be replicated for the other gender. Women, more than men, are interested in relationship issues more than institutional ones. Men, more than women, are interested in institutional issues more than relationship issues. The loss of trust may point out these differences. Trust at least from the community is what sociologists would mean by "institutional norms." Personal trust is something a woman might be more sensitive to, but 'community trust' is more like prestige, esteem, or honor. Men appear quite sensitive to these aspects of their relationships,[145] while women seem much less sensitive to them. We are therefore not certain whether these differences are reciprocal. Further, in the early 1990s, when the custody data was collected, it was still quite unusual for women to lose custody of children. The noncustodial mothers may well have had significant problems, including emotional issues like depression, that caused their loss of custody.

We also ran precisely the same regressions using an additional variable, joint legal custody. Lawmakers and attorneys who dreamed up joint legal custody in the first place or who advise men to seek joint legal custody presumably do so in order to make them feel better, or to give them some role in their absent child's upbringing. They may also have thought, contrary to what Seltzer has found, that children would do better, through either increased visits or more faithful child support payments. Of the 380 couples affected by legal agreements, 204 had a joint legal custody arrangement. Our analysis showed that those who receive joint legal custody are not (statistically) *significantly* more depressed than those who simply lost physical custody between the first and second waves. However, the direction of the effect of joint legal custody (even if statistically significant at $p = .10$) is positive (and of comparable magnitude) and consistent with results already presented (that loss of physical custody is associated with more depression). That is, joint legal custody may not have achieved any of its goals. To repeat, this is independent of the effect of how depressed the man was at the first wave, the impact of the divorce itself, or the loss of custody of the child.

Let us look again at the facts and assertions with which we began—marriages break up when parents no longer trust each other, and the depression level for divorced men is much higher than that of married men (while with women, marital status makes no difference). It may seem somewhat incongruous to equate the two types of trust—the private one of wife for husband that, when violated, causes divorce, and the public one signifying trust for married parents or after divorce for the custodial parent only. Several generations ago, that was how custody was allocated.[146] The parent who was at fault in breaking up the marriage was presumptively unfit to raise the child, since divorce harmed children. But, at that time, divorce could be granted only upon proof of fault grounds that were also publicly set. In other words, both the divorce and the awarding of custody involved expression of community norms. With no-fault divorce, the two determinations become legally quite distinct. The within-couple or personal trust becomes the focus for the no-fault divorce proceeding. Once it is lost, a disappointed spouse may nearly automatically obtain a divorce. The custody determination, based upon "best interest of the child" remains rooted in community, or what we have called institutional, norms. Yet it may still be true that by a declaration that one parent is a "visitor" or noncustodial parent, the court places him or her outside the publicly recognized norm for parents.

How much of the increase in depression is due to the lack of a trust norm for noncustodial parents? There are alternative explanations, of course. One is that men who divorce are more inclined to have depression problems anyway. (This is why we held divorce and depression constant in the regressions.) Another is that divorced men miss their children more keenly than they feel the loss of their wives—that it isn't the trust over parenting that makes the difference, but the lack of contact with the children.[147] This is less likely, however, because separation from one's child was not statistically significant (though this did not measure a change between the two waves of the study as the legal loss did). That is, separation from the child was held constant in all the equations.

When men remarry, their depression decreases even though their children live elsewhere (see table 2.6). This may be because their new wives give the noncustodial fathers many psychological benefits, or because they have assumed new responsibilities (and norms) to children of their second marriages or their stepchildren. In fact, their higher remarriage rate (compared to that of their former wives) may not only be because the noncustodial fathers have higher human capital, as has long been suspected,[148] but also because they are more *eager* than their former wives because of the need to reestablish the societal trust. We will postpone discussion of the legal implications of the two different kinds of trust involved until later in this chapter and in chapter 4.

But other implications of changing custody rules are worth pondering. As a society, we should be careful to allow the "property rules" that come with a grant of status in family law (like presumptions that one's parenting is in the child's best interests) to develop only where the essential societal trust in a relationship overcomes possible harm to or confusion on the child's part. Otherwise, we should leave romantic partners or adults who at the time are responsible for our children to "liability rules," such as suits for damages, only. As I discussed in the preceding chapter, this is the mistake I believe the ALI[149] makes in its domestic partnership chapter, which effectively equates cohabitation and marriage for actions between the parties. Unlike the New Jersey or Connecticut "civil union," which for all purposes recognizes same-sex civil unions as the legal equivalents of marriage (let alone the rules allowing same-sex marriage in Massachusetts,

Vermont, Iowa, and formerly California), the ALI domestic partnership provisions withhold the societal judgment that the partners are worthy of trust in their relationship. Domestic partnerships, though they may be the numerical norm in the United States, are not a trust-imbued institution. Nothing we have seen thus far shows that noncustodial fathers' relationships with their children deserve the protection of family status either.

Another implication of the distinction I am drawing between types of family norms might affect premarital counseling. Couples might be taught that once they begin trying to quantify what should be unconditional love, they are revealing a lack of trust in each other. If they do not trust each other before marriage, they probably should not get married. If they see this happening once they are married, they should realize their relationship is in jeopardy and seek counseling. We might consider second-guessing a couple's decision making, even regarding their children, more carefully when they seem to be in an adult exchange relationship.

While Steven Nock and I would have liked to have seen what happened with joint *physical* custody, the number of couples who had some form of this in the NSFH (34) was so small that no conclusions could be drawn. However, Douglas Allen and I developed different data using divorces from four states to measure divorce filing patterns. The bottom line is that women file for divorce most of the time and that they probably do so because they expect to receive physical custody of their children (which, assuming equal amounts of marital unhappiness, lowers the costs of divorce for them).[150] I have more recently studied other legal behavior in Oregon (prior to and after divorce) following a change in the custody rules to prefer joint physical custody. We turn now to this other work.

Divorce filing, custody, and social norms

As I have observed, because of the financial and social hardship faced after divorce, most people assume that generally husbands have instigated divorce since the introduction of no-fault divorce. Yet *women* file for divorce and are often the instigators of separation, despite a deep attachment to their children and the evidence that many divorces harm children.[151] Furthermore, divorced women in large numbers reveal that they are happier than they were while married. They report relief and certainty that they were right in leaving their marriages. This fundamental puzzle suggests that the incentives to divorce require a reexamination and that the forces affecting the net benefits from marriage may be quite complicated, and perhaps asymmetric between men and women. Women's filing can be seen as rational behavior, based on their relative power in the marriage, their opportunities following divorce, and their anticipation of custody.

Throughout most of American history, wives rather than husbands have filed for divorce. The proportion of wife-filed cases has ranged from around 60% for most of the nineteenth century[152] and, immediately after the introduction of no-fault divorce, to more than 70% in some states.[153] Today, with some variation among states, it remains slightly above two-thirds. The standard explanations for this behavior are as follows: women file because of tradition;[154] women file to assure their innocence in the underlying proceeding;[155] women file to secure rights to custody, support, and attorney's fees;[156] or women file simply because it is more convenient for them to do so. While these explanations have some merit, even in combination they cannot explain the variation in divorce rates across states (see table 2.7), the persistence of the "gender gap" in who does the filing, nor the systematic filing behavior we explore later on.

Economic explanations of divorce, beginning with Gary Becker, stress the rational weighing of remaining married over becoming single. When remaining married is no longer attractive, a spouse files for divorce, and, on the surface, it is unclear why the bias should be toward women filing. What makes the high filing rate for women most puzzling, however, is that it is generally assumed that, overall, husbands should be the ones most wanting out of marriage—particularly since the introduction of no-fault divorce. This understanding results from the focus on postdivorce financial status. Even by the most conservative accounts, the average divorced woman's standard of living declines from the one she enjoyed during marriage, and it declines relatively more than does the average husband's standard of living. Men often have an increase in their material well-being after divorce.[157] Furthermore, women face longer terms of low wealth and consumption when they divorce, because they are less likely to remarry than their former husbands are, though most eventually do, as we have seen.[158] This lower remarriage rate and longer unmarried period are exacerbated when the wife has custody of the children. Some analysts claim that part of the reason for this disparity is that a woman's value on the marriage market tends to depreciate with time, while her husband's tends to appreciate.[159] In addition to the other problems, newly divorced women encounter tremendous obstacles performing their role as parents. Studies of their performance as parents prior to and after divorce reveal weaknesses in consistency and ability to cope with the stress of single parenting.[160]

TABLE 2.7 **Comparative divorce rates, 1995**

State	Divorces	Population (in thousands)	Divorce rate
Maine	5,467	1,241	4.405318
New Hampshire	4,871	1,148	4.243031
Vermont	2,786	585	4.762393
Massachusetts	13,453	6,074	2.21485
Rhode Island	3,654	990	3.690909
Connecticut	9,597	3,275	2.930382
New York	55,999	18,136	3.087726
New Jersey	24,293	7,945	3.057646
Pennsylvania	39,439	12,072	3.266981
Ohio	48,682	11,151	4.365707
Indiana	—	5,803	−99
Illinois	38,784	11,830	3.278445
Michigan	39,910	9,549	4.179495
Wisconsin	17,522	5,123	3.420262
Minnesota	15,828	4,610	3.433406
Iowa	10,504	2,842	3.695989
Missouri	26,844	5,324	5.042074
North Dakota	2,204	641	3.438378
South Dakota	2,888	729	3.961591
Nebraska	6,256	1,637	3.821625
Kansas	10,732	2,565	4.184016
Delaware	3,671	717	5.119944
Maryland	15,025	5,042	2.979968
Virginia	28,897	6,618	4.366425
West Virginia	9,393	1,828	5.138403
North Carolina	36,978	7,195	5.139402
South Carolina	14,753	3,673	4.016608
Georgia	37,209	7,201	5.167199
Florida	79,528	14,166	5.614005
Kentucky	22,883	3,860	5.928238
Tennessee	33,081	5,256	6.29395
Alabama	25,957	4,253	6.103221
Mississippi	13,076	2,697	4.84835
Arkansas	16,041	2,484	6.457729
Louisiana	—	4,342	−99
Oklahoma	21,829	3,278	6.659243
Texas	98,373	18,724	5.253845
Montana	4,179	870	4.803448
Idaho	6,770	1,163	5.821152
Wyoming	3,197	480	6.660417
Colorado	18,795	3,747	5.016013
New Mexico	11,279	1,685	6.693769
Arizona	27,633	4,218	6.551209
Utah	8,892	1,951	4.557663
Nevada	12,355	1,530	8.075163
Washington	29,677	5,431	5.464371
Oregon	14,982	3,141	4.769819
California	—	31,589	−99
Alaska	2,999	604	4.965232
Hawaii	5,494	1,187	4.628475

Source: From Margaret F. Brinig and Douglas W. Allen, "'These Boots Are Made for Walking': Why Most Divorce Filers Are Women." *American Law and Economics Review* 2 no. 1 (Spring 2000): 152, table 5.
Note: N = 3,549; $R^2 = .083$. Widowed, never married, and unknown omitted. Data from NSFH (1987–88 and 1992–93).

TABLE 2.8 **Frequency Distribution of Respondent's Reports of Which Spouses Wanted the First Marriage to End, 1987–88 and 1992–94**

	Women		Men		Total	
Item and response categories	N	Percent	N	Percent	N	Percent
1) I wanted the marriage to end BUT my husband/wife did not	338	27.2	67	9.6	405	20.7
2) I wanted it to end MORE THAN my husband/wife did	239	19.4	70	10.0	309	16.0
3) We both wanted it to end	223	17.8	197	28.1	420	21.6
4) My husband/wife wanted it to end MORE THAN I did	110	9.0	113	16.2	223	11.6
5) My husband/wife wanted it to end BUT I did not	116	9.5	142	20.3	258	13.4
Inappropriate/no answer	211	17.1	111	15.8	322	16.6
Total responses	1,237	100.0	700	100.0	1,937	99.9

Source: From the NSFH, Wave 2, Self-Enumerated Codebook Primary Respondent and Ex-Spouse, Which Spouse, SE-3, MT308 0173. Data acquired from James A. Sweet and Larry L. Bumpass, "The National Survey of Families and Households, Waves 1 and 2: Data Description and Documentation." Center for Demography and Ecology, University of Wisconsin–Madison, 1996, http://www.ssc.wisc.edu/nsfh/home.htm.

Question: "Sometimes both partners equally want a marriage to end, other times one partner wants it to end much more than the other. Circle the number of the answer that best describes how it was in your case."

Because of the financial and social hardships faced after divorce, it has been commonplace, in the law and economics world at any rate, to assume that husbands have at least instigated divorce.[161] This position has also been supported by the tidbit of information suggesting that male filing rates increased right after the introduction of no-fault divorce.[162] The standard view is that the increases in divorce rates brought about by no-fault were the result of husbands unilaterally absconding with disproportionate shares of marital property.[163] Yet, women file for divorce more often than men do. Not only do they file more often, but some evidence suggests they are also more likely to instigate separation[164] despite a deep attachment to their children and the evidence that many divorces harm children.[165] Because the connection between filing and initiation of breakup is important to the analysis, I reproduced a table from the NSFH data as table 2.8.[166] Furthermore, divorced women in large numbers reveal that, unlike the noncustodial fathers discussed above who tended to be more depressed, they are happier than they were while married.[167] They report relief and certainty that they were right in leaving their marriages.[168]

It should be noted that divorce itself is costly and still carries some stigma. Divorce contains costs in the form of attorneys' fees, harm to children, financial losses, and even today the loss of the comfort of being

TABLE 2.9 **Effect of Custody on Who Files for Divorce**

Case 1: Wife married at 16, husband at 26. They've been married 20 years and have three kids. The husband gets custody. Husband has 7 years more education than the wife, and they live in a fault state. Wife is white. Probability that wife files = .095.	However, if the wife got custody, the probability that she would file increases to .69.
Case 2: They married when both were 26 and have been married 5 years. They have two children, and the wife will get custody. The husband finished college and the wife a law degree (three more years of education). They live in a no-fault state, and wife is white. Probability that wife files = .79.	However, if the husband got custody, the probability that wife files would decrease to .32.

Source: From Margaret F. Brinig and Douglas W. Allen, "'These Boots Are Made for Walking': Why Most Divorce Filers Are Women." *American Law and Economics Review* 2, no. 1, 2000.

married. As a result, the divorce event (or process) provides a hurdle that "channels" people to remain married even though the union is marginal at best.[169] The marriages that eventuate in divorce, therefore, belong to those couples in which at least one individual believes life is better after divorce in spite of these costs. This one individual tends to be a woman who files with the expectation she will receive custody (who at least does not suffer the additional cost of losing her children and the status that comes with them).

Table 2.9 displays the strength of the custody coefficients under the conditions where the other variables are at their most extreme. In case 1, we have a situation biased in favor of the husband filing. Merely switching the anticipation of custody in this case from the husband to the wife changes the probability of the wife filing from .095 to .69—slightly more than a seven-fold increase. In case 2, the bias is in favor of the wife filing. Yet switching the anticipation of custody from the wife to the husband results in a fall from .79 to .32 in the probability of the wife filing for divorce, even in those situations in which her outside options look the best.

As I have stressed throughout the preceding text, filing behavior can be interpreted as either primarily an attempt to leave a bad situation or primarily an attempt to leave the marriage with a disproportionate share of the marital property. Outside of the custody variables in our regressions, we find little evidence for the exploitation theory and more for the appropriation one. The question is, which theory best explains the remarkably strong custody-related coefficients we observed?

To understand how custody-related filing might be considered appropriation, we could simply describe children as assets—usually the most valuable and sometimes the only assets produced by the marriage.[170] A variant of this idea that might avoid concerns about commodification of children would be that children are not exactly like other assets, but that wives, as a general rule, place higher value upon their offspring than do their husbands.[171] Under either explanation, when a marriage becomes shaky, the party placing the highest value upon the children files. (In an extreme case, ending the marriage may even be beneficial for the children. For example, a loving parent might remove the children even at some financial cost in order to spare them continued contact with an unstable or impaired parent.)[172]

Alternatively, and more persuasive to me, custody outcomes may strongly correlate with divorce filing because the spouse who desires custody upon divorce has been more involved with the children during marriage. Such involvement, which may require some withdrawal from the paid labor force, sets up a dependence relationship that is not captured by the human capital (education or age) variables. That is, even if a wife has an undergraduate or graduate degree, or even if she is more educated than her husband, she may remain out of the labor force during her children's infancy, suffering a diminished lifetime income. She may thereafter need to make accommodations to child rearing even when she returns to full employment. Once she becomes dependent in this way because of childbearing or child rearing, she is subject to the same exploitation described earlier. In this view, she files when the marital situation becomes intolerable, usually for some reason not directly related to custody issues. But having custody following divorce lowers the cost of divorce to her.

Having custody of children may even be a way of asserting control over a noncustodial parent,[173] either personally[174] (placing restrictions on religious exercise, smoking, moving, and so forth) or through the child support that usually goes along with the children.[175] The tremendous quantity (and frequent vindictiveness) of litigation over these postdivorce custody problems suggests that perpetuating relationships in this way indicates that custody may be a different type of asset, if it is indeed an asset. Modern divorce theory spouses a "clean break" concept,[176] while these postdivorce custody battles suggest a relationship that continues despite divorce.[177]

Although in a number of state legislatures are currently considering some change in divorce grounds (such as covenant marriage or even a return to fault grounds), in nearly all states, as well as in the scholarly literature, custody standards and rules are, as I have mentioned, "ground zero in the gender wars."[178] Because there is so much ferment over custody standards and because, whatever the custody rules impact upon parents, the outcomes are so important to children,[179] Douglas Allen and I suggested further study to sort out the most important reasons that filing corresponds so closely to custody. We also suggested that because custody outcomes are so obviously important to who files for divorce, changes in custody rules are likely to have a major impact not only upon divorce filings but also upon the conduct of marriage itself.[180]

As we saw earlier in the chapter, in many modern marriages, men seemingly hold up their parts of a traditional bargain in a world where many, if not most, women have changed their roles dramatically, work more total hours, and seek some relief on the home front. Men who see dual earner parents divorcing tend to see the wife's filing (and probably getting custody) as taking the children from the husband and may suggest some sort of joint custody presumption as a remedy.[181] Women who view the same situation overwhelmingly see a working mother who files as being pushed out of an apparently bleak and hopeless situation, filing because she is simply exhausted. They prefer a custody pattern more closely mimicking the one set in the marriage, where the husband would have some meaningful parenting opportunities but the wife would remain the primary custodian.[182] Such women suggest, not only has she "earned custody" in a way her workaholic husband has not, but also that the children would not be as disrupted by such an arrangement.

One way in which the implications of whether women with children who file do so to "take assets" or because they are "exploited" might be teased out from a different data set. One could examine work and household patterns of both divorcing spouses at an earlier time (t) holding constant race, age, income, length of marriage, and education. An additional variable would indicate whether each spouse was satisfied with the fairness of the household and labor-market arrangements. If the husbands' and wives' working and household patterns were similar at time (t), and if they did not see their division of child care and housework as a big problem in the marriage, a divorce by some later time (t+1) would probably be for other reasons than "exhaustion," and child custody might indeed simply be asset appropriation. If there was strong evidence of inequality in child care and housework and unhappiness about it in the earlier period, a subsequent divorce would seem more likely to be because of a felt exploitation coming out of the way child care and other household responsibilities were handled during the marriage.[183] I have already presented the data from the

NSFH indicating that fairness in housework is not determinative of stability but did not consider custody. Recent work from the third wave of the NSFH indicates that the child-care patterns have not changed much[184] and might prove a basis for this type of study on custody-related matters.

The results Allen and I found, using divorce statistics, were consistent with our hypothesis that filing behavior is driven by some sort of self-interest at the time of divorce. Individuals file for divorce when there are marital assets that may be appropriated through divorce, as in the case of leaving after receiving the benefit of educational investments such as advanced degrees. However, individuals may also file when they are being exploited within the marriage, as when the other party commits a major violation of the marriage contract, such as cruelty. Interestingly though, cruelty amounts to only a small percentage of all divorce filings in Virginia (6%), the only state whose data permitted us to sort out the proven reasons for divorce. We found that who gets the children is by far the most important component in deciding who files for divorce, particularly when there is little quarrel about property, as when the separation is long.

What does all this mean for divorce reform and for predictions of future filing behavior? It suggests that as men's and women's labor-force income becomes more nearly equal, the state difference in filing rates should disappear and will likely be determined by custody alone. The legal ramifications of the no fault variable are perhaps the most interesting. In the jurisdictions we studied, even taking into account the higher divorce rates, in no-fault states women take advantage of the no-fault option more than do their husbands.[185] From the woman's perspective, repealing no-fault laws might cause harm as compared to investing in making marriages better. However, if filing behavior is mostly driven by attempts to exploit the other partner through divorce, tougher laws may be socially more beneficial. Because the custody coefficients were the largest by far, family law reformers may want to concentrate on formulating custody rules that will alter the spouses' relative gains from marriage. Allen and I favor custody rules that replicate the patterns in marriage as closely as possible while giving each spouse a meaningful role (i.e., not zero) after divorce, as opposed to either a "winner takes all" rule like "maternal preference" or "primary caretaker" or a presumption of equal joint custody shares.[186] A "replication" rule would not make either spouse better off divorced than during marriage. It might encourage the sharing of child rearing and other associated tasks, allowing more equal participation in the labor force. It would be less likely than any "winner takes all" rule to give the status of custodial parent to only one former spouse.

Is joint physical custody already a norm?

We conclude this chapter with another related instance where law may have outstripped social norms. Oregon in 1997 changed its divorce law to strongly prefer joint physical custody and to make it easier and less expensive for noncustodial parents (mostly fathers) to enforce visitation rights. In a series of papers[187] I explored empirically whether these changes in the law in fact did what their promoters wanted.

While the Oregon statutes that frame our discussion here, like most state laws, do not state an explicit preference for joint custody, shared custody (or shared parenting) is certainly encouraged by §107.179, which refers cases in which the parties cannot agree on joint custody to mediation and by § 107.105, which requires the court to consider awarding custody jointly. In addition, 1997 legislation noted in its very first section that it was state policy to "[a]ssure minor children of frequent and continuing contact with parents who have shown the ability to act in the best interests of the child." The effect of this legislation was to strengthen the power of noncustodial parents, since denial of access to the children would give the right to terminate spousal or child support, change the parenting plan, or obtain an award for "makeup" visitation. The legislative history for the bill shows that it was a compromise between men's rights groups and those concerned about domestic violence. The empirical work is fully explained elsewhere, so only a summary is included here: a random sample of about 500 divorced couples with children was extracted from the divorce certificates for the years 1995–2002 and was matched with court records for each of the cases, including not only the divorces but also domestic violence filings.

At first glance, the change in the statute did apparently have one desired effect: there is significantly more joint physical custody (about 1.3 times the amount from prior years, or 30% more) in cases where the couple separated after the statute took effect than before (see table 2.11).[188] However, this increase is not inconsistent with the trend toward joint custody in Oregon (see fig. 2.1). Although there are more joint custody awards for the couples who separated after 1997 than in the preceding years, a longer view shows that this might have occurred even without the change in statute.[189] In other words, the slightly increased joint custody follows a trend. The increase comes out of the wives' share—they have custody less

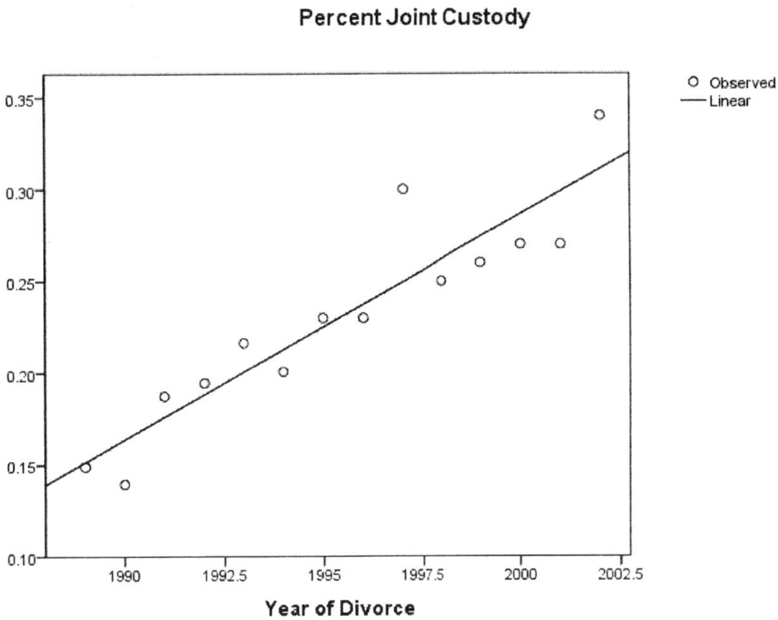

FIGURE 2.1 Joint custody orders. (Data acquired from the National Center for Health Statistics, Marriage, and Divorce Data, 1989–95. I extracted the Oregon divorces [a sample of the total divorces in the state, a total of 22,019 for the seven years] and eliminated those with missing custody data or those with no children. I totaled the number of children in each custody arrangement and divided the "joint custody" number by the "total number of custody children.")

often, while husband and split custody also increased, though less dramatically (see tables 2.10 and 2.11). After reading Mnookin and Kornhauser on divorce bargaining,[190] we might expect a change affecting custody rules to cause would-be-sole custodial parents to settle for lower child support in order to get the custody they wanted. As far as the correlations and regressions show, this also occurred: there were statistically significantly lower dollar amounts of child support (see tables 2.12 and 2.13). In addition, the real amount decreased further, given inflation.[191] The law also apparently decreased the number of domestic violence complaints (insignificantly) but decreased the number of complaints that resulted in domestic violence orders (significantly). The change in the law apparently is also related to an increase in the petitions for modification of custody and visitation (following divorce). (For the remaining observations, see table 2.10 and the lines indicated.) It also is related to increases in the amount of litigation

TABLE 2.10 **Relationship of Child's Depression to Characteristics of Noncustodial Father**

	Unstandardized coefficients		Standardized coefficients		
	B	Std. error	Beta	t	Sig.
Constant	14.237	1.811		7.863	0
Kid age at time of interview in 1995	0.194	0.085	0.052	2.272	0.023
Kid sex	1.318	0.278	0.104	4.741	0
Household income in 1,000s	−0.004	0.005	−0.017	−0.742	0.458
Mom is Hispanic	2.148	2.621	0.018	0.82	0.413
Mom is black	0.695	0.311	0.05	2.236	0.025
Mom is Asian	0.156	0.938	0.004	0.166	0.868
Mom is Native American	2.979	1.227	0.053	2.428	0.015
Mom is other race	1.111	0.605	0.04	1.835	0.067
Mother's years of schooling	−0.311	0.066	−0.108	−4.731	0
Mom age	−0.021	0.027	−0.018	−0.784	0.433
Seldom does kid stay w/dad once or twice? 1=y, 0=n	0.671	0.444	0.035	1.511	0.131
Several does kid stay w/dad several times? 1=y, 0=n	1.33	0.422	0.078	3.153	0.002
Monthly does kid stay w/dad once a month? 1=y, 0=n	−0.024	0.573	−0.001	−0.043	0.966
Weekly does kid see dad more than weekly? 1=y, 0=n	−0.193	0.607	−0.008	−0.319	0.75
Often	0.278	0.587	0.012	0.474	0.635
Times last year kid talked with bio dad	2.73E−03	0.004	0.018	0.671	0.502
How close kid feels to bio dad	−0.595	0.124	−0.13	−4.814	0

Source: From Margaret F. Brinig, "Does Parental Autonomy Require Equal Custody at Divorce?" *Louisiana Law Review* 65, no. 4, 2005, originally titled "Depression (CESD2 19-item Depression Scale) (R^2 (adj.) = .047)."

TABLE 2.11 **Predicted Joint Custody Percentage**

B	SE		Wald	df	Sig.	Exp(B)
Separation after custody statute	0.256	0.080	10.324	1	0.001	1.292
Length of marriage	0.033	0.006	27.662	1	0.000	1.033
Spouse on welfare	−0.454	0.143	10.043	1	0.002	0.635
Husband's number of marriages	−0.117	0.071	2.745	1	0.098	0.890
Protective order issued?	−0.721	0.114	40.154	1	0.000	0.486
Number of children in household	−0.099	0.043	5.471	1	0.019	0.905
Constant	−0.970	0.148	42.785	1	0.000	0.379

Source: From Margaret F. Brinig, "Does Parental Autonomy Require Equal Custody at Divorce?" *Louisiana Law Review* 65 no. 4, 2005.
Note: Cox & Snell R^2 = .036

TABLE 2.12 **Predicted Child Support Amount**

	Unstandardized coefficients		Standardized coefficients		
Variables	B	Std. error	Beta	t	Sig.
Separation after effective date of statute (1=yes)	−63.463	19.953	−0.067	−3.181	0.001
Children in household	52.480	9.430	0.109	5.565	0.000
Wife represented by counsel (1=yes)	164.473	19.117	0.173	8.604	0.000
Incidents/years 2004–year of divorce (#/yr)	5.797	1.198	0.102	4.840	0.000
Either lives out of state (1=yes)	32.249	28.866	0.022	1.117	0.264
Wife's age	3.693	1.226	0.059	3.012	0.003
Per capita income of county (#)	0.012	0.003	0.106	4.461	0.000
Population density (#/mile)	−0.134	0.026	−0.120	−5.127	0.000
Logit residual of joint custody	−7.856	3.856	−0.040	−2.037	0.042
Constant	−239.899	78.406		−3.060	0.002

Source: From Margaret F. Brinig, "Penalty Defaults in Family Law: The Case of Child Custody." *Florida State University Law Review* 33, no. 3, 2006.
Note: Child support amount ($/month); R^2 (adj.) = 0.083.

TABLE 2.13 **Predicted Child Support, Holding Predicted Probability of Joint Custody Constant**

	Unstandardized coefficients		Standardized coefficients		
Variables	B	Std. error	Beta	t	Sig.
Separation after effective date of statute (1=yes)	−70.832	21.692	−0.075	−3.265	0.001
Children in household	51.570	9.578	0.108	5.384	0.000
Wife represented by counsel (1=yes)	165.756	19.115	0.175	8.671	0.000
Incidents/years 2004–year of divorce (#/yr)	6.097	1.209	0.107	5.042	0.000
Either lives out of state (1=yes)	36.400	28.729	0.025	1.267	0.205
Wife's age	2.846	1.400	0.046	2.033	0.042
Per capita income of county (#)	0.012	0.003	0.103	4.334	0.000
Population density (#/mile)	−0.132	0.026	−0.119	−5.058	0.000
Predicted probability of joint custody	152.148	136.591	0.027	1.114	0.265
Constant	−242.748	79.459		−3.055	0.002

Source: From Margaret F. Brinig, "Penalty Defaults in Family Law: The Case of Child Custody." *Florida State University Law Review* 33, no. 3 (2006): 779, table 4b.
Note: Child support amount ($/month); R^2 (adj.) = 0.081.

(per year) couples experience in Oregon (incidents/years between divorce and 2004), the number of failed mediations (mediation, no settlement), and the fees paid to the court (fees charged). Contrary to the prediction made by the task force in Oregon, the number of pro se petitioners, even for parenting time modifications, did not increase following the enactment of the legislation[192] (see neither represented by attorney), nor was there a statistically significant increase in filings to enforce visitation per year by pro se petitioners (pro se parenting time/custody motions per year), though there was a significant increase in these motions when either party was represented.

Evidence of "bargaining around" the joint custody presumption comes from the decline in the value of child support (including the absolute dollar amount) since enactment of the statute. While the absolute dollar number has been remedied somewhat under the revised guidelines that took effect in 2003,[193] the lack of significant clustering at guideline amounts and the fact that higher child support awards are made more often in rural counties indicates that in many, if not most, cases the amount is individually tailored, leaving room for bargaining despite the apparent rigidity and statewide applicability of child support guidelines. The data did not permit an analysis of property awards.[194] Perhaps more troubling evidence of strategic behavior can be found in the increase in the number of allegations of domestic abuse where orders did not issue. Although the child support amount did not change much, the number of motions to modify or enforce it did increase significantly following enactment of the statute. Together with an increase in custody and parenting time change or enforcement motions as well as increases in the number of cases in which mediation failed and in the average number of court contacts per year, the statute seems to have failed in its purposes of keeping family law cases out of the court system and in making access more available to pro se litigants.

Although I am trained in family mediation myself, I cannot find evidence that the mandatory or court-referred mediation plans put into place in Oregon have been particularly successful. Although the percentage settled by mediation changed from 4% to 13%, the percentage of failed mediations increased as well, from 2% of all cases, not just the mediated ones, to 6%.[195] Particularly disappointing, many cases involving domestic violence restraining orders seem to be mediated (and to fail).[196]

This chapter shows that marriage and parenting are governed by strong norms that operate both within and external to the family. Considering this strong normative influence as trust explains more than does reputation (in Posner's explanation) or esteem (in McAdams's), though trust is related to both. I have also provided several more examples of times when law (urged by government, interest groups, or academics) pushed beyond the prevailing social norms. Each time this happens, families respond in seemingly unanticipated ways, and typically not in terms of new norm creation. We will turn next to the way that the soft norms we have described encourage family autonomy.

PART II

The Boundaries of Family Communities

CHAPTER THREE

The Limits of Community and the Role of Autonomy

So far we have discussed why some family relationships are given special status and why others are not, and we have considered the idea of family norms as featuring trust, some sort of networking, and very long time horizons. We have distinguished these concepts from norms discussions solely relying on reputation or self-esteem, which may be entirely adequate paradigms in contexts other than the family, and have noted the pitfalls associated with thinking of family dynamics as exchange relationships. In this chapter, we will be examining the mechanisms by which the community aids families that are given the status of "domestic relations," and then, in chapter 4, we will model the limits on appropriate community involvement.

There are three main ways in which communities support families, though that support may be combined in various ways. Firstly, communities may strengthen families directly and tangibly, as with giving financial support, doing tasks for family members, or providing the tax and other relief so sought after by same-sex couples seeking to marry. Secondly, communities may furnish emotional or spiritual support, such as by listening, providing sound advice, mediating disputes (or teaching family members to do so), or even offering their prayers. Finally, and most often studied in law school classes on the family, the state may create a zone of family privacy and autonomy within which the family is free to act (so long as norms aren't violated too egregiously). Obviously, upon violation of the norms, any excommunication or loss of status, as for noncustodial parents, will be accompanied by loss of self-esteem as well as the esteem of others—the phenomenon called loss of trust in the last chapter.

Though many writings about marriage, including legal opinions, extol its virtues as a building block of community and society, very few, especially in the legal context, look at the relationship from the inside out.[1] The thesis here, however, is that good family relationships very much need larger communities to begin them right, support them, and effect necessary repairs when they founder. Presently, I will argue that the usefulness of outsider involvement is limited. In legal terms, we reach these limits when third-party claimants assert rights to access spouses and children in ways that conflict with the autonomy families need. When autonomy becomes atomistic individualism, the family network may fragment into its constituent parts.

This chapter begins with the description of the ways community aids—in fact is essential to—marriage and parenting. Relationships invite community recognition, or what I have called covenant, when they possess characteristics of permanence and unconditional love.[2] Once the community trusts that partners or parents are capable of thinking unselfishly and over the long run, it lends vital support to the marriage or parenting relationship. However, we will see that this community sanction and support does not give individual outsiders the power to interfere with autonomy that married couples and parents possess. When third parties claim "rights," they undermine marriages and parenting. When family members begin to claim rights against each other, the families often become troubled.

Ways in which communities enhance marriage and parenting

Information and signaling

In addition to what was discussed in chapter 1, investments in resources specific to a relationship between identified parties give rise to what economist Yoram Ben Porath called "specialization by identity."[3] Such relationships exist over long periods of time, encompass a large variety of activities, involve many implicit terms, and have no explicit balancing of the exchange. They also have three features that are especially pertinent to this discussion. Consistent with Eric Posner,[4] Ben Porath's first characteristic is that enforcement is mostly "internal to the contract" (or by the family itself),[5] while another is that the family contract "creates a collective identity that affects the transactions of each member with people outside the family."[6] Finally, it is embedded in the identity of the partners, without which it loses its meaning—it is thus nontransferable.[7] The family (or family firm) thus gives the person an identity "in addition to a past and a future."[8] To the extent that outside forces, including private market forces, intrude upon the province of the family, the signal given by "family affiliation" becomes diluted.[9]

Marriage, at least to the extent the parties live together, also proves an efficient way to monitor the activities of the other spouse. In particular, as Frank Buckley and I have written elsewhere, marriage provides an excellent way to make sure that the other spouse is performing well as a parent.[10] Although cohabitation might perform this function, marriage solves the "principal-agent" problem very effectively. That is, each spouse is able to see for him or herself how time and money are spent on other members of the family.[11] Similarly, spouses can act as curbs on ineffective or excessive discipline or extreme parenting in any form.[12]

Insurance, or "distributing the risks of regret"[13]

Any long-term relationship, and particularly marriage or parenting, involves risks. A former student told me the wavy pattern of her Hindu wedding ring signifies not only the permanence of marriage but also its ups and downs. The risk allocation is expressed by the traditional marriage vows: "For richer, for poorer, in sickness and in health." Elizabeth and Robert Scott note in their article about marriage that "interwoven and continuously changing factors" will affect the emotions of a marriage and each party's happiness in it. These constant changes will lead the couple to adopt a broad strategy of shared responsibility and cooperative adjustment rather than one of trying to specify each contingency.[14] Parenting, too, is risky. Children can make one proud or disappoint. They may be healthy athletes or have a whole series of serious physical or behavioral difficulties. Thus, one so-called wrongful adoption case pointed out that even biological parents cannot be the guarantors of their children's future good health and well-being.[15]

Investment in identity is rewarding in families, trust is mutually beneficial, and "proximity and general involvement create at little expense the information that is lacking among strangers and generate incentives for proper behavior. Typically insurance between family members is mutual, an exchange of promises for aid contingent on the situation of both (or all) parties."[16] In guaranteeing, for example, support in time of sickness, or in averaging the randomness of individual incomes, the family can be an effective insurer, and larger families may serve this function either through many children or through ties extending beyond the nuclear family.[17]

Marriage often serves an insurance function.[18] On a basic level, a marriage contains two potential labor-force participants—one can work if the other becomes unemployed or unemployable. Historically, couples might have many children to insure that at least some offspring could support their parents in old age or carry on the family name. In day-to-day life, many parents will rely on each other's availability to do chauffeuring and other child-care tasks if a child gets ill or there is a "snow day" from school.

Parents rely upon the wider community as well. From the frontier[19] or the Amish family's shared barn building popularized in the movie "Witness," to the 1960s "coffee klatches,"[20] other families, and especially other women, have long provided support for each other. Whether it was an additional hand in hard work, help when someone was sick, child-rearing advice, or the shared recipe, the broader community has always taken an interest in strengthening the family. In fact, these acts of help encourage neighbors to provide efficacious environments for child rearing.[21] In a more organized vein, such insurance-type functions may be typical of job sharing between two mothers (or two spouses) in the paid labor force.[22]

Investment in capital

Historically, many families seeking to immigrate to this country have sent a potential high earner along first to establish himself (most often) and then pay for the others' passage. Such investments by families can also be made by the wider community. In the business and corporate world, much has been made of the ability of new Asian immigrants to the United States to pool assets and earnings to establish an investment fund from which all members can draw.[23] Observers have credited much of the success of the small businesses run by first-generation Asian Americans to such cooperative financial support (coupled, of course, with the tremendous industry of the individuals involved).[24]

Similar financial arrangements called *roscas*, *kye*, *cundinas*, and *tontine* all serve the important function of allowing people to borrow and save when they otherwise would not have credit markets available to them. For immigrants who have neither high incomes nor established credit ratings, purchasing durable goods, a key function of these credit associations, would otherwise become an impossible, or at least a time-consuming task. The *rosca* or *kye* allows the newcomer to trade on his reputation and close social and blood ties to the community (his social capital).[25] In fact, the community will sanction him strongly or make him feel ashamed if the loan is not repaid or the member does not keep contributing to the monthly or weekly pot after he has taken his draw. Francis Fukuyama claims that networks that require and engender trust are essential to the flexible social capital needed for sustained economic growth.[26]

The *rosca* arrangement is not particularly effective as insurance, however, because there is no guarantee that the "winning" turn of the individual will coincide with his need. Even where he can "bid" for an earlier-than-random share, others in the community may well suffer precisely the same tragedies (such as property losses due to riots or crop damage due to flood or drought) at the same moment.

The revolving credit association gives its relatively low-income members opportunities to purchase goods or invest in their own businesses that otherwise would not be available and functions to strengthen the community itself. Not only are all members financially tied to one another, but they also meet periodically at the "winner's" home or an ethnic restaurant (from the same ethnic group), usually in the context of a feast or other celebration (for which the "winner" pays).[27] This regular meeting, available only to members of the credit association, serves as a time to exchange information, develop additional social ties (for example, allowing the children of group members to meet and perhaps court), and promote the affinity Anthony Kronman calls "union."[28]

"Venting" and dispute resolution

When we have had rough days at the job, whether outside or inside the home or at school, our families, and particularly our spouses and parents, provide helpful ears for our venting. Social science support for what may seem a common sense proposition is quite extensive. In fact, a paper by Bryant and Conger both reviews the literature and establishes a new point—even in marriages of more than fourteen years, relationship-specific support significantly predicted more stable and successful marriages, while friends in common and general personal support did not.[29]

Our children vent too. They tell us (and especially their siblings) about fights on the playground, the teacher's or others' (if not their own) latest classroom antics, and their distress at missing the last spot on the varsity team. If we have particularly close relationships with them, they may report to us the anguish of being date raped or the sadness of breaking up with their girl- or boyfriend. Cultivating this close sharing with our children may be the most important thing we do for children after donating DNA. (Hence, the national campaign with the slogan that parents are the "anti-drug.") Interacting like this of course means sharing (appropriately) some of our own mistakes and regrets and failures around the dinner table or in a rare moment of no distractions from phones, TVs, or Facebook.

Mutual support is at least part of what Milton Regan celebrates in *Family Law and the Pursuit of Intimacy*.[30] As Regan notes, one of the home qualities promoted by the "Separate Spheres" doctrine of the nineteenth century was the ability of the peaceful and clean home to cleanse the worker, tired and at least figuratively dirty from his day earning money.[31] Thus, we complain to our families about people and events from outside. We also use our families to resolve disputes we have with each other. When our parents teach us about how to forgive our siblings or our parents or how to admit blame for our mistakes, we are better able to do the same with outsiders.

On a broader basis, communities can also function to resolve disputes, sometimes much more effectively than the civil or criminal justice system. Professor Lawrence Sherman has studied dispute resolution for juvenile offenders in New Zealand,[32] and reports that when the offender and his or her chosen supporters meet with the victim and supporters, real healing occurs. A neutral third party, usually a police officer, asks both "sides" to report what happened as well as the results of the incident. The offender almost always admits responsibility and the victim forgives. There is some direct restitution, which may come from the offender or his family and may be in kind rather than simply financial. At least in New Zealand, this process has been much more successful in lowering recidivism than has the public justice system.[33]

Such a practice has an older analog in the Native American peacemaker court. The Native American community began the Navajo Peacemaker Court in 1982 because the civil state courts were thought contrary to Navajo tradition.[34] The state courts present what economists call a "zero sum" game, with a necessary winner and loser: "One goes out of the [state] courtroom with his tail up, and the other goes out with his tail down."[35] Navajo philosophy centers around the concept of *hozhó* (everything is in its proper place and functioning in harmonious relationship to everything else[36]) and *K'e* ("all those positive virtues which constitute intense, diffuse, and enduring solidarity"[37]). Traditional Indian justice involves the perpetrator and the victim directly talking out the problem, involving their family and clans. For example, in domestic violence situations, the Peacemaker Court would restore the victim to her former self—back into her state of *hozhó*—and the perpetrator, with the assistance of his family and clan, do the restoring.[38]

A skeptic's question is whether this system works for the Navajos because the Native American community is relatively small and homogeneous, or whether it works because the community is personally involved in the justice system, as its proponents hope. The relationship between the dramatic New Zealand and Navajo nation findings on restorative justice and the much less positive ones done by Sherman and colleagues on mandatory arrest in American cities[39] is that both involved the status—prior to and after the offense—of the offender in the community. When the extended family and friends are involved in the proceedings, the offender can maintain dignity and feelings of self-worth, feel supported, and explain his side of the story. Therefore, he is much less likely to repeat the offense. More broadly speaking, the salutary results occur precisely because the community becomes involved with the relationship. When the offender has little to lose, because community ties are weak or nonexistent, restorative justice is less effective than the judicial system.

The New Zealand tribal court successes suggest an answer to another related question, whether community involvement will lessen given the growing rate of childlessness and smaller families generally. The tribal court results have nothing to do with the presence of children (and the New Zealand replications involve youthful offenders with no children).[40] The community interest may not, therefore, exist primarily to benefit (and encourage the production of) children and may be strong even for childless marriages, though clearly the networks are important.

Communities handle family conflicts in many ways that extend beyond the domestic violence setting. As I have mentioned, the recent interest in community involvement with parenting can be demonstrated in the popularity of *It Takes a Village*,[41] but it clearly antedates Senator Clinton's thoughts. Legislation of some states[42] and the writing of some commentators[43] suggest different divorce regimes for marriages without minor children. Others[44] suggest protection of the children of divorce by giving them the marital estate or some share in it. Some states extend parental support to include college education for children of divorce.[45] The open-adoption movement[46] and the recent legislation allowing more access to information identifying birth parents,[47] when looked at from the perspective of the adopted child, arguably demonstrate the child's desire to establish his or her roots in the community.

Dispute resolution can frequently be accomplished more efficiently and effectively by communities (if not within the families themselves) than the legal system.[48] The "neutrals" often have a stake in the relationship's continuing and will know more about the particular parties and their circumstances than will judges in the divorce or municipal court (in cases where family violence ensued). Restorative justice, just described, can heal such broken relationships, at least where communities are tight and reputation within them important.

Sources of information about the relationships

Our social networks educate us about what to expect from relationships. We will explore the way such information is transmitted at some leisure in chapter 5. There is obviously a continuum between the proverbial locker room conversation about sexual exploits and the hopefully more useful things parents teach children about dispute resolution, childbearing and child rearing, and even manners. Much of this education goes on before we begin grown-up relationships, but parents remain sources of support and guidance long after children become adults. Grandparents and others in the wider community also provide cultural guidelines within which to pursue relationships as well as experience about relationships that last. This type of help is particularly celebrated in African American and first-generation American communities. Sometimes such information passing is more formalized. In some religious traditions and for those electing covenant marriages in Arizona, Arkansas, and Louisiana, couples are required to attend marriage preparation classes. A recent Georgetown University survey indicates that many currently married Catholics attend marriage preparation events such as weekend "encounters" or evening marriage preparation classes or meetings with Catholic mentor couples.[49] Generally speaking, this more formalized community involvement is designed to continue during marriage as well.

CONVENTIONS AND BEHAVIOR CHANNELING. As mentioned earlier, spouses, families, and the wider community are useful in establishing norms or, more broadly, culture.[50] As children, we may learn acceptable ways of dealing with older people.[51] In fact, one team of economists claims that parents use their behavior to their own parents specifically to indicate to their children how they wish to be treated when they become aged and dependent.[52] Further, we learn how to act as social beings in our own ethnic groups. Thus, some of the opposition to interracial adoption has been on grounds that African American children need to be educated about not only African traditions and history but also how to fortify themselves against a racist society.[53] Parents and the wider community also teach children about law, respect for law, and limits they should set for their own behavior.[54]

For marriages, culture in this sense includes such mundane items as whether and in what way to celebrate one's anniversary (hence the conventional lists of gifts, beginning with paper and ending with diamonds),[55] Valentine's Day, or Father's Day. More importantly, conventions and behavior channeling include expectations about the duration of marriage, of what justifies leaving one's spouse or divorcing, and of what conduct is considered acceptable or what is cruel. We have seen already, for example, that in places where there are more births to unwed parents or more divorces—in stronger terms, a culture of single parenting or divorce—more occur even holding other explanatory variables constant.[56] Conversely, where there is a culture or tradition of extramarital chastity and lifetime marriages, less of the more socially costly behavior occurs.

Union building

Community involvement in marriage can certainly be seen in courtship rituals.[57] Parents and other family members are, and always have been, involved when relationships progress from the casual to the serious stage. Some religious groups still require something akin to the historical publishing of banns well before a couple can marry. Ceremonial marriage requires a license[58] and the meeting of certain requirements involving contractual capacity (age and mental capacity)[59] and what might be thought of as social capacity (no continuing other marriage, no overly close family relationship to the prospective spouse, and, in most states, different genders).[60] The community is also vitally involved in the marriage ceremony, as necessary witnesses to the couple's exchange of vows and, particularly in the Jewish and covenant marriage contexts as well as in the Hawaiian marriage from the introduction, as guarantors of support.[61] Other examples can be drawn from the regulation of ongoing marriages. These include the necessaries (or "family support") doctrine, which allows third parties to recover if they advanced credit to a spouse for something needed to maintain the standard of living[62] and prohibitions against contracts that contradict the essence of marriage.[63] Of course there are rules involving the exit from marriage (divorce grounds and, for example, the required viewing by divorcing couples of films on the effect of divorce on children).[64] We do significant community building with our children as well.[65]

In his book *Family Law and the Pursuit of Intimacy*, Milton Regan mentions the rituals that hold us together as families. This particularly includes family holidays such as Thanksgiving, the Seder meal, and Christmas.[66] All of these include "outside" traditions—turkey, football, and cranberry sauce; lamb, specific prayers, and bitter herbs; and decorated trees, nativity scenes, and carols—and special customs that run within particular families. Such traditions give us a sense of shared identity and help support the unity necessary to foster family cooperation on harder questions.[67] They can be said to strengthen family networks.

THE CENTRAL PLACE OF RELIGION IN RELATIONSHIPS. An old slogan postulated that "the family that prays together, stays together."[68] Many of my earlier observations might suggest a linkage between community involvement (particularly involvement from outside the nuclear family) and religion. Obviously religious authorities can perform marriage ceremonies (and in some countries this is exclusively true). Marriages "in" a religion can subject couples to a set of ecclesiastical rules as well as the secular ones.[69] Certainly there are strong marriages that are not part of a religious tradition, and a religious affiliation does not guarantee success. Data suggests that Catholics and fundamentalist Protestants, for example, divorce at about the same rate (or a higher rate) as the general public.[70] My own research on Iowa divorcing couples suggests that religious couples may have extremely difficult (and litigious) divorces when they do split up.[71] If this is so, is it strong religious tradition or personal adherence that is important in maintaining marital stability?

Most studies find that the stated religious preference at the time of marriage has very little effect on marital stability.[72] Two Methodists marrying, holding other things constant, will divorce about as often as two Catholics, two Jews, or two atheists. Steven Nock and I wondered whether it might not be religious intensity rather than affiliation that was important. We found, using the NSFH, that difference in religious observance and the importance of God in one's life did affect couples' ability to stay together over the period in question. Our unpublished work to a large extent duplicated that of Brigham Young University sociologists who used the same data set. Call and Heaton found that when both spouses attend religious services regularly, the couple has the lowest risk of divorce, while a difference in church attendance increases the risk of divorce.[73] They posit that church attendance "can either provide a common forum for a couple's religious orientation and family commitment or become a conflict for couples who do not share the same levels of personal dedication."[74] They note that joint participation in church gives a family a sense of purpose and similar values that increase family commitment and social integration.[75] However, the Call and Heaton study found (as did we) that all significant religious *affiliation* influences disappear once the authors controlled for demographic differences. Call and Heaton continued to find significant results in cases where the spouses differed in church activities, because "joint socialization in religious teachings that support family values and stability affirm the importance of marriage and family," and "joint participation in friendship networks provides a greater potential for interaction with friends in a context that generally supports positive communication between spouses."[76] Consistent with their finding, another study more recently found that marriages where both spouses were Catholics and attended church regularly together tend to last longer than "mixed marriages."[77]

One secular reason religious homogeneity may be important is that it increases attachment to the community in which the couple lives. A number of papers suggest that community attachment affects family stability. In one such example of many, home ownership apparently increases marital stability, while living in a large metropolitan area (whether in a suburb or central city) decreases it.[78] In another, Frank Buckley and I found that divorce rates from 1979 to 1991 were higher both in metropolitan areas, where many people are transients, and in "frontier" states.[79] Organized religions may provide outside communities that replace or supplement the support extended families used to provide.

Religious tradition also suggests (more than does civil law)[80] that children should be respectful of parents[81] and should support them in old age.[82] These would certainly seem to be positive, community-building and supportive, features of families.[83] But religious tradition may also be mutated into allowing an over-disciplinary father and a pious, noninterfering mother.[84]

Investment at the time of marriage

EVIDENCE OF THE POSITIVE RELATIONSHIP BETWEEN MARRIAGE AND COMMUNITY. I have been very fortunate to have read the stories of many students who have shared with me something of their lives and their families. Two in particular have written about arranged marriages in twentieth-century America. I have already mentioned how a second-generation Indian American sent me an exceptionally moving and interesting account of her own arranged marriage. Not surprisingly, as an American-educated and very Americanized young person, she was skeptical that her parents could find someone right for her. Surprisingly, she fell in love with the man she was to marry after her first year in law school, though she became acquainted with him largely over the phone and only met him briefly shortly before their wedding. She wrote me:

> However, deep down, I had always harbored secret thoughts of doubt about arranged marriages. My parents had a great marriage, but I had also observed some unhappy Indian couples. I knew that just because a marriage is arranged does not guarantee that it would work. Another problem with arranged marriages is that there is an immense social stigma to ending that marriage in divorce. Even today, Indian couples rarely choose that course of action, regardless of abuse or other serious marital problems.

On balance, she thinks they are more successful than many of their Western counterparts.[85]

My student was not unique in her feelings about community support for such a marriage. The community's involvement in Hindu weddings and marriages is evident in "The Song of the Groom's Anointment," or "Ābtauni," that is sung in rural India when the bridegroom is rubbed with saffron prior to his returning home. It illustrates the involvement of the extended family in the successful union:

> In a gold cup
> I make the saffron paste
> And rub it on the bridegroom's body
> The Brahman utters prayers,
> The women sing their joy.
> The mother wipes his mouth with her sari
> The father's sister pencils his eyes

The elder brother's wife fans his head,
The women sing their joy.
The father's brother's wife wipes his mouth
The elder sister pencils his eyes
The mother's brother's wife fans his head,
The women sing their joy.[86]

Another of my students, a Navajo American, wrote me that in the Navajo tradition:

> [M]arriages were arranged between families, which included not only the parents, but also grandparents, uncles, and aunts of the "husband to be and wife to be." Furthermore, traditionally the bride and groom really did not have a say as to whom they would marry. Negotiations between the families included what the groom's family would give to the bride's family . . . horses, sheep, cows, jewelry—a sort of dowry. A date for the ceremony was chosen. More importantly, the clans of the couple were stated and approved by the family to ensure against intermarriage. "The bloodlines were kept clean and everyone was knowledgeable about the clanship system and the whole society was kept in balance in that manner."

Not all arranged marriage forms seem more successful than love matches. A study of divorce rates in China using a 1985 survey sample from two provinces and the municipality of Shanghai, including more than 13,307 women, found that the arranged marriages ended in divorce more than twice as often as "free choice" marriages.[87] The Chinese apparently date following the commitment to marry rather than before, and, regardless of marriage type, know each other for longer before marriage than their American counterparts.[88]

The community was involved in traditional (usually arranged) Chinese marriages, too. Consistent with the Chinese emphasis on reverence for ancestors, note the respect paid by the bride to the groom's senior relatives.

> When the chairs arrive in the bridegroom's home, three ritual offerings are made: the couple first pays homage to Gods of Heaven and Earth, then to the Kitchen God, and then to the ancestors. At each altar offerings of food, fruit, and flowers were laid before the actual rituals were begun. The bridegroom inserts fresh incense sticks into the bowls before kowtowing side by side with his bride. These rites are necessary to give spiritual validation to the marriage.

> Then the couple is led by an elderly woman, usually of the same clan, to pay respect (by kowtowing) to the boy's parents, uncles, aunts, the older brothers and sisters-in-law, and any other senior relatives present. This is the formal introduction of the bride into the house and clan, and is the social validation of the marriage.[89]

Many of us are most familiar with another incarnation of arranged marriage—the early nineteenth-century Russian-Jewish tradition that we know through our reading, viewing, and listening to *Fiddler on the Roof*.[90] Like the more recent versions of arranged marriages discussed, even modern Jewish ceremonies include community involvement. The *ketubah* is a set of solemn promises regarding the mutual obligations of husband and wife. It is signed by the bride and groom in front of a community of witnesses who promise to be supportive of the couple.[91]

I wonder which of the traits my students identify as stabilizing is the more important. They initially pointed to the lack of dependence on sexual love and expectations of romance as what makes arranged marriages so stable. Perhaps, instead, it is the qualities of community support, interrelatedness, and approval they also mention that make the difference.

Finally, the African American broom-jumping ceremony involves community, though not the other features of arranged marriage. Instructions for the contemporary wedding include the following:

> Have your host ask guests to form a circle around the couple as they stand in front of the broom on the floor. The host should discuss the symbolism behind the broom as it relates to the joining of the couple and the combining of two families, and the need for the community to support the couple. Meanwhile have the couple hold the broom handle together and sweep around in a circle until the host or designated person is finished talking.[92]

In What Direction Does Causation Move?

Does the community become involved to strengthen marriages (advancing the individual goals of the couple)[93] or is the relationship more reciprocal than that—one where marriages also strengthen the community? This latter explanation would fit better with Eric Posner's theory of how individual practices become norms,[94] discussed in chapter 1. Further, marriages historically were integral to the passing on of land and creation of wealth.[95]

Children somehow turn marriages into communities.[96] Many studies,[97] including some of my own,[98] have noted that the divorce rate falls when the family includes children born during the marriage. This is despite the fact that social scientists have found a decrease in marital happiness, which follows a U-shaped curve that reaches its lowest point when children are born.[99] The interesting question for this chapter is why most less than blissfully happy couples remain together. The obvious reasons from the point of view of individual spouses include an increased sense of responsibility,[100] inculcation of altruism,[101] investment,[102] or joy in creation.[103] Perhaps a more subtle reason is that children teach us to give unconditionally and to think of others first. Their presence insures a more permanent relationship between the adults involved (since parenting will go on after divorce, even if marital relations do not).[104] Hence, two of the three conditions I earlier ascribed to the covenantal nature of families are present even without outside involvement. And, of course, the presence of children assures that the state will also be interested in the family, for with children come such things as state-mandated education, compulsory use of child car seats, required vaccinations, and mandatory issuance of social security numbers.

Theoretical Cases for Community: Norms Discussions in the Literature

We have already examined family and community relationships ethnographically. We can repeat the exercise by examining the relationship between family and community using the tools of institutional economics.

Reputation effects

While we have already discussed the work of Eric Posner in chapter 1, David Charny, who writes from a more politically communitarian background, also theorizes based on reputation and its effects.[105] Charny posits that although there are legal sanctions for breaking promises, "virtually all commercial transactions involve nonlegal commitments—commitments enforced only or predominantly by nonlegal sanctions such as concern for reputation."[106] Charny would allow legal intervention when the parties had elected nonlegal commitments only when they were gravely mistaken when the contract was made.[107] Charny contrasts what he calls an autonomy or rights-based system of contract[108] with a communitarian system. "An emerging alternative approach to the problem of nonlegal commitments seeks to go beyond conceptions of contract based on free choice. This communitarian approach purportedly accommodates a range of community interests rather than simply enforcing choices made by the contracting parties."[109]

Like Posner, Charny suggests that sometimes using legal sanctions where the parties intended nonlegal ones may distort the remedies the parties chose for themselves. He notes that according to communitarians, intervening may run counter to the framework of trust the parties established for themselves.[110] Or, as Michael Trebilcock has written, "[t]he adversarial character of legal enforcement means that once resort is had to the law to enforce commitments in an on-going relationship, it is or shortly will be at an end."[111] Charny continues:

> In the employment relationship, for example, nonlegal sanctions arguably enforce systems of reciprocation by encouraging mutual gift-giving or by monitoring effort, and thereby make superfluous the legal rules of contract and restitution that are largely directed to the same goal. By disrupting nonlegal systems, legal enforcement of implied limitations on employer discretion may impoverish rather than empower workers.[112]

Furthermore, some communitarians, inside and outside the legal community, suggest that the intrinsic value of social collaboration may depend on the parties' experience of a sense of trust not dependent on coercive public intervention.[113] Some situations suggest that nonlegal sanctions may in fact work better than the standard legal remedies: for example, those cases involving "vaguer commitments whose interpretation depends on 'embedded' norms or expert decision making,"[114] and commitments that have low stakes relative to litigation costs.[115]

A related strand of this work we have already discussed at length in chapter 1 is found in the social norms literature. Although as a branch of law and economics the field is vast enough to spawn its own conferences,[116] it has flourished in sociology for many years,[117] in economics for at least a generation,[118] in law for at least 15 years,[119] and in psychology for nearly twenty.[120] "In a sufficiently close-knit group, where norms are well-defined and nonlegal sanctions are effective, the law has little impact on behavior."[121] The way it does influence behavior is quite complex, so that sometimes the group's own norms dominate, sometimes the external law does, and sometimes law "reduce[s] the group's ability to regulate its members."[122]

In many communities, outside norms and legal rules both operate to regulate various aspects of family behavior. For example, community norms will determine the mechanism for courtship,[123] while legal rules will govern the exact requisites for marriage. The intragroup or community norms are frequently more efficient than the "blunt instrument" of the law because they take advantage of the common language, features, and traditions of the group.[124] For example, the Native American peacemaker court discussed earlier probably functions better than the civil justice system for members of the Navajo tribe because it accounts for *hozhó* and each community member's desire to be restored to balance. The difficulty, as Eric Posner might describe it, occurs when the legal system attempts to regulate or otherwise interfere with the valid operation of intrafamily, or transactional, norms.[125]

A related strand of the law and economics explanation of the importance of community is the idea of *network externalities*.[126] This concept means the web of effects a single action (or nonaction) has on a larger whole because of other existing relationships.[127] The relationship may be one of affinity (like marriage) or status (such as that of parent and child). For example, assume that a couple has tried for many years to have children, but is plagued with infertility problems. Their ensuing marital problems will no doubt be a source of concern to their parents and siblings, stretching out to the wider family community as well.[128] All of these family members may offer advice or sympathy, will in some way feel the loss as their own, and will rejoice with the couple when they adopt a child or finally conceive.

Mediating Institutions in the Community: All Communities Are Not Alike

One of the puzzles left over from the first chapter on the importance of legal family status is posed dramatically by a comparison of the general effects of family status (table 3.1) and those involving African American children (table 3.2, which concerns the relative lack of effect of formal family status on African American children). The fact that, controlling for poverty, black children tended to be significantly less likely to be anxious or depressed and more likely to have high self-esteem suggested that it

TABLE 3.1 **Effect of One Unit Change in Predictor on Child Outcomes**

	BPI			Self	
Outcomes (dependent variables)	Total	Externalizing	Internalizing	Efficacy	Esteem
Predictors (independent and control variables)					
Household income divided by census needs standard				0.0013738	0.001497
Sex of CDS child	−0.21908	−0.115438327			
Child's age at time of interview	−0.03797	−0.014294594	−0.015058213		
Age of mother or mother figure		−0.005854695			
Head is black			−0.216597424		0.029742
Head is Hispanic-Latino/a		−0.090871125	0.286641915	−0.0668909	−0.07054
Head is Asian PI	−0.72765	−0.255136174	−0.371089142		
Head is other race (American Indian, etc.)					
Head is white (ref)					
Kid lives with bio mom and no bio dad?	0.474498	0.178395398	0.264718657	−0.0217882	−0.02387
Kid lives with bio mom and adoptive dad?		0.4729471			
Kid lives with bio mom and step dad	0.726571	0.24945777	0.357231368		
Kid lives with bio mom and other dad figure	0.53186		0.359946476	0.0438003	0.047995
Kid lives with two adoptive parents					
Kid lives with both biological parents (ref)					
Mom married and widowed at least once		0.28684173			
Mom married, divorced, remarried still intact					
Mom married, divorced, remarried, now divorced					
Mom never married	0.390665	0.163012554		−0.0347441	−0.03805
Mom married, divorced, never remarried					
Mom married once – marriage intact (ref)					
Parental warmth scale 02	−0.40525	−0.187898811	−0.10754948	0.0366067	0.040045

Source: From Margaret F. Brinig and Steven L. Nock, "Legal Status and Effects on Children," *Saint Thomas Law Review*, 548, 2009.

TABLE 3.2 **Comparison of Associations with Behavioral Problems for White and Black Children**

	Whites only					Blacks only				
	Unstandardized coefficients		Standardized coefficients			Unstandardized coefficients		Standardized coefficients		
	B	Std. error	Beta	t	Sig.	B	Std. error	Beta	t	Sig.
Constant	16.128	1.865		8.649	0.000	24.671	3.805		6.484	0.000
Household income div census needs standard	−0.001	0.028	−0.001	−0.026	0.979	−0.721	0.292	−0.157	−2.469	0.014
Kid lives with bio mom and no bio dad?	4.109	1.105	0.229	3.717	0.000	−1.966	1.461	−0.130	−1.346	0.179
Kid lives with bio mom and adoptive dad?	5.119	2.204	0.064	2.322	0.020	−8.723	21.491	−0.022	−0.406	0.685
Kid lives with bio mom and step dad	3.250	0.833	0.132	3.948	0.000	2.664	1.567	0.107	1.700	0.090
Kid lives with bio mom and other dad figure	4.281	1.392	0.117	3.074	0.002	−0.539	2.322	−0.015	−0.232	0.817
Kid lives with two adoptive parents	11.299	9.129	0.034	1.238	0.216					
Mom married and widowed at least once	−1.955	1.784	−0.033	−1.096	0.273	5.962	2.458	0.157	2.426	0.016
Mom married, divorced, remarried still intact	0.400	0.582	0.023	0.688	0.492	−0.647	1.743	−0.023	−0.371	0.711
Mom married, divorced, remarried, now divorced	−0.500	1.287	−0.016	−0.389	0.698	1.463	2.763	0.033	0.529	0.597
Mom never married	4.140	1.468	0.103	2.820	0.005	1.112	1.629	0.072	0.682	0.495
Mom married, divorced, never remarried	−1.702	1.093	−0.086	−1.557	0.120	1.558	1.765	0.080	0.883	0.378
Parental warmth scale 02	−1.725	0.302	−0.163	−5.717	0.000	−1.517	0.582	−0.148	−2.608	0.010
Sex of CDS child	−0.169	0.340	−0.014	−0.496	0.620	−2.412	0.874	−0.159	−2.759	0.006
Child age at time of PCG IW – years 02	−0.183	0.064	−0.091	−2.864	0.004	−0.269	0.158	−0.107	−1.700	0.090
Age of mother or mother figure	0.022	0.028	0.026	0.803	0.422	−0.032	0.061	−0.034	−0.521	0.603

Source: Margaret F. Brinig and Steven L. Nock, "The One-Size-Fits-All Family." *Santa Clara Law Review* 49, 2009.

would be worth running the equations predicting depression, behavioral problems, self-esteem, and self-efficacy again just with the black children. What I found placing black and white children side by side were the surprising results shown in table 3.2.[129] For whites (and for the whole sample), income did not have a statistically significant effect when coupled with all the other variables (listed in table 3.1). However, for black children it did. For whites (and for the whole sample), what mattered a great deal was whether the parents had ever been married. For blacks, this was not significant at all, nor is the mother's living with a cohabitant (something significantly related to white and other children's problems). For blacks, but not whites, losing a father through his death was significant.

The first obvious conclusion is that for black families, income really matters. This would tend to support the writings of social policy critics like Dorothy Roberts who urge that preventing poverty should be a top priority, especially for the black community.[130] As I noted in the first chapter, income may help to prop up families that lack one of the supporting features (formal status). The second observation might be that for black children, what seems to matter is loss of a parent, not necessarily the absence of one. This would account for the difference in significance of Mom Never Married and Mom Married and Widowed at Least Once but not the lack of significance of divorce (another at least partial loss of a parent). A possible answer for the observation about divorce might be related to what we noted earlier about social norms: because black marriages are so much more likely to end in divorce than white ones (and imprisonment of a parent occurs more frequently as well), there may be more resources with dealing with absent fathers than is present in the white community. But what kind of resources are there?

The folk wisdom maintains that reliance on the extended family is more prevalent in black America than in the majority culture.[131] In fact, we have already noted this in the section dealing with kinship care. Then the empirical question is whether black children do better when their mothers are receiving assistance from their own mothers, controlling for everything else. Fortunately, the PSID and the CDS provide us with data we can use to resolve the question. As mentioned previously, there are at least three generations of respondents now in the data: original respondents, those who were "target children" originally, and now children of the "target children." Steven Nock and I began with the latter, matched them to their mothers and then to their grandmothers. In 1987–88, the mothers were asked whether, and how much, hourly and monetary support they

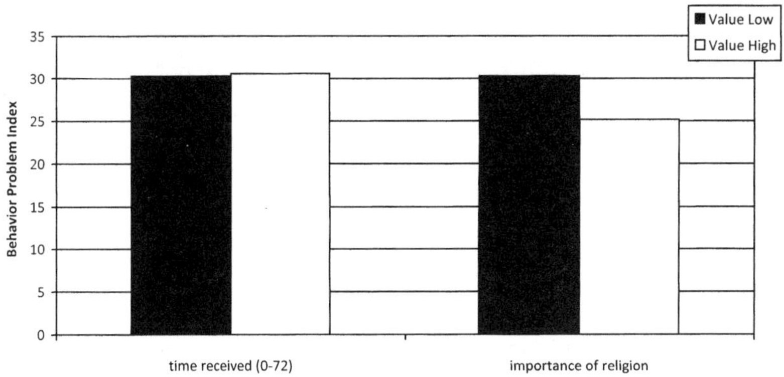

FIGURE 3.1 Total behavioral problems with relative effects of grandmother time and importance of religion to mothers. (Based on the PSID and CDS public-use dataset [1997 and 2002]. Data is available from the author.)

had given to or received from various people, including their own mothers, during the preceding year. We selected black CDS children born at the time the "help" questions were asked, a total of 392 children. We found that to the extent the hours of help (or dollar assistance) was significant, there followed a negative effect on children's well-being, that is, it was a signal of problems in the family.[132] What was positive, even with everything else (income, age, family structure, education, gender) held constant, was the importance of religion to the child's mother.

Figures 1.4, 1.5, and 3.1 all show the relative effect of a change from the low to the high end of grandmother's (hourly) help to mother in 1988 and the importance of religion of mother in 2002 on various aspects of the child's behavioral problems in 2002. These are all taken from the full equations, holding constant, or net of, all the variables listed in table 3.1. Similarly, both self-efficacy and self-esteem show an insignificant coefficient for the help by grandmothers and a positive and significant coefficient for importance of religion (not shown in figures). What could this mean? The most likely meaning of the negative results for help from grandmothers is that the grandmothers provided hours of help because the mothers were really having difficulties when the children were small, either because the father had recently left or because the mother had her own problems at that time. Importance of religion is hard to translate into a secular value, particularly because religious attendance or participation in religious groups did not have the same significant results. As noted previously,

African Americans are said to be the most religious of our society.[133] These mothers may receive strength from their religious beliefs or may be more inclined to use successful parenting techniques (said to be "authoritative" as opposed to "authoritarian") for dealing with their children because they are consistent with religious (heavily Protestant) values.[134] But the results do not show that involvement with church groups made a difference.

Autonomy

All this emphasis on community runs counter to another distinctly American trend—that of family autonomy.[135] For example, in the early Puritan colonies, families were expected to deal with their own problem children. It was only if they could not that the community, through its appointed elders, would adjudge whether a son was "rebellious" and ungovernable by his parents.[136] In a similar vein, it was the head of household (usually the husband) who was responsible for his wife's and children's attendance at church services.[137] A number of legal academics have written favorably and unfavorably about family autonomy. We will begin with the favorable treatment. Carl Schneider, for example, has argued that courts give parents autonomy in dealing with children for a number of reasons, among which are the courts' relative lack of knowledge and expertise.[138] Elizabeth and Robert Scott, as part of their fiduciary principle, treat being "left alone" (autonomy) as part of the reward of good parenting.[139] The Scotts are apparently writing about the informal rules couples and parents and children set up to regulate the behavior within the family—rules like bedtimes or the observance of birthdays. To the Scotts, marriage, like adoption or biological parenting, carries with it a commitment toward permanence that places it in a different category of relational interests than if it were temporary. And the freedom from outside rules that comes with the permanence is an important part of Eric Posner's social norms story as well. Bruce Hafen noted twenty-five years ago:

> A "justifiable expectation . . . that the relationship will continue indefinitely" permits parties to invest themselves in the relationship with a reasonable belief that the likelihood of future benefits warrants the attendant risks and inconvenience. There is a clear analogy between the motivational factors that influence human investment and those that influence economic investments. Jeremy Bentham believed that private ownership of property is more likely to maxi-

> mize social utility than is collective ownership because "the human motivations which result in production are . . . such that they will not operate in the absence of secure expectations about future enjoyment of product." The will to labor and the will to invest "depend on rules which assure people that they will indeed be permitted to enjoy a substantial share of the product as the price of their labor or their risk of savings."[140]

We know, as legal and social science students of the family, that marriages and families are societies' essential building blocks.[141] Parenting is as important as marriage from society's and the child's perspective, and interference with it a threat to be avoided. Thus the supreme court of Alabama, opining in *Kilgrow v. Kilgrow*,[142] a dispute between two parents over religious or public education for their child, wrote:

> Intervention, rather than preventing or healing a disruption, would quite likely serve as the spark to a smoldering fire. A mandatory court decree supporting the position of one parent against the other would hardly be a composing situation for the unsuccessful parent to be confronted with daily. One spouse could scarcely be expected to entertain a tender, affectionate regard for the other spouse who brings him or her under restraint. The judicial mind and conscience is repelled by the thought of disruption of the sacred marital relationship, and usually voices the hope that the breach may somehow be healed by mutual understanding between the parties themselves.

Similarly, John Locke, in his *Second Treatise of Government*,[143] reveals that as a political matter, the "right to discipline" belongs not to parents, but to children. As many papers note, this theoretical allocation of limited[144] power, however, has only recently mustered a majority of the Supreme Court.[145] This mutation of what was simply a family law principle into a constitutional right will be discussed in chapter 4.

All this freedom from intervention of course creates an environment for opportunism. This dark side has been commented on repeatedly by feminists.[146] For example, in an infamous nineteenth-century case, the assault case against a husband who had beaten his wife with a switch "no larger than a man's thumb," was dismissed because the harm from "raising the curtain and exposing to public curiosity and criticism, the nursery and the bed chamber" would outweigh the lesser evil of "trifling violence."[147]

Arguably, the autonomy principle is related to the behavioral economics concept of the framing effect:[148] the ability to make decisions without outside interference, once possessed by family members, is worth more to them than to the third parties outside the family circle. But I argue, like the communitarians, that the ability of family members to make good decisions and otherwise self-govern is normatively better than for outsiders to attempt the same task.

Changes in prescriptions for the problem of repeated marital violence as seen through the eyes of one leading researcher provide a snapshot of this problem.[149] The most popular current legislative solution, mandatory arrest, began in the early 1990s based on the findings of social science research done initially by Lawrence Sherman using randomly assigned control groups in Minneapolis.[150] Sherman has since obtained grants to replicate the study in six American cities and has found that in some instances, particularly where the husband-assailants were unemployed, mandatory arrest worsens the chance of recidivism rather than improving it.[151] In a talk at the University of Virginia during the fall of 1999, Sherman spoke of a new youthful offender "restorative justice" program tested in New Zealand, based upon community involvement much like that of the Navajo nation.[152] From Sherman's work I have learned that if there is not already a network of shared values in the community, procedures that rely upon community sanctions will be ineffective.

One obvious way in which the state's lack of interference privileges families (abuses of that power aside) stems from the additional opportunities for agreement and growth bestowed on marriage. This protection from third-party claims of rights will be discussed at considerable length in the following chapter. When others—putative fathers, grandparents, well-meaning strangers—cannot second-guess decisions, families can thrive.[153] This is of course not arguing that others cannot have a positive influence in children's lives. Of course they can, and do. Sometimes, in fact, the grandparents or other relatives have the most important and most stable relationships.[154] In such cases, they should be treated precisely like parents for custody and visitation purposes.[155]

Using a corporate law and economics analogy, investment in relationships will be more efficient if third-party monitors have some residual claims to the benefits of the relationship. The paradigm suggests that stockholders, because they own shares (or residual rights) in the corporation, will have incentives to monitor the managers who actually run its day-to-day operations and who otherwise might tend to shirk. Because there are limits on how much decision-making power these outsiders should possess, we will take this topic up again in the family context in the next chapter. Further, social norms and conventions enhance relationships because they provide verbal and behavioral short cuts for us.[156] "Network externalities" or "social capital" enhances our undertakings in part because of this common language and in part because they provide a kind of insurance for us.

CHAPTER FOUR

Reaching the Limit: Granting Insiders and Outsiders Rights

Chapter 3 concluded with a very brief description of what in family law is known as the doctrine of family autonomy: that is, a common law–based strategy of nonintervention in the family (involving either marriage or parenting). Autonomy protects participants in "private families" from most government intervention or even suits between family members. For example, in the previously mentioned case of *Kilgrow v. Kilgrow* regarding the parental dispute over whether or not to send a child to parochial school, the court noted that "[i]t seems to us, if we should hold that equity has jurisdiction in this case such holding will open wide the gates for settlement in equity of all sorts and varieties of intimate family disputes concerning the upbringing of children."[1] It is only when people seek access to government services through public assistance or become involved with the child welfare system that the "veil" of family privacy is pierced, allowing outsiders intimate views. Families then become "public families."[2]

Traditionally, family law scholarship has seen the autonomy doctrine as the source for important presumptions of parenthood (such as the doctrine that husbands of new mothers are presumed to be the children's fathers[3] and the very strong presumption that parents are acting in their children's best interests)[4] as well as the demarcation of what is largely outside governmental scrutiny. A historical description of family law will then describe how this unitary and autonomous citadel has been battered from above and below so that the ideal remains unrealized.[5] The first incursions came from the state in its *parens patriae* function, initially through such measures as compulsory education and child labor laws.[6] These are described by economists as largely mirroring what the parents themselves would do anyway but are government provided to take advantages of economies of scale.[7] The second pincer of the attack, according to the family law literature already mentioned, comes from the growing decision-making authority given to the child, proceeding from cases like *Tinker v. Des Moines Independent School District*[8] and *Bellotti v. Massachusetts.*[9]

This chapter, unlike most family law scholarship, will look at family autonomy from a more structural stance, as a network of relationships best calculated to create social capital[10] for the couple and their children (as well as for society as a whole). Instead of looking at incursions from the bottom up, it will look at what happens to social capital if insiders (spouses or children) are accorded (or seize) individual rights that conflict with well-functioning family networks. Instead of looking at invasions from above, this chapter will examine attempts by outsiders to claim rights to share in family networks. Unlike the other chapters in this book, this one will not draw heavily on empirical work. Throughout, please bear in mind that the Supreme Court first and foremost considers what the Constitution means, not what society values.

We have already discussed how families, especially those with long time horizons and support from outside, tend to promote well-being for both the adults and children. We have talked in terms of relationships, status, networks, covenant, and trust, but until now have not developed the social science framework that uses all these terms and has relatively recently been recognized to aid in the creation of wealth: social capital. Put forward originally by sociologist Mark Granovetter[11] as a correlate of the new institutional economics, this theory recognized that the market system proposed by Adam Smith did not completely depend upon individual pursuit of self-interest, but rather was "embedded" in social relationships, which generate trust, establish expectations, and create and enforce norms. James Coleman used the term social capital three years later,[12] it became popularized by Robert Putnam's *Bowling Alone*,[13] and it has become the focus of not only a good deal of sociology scholarship but also that of economics.[14] In his article "Economics of Social Capital," Cambridge economist Partha Dasgupta describes social capital as a means to create trust.[15] He maintains that social capital (which he also sometimes calls interpersonal networks) can stem from a number of sources but should never resort to an external enforcer of agreements (that is, as in government enforcement of contracts).[16] Interpersonal networks cost something to establish. In other words, they involve transaction costs (the costs of contract negotiation, making, and enforcement) and opportunity costs, meaning that the participants could be spending their time and money doing something else. Eventually, Dasgupta argues that social capital will not only eliminate transaction costs in dealings among network members but also that it has (typically positive, but not always) external effects. Social networks help us to produce human capital[17] and are sometimes better, sometimes less effective, than impersonal markets.[18] Briefly, they will be more effective when they function in a complementary, as opposed to a substitutionary, way. That is, some kinds of networks can prevent markets from functioning well, because they dilute personal incentives to invest for prosperity. Networks will be ineffective when they and the market are substitutes. On the downside, because they are exclusive by their very nature, they can act to reinforce inequalities and prejudice, and because they generate trust (and therefore vulnerability), they may be subject to opportunism.[19]

In the social capital literature, just as they are "gender factories,"[20] families are a chief, perhaps the chief, producer of social capital. As we will see in the last section of the book, social capital is passed on through parental investment in networks and through their transmitting cultural values, as well as through children's imitation of parents, close adults, or peers.[21] So let us for now think about families as exclusive social networks functioning on many channels or linkages and promoting and generating trust. As Robert Putnam put it, "By analogy with notions of physical capital and human capital—tools and training that enhance individual productivity—"social capital" refers to features of social organization such as networks, norms, and social trust that facilitate coordination and cooperation for mutual benefit."[22] What does constitutionalization of various individual rights do? I will argue that to the extent that a right belongs to an individual within the family (a spouse or a child), creation of, and especially enforcement of, that right blocks or partially impedes the trust flowing through that channel or network. To the extent that it belongs to someone outside the family, for example a grandparent or stepparent, creation of the right makes the network less exclusive and gives less incentive for parents (or spouses) to spend time investing in it. In either event, there will be less trust generated by the particular family and, ultimately, less for society as a whole.

The "Inside Job": Clogging Trust Networks

Money for love

We have already discussed the ongoing battle of the sexes over housework during marriage, as well as my prediction that legislating that each do equal work will not succeed. One solution academics have proposed for both the lack of market respect given to household work and for the unequal bargaining positions married men and women face is to somehow compensate women for the excess home work they provide. That is, not only would each spouse presumptively get 50% of the assets on dissolution of the marriage, but there would also be compensation during the ongoing marriage. In other words, each spouse would have a right to be fully compensated for whatever he or she brought to the relationship. While this would obviously bring to the table all the "returning to exchange" problems noted in the first chapter, direct compensation during marriage is also likely to block the free flow of trust between the spouses.

Thus, in her article "Marriage Contracts and the Family Economy,"[23] Professor Katharine Silbaugh struggles with the problem of whether or not women should be compensated for household services performed during marriage. In an earlier piece,[24] Silbaugh argued persuasively that married women are undercompensated for the work they do (and consequently will probably always be at a financial disadvantage to their husbands), because they have no legal entitlement to recover for their significantly greater work around the household, which contributes something in excess of a quarter of total Gross Domestic Product.[25] In the "Marriage Contracts" article, Silbaugh first argues that corrective legal rules should not just compensate for *losses* that are themselves the result of legal rules, but instead should view nonmonetary contributions as a *gain* to the family.[26] However, instead of arguing that both paid and unpaid labor should be subjects of compensation worked out through premarital agreements,[27] she argues that children, whom she treats as belonging to both parents but not proper subjects for premarital bargaining, wage labor, and even money itself,[28] all become highly intimate within families.[29] Wage labor and housework are treated as equivalent in her analysis because housework and wage labor "are both expressions of affection as well as materially beneficial."[30] In my opinion, one of the powerful arguments fathers make when seeking custody upon divorce is that their work hours, and especially overtime work, was done for the family and was not something they would have contemplated in the abstract. They therefore find it difficult to swallow the idea, present in its most vivid form in the "primary caretaker" custody rules (meaning that the parent who was the primary caretaker should be given full custody of the children) that time spent directly with children is somehow qualitatively different from time spent working for them. At the end, Silbaugh finds that "the goal of legal parity necessitates a solution that changes the legal status of wage labor within marriage, rather than the status of domestic labor. In order to treat the monetary and nonmonetary aspects of marriage equally, we should not enforce monetary premarital agreements."[31] Because the husband's work for his family and the wife's work for hers are done out of love as well as for gain, Silbaugh argues that both should be compensated outside a marital exchange system. Thus, as others have argued, attention should be paid to equal labor-market compensation rather than expecting marital payments to do the job.

Thinking about the problem in terms of trust and social capital, we can see obvious parallels. Enforcement of contracts through the court system would obviously impair a healthy, functioning marriage network as would the precise weighing of exactly how much, and of what quality, household labor was done.[32] As Partha Dasgupta writes, "the clause 'personal relationships' in the notion of networks is central. It involves trust without recourse to an external enforcer of agreement."[33]

Rights over procreation

Cases involving rights to procreate (or to refrain from procreating) may seem to have little to do with the general problems we have been discussing, but in fact they not only set the stage for all the political fervor surrounding *Roe v. Wade*[34] but also set in motion conflicts based upon claims of rights that can give spouses language inconsistent with the unconditional nature of marriage and even endanger already fragile marriages.[35] The conflicts arise because the right to decide whether or not to bear a child belongs to an individual, the pregnant woman, married or single.[36] She need not get her husband's consent to make her choice, nor need she notify him that she is contemplating it.[37]

One unfortunate couple who fell into this particular maelstrom was Junior and Mary Sue Davis.[38] They had been unsuccessful in their attempts to have children for several years because Mary Sue miscarried multiple times. They then tried various fertility treatments, one course of in vitro fertilization, and what was then an experimental procedure, in vitro fertilization of Mary Sue's ova using Junior's cryogenically preserved (frozen) sperm. After one more failed implantation, their marriage was sufficiently troubled that Junior filed for divorce. The parting of ways itself was nowhere near as rancorous as the couple's subsequent battle over possession and disposal of the embryos. At the time of the original hearing, Mary Sue wished to go ahead with the original plan and implant them so that she could have at least one biological child. Junior did not want to become a noncustodial father and did not want his biological child to be born into a broken family. By the time the case reached the Tennessee Supreme Court, the lines had been drawn differently—Mary Sue wanted to donate the embryos to another infertile couple. Each maintained the same genetic connection to the embryo, so the court was faced with a right-to-life claim (separate from the fact of an ongoing pregnancy) versus Junior's claimed (and eventually legally vindicated) right not to procreate.

Davis, like *Roe*, sets an endpoint on a woman's exclusive right to choose whether or not to bear a child: the equal privacy right the father has to choose not to procreate prior to implantation. Only after the child is born does the father's right "to grasp the opportunity" of parenthood become important.[39] Only then must he, like the mother, be given procedural protections before his parental rights are terminated. His right to parent is so important that it cannot be conclusively presumed away, as Illinois attempted to do in the unwed father case of *Stanley v. Illinois.*[40] On the other end of the process, the right to procreate or to choose not to procreate is fundamental as well[41] and ordinarily may not be interfered with even indirectly and for a legitimate public purpose. For example, in *State v. Oakley*,[42] a divided Wisconsin Supreme Court allowed, as a provision of probation for the willful failure to pay child support, the condition that the defendant take steps not to father more children without paying the support already owed. Each spouse has an equal right at least until implantation in a woman.

The story of the Davises' frozen embryos, like other couples' struggles surrounding procreation, ultimately became a political conflict. Such wider implications of control over procreation have not been lost on the Supreme Court. In the abortion case of *Planned Parenthood of S. E. Pennsylvania v. Casey*,[43] in the section dealing with spousal notification of the pregnant woman's intent to abort, Justice O'Connor noted:

> Abortion is a unique act. It is an act fraught with consequences for others: for the woman who must live with the implications of her decision; for the persons

> who perform and assist in the procedure; for the spouse, family, and society which must confront the knowledge that these procedures exist, procedures some deem nothing short of an act of violence against innocent human life; and, depending on one's beliefs, for the life or potential life that is aborted. . . . The mother who carries a child to full term is subject to anxieties, to physical constraints, to pain that only she must bear. . . . Her suffering is too intimate and personal for the State to insist, without more, upon its own vision of the woman's role, however dominant that vision has been in the course of our history and our culture.[44]

Further, the spousal notification provision struck down in *Casey* also ran counter to a generation's post-*Roe* reliance on control over reproduction:

> But to do this would be simply to refuse to face the fact that for two decades of economic and social developments, people have organized intimate relationships and made choices that define their views of themselves and their places in society, in reliance on the availability of abortion in the event that contraception should fail. The ability of women to participate equally in the economic and social life of the Nation has been facilitated by their ability to control their reproductive lives.[45]

Davis sets a limit on the supremacy of women's privacy rights in reproduction. To be sure, it affects only the relatively small number of couples using in vitro fertilization and cryopreservation technology. Purely on political terms, then, *Davis* represents the winning of a battle in the war between the sexes but not the war itself. This war continues, but within the purview of family law, it is now sometimes fought in the context of child custody, where fathers are pursuing claims of rights to be equal custodial parents. So far, fathers have not been successful in their constitutional challenges to the "best interests" custody test,[46] though they have convinced a couple of legislatures that equal physical placement of children is best.[47]

My own father, an avid football fan, used to say, "You live by the bomb, you die by the bomb."[48] When women and men are treated equally with regard to procreation and parenting—when the reproductive battle between the sexes takes place on a level playing field—women will necessarily lose some cases, as in *Davis.* Sometimes, too, the facts of particular cases will make it unlikely that a particular heroine will succeed. Sometimes to win a particular game in the battle of the sexes, the cost will just be too high, as it ultimately was for Mary Sue Davis. But the game would never have been played at all had it not been for the constitutionalization of rights surrounding procreation. And the idea that it is a game at all played with endowments of rights represents something new and perhaps dangerous for the family.

Biology inside and out

If parents acquire definitive rights to parent only after conception (and in the case of men, birth) of their children, does biological parenthood automatically confer the rights? A series of Supreme Court cases has qualified the parental rights, at least for men. Beginning in the 1970s, unmarried fathers of children acquired rights to hearings (and sometimes custody), but only when they "seized the opportunity" to become social (or at least supportive) fathers.[49] And that is not the only limitation. In a case that might be seen as a declaration of a right by someone inside the relationship (after all, a biological father) or as an attempt to invade the marital space by an outsider (since the mother was married to someone else who had taken on many parenting duties), *Michael H. v. Gerald D.*[50] declared that biological fatherhood is not enough.

In this case, Gerald D., "a top executive in a French oil company," married Carole D., "an international model," in 1976. In 1978, Carole became involved in an adulterous affair with a neighbor, Michael H., producing a child, Victoria D., in 1981. Gerald was listed as the child's father on the birth certificate and always held Victoria out to the world as his daughter. However, a blood test revealed a 98.07% probability that Michael was Victoria's father. During the next three years, Victoria stayed with Carole, but Carole moved among the households of Gerald, Michael, and yet another man, Scott K. It is hard to tell just how much contact the biological father Michael had with Victoria during this period, but at a minimum Michael spent three months with Carole and Victoria in St. Thomas, Virgin Islands, and he stayed with Carole and Victoria whenever he was in Los Angeles. In addition, it also appears that Victoria called Michael "Daddy,"[51] Michael contributed to Victoria's support, and Michael was eager to continue his relationship with the little girl.[52]

Michael eventually filed an action to establish his paternity and win visitation rights.[53] Meanwhile, Carole had reconciled with Gerald and joined him in New York, where they lived with Victoria and their two children in common. During this time, Michael's suit encountered a California statute providing that the child of a wife cohabiting with a husband who is not impotent or sterile was conclusively presumed to be a child of the marriage. Oddly, this conclusive presumption could be rebutted, but only if the husband or wife (not a biological father) made a motion for paternity tests within two years of the child's birth.[54] In its ruling, the Supreme Court upheld the constitutionality of this presumption against Michael's Fourteenth Amendment liberty interest challenge. The Court held that presumptions of paternity rest upon "the historic respect—indeed, sanctity would not be too strong a term—traditionally accorded to the relationships that develop within the unitary family."[55] In doing so, the Court quotes an earlier case dealing with an extended family, *Moore v. East Cleveland*,[56] noting how deeply the family is rooted in the nation's "culture and tradition."[57]

The Court did briefly consider the child Victoria's interest but found it weaker than Michael's:

> We have never had occasion to decide whether a child has a liberty interest, symmetrical with that of her parent, in maintaining her filial relationship. We need not do so here because, even assuming that such a right exists, Victoria's claim must fail. Victoria's due process challenge is, if anything, weaker than Michael's.[58]

Why would it be weaker? Presumably, because Victoria's interests were, at least in theory, already protected by the idea that the parents would be looking out for her best interests. Protection came from the precedent set by *Parham v. J. R.*,[59] which held "[t]he law's concept of the family rests on a presumption that parents possess what a child lacks in maturity, experience, and capacity for judgment required for making life's difficult decisions. More importantly, historically it has recognized that natural bonds of affection lead parents to act in the best interests of their children." Further, Victoria's interests were guarded by the California presumption, which relieved the Court from having to decide who her father was if neither spouse asked. That is, if the Court was not being asked to make the determination, there would be no need for litigation that might exacerbate family conflict. As the Court noted, however, Victoria was not trying to assert her rights here, so there was no existing conflict between parent and child.

How then can we characterize what Michael was trying to do in terms of networks and rights? Michael claimed that as a biological and what he called a social father he had a constitutional right to nurture his relationship with Victoria. Carole (speaking for Victoria) and Gerald maintained that as a committed married couple they had already set up the best situation for Victoria's upbringing. Any claim of rights by Michael would clog up the trust relationships in their household and would, at a minimum, confuse Victoria. Alternatively, we can look at the case as one between a would-be insider and an existing nuclear family because of the presumption and Gerald's marriage to Victoria. Michael was asserting that because of his unquestioned biological fatherhood and his claimed social parenthood he had a right to spend time with Victoria, support her, and potentially have custody of her.

Rights to inculcate religion

In the discussion in chapter 3 of family autonomy, we noted the famous *Kilgrow* case dealing with the parents' dispute over whether their child should attend a parochial or public school. The court determined that this was a matter best left to the parents, who ultimately did work out a satisfactory solution, educating Margaret half in Catholic and half in public schools. But can and should a parent be able to maintain his constitutional right to bring up the child as he sees fit? What about the child's right to exercise her own religious beliefs? The context here is typically not the ongoing family but the postdivorce family. We will begin, however, with a case that follows shortly after *Michael H.*

Board of Education of Kiryas Joel Village Sch. Dist. v. Grumet[60] does not seem to consider the children's independent interests at all.[61] In this case, suit was brought by taxpayers and others who sought to invalidate special New York legislation creating a school district for a religious enclave of strict Jewish practitioners.[62] Justice Souter, for the Court, declared that the special legislation violated the Establishment Clause because of its "purposeful fusion of religious and governmental functions."[63] Justice Stevens, in his concurring opinion, focused on the statute's effect on children. At this time, Justice Stevens was still writing for a minority of three members of the Court.[64] He maintained:

> The isolation of these children, while it may protect them from 'panic, fear, and trauma,' also unquestionably increased the likelihood that they would remain within the fold, faithful adherents of their parents' religious faith. By creating a

> school district that is specifically intended to shield children from contact with others who have 'different ways,' the State provided official support to cement the attachment of young adherents to a particular faith.[65]

Carl Schneider discusses this problem of isolation at some length in "Religion and Child Custody."[66] He recognizes the difficulty of courts, as opposed to parents, making this sort of decision without running afoul of the Establishment Clause and therefore argues for a hands-off approach unless, in a custody case, the child's best interests are directly threatened.[67] Another way to think of the isolation would be to locate the children in the very strong web of networks that made up their religious community. Not only were the channels between parent and child threatened by state action, but also those between child, parent, and other residents of Kiryas Joel.

Justice Stevens's concern for children's relationship rights as distinct from their parents' emerges yet more clearly in *Troxel v. Glanville*,[68] where the Court upheld a fit parent's constitutional right to determine whether, and under what conditions, visitation by third parties (in this case grandparents) was appropriate. Broadly speaking, the case reaffirms the right of fit parents "to control and direct the upbringing and education of their children."[69] Justice Stevens, in his dissent,[70] stressed that the broad parental rights articulated by the majority might not always concur with what was best for their children:

> [W]e have never held that the parent's liberty interest in this relationship is so inflexible as to establish a rigid constitutional shield, protecting every arbitrary parental decision from any challenge absent a threshold finding of harm. The presumption that parental decisions generally serve the best interests of their children is sound, and clearly in the normal case the parent's interest is paramount. But even a fit parent is capable of treating a child like a mere possession. . . . Cases like this do not present a bipolar struggle between the parents and the State over who has final authority to determine what is in a child's best interests. There is at a minimum a third individual, whose interests are implicated in every case to which the statute applies—the child.[71]

Justice Stevens's point, centered on preserving "established familial or family-like bonds," is so central to this chapter and the discussion of family social networks that I set it out at some length:

> While this Court has not yet had occasion to elucidate the nature of a child's liberty interests in preserving established familial or family-like bonds, it seems to me extremely likely that, to the extent parents and families have fundamental liberty interests in preserving such intimate relationships, so, too, do children have these interests, and so, too, must their interests be balanced in the equation. At a minimum, our prior cases recognizing that children are, generally speaking, constitutionally protected actors require that this Court reject any suggestion that when it comes to parental rights, children are so much chattel. . . . The constitutional protection against arbitrary state interference with parental rights should not be extended to prevent the States from protecting children against the arbitrary exercise of parental authority that is not in fact motivated by an interest in the welfare of the child.[72]

Children thus have an important interest in the bonds they maintain with their parents. In addition, Justice Stevens recognizes that despite best interests presumptions, parents may not always act unselfishly even when their decisions affect their children. Francis Fukuyama, you will remember, also observes that rights discourse may be used as a "kind of cover for selfish individuals to pursue their private aims."[73]

Justice Stevens's opinion in *Troxel* nevertheless begs the question of how the child's relationship interests mesh with their strong interests in being part of a family sufficiently powerful (as against the state and third parties) to be a place where parents can do their jobs and children flourish,[74] a topic we will take up next.[75] Justice Stevens's position in *Troxel* was, of course, taken in dissent. The majority extended privacy doctrines to protect the decisions of the parent.

A fourth case, *Lawrence v. Texas*,[76] invalidated laws against consensual same-sex sodomy.[77] This case could be considered a victory for strengthening privacy rights because of the Court's reliance upon search and seizure cases and concern about police interference with intimate conduct.[78] Although the Court cautions that it is not considering a statute recognizing the status of same-sex relationships,[79] *Lawrence* can also be considered in a broader sense as involving the content of a couple's relationship itself. Justice Kennedy, writing for the Court, distinguishes between "mere sex" and "relationship" in these words:

> To say that the issue in *Bowers* was simply the right to engage in certain sexual conduct demeans the claim the individual put forward, just as it would demean a

> married couple were it to be said marriage is simply about the right to have sexual intercourse. . . . The statutes do seek to control a personal relationship that, whether or not entitled to formal recognition in the law, is within the liberty of persons to choose without being punished as criminals. . . . This, as a general rule, should counsel against attempts by the State, or a court, to define the meaning of the relationship or to set its boundaries absent injury to a person or abuse of an institution the law protects.[80]

Therefore, while *Eisenstadt*[81] brought privacy to the individual woman regarding contraception,[82] *Lawrence* returns privacy not just to the gay man involved but also to his relationship with another.[83]

Finally, *Oak Grove Unified Sch. Dist v. Newdow*[84] may be best remembered as the case where the Court refused to consider whether "under God" could remain part of the Pledge of Allegiance.[85] Again, this is a case in which someone once part of the innermost family circle has been moved toward the periphery because the parents had broken up. The Court found that Michael Newdow, who had joint physical custody of his daughter but not the power to make ultimate decisions when he disagreed with her mother, lacked standing as a parent to make his claims because of the California court's custody determination.[86] Authored by Justice Stevens for the Court, the opinion stated:

> This case concerns not merely Newdow's interest in inculcating his child with his views on religion, but also the rights of the child's mother as a parent generally and under the Superior Court orders specifically. And most important, it implicates the interests of a young child who finds herself at the center of a highly public debate over her custody, the propriety of a widespread national ritual, and the meaning of our Constitution. . . . The interests of the affected persons in this case are in many respects antagonistic. Of course, legal disharmony in family relations is not uncommon, and in many instances that disharmony poses no bar to federal-court adjudication of proper federal questions. What makes this case different is that Newdow's standing derives entirely from his relationship with his daughter, but he lacks the right to litigate as her next friend. In marked contrast to our case law on *jus tertii*, . . . [t]he interests of this parent and this child are not parallel and, indeed, are potentially in conflict.[87]

Newdow shows us clearly, as *Troxel* did not, that sometimes parents' and children's rights may conflict. To take another example, statistics show us both that interracial marriages are more likely to dissolve than to remain intact (since they divorce at a rate more than 50% higher than the rate for others, even controlling for other factors typically leading to divorce or their "selection into" interracial marriage) and that divorce is particularly hard on biracial children.[88] Yet the rights of the Lovings (of *Loving v. Virginia*,[89] the case invalidating prohibitions against interracial marriages) and their children clearly did not conflict, since the family could not live together legitimately in Virginia without the Court's decision. The rights will be more likely to conflict, with the consequent disruption of channels of trust, when divorcing parents hold strong—and potentially opposing—religious beliefs, as was the case in *Newdow*.[90] In fact, I have found in a study of Iowa divorces that there was a statistically significant relationship between parents who decided religion was important enough to mention in their separation agreements[91] and those who divorced on fault grounds and who continued disputing after the divorce decree.[92]

Fights about visitation often center on religion itself or disciplinary views strongly colored by religious views. For example, in *Baker v. Baker*,[93] the mother was Baptist and the father was a Jehovah's Witness. The court originally awarded the mother custody. Both parents were taking the children to their respective religious services and training, and each attempted to undermine the other's religion. At trial, the mother petitioned for, and won, affirmation of her exclusive right to determine the children's religious upbringing, based on the physical and psychological effects the conflict was having on the children. In another visitation case, *Brown v. Szakal*,[94] the court refused to order the non-Jewish father to observe the Sabbath and keep kosher when he visited his seven- and nine-year-old daughters. The court found that "absent a showing of emotional or physical harm to the children, courts . . . will not impose upon the non-custodial parent the burden of policing the religious instructions of the custodial parents."[95] A third-party visitation case, a subject we will take up presently, involved a conflict over discipline (with a belt),[96] where relationships with the grandparents were fairly close and cordial until the attempted discipline.[97]

Threats to Exclusivity: Diluting the Networks

One of the most poignant cases in family law textbooks presents two families in tragic circumstances. The parents of Phillip Becker, a Down syndrome child, after some anguish and consultation with numerous advisors, including doctors and their priest, had placed Phillip in an institution. They did not visit him often, left him primarily on public support, and refused to consent to heart surgery that might prolong his life,[98] a decision that resulted in the whole matter being aired on national television. Meanwhile, a couple who volunteered at the institution were taking more and more interest in Phillip, successfully teaching him a number of life skills and allowing him to spend most holidays and many weekends with them and their children. When Phillip's parents refused to allow the Heaths to take Phillip for any more overnight visits, the Heaths sought to become his legal guardians. With the help of a young attorney working pro bono and then-Stanford law professor Robert Mnookin, the Heaths won their case and eventually adopted Phillip, who had successful heart surgery.[99] As a matter of simple humanity, this was the only right conclusion. As a legal precedent, however, this was a dangerous opinion that needs to be confined as narrowly as possible to its facts (near abandonment, emotionally and financially, by biological parents and a close and long-lasting relationship with parent surrogates who are willing to adopt).

Here is the problem, at least as Phillip's parents portrayed it: They stressed the "agonizing discussions with medical and spiritual advisors" that resulted in their refusal to "consent to risky, painful, and questionable open-heart surgery." They noted that they had never been found to have abandoned, abused, or neglected Phillip but that nonetheless he was given to "a couple our age whom we have never met," according to them because someone else convinced the judge that the Heaths were more involved with the child than the parents and would make better decisions for him.[100] In other words, outsiders were permitted to intervene in an undoubtedly stressed and stretched, but intact, family over the objection of fit parents. Should outsiders be allowed to do this routinely?

Most of the time, at least without proof of unfitness on the part of parents, outsiders are excluded from the family except as parents consent, according to the landmark case *Troxel v. Glanville*,[101] the grandparent visitation case mentioned earlier in the chapter. The statute the Court found unconstitutional in *Troxel* allowed "any person" to petition the court "at any time" for visitation rights if visitation would be in the child's best interests and did not presume that the parents who disagreed were acting in the child's best interests. This, the Court held, violated the fit mother's liberty right "to control and direct the upbringing of her children," in part because it was "breathtakingly broad" and in part because it gave no deference at all to the presumption that the parent was acting in the child's best interests. The grandparents, who claimed that they had a right to maintain their substantial ties with their grandchild, simply did not have an interest that would trump the parent's. The Court went to some pains not to invalidate the less sweeping third-party visitation statutes enacted in all U.S. states, most of which allowed visitation only when the relationship with the child was substantial, the person petitioning was a grandparent, and an enumerated set of circumstances such as divorce or death of the petitioner's child disrupted the family anyway or perhaps made it more likely that the parent was acting selfishly.

But outside the legal holding, is there a broader explanation for what the Court did in *Troxel*? I believe there are two alternative rationales, either of which fits within the theories of this book, and both of which could also be said to fit within the exclusivity idea of Dasgupta's "Economics of Social Capital" piece.[102] One draws on a twist to the classic Tragedy of the Commons (a problem interesting to writers on norms and social capital as well as property rights theorists), while the other is borrowed from the literature on corporate stakeholders. Both of these theories suggest restrictions on outsiders who claim rights that would dilute the parents' ability to generate human capital.

In his ingenious article, *The Tragedy of the Anticommons*,[103] Michael Heller writes about the privatization of Soviet housing stock. The problem he describes is that too many people have ownership interests in the same units. In a commons, to which he contrasts the Soviet situation, multiple owners are each given a privilege to use some resource, and no one has the right to exclude another. The resource will then be overused.[104] With the anticommons, multiple owners are each given the right to exclude others from a scarce resource, and no one can effectively use it.[105] The resource is therefore prone to underuse—hence the tragedy. He writes that empty Moscow storefronts are a good example, but that others include Irish property before the "potato famine," and "upstream" biotechnology patents that must be secured before new products can be brought to market.[106] In fact, he notes, an anticommons tragedy can appear whenever governments create new property rights.[107]

In some ways, children possess many of the properties of a commons shared between their parents. In fact, they have been described as "public goods" of their parents' marriage.[108] Unlike the pond that can be overfished, parents cannot "over love" (though they may smother) their children.[109] Managing the scarce resource that is children's time can effectively help parents develop informal norms and institutions. Carol Rose[110] and Elinor Ostrom[111] have shown how people sometimes develop informal norms and institutions to manage commons property efficiently. As Rose notes, when the parents are "locked together" in their relationship, their common task may reinforce communitarian values and help them learn to work together.[112] Informal coordination and the nonutilitarian value of overlapping ownership apply on the anticommons end of the property spectrum as well.[113] Whether anticommons ownership of a particular resource results in tragedy depends in part on people's ability to cooperate informally. And this ability, of course, is precisely what is threatened by granting parental prerogatives[114] to third parties. If the parties all get along and are willing to accommodate (as will be the case in most grandparent/parent relationships), no tragedy will be involved. But when they can't make joint decisions, as in the *Troxel* case or any other in which the grandparents are likely to resort to lawsuits to enforce visitation, many of the good things flowing from the autonomy right are likely to evaporate.

> Marriage, like adoption, carries with it a commitment toward permanence that places it in a different category of relational interests than if it were temporary. A 'justifiable expectation . . . that the relationship will continue indefinitely' permits parties to invest themselves in the relationship with a reasonable belief that the likelihood of future benefits warrants the attendant risks and inconvenience. There is a clear analogy between the motivational factors that influence human investment and those that influence economic investments. Jeremy Bentham believed that private ownership of property is more likely to maximize social utility than is collective ownership because 'the human motivations which result in production are . . . such that they will not operate in the absence of secure expectations about future enjoyment of product.' The will to labor and the will to invest 'depend on rules which assure people that they will indeed be permitted to enjoy a substantial share of the product as the price of their labor or their risk of savings.'[115]

With visitation rights, as with issues discussed in the Scotts' article "Parents as Fiduciaries,"[116] ill-considered law may reduce the incentives (rewards) for optimal behavior by parents. We are also reminded of the previous discussions about the signal marriage gives. When many people have rights, as opposed to moral justifications, to pieces of marriage or children, the signal becomes confused, as Michael Trebilcock notes when he criticizes enacting multiple choices of marriage type.[117] When the signal becomes dilute, the benefits from marriage will not be as strong, nor will marriage be as well differentiated from, say, cohabitation.[118]

Stakeholders

Corporate scholars outside the law and economics world tend to speak of stakeholders in the same breath as the business judgment rule.[119] That is, they ask whether the director in question acted within the protections of the business judgment rule if he granted a voice to stakeholders.[120] Conversely, might he have violated the business judgment rule if he did not?[121] In law and economics, however, the questions change. They still deal with the director's duty, but the underlying question is to whom the duty is owed. What is "the corporation," and if the director does his duty, what values must he maximize? (Of course, corporations can also take advantage of social capital.[122])

From the early writings of Ronald Coase,[123] law and economics scholars have conceptualized the business firm as a collection or nexus of contracts.[124] Corporations exist, the theory goes, because they save on transaction costs that would otherwise thwart principals who would have to make contracts for every input and service necessary to produce. The corporation is also organized to take advantage of team production (or multiple people working at one or more step).[125] The problem created by team production, in turn, is that it is difficult to see what any one team member contributes to the collective output.[126] Thus, as Butler and McChesney put it, "The nature of the firm, then, is the use of ongoing internal direction by the firm's managers to control labor and other resources, rather than negotiating a series of external contracts in the marketplace as needs arise."[127]

Following Coase, much of the debate has centered on the roles for and incentives of various players in the corporate process—shareholders, managers, employees, and boards of directors.[128] Thus, according to Alchian and Demsetz, corporate managers exist to monitor the behavior of other employees who would otherwise, as agents of the owners, shirk. Stockholders become residual owners in order for them to have appropriate incentives to "monitor the monitors."[129] Managers have independent incentives to act to further corporate interests because they participate in a "market for managerial control."[130]

Of late, the discussion has returned to the essential question of what the corporation is and what its goals must be. Does it exist solely to fulfill the interests of its stockholder-owners?[131] Are these interests confined solely to making money over the short term, or more broadly, does the corporation have a mission for the long-term holders,[132] the general community, or to society in future generations? Does the corporation, like *Homo economicus*, have a conscience?[133]

At least since the 1960s, corporations themselves have realized that giving employees some stake in the firm makes them more productive. They have instituted stock ownership plans, T-groups, work-clusters, incentives for suggestions, and sometimes, apart from organized labor, placed employees on the corporate board.[134] They sometimes organize, as in Japan, precisely to take advantage of employees' team-working capabilities—in other words, their social capital.[135]

Corporations have also become large donors, not only to political campaigns (obviously a form of taking advantage, or what economists call "rent seeking"), but also to community causes and more general charitable endeavors.[136] Sometimes corporate giving is seen as selling not only the product but also the image of the firm.[137] Thus, Ben and Jerry's ice cream is identified with "green" causes and generally liberal politics.

When corporations have talked about closing plant doors, perhaps to seek cheaper forms of labor outside the country, their relocation plans have drawn vigorous community opposition. Not only will many jobs be lost, protest the communities, but also the support services that thrive on the presence of the industry in the community will lose out. Somehow, the corporation has acquired a duty to the community besides making a profit. But viewed another way, because these outside stakeholders have more acute needs than the stockholders, they may well contract for job security or other entitlements. The firm will give them job security or higher wages to attract the best workers. Better workers make the firm more productive, so this activity furthers stockholder interests (at least over the long run).[138] Organized labor and institutional interests, such as pension plans, also depend upon corporate vitality in a fashion the "theory of the firm" originators probably did not find important to include in the 1960s.

No one doubts that all or at least some of these stakeholders, as they are called, ought to be given some deference in corporate day-to-day decision making. The real question is whether they ought to be given not only a voice but also a vote.[139] Should they be able to interfere with corporate plans that would otherwise be profitable?[140] Does the corporation belong to them in some meaningful sense?

Some writers claim that the goal of the firm must be to work in the interests of the "corporation," a more inclusive concept than merely its stockholders.[141] Alternatively, the interests of the stockholders are seen as not being merely monetary ones and not ones limited to the short-term. It is clear, though, that managers will be acting outside their authority and in violation of the business judgment rule if they ignore stockholder interests to pursue their own. In other words, the actions of the managers cannot lawfully conflict with or dilute the residual interests of the shareholders.[142] Such a conflict would be inefficient and would violate the principle that the corporation exists to serve a public purpose of creating economic wealth for its owners and therefore the larger society.[143]

My argument here is that giving "ownership rights" to third-party family stakeholders (grandparents like the Troxels, excluded biological parents like Michael H., or even volunteers like the Heaths) would wreak the same kind of mischief as giving "ownership" rights to corporate stakeholders who aren't stockholders. Families obviously aren't corporations. There is a great deal more going on in family life than maximizing profits and producing monetary wealth. But the ability to parent effectively, like the ability of a corporation to produce or serve efficiently, requires some noninterference from outsiders, whether the state or interested private parties. This has long been protected (at least vis-à-vis the state) by the autonomy doctrine and the parental preference doctrine, both discussed previously.

A good bit of my work on the economics of the families analogizes marriages and families to firms. In fact, *From Contract to Covenant* contains a whole large section entitled The Family as Firm.[144] In my earlier work,[145] my concerns with stakeholders are mostly vertical—that is, intergenerational—ones, though the outsiders occasionally may be peers like the Heaths and Michael H. or former same-sex partners.[146] To be clear, I believe that "contracts" between parents and children should remain implicit and unenforceable.[147]

Here I wish to enlarge the thought to consider what happens when what might be called horizontal communities—extended families and kinship groups—become involved. I do not mean to suggest that extended families or kinship groups are not extremely important[148] or that they do not benefit parents and their minor children in many ways. For example, remember the importance of the witnesses to the Hawaiian wedding with which we began? I just do not believe, as the Court apparently does not, that these admitted stakeholders should be able to interfere and dilute the effectiveness of the parenting done by fit parents. Thus in cases like *Troxel* and *Michael H.*, I would urge the stakeholders to forge bonds with the parents or spouses involved,[149] rather than to stress whatever ties may be in place by bringing lawsuits or claiming "rights."

Similarly, Fukuyama and Dasgupta found some problems with kin networks, in stifling what Fukuyama calls "flexible networks" and Dasgupta calls impeding the movement of labor or capital. Just because the network is broader does not mean that it is more effective. For example, recent research has shown that having multiple kin networks because of parenting children with more than one woman[150] or man[151] (or multipartnered fertility) does not promote child well-being, and even inhibits the resources kin normally provide, perhaps because of "too many trips to the well," perhaps because of lack of trust. Both of these studies were made on African American families, long thought of as relying heavily on kin support. As James Coleman would say, the networks become open as opposed to having closure.[152] All the intermediate "nodes" are no longer linked. Alternatively, in Francis Fukuyama's terminology, the free-rider problem becomes more severe as group size increases because of difficulties in monitoring.[153] We cannot know precisely what each family member is contributing to the overall welfare as we could with a smaller group.

Brief Conclusions

Communities are vital for marriage and parenting. Informal communities should be encouraged socially and through channeling legislation.[154] However, turning these informal ties into legal rights destroys the relationships. As Carl Schneider wrote some years ago,

> Where a right exists, we prima facie prefer the individual, as the law of substantive due process illustrates. But the rights schema is often inapposite in the family context, since there a right against the government is also a right against other family members. And because we dislike compromising a right against the government, we are inhibited from looking for ways to encourage compromises or even discussion within the family. Indeed the very appeal to law—to an external set of standards enforced by might—is atomistic in that it circumvents the (no doubt idealized) standards of family decision: private persuasion and eventual accommodation based on solicitude for the person with whom one disagrees.[155]

On the other end of the spectrum, community parenting, despite its superficial attraction,[156] just isn't a good idea.[157]

PART III
Families, Mimetics, and Community

CHAPTER FIVE

The Family as "Little Commonwealth": The Role of Mimetics

In earlier chapters, we have seen how trust is related to society's choice of which relationships are deemed to be family, how the family works in creating social capital, and how burgeoning rights may threaten social capital (or, in Fukuyama's term, reduce the "radius of trust").[1] We turn now to questions of how trust in particular, or social capital in general, is created in families and how that same mechanism of mimetics, or imitation, may, as it does in larger communities, become destructive through scapegoating. We will take models worked out for macroeconomic behavior (on the labor-force, country, or societal level) and apply them to the microeconomic level of family units. We will end with some ways in which the destructive path may be avoided and some roles public policy and especially law can take to promote the creation of social capital. In our discussion we will revisit some scholars we have treated before, especially Richard McAdams and Francis Fukuyama, but will add some new ones, particularly Robert Frank, René Girard, and Gil Baillie.

We begin with what probably seems only common sense: looking at what parents typically want for their children and how they go about creating these things. On the absolutely most basic, biological level, parents want their children to grow to become adults and have their own children.[2] Amplifying this idea a bit, we, as parents, love them because they are in a sense part us, because they are familiar through constant interaction[3] (particularly for those who provide the most child care), and because we feel hope through them. As John Locke wrote, we equip our dependent children with the things they need to grow into adults who can make decisions for themselves.[4] This means that parents equip their children with the material needs of food, clothing, and shelter. Because we live in a complex society, we provide our children with human capital in addition to this physical capital: we educate our children.[5] We hope that they will be able to do at least as well as we did, materially and in terms of happiness. And so, as we have seen already, we give them the social capital that they will need to be able to prosper in human communities.

One of the continual debates in the human studies literature is whether it is nature or nurture that ultimately makes the child: whether children are destined to be "naughty or nice" because of their genetic heritage, or rather because of what parents do after the child is born. Clearly, as we saw in earlier chapters, both nature and nurture play a role.[6] For example, a team studying pairs of children adopted close to birth during the 1950s and 1960s has shown that it is the interaction between parenting and biological traits that seems to matter.[7] In the Iowa Adoption Study, children were matched by date of birth, child placement agency, and age of adopting mother. One child in each pair had at least one parent with a history of alcohol or drug abuse, mental illness, or antisocial behavior. The other did not have a parent with known problems. The children have been followed continuously for more than forty years, so much is known about their later history. Children with genetic indications of problems were in fact more likely to follow the same patterns as their biological parents,[8] but the latent tendencies in the main required activation by something in the adopting parents' household—something like alcoholism in an adopting parent or a parental divorce in the adoptive family.[9] But even absent such a big change (known to produce problems even without genetic proclivities), when the adoptive parents knew about the problems in the birth family, the children were significantly *more* likely to replicate the problem behaviors.[10] Thus, parents influence their children in more than just their selection of a mating partner.

In her important book *Love and Economics*,[11] Jennifer Roback Morse powerfully argues that parents change children from *Homo economicus*, the rational self-interested creature of classical economics, into people capable of love. Parents do so first by providing children with their material needs in a regular and prompt way that creates trust and then, beginning when the child starts to acquire reasoning capacity, by setting appropriate limits (even though not appreciated, followed by the child because of the trust that has been inculcated before) within which the child can develop her own sense of identity and decision-making capacity without permanently damaging herself. Children can grow physically, Morse writes, they can thrive intellectually and can even make calculating economic choices. But in a profound sense, they will be less than fully human if they cannot trust and therefore cannot think beyond themselves except in strategic ways.[12]

What we all recognize is that children learn not only through independent observation but also through imitation of those around them.[13] This is of course true of language acquisition and even learning about more primitive communication, such as facial expressions like smiling. It is true of the basic life skills we learn as children (like tying shoes or doing hair) and the more complicated ones (like home repair, table or classroom manners, or dating etiquette). And the characteristics of social capital (and particularly trust)[14] are also learned through imitation, both of our parents and others close to us. In the section that follows, we will talk about the development of trust as the manifestation of social capital found and formed in families.[15]

What Should be "Maximized" in Families?

At first glance, deciding what values society should seek to maximize in families sounds like a silly question. Once we think about it, though, our disciplinary focus takes over our impulse as parents. As parents, we are apt to answer the question of what we want for our children by saying we want them to be happy. Happiness is not necessarily tied to wealth, as an interuniversity World Values Survey reported in 2003.[16] In this study, the happiest people lived in Nigeria, Mexico, Venezuela, El Salvador, and Puerto Rico, while the least happy resided in Russia, Armenia, and Romania. Jonathan Power, a journalist interviewing people in the happiest country,[17] writes that it is because "we all have a great religious faith" and "We Nigerians look after each other. If I know you and you are hungry or ill I will try and help." Psychologists report that happiness is based on autonomy, competence, relatedness, and self-esteem.[18] In alternatives to volunteering child happiness as a goal, though these characteristics may lead to happiness, some parents will say they want their children to develop their talents fully, to have the advantages they never had, or to at least not to make the same big mistakes.[19]

Once academics are asked the same question about what parents maximize, they give different answers. Nobel Laureate Gary Becker writes that families seek to maximize utility, which he says is related to the production of "commodities" that cannot be purchased in the marketplace but are produced as well as consumed by households using things that are purchased, the couple's time, and environmental inputs. He enumerates these as "children, prestige and esteem, health, altruism, envy, and pleasure."[20] In other work, he writes about the tradeoffs between the quantity and quality of children.[21]

Another suggestion comes from law professor Milton Regan, who argues that families were the best sites for the production of intimacy. Quoting various researchers,[22] he notes that the primary function of family is "caring, nurturing, and loving" and prescribes a return to the legal concept of status to promote the intimacy people seek as an antidote to the alienation of the postmodern world.

This section builds on the earlier work by showing how trust and its close relative, unconditional love,[23] might be the values for the family to maximize that are most critical for social capital. Although the exact prescriptions may vary with cultural groups, the abilities to trust, to love others well, and to give selflessly do not recognize cultural, socioeconomic, or physical boundaries. Children are not born trusting or loving unconditionally, but acquire these abilities over time, primarily through experiencing (and imitating) other models of love: their parents' love for each other, their parents' love for them, and for many, love in a religious or spiritual context. In this chapter, I will support these claims about acquisition of the central family values through a variety of empirical strategies: experimental, survey, diagnostic tests, and real-life behavior.

First, there is a nomenclature question. Psychologists are apt to equate the acquisition of trust and the ability to love with the creation of the child's prosocial[24] or altruistic behavior. Sociologists focus on altruistic volunteering or donating time or money to others and term its opposite exchange-based behavior.[25] Economists, perhaps Frank and Dasgupta excepted, will call it altruistic, with its opposite tit-for-tat exchange.[26] Those who write about families may well claim that children who "best love" (or who are at least altruists) possess "interdependent utility functions" with those others:[27] they are made happier when the others are happier.

Given my past work, it is perhaps not surprising that I see acquisition of trust as requiring permanence in the relationship.[28] I hypothesize that children acquire this tendency (or longing, as Aristotle and Morse[29] would term it) as they see it around them (in a less superficial way than the Troggs' "Love is All Around").[30] As mentioned previously, the observation that we acquire values as well as other things through observation of others comes initially from learning theory.[31] For example, children pick up behavioral cues from their parents, particularly in ambiguous situations. The moral viewpoint learned primarily from parents will guide their learning throughout life.[32] They may also learn about intangible things, such as science concepts and about God.[33]

The parents' love for him or her is likely the first example of unconditional love worthy of trust noticed by the child.[34] Outsiders can see it in what the parent says about the child, what kinds of activities he or she does with the child, and how close the child feels to the parent, and perhaps by whether the child feels the parent stands up for him or her or acts as an advocate.[35] (Remember that a scale built from these elements was the parental "warmth" variable so important to child success in chapter 1.) From an absent parent, we can still get some glimpse of parental love through continued contact, attendance at the child's activities, and even faithful payment of child support.[36] From a negative perspective, we see the absence of unconditional love in parents who say they are disappointed with their child, who neglect their child (when they have the means of support), perhaps when they engage in custody battles,[37] and certainly when they abuse the child. As I will argue, law can strengthen parental relationships with children and therefore make it more likely that they will learn to love well and to trust.

The parents' love for and trust in each other also can serve as a model for children. We have seen already how unconditional love and trust are most likely to flourish in marriage as opposed to cohabitation. It is also most evident in what Judith Wallerstein calls the "good marriage,"[38] whose opposite is the "separate spheres" (or marriage reduced to its lowest common denominator) discussed by Lundberg and Pollak[39] or the "exchange relationship" described by Gary Hanson.[40] As I have argued throughout this book, from a nonlegal perspective, marriage is strengthened by increased support from extended family and the community, secular and religious, as well as through less reliance on "rights" as a source of relationship.[41]

God's love is, for the believer, the model for all human unconditional love.[42] We might see parents' response to it in the frequency of their church attendance or how important they say religion is in their lives.[43] The ability of law (at least in the United States) to influence belief and the exercise of it is undoubtedly a delicate constitutional question.[44] The law can certainly continue to refrain from discriminating against religion and to allow such benefits as charitable tax deductions for religious contributions[45] and tax exemptions for religious properties.[46] Tuition vouchers may act to make religious education more available for the poor as well.[47] But the controversy in Massachusetts surrounding Catholic Charities' adoption policies (that is, rather than consent to place adopted children with same-sex couples, the charities ended adoption services)[48] shows how politically and legally fragile this balance has become.

These ideas can be tested to some extent. I have already published data on altruism as it relates to age, gender, and marital status (including some original experimental research),[49] which I will report briefly here as well as a study by sociologists relating obligation for others to family structure and early experiences. We can also get at least some rough measures of religiosity of parents, their own parents' marital status, and closeness to them, as well as how they contribute (in terms of time and money) to various kinds of charitable organizations and to their aging parents, how they interact with and feel about their children, and how the children are turning out using the PSID and the CDS (now in its second round).

Altruism, Trust, and Unconditional Love Develop Over Time

Altruism in its simplest form is care for another. The altruist and the other, as defined by economists, have interdependent utility functions, as economists Becker[50] and Posner[51] have noted, so that the altruist is willing to reduce his or her own consumption to increase the consumption of others.[52] The altruist takes the other's utility or happiness into account, so that the other's utility is an extension of the altruist's own.[53] As Paula England puts it,[54] neoclassical economists assume that *A* is altruistic toward *B* when whatever gives *B* utility contributes to *A*'s utility.

Sometimes this connection provides the altruist with a kind of pleasure; at other times the altruist acts out of a sense of duty. Thus Jon Elster writes,[55] "[H]elping or giving out of love is instrumental behavior, that is, concerned with outcomes. If I help my child, I seek the best means to make that child happy. . . . The concept of duty is more ambiguous: It can be instrumental or squarely noninstrumental." Milton Regan, in one of his books, argues that the altruist perceives the self as part of a common humanity: as a relational self.[56]

TABLE 5.1 **Preferences for Altruism on Behalf of a Group**

Variable	Coefficient	Std. error	t-ratio	Prob\t\òx	Mean of X	Std. of X
Age	.293139E−01	0.502634E−02	5.832	0.0000	18.941	11.195
Sex	−0.14587	0.152909	−0.954	0.34018	0.45098	0.49857

Source: From Margaret F. Brinig, "Does Mediation Systematically Disadvantage Women?" *William and Mary Journal of Women and the Law* 2, no. 1, 1995.
Note: The chi-squared for the equation was 21.058, showing that the results in all probability did not happen by chance.

Using the experiments of Robin Dawes and others[57] as a model, I devised a simple test originally planning to determine whether women are more willing to give than are men.[58] A sample of 255 people ranging in age from five to sixty-six years was divided into groups of five. All members of each group were about the same age, with no member more than two years older or younger than any other member of the group. Each participant indicated age, sex, and zip code (used as a proxy for income). The participants were given five chocolate candies each. They were told that if three people in their group would contribute their five candies, everyone in the group would receive ten more. Thus, if three contributed, they would receive ten candies, and the others would receive fifteen. If less than a majority contributed, those who had contributed would lose their five candies while the others in the group would keep their original five. Those choosing to contribute were the altruists, since they could in no event do as well as those who more selfishly kept their own candies. However, their contribution increased the probability of a larger reward for the other members of the group. The results of a probit regression[59] using the choice of contributing or not as the dependent variable are shown in table 5.1.

What table 5.1 demonstrates is that age was significantly related to altruism in this simple setting: as the experimental subject's age increased, so did the probability of choosing to contribute to the group. However, gender did not predict altruism in this pure sense (although the negative sign indicates that girls and women were slightly more willing to contribute, controlling for age).

Learning from relationships: The study of Nock et al.

In their piece "The Distribution of Obligations," Nock and his coauthors explored the extent to which particular needs are considered personal obligations, a legitimate concern for government, or some mixture of the two.[60] They found that personal obligations appear to be conditioned by what people believe others (relatives, charities, and the government) owe to a needy individual. In their study of 507 broadly representative people in Richmond, Virginia, they sought to establish whether social groups actually differ in how they allocate responsibility in a number of realms (e.g., health care and job training). They framed their questions only in terms of obligations that involved financial costs, reasoning that individuals who differ in how many dollars they are willing to give someone in need may be said to differ in their sense of obligation to that person.

The authors asked subjects to indicate how much they personally would be willing to contribute to solving another's hypothetical need, as well as the amount they thought other relatives, churches and charities, and the government should contribute. The vignettes were randomly altered to reveal the effects of different relationships between the needy person and the respondent and varying culpability of the needy person. The situations reflected various common kinds of need: unemployment with a need for job training, health issues with a need for nursing care or medical care uncompensated by insurance, and eviction with a need for new living arrangements. The relationships the authors varied included: parent, child, brother or sister, grandparent, grandchild, aunt or uncle, niece or nephew, cousin, son- or daughter-in-law, mother- or father-in-law, close friend, coworker, close neighbor, and a person in Richmond unknown to you.

The largest difference in personal obligations found by the authors was associated with the hypothetical relationship implied in the vignettes. Compared with an unknown stranger, a coworker evinces only $58 more personal obligation. On the other hand, a child or parent produces vastly greater obligations—$2,536 and $1,778, respectively. For this reason, Nock and his coauthors focused primarily on the role played by relationship distance.

Norms of personal obligations distinguish sharply among close relations (child, parent, grandchild) but less so as relationship distance increases. In-laws, grandparents, and siblings occupy a similar position in the relationship dimension of personal obligations. All other relatives and close friends also constitute a cluster. Finally, tangential figures in most lives, to whom Fukuyama's "radius of trust" may not extend,[61] represent the least compelling object of personal responsibility. Not surprisingly, as personal obligations decline, the help expected from other relatives, churches and charities, as well as the state increases.

Personal and demographic factors did not explain the differences found for relationship categories. The authors' final analysis, therefore, focused on a range of childhood experiences reported by respondents. Nock and coauthors' initial research plan proposed that obligations would be a result of (among other things) relationships and experiences in childhood. They reasoned that an adult's account of her or his childhood, for example, would help explain how needs were seen. Adults who recall their parents (or primary caretakers) as warm and trusting, for example, would differ from those who had different recollections. Most importantly for this study, the relationship between the respondent and his or her parents was measured by a scale of parent-child trust (e.g., my mother/father trusted me, I trusted my mother/father) and closeness (very distant to very close). Their findings are presented in table 5.2. To summarize, to the extent that childhood experiences matter, they do so selectively. For example, adults who remember that a nonrelative gave them significant help respond more generously to a wide range of others but are less generous with respect to their own parents. Memories of helping others as a child do not matter much if at all. The last three items in table 5.2 refer to memories of intergenerational trust and closeness. All three are uniformly positive in their effects, even if weak and inconsistent. Adults who recall their parents as having trusted them respond more generously to the problems of children, siblings, and friends. There is only one significant effect for having trusted parents: more generosity to nieces and nephews. Finally, those who reported their family as having been close assume more personal obligations for both parents and grandchildren.

The PSID revisited: Intergenerational influences on unconditional love

The PSID is a nationally representative longitudinal study headquartered in the Institute for Social Research at the University of Michigan and is detailed at greater length in chapter 1, though a brief summary appears here as well. The CDS is one research component of the PSID. While the PSID has always collected some information about children, in 1997 the PSID supplemented its main data collection with additional information on children 0–12 years old and their parents. The objective was to provide researchers with a comprehensive, nationally representative, and longitudinal database of children and their families from which to study the dynamic process of early human capital formation. The CDS-I successfully

TABLE 5.2 **Childhood Predictors of Variations in Personal Obligation**

	Parent	Child	Sibling	Grandparent	Grand-child	Aunt/uncle	Niece/nephew	Cousin	Child-in-law	Parent-in-law	Close friend	Coworker	Close neighbor
Respondent traits													
Intercept	1256.99**	1812.27**	405.21	782.63*	2042.47**	162.59	−41.81	71.68	162.61	549.98	325.08	1.69	99.47
Age	13.85**	3.41	9.62*	12.23**	9.57**	8.99*	1.08	3.33	8.44*	8.71*	2.52	1.31	2.21
Education	45.89*	12.91	7.47	50.87*	9.62	−9.32	−2.1	25.96	−9.95	46.54*	4.82	6.94	−4.59
Income	3.97**	11.71**	0.98	4.398**	4.33**	3.38*	1.51	2.54	4.449**	5.67**	2.25	−1.3	0.75
Male	245.97**	560.99**	137.94	109.73	244.70*	226.55*	284.61**	143.42	434.97**	372.46**	167.33	182.78*	179.24*
Black	210.73*	−232.44*	−5.56	138.82	−246.16*	−31.51	232.42*	207.81	−125.48	−325.63**	151.7	−2.14	77.58
Other races	339.39	296.01	−132.34	−394.65	−639.78**	−40.16	−371.02	260.89	−176.89	−523.37*	−8.82	204.7	−152.58
White	Ref												
Any children	−264.99*	212.64	−437.69**	−60.14	−241.04*	−102.78	−12.82	−117.78	53.23	−82.65	−204.22	83.72	−150.72
Childhood													
Pro-social experiences													
Youth group	215.98	448.39**	51.29	75.99	−154.59	104.71	−59.53	−14.75	126.48	−288.60*	159.46	−53.21	−91.57
Volunteer?	−231.68*	−220.55	−61.05	173.37	−237.09	179.96	72.92	84.48	9.07	182.49	68.61	44.28	44.99
Raised money	−83.12	−221.96*	18.76	−153.55	100.33	−135.33	−75.48	−127.26	26.19	−118.94	−33.59	−7.08	−47.54
Active relig	37.61	−136.07	287.71*	97.27	43.51	−74.99	31.15	43.35	92.24	90.54	75.35	−11.22	8.09
Experience with acute need													
Seriously ill	162.93	226.95	−128.5	95.28	−100.86	30.39	−126.61	96.29	−34.58	−11.79	11.3	−53.11	−58.16
Grew up poor	68.27	−180.07	−90.36	464.92**	−176.89	194.62	−205.14	−60.05	422.36**	236.98	256.79	25.84	−17.97
Saw poverty	−168.69	−261.42*	57.78	−177.55	−222.86*	88.32	−4.09	6.35	−267.27	−258.19*	−193.51	−37.42	131.38

Experienced help													
Non-rel helped	−302.77**	308.99**	−95.05	−39.5	229.80*	−120.17	264.75**	12.65	153.65	51.41	−28.92	158.69*	28.92
Bio parents	170.29	−175.03	−25.78	−250.24*	−24.05	−187.25	61.62	13.78	−101.02	84.65	−133.91	29.78	−23.01
Trusted by parent	−5.55	132.89*	166.55*	81.04	−15.07	30.47	−78.77	13.59	87.74	75.53	146.77*	−4.19	78.1
Trusted parents	4.21	64.54	105.95	−70.47	−117.45	50.4	168.73*	59.5	85.48	74.91	−66.98	−32.53	−58.19
Family close	85.49*	−34.7	−26.94	42.15	66.65*	7.59	−2.16	−19.19	−10.05	10.97	−11.16	3.11	−1.96

FIXED FOR ALL OUTCOMES:

Intercept	160.14**			
Degree	57.02**			
Culpability	−27.59**	n	38,532	Outcomes
Thanks	7.71	n	9,663	Vignettes
Repayment	65.12**	n	507	Respondents
Nursing	151.92**			
Training	−120.71**			
Medical Care	154.62**			
Housing	Ref			
Cost to Solve	0.1744**			

Source: From Steven L. Nock, Paul William Kingston, and Laura M. Holian, "The Distribution of Obligations." In *Intergenerational Caregiving*, edited by Alan Booth, Ann C. Crouter, Suzanne M. Bianchi, and Judith A. Seltzer. Washington, DC: The Urban Institute, 2008.

* $p < 0.05$

** $p < 0.01$

completed interviews with 2,394 families (88%), providing information on 3,563 children. In 2002–3, the CDS recontacted families in CDS-I who remained active in the PSID panel as of 2001. CDS-II successfully reinterviewed 2,021 families (91%) who provided data on 2,907 children and adolescents aged 5–18 years.

Because the CDS is a supplement to the PSID, the study takes advantage of an extensive amount of family demographic and economic data about the CDS target child's family, providing more extensive family data than any other nationally representative longitudinal survey of children and youth in the United States. In addition, the PSID and the CDS data are intergenerational in structure with information contained in several decades of data about multiple family members. This rich data structure allowed a unique opportunity to fully link information on children, their parents, their grandparents, and other relatives to take advantage of the intergenerational and long-panel dimensions of the data. In particular, Steven Nock and I were interested in relationships with parents, parent-parent relationships, and religiosity and these variables' effects on child outcomes.

Based upon our prior work, both the studies previously reported in this chapter and others we have done together and separately, we theorized that social capital in the forms of trust and unconditional love will develop throughout childhood (and thus should be related positively to the child's age). We see trust and unconditional love as growing primarily from the three models to which children are exposed: the parents' love for each other, love of parents for the child, and, where applicable, love in a religious sense. Again, based upon prior work, we believe that social capital, shown by trust, is most likely to develop in a relationship that the participants (at least the adult participants) view as permanent and stable and that turns out to be stable.[62] Many studies, both in the United States and Western Europe, have shown that marriage is more stable than cohabitation. Further, many studies (ours included),[63] have shown that parents' or one's own prior divorce predicts instability in one's own marriage.[64] The more permanent the marriage (e.g., choosing covenant versus standard marriage in Louisiana), the more the parties change during the first years of marriage to become committed, interdependent spouses.[65] We have also shown previously that adolescent children do better (at least in terms of depression) if their parents are living together and if their mother's last relationship did not end in divorce, and worse, for all groups of children, in foster care than in marriage, adoption, or kinship care. We also hypothesized that the causality runs in both directions—that community recognition, or status, should encourage the kind of trust needed for unconditional love to develop. Thus, interracial marriages may be less stable than intraracial marriages because of the lack of outside support.[66] Again, cohabitation, an informal relationship, provides fewer benefits and is less stable than marriage.[67]

Because we saw that more than 95% of the children in the CDS lived mainly with their biological mothers, we excluded most other living arrangements (other than children living with two adoptive parents). First, the sample size in these groups was simply too small to draw valid conclusions. (The largest is for children living with biological fathers, and it is only 83 children.) Second, these families were likely to differ on a large number of other dimensions that we could not account for but which involved separation from biological mothers. A child is highly likely to live with his or her mother, and if not, it is typically because of the mother's death or because of her abuse, neglect, or abandonment of the child, all of which would undoubtedly have major influences on our dependent variables of interest. (See table 5.3 for descriptive statistics and fig. 5.1 for one example of the findings.)

Here is what we found, using words instead of regression results. We began with the typical economist's explanation: wealth. After controlling for it and a host of usual suspects (race, age, etc.), we found, as we explained in chapter 1, that any exposure to being married has more favorable outcomes than having a parent who never married, regardless of cohabitation experiences. In short, children pay a price on a very wide range of outcomes for having parents who never marry. It is even better to have divorced parents than never married parents. Again, as reported in chapter 1, we found that a very simple measure of parental warmth (saying I love you, hugging the child, praising the child, telling the child nice things about him- or herself, telling others good things about the child) strongly predicts better outcomes on a wide range of child traits, even when everything else is controlled.[68]

The new information reported here is that we found that a child's attendance at religious services is related not only to his or her lower problems (both depression and delinquency) but also to lower estimates of self-esteem and self-efficacy. (We have more to say about the mother's religion, but a measure of strength of religious importance was not significant in these particular equations. We suspect that this is so because of a high coincidence of child attendance and maternal attendance at services.

TABLE 5.3 **Descriptive Statistics**

	N	Minimum	Maximum	Mean	Std. deviation
Kid lives with two bio parents	2,681	0.00	1.00	0.6832	0.46532
Kid lives with bio mom and no bio dad	2,681	0.00	1.00	0.1917	0.39367
Kid lives with bio mom and adoptive dad	2,681	0.00	1.00	0.0063	0.07922
Kid lives with bio mom and step dad	2,681	0.00	1.00	0.0759	0.26489
Kid lives with bio mom and other dad figure	2,681	0.00	1.00	0.0344	0.18226
Kid lives with two adoptive parents	2,681	0.00	1.00	0.0086	0.09219
Head is white	2,681	0.00	1.00	0.6316	0.48246
Head is black	2,681	0.00	1.00	0.1462	0.35335
Head is Hispanic-Latino/a	2,681	0.00	1.00	0.1321	0.33866
Head is Asian PI	2,681	0.00	1.00	0.0278	0.16437
Head is other race (American Indian, etc.)	2,681	0.00	1.00	0.0432	0.20124
Estimated attendance of kid at services drawn from 2 variables 6–9 and 10+ age (religious attendance)	2,030	1.00	6.00	4.2156	1.37686
Importance of religion to primary caretaker	2,672	1.00	3.00	2.6385	0.59797
Age of mother or mother figure	2,582	20.00	81.00	41.9310	7.44560
Household income divided by census needs standard (needs)	2,583	0.00	113.39	3.7756	4.78121
Mom married once, still intact	2,681	0.00	1.00	0.5833	0.49311
Mom married and widowed at least once	2,681	0.00	1.00	0.0153	0.12274
Mom married, divorced, remarried, still intact	2,681	0.00	1.00	0.1251	0.33093
Mom married, divorced, remarried, now divorced	2,681	0.00	1.00	0.0316	0.17483
Mom never married	2,681	0.00	1.00	0.1168	0.32119
Mom married, divorced, never remarried	2,681	0.00	1.00	0.1176	0.32221
Positive behavior scale 02	2,681	1.00	5.00	4.1270	0.59692

Source: From Margaret F. Brinig and Steven L. Nock, "Can Law Shape the Development of Unconditional Love in Children?" Notre Dame Legal Studies Paper No. 07–20, available at http://ssrn.com/abstract=973821 as "Best Love of the Child."

Since child variables are the outcomes, the child's attendance swamps the parent's.) Because of significant and large coefficients for race shown in these equations, we will later discuss what may be occurring with the African American families in the sample.[69]

As noted in chapter 1, in every case, family structure matters in addition to marriage and/or marital history. So while children are affected, for example, by having parents who were divorced before forming their current family, those kids are also affected by the arrangements in which they now live. Family structure is more than simply marital history, and vice versa, and this holds true regardless of wealth.

While children may be affected most by their parents when they are small, there has been significant argument that peers affect them at least as much when they reach adolescence.[70] My research leads me to conclude that the answer is that both parents and peers appear to matter. In another empirical paper, Steven Nock and I found, this time using data from the National Longitudinal Survey of Youth (NLYS),[71] that as far as innate traits like optimism (good things are likely to happen to me), holding constant all the socioeconomic, legal, and family structure variables we have used repeatedly throughout this book, the parent's religiosity (not the child's and not the peers') was most important. (See fig. 5.2, with an abbreviated version at fig. 5.3.) However, when it came to outward (or external) behavior like delinquency, it was not the parent's religiosity (or the child's) that mattered but two things: whether or not the child's closest friends attended religious services frequently and whether the family participated in nonreligious activities together. (See fig. 5.4, with an abbreviated version at fig. 5.5.) The different findings for internal ("innate") and external

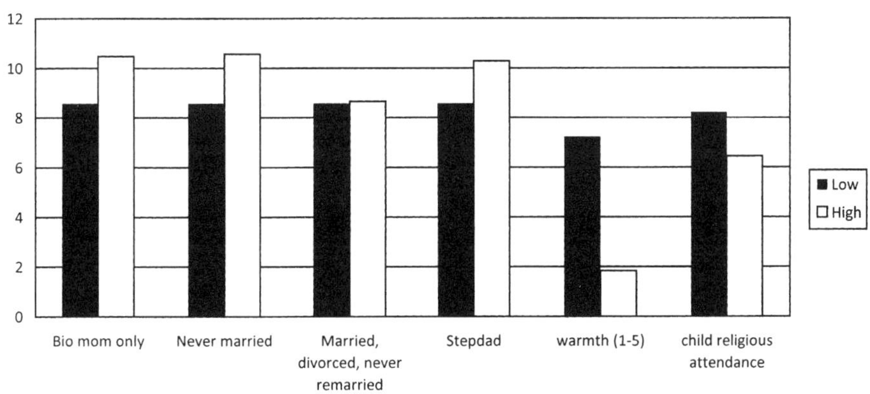

FIGURE 5.1 Total behavioral problems with importance of religious attendance of child. Adjusted R^2 for equation, controlling for wealth, race, age, etc. (as in Table 5.4) is 0.06. (Based on the PSID and CDS public-use data set, 1997 and 2002. Regressions available from the author.)

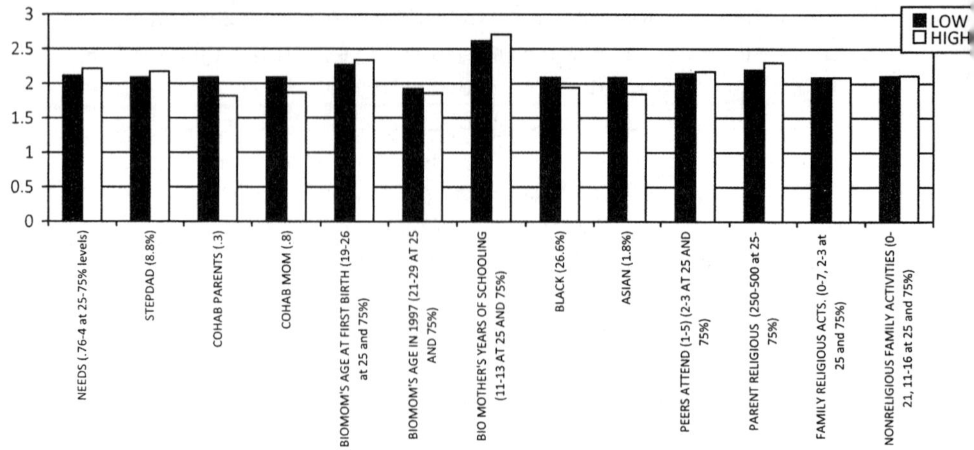

FIGURE 5.2 Good things happen to me with importance of religion to mothers and religious attendance of peers. R^2 (adj.) = 0.06. (Data from the NLSY. Regressions available from the author.)

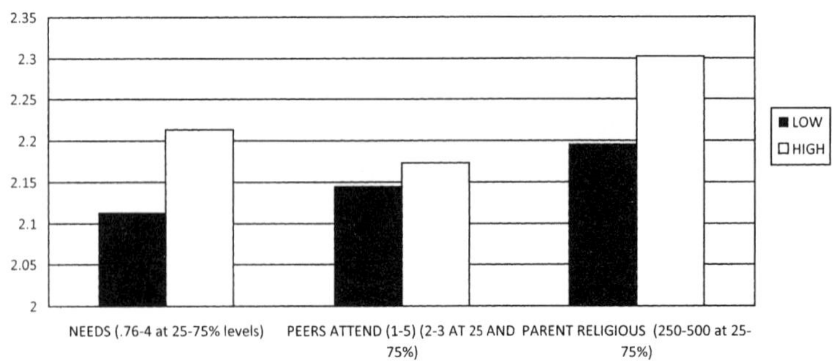

FIGURE 5.3 Good things happen to me, key values of needs, importance of religion to mothers, and religious attendance of peers. (Data from the NLSY. Regressions available from the author.)

("outward") measures lead to the idea that day-to-day behavior may be most influenced by peers, while innate attitudes may come from parents.[72]

Although the children of the PSID and the NLSY are not yet adults, what we concluded is that certain internal and external traits in adolescents are statistically and actually far more likely to be present under some conditions than others. These have to do with the family structure and legal relationship factors mentioned in chapter 1 as well as trust among family members and some religious influence. If other social scientists'

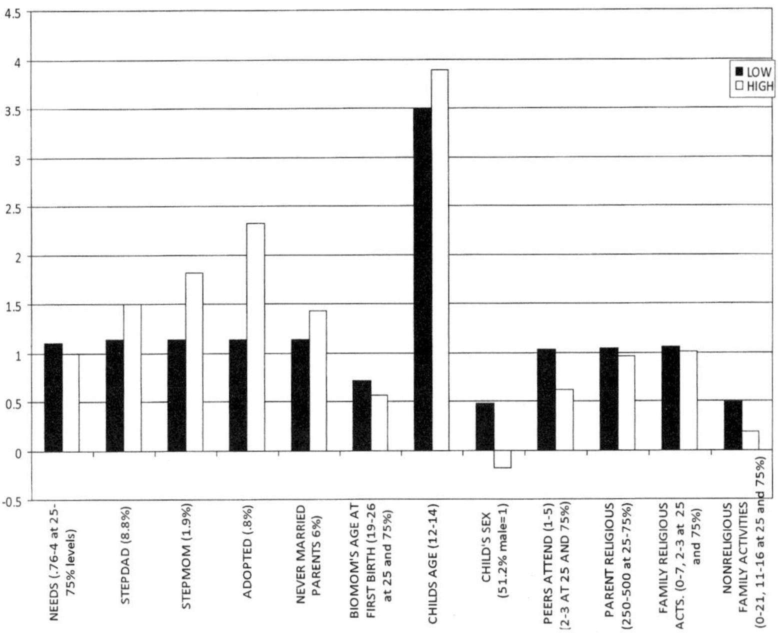

FIGURE 5.4 Delinquency of children with importance of religion to mothers and religious attendance of peers. R^2 (adj.) = 0.06. (Data from the NLSY. Regressions available from the author.)

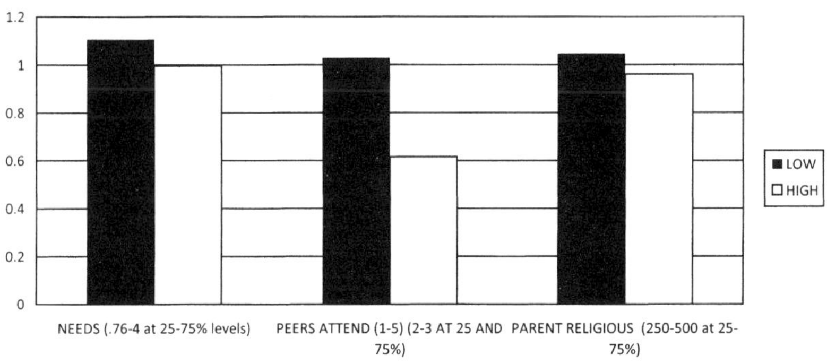

FIGURE 5.5 Delinquency of children with key values of needs, importance of religion to mothers, and religious attendance of peers. (Data from the NLSY. Regressions available from the author.)

findings are correct, the group with what I believe are characteristics of the ability to love unconditionally, to trust, and to build social capital, will do better as spouses, parents, and givers to community than those without them. Much of what I have to report here is not new: the differences are the large, nationally representative data sets we have used, the longitudinal nature of our data, the introduction of religiosity in some of our equations, and the emphasis upon the mediation of legal (and otherwise stable) relationships.

Psychologists have long understood the relationship between children's attachment to their parents and their own ability to form later relationships.[73] A recent study suggests that young adults' retrospective reports of parenting by their mothers and fathers are associated with their current romantic relationship quality.[74] However, most of these psychological studies have small samples, and they typically do not move from adolescent characteristics to adult outcomes. However, there are a few exceptions, still using limited samples in particular geographic areas. Some have also looked at the relationships between parents and with siblings in terms of young adults' own romances.[75] In earlier work, Conger and coauthors found that such behavioral characteristics in parents promoted prosocial behavior and inhibited antisocial behavior in both boys and girls.[76]

The parents' marriage also has an effect on the child's later transition to parenthood in his or her own marriage.[77] Apparently, if the couple honestly realized the adjustments their own parents faced in passing through the transition, they themselves did better (meaning they were emotionally more attuned to each other) than those who overromanticized or understood the difficulties with low insight about them.

A longitudinal survey in New Zealand of 141 children found that even tendencies as young as age 3 (on scales of "undercontrolled, inhibited, or well-adjusted") could predict the same traits in adolescence and even at age 21 when they were young adults. Although the ways in which the original traits manifested changed over time, the common patterns were revealed in a significant number of the subjects.

Similarly, sociologists have noted the relationship between earlier parental divorce (or nonmarriage) and various child behavior difficulties. In their pathbreaking book, *A Generation at Risk*,[78] Paul Amato and Alan Booth show the effects of divorce and separation on children's later success as young adults, measuring education, earnings, and relationship stability. Amato and Booth studied children born to married parents over approximately a twelve-year period, measuring variables supplied by parents in the 1980s and children in the 1990s. They found that support from mothers and fathers was positively associated with church involvement, community attachment, and the number of relatives and friends to whom the children feel close.[79] In keeping with other work, they noted that relationship quality tends to be transmitted across generations[80] because children who are exposed to poor-quality marriages are deprived of appropriate models of relationship functioning.[81] In addition, marital conflict affects children's social competence because it leads parents to be less affectionate, less responsive, and more punitive toward their children, in turn leaving children feeling emotionally insecure.

Amato and Booth found[82] that parents' marital conflict was associated with fewer relatives and with marginally lower religious involvement and community attachment. In contrast, by itself, parental divorce was not associated with children's levels of social integration.[83] Divorce decreases problems for children when it provides relief from high-conflict situations but is problematic for children when it removes a parent from the more common and typical low-conflict household that divorces.[84] The authors suggest that "family characteristics measured when most children are preadolescents or adolescents have lingering consequences for the quality of the offspring's social relationships, including aspects of both structural integration (church involvement and membership in clubs and organizations) and psychological integration (feeling close to others and attachment to one's community)." Further, intraparental conflict has long-term negative consequences for children's psychological well-being, while a stable, high-quality parental marriage maximizes offspring's mental health.[85]

More recently, Amato and DeBoer[86] found that the transmission of divorce between generations occurs primarily because the children, particularly of those following a low-conflict divorce, had a comparatively weak commitment to the norm of lifelong marriage. This difference in reaction based upon the context of divorce is also discussed in the literature review also written by Amato.[87]

In a still more recent piece, Page and Bretherton reported that when parents of preschoolers divorce, girls and boys differ in their attachment to their noncustodial fathers. Boys who were more attached to their fathers had higher preschool teacher ratings for social behavior, while for girls the opposite was the case.[88] With adolescents, attachment to noncustodial fathers did not seem to matter unless their mother remarried (or formed another residential adult relationship). At that point, lack of closeness is associated with psychological distress.[89]

Further, pre-labor-market attitudes of high school graduates (admittedly slightly older than our sample children) predict real economic consequences for them later.[90] Glen R. Waddell found that poor attitude and self-esteem (using the Rosenberg Self-Esteem Scale) were followed by fewer years of postsecondary education, less employment fourteen years after high school, and lower earnings. Waddell used the NLSY, in which the participants also reported on the importance of various outcomes to their lives. These teens rated being successful in work (.850 of those surveyed) and finding the right person to marry and having a happy family life (.832) as very important to their life. The third highest rated outcome was having strong friendships (.815). Friendships were also discussed by Engels, Dekovic, and Meeus,[91] who noted the continuing influence of parenting practices and family structures as well as adolescent social skills on the quality of the older children's peer relationships.

In groundbreaking work in psychology, Vaughn and Block[92] showed that parental agreement about values and in other psychological measures in early childhood was strongly related to their characteristics later. Parental intelligence showed up in harmony and moral development in boys, while ego control later appeared in girls' independence and harmony. As Elizabeth Marquardt points out, it is the lack of agreement on values in the "different worlds" of their parents that makes children of divorce have to take on adult roles prematurely.[93]

As I suggested earlier, children apparently pick up their models for loving behavior from their parents, at least according to Morman and Floyd.[94] They look to the father for open expressions of love for the mother and wife and for spirituality.[95] Adolescents also model volunteer and other activities after their parents (although these work differently in boys and girls).[96] Boys were more likely to feel more connected to their community and more likely to be involved with their community when their parents had been. For girls with more community-involved parents, the result was more likely to be more involvement in school- and community-based extracurricular activities. However, you will recall that Nock and his colleagues found no inference of parental prosocial activities on respondents' feelings of obligation to others.[97]

Where families no longer live together, as might be expected, the quality of residential parent-adolescent relationships explained the most variation in adolescent psychological distress. In a study using the NLSY, Christina Falci recently found that the quality of relationships with nonresidential fathers only had a significant association with adolescent psychological distress for adolescents in blended families.[98]

Of course, many of the characteristics of family structure are interrelated in complex ways. For example, both depression and conduct problems (similar to Nock's and my internal and external measures of behavior problems) are associated with a lack of family cohesion and expressiveness and a lack of exposure to intellectual and cultural activities or to family activities and recreation.[99] Depression, in particular, was associated with higher levels of family conflict and low cohesiveness[100] and with family insularity. Conduct problems (similar to our external behavior problems) were uniquely associated with low cohesion, low intellectual/cultural orientation, and high conflict. However, attention deficit hyperactivity disorder (ADHD) did not contribute significantly to predictions of family environment characteristics. This may be surprising when considered with evidence that will be reported in chapter 6 pointing toward more abuse of ADHD children, but of course abuse occurs in only a tiny percentage of families. This result is suggestive, though, of the idea that the child's disability does not provoke or cause the abuse, but rather that once abuse occurs, it predicts which child will likely be the target.

Religion and the Black Family

We have already noted in chapter 1 that black families, who are less likely to be involved in formal relationships, do not appear to rely as much on formal legal status as do whites. Instead, for African Americans, income makes more of a difference (at least as perceived through the eyes of children), and the mother's religiosity seems to mediate in troubled times. At this point, I would like to repeat another data point from chapter 1: In her dissertation research on interracial marriages, demographer Rose Kreider examined black-white couples and found that they had nearly twice the likelihood of divorcing as did homogenous couples of either race.[101] Controlling for other variables predicting divorce, if the respondent wife saw her mother infrequently, the chance of dissolution between waves of the survey increased by 8%. On the other hand, if the husband attended religious services frequently, the relationship dissolved only about two-thirds as often.[102] The question is whether religiosity (particularly on the part of husbands) and family support (but not in the sense of direct help provided) affects African American marriages in general as well. It is certainly true that African Americans who are more religious are more likely to marry, and those who are married are more religious (see fig. 5.6).[103] Also, the religiously compatible divorce at a lower rate than the general African American population,[104] which usually experiences a higher rate than that of Americans as a whole.[105] Wilcox and Wolfinger maintain that the greater willingness of the religious to marry comes from more viable networks:

> We speculate that the family-oriented networks grounded in religious congregations may provide churchgoing mothers with helpful models of married life, social and economic support, and monitoring of their partners—all of which can help improve their relationship and their odds of marriage. Indeed, research on urban family formation suggests that networks play a central role in the transition to marriage for urban couples.[106]

In Orbuch et al.'s longitudinal study of black and white couples in Detroit, the black couples were different, not only because of lower socioeconomic status, but also for two reasons related to subjects we have already discussed. One was that the norm for the black, but not the white, couples was for husbands to take an active and relatively equal role in housework and child care. Marriages where the husband did not were more apt to end in divorce or separation by the end of the study.[107] The second was that for the black couples, it was important for the husband, but not the wife, to receive affective information. (In contrast, in Sayer and Bianchi's work on the general population, it was *wives'* satisfaction with the emotional content of the marriage that predicted divorce.[108]) Orbuch and his coauthors deduce that the African American wives, but not husbands, were receiving the necessary social support from their children or the outside community.[109] In contrast to the differences between blacks and whites we have focused on so far, Mexican Americans seem to marry and divorce at about the same rates as whites and have a higher level of marriage and much lower level of divorce than blacks, despite very similar levels of poverty and unemployment. In a new paper, Jennifer Roebuck Bulanda and Susan L. Brown[110] contrast marriages in these three large ethnic groups using the two waves of the NSFH (as Nock and I did in research reported in chapter 1). They find evidence that two cultural differences help explain the differing marriage and dissolution rates. One

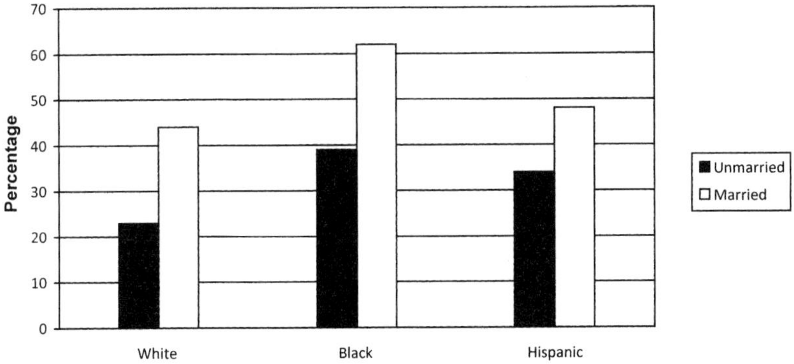

FIGURE 5.6 Relationship between the percentage of those marrying and religion among African American mothers. (From W. Bradford Wilcox and Nicholas H. Wolfinger, "Then Comes Marriage? Religion, Race, and Marriage in Urban America." *Social Science Research*, 36, no. 2, 2007.)

is the greater reliance on social relationships evidenced in the Mexican American marriages.[111] Though, as with blacks, marriages are significantly more likely to be stable with greater religious participation (more than three times as likely in both cases), Mexican American families also show what the authors term a more collectivistic than individualistic orientation (with the individualistic orientation present in both white and black marriages).[112]

Where does all this literature lead us? We are back to considering networks and trust. While there are unquestionably selection effects influencing which couples marry and which do not, as Wilcox and Wolfinger realize,[113] having a rich outside community for support, including religious support as a couple, seems critical,[114] especially where there are not many financial supports. This might remind us of another finding from chapter 1: couples in covenant marriages in Louisiana (which have a far lower divorce rate than standard marriages)[115] had more parental approval and more people in attendance at their ceremonies than those from standard marriages.

Finally, I would like to turn briefly to what is being noted as one of the great social issues of our time: that of fertility and specifically reproduction at a rate that will not produce decreases in population. Many have found that in Western Europe and in some parts of Asia, current reproduction rates are far below the 2.1 needed for a stable population. Children signify hope for the future, as well as greater concern about others (as I maintained when I said in chapter 3 that children somehow create community). A simple correlation between the happiness studies reported by the International Social Survey program[116] and fertility rates[117] shows some relationship (at .545) (see fig. 5.7). So, for the United States, one wonders whether fertility relates to religious attendance (see table 5.4), as has been suggested by those who note that the Muslim immigrants to Europe are reproducing at a much higher rate than native Europeans, though only for the first generation.[118] Apparently, at least for some and holding other things constant, fertility relates to a concern for the future, which corresponds with religiosity in the Judeo-Christian-Muslim tradition.

Values of social capital in general, evidenced by trust, are created largely within the family as children imitate their parents. The values are influenced by peers as children grow older and are passed along, as all

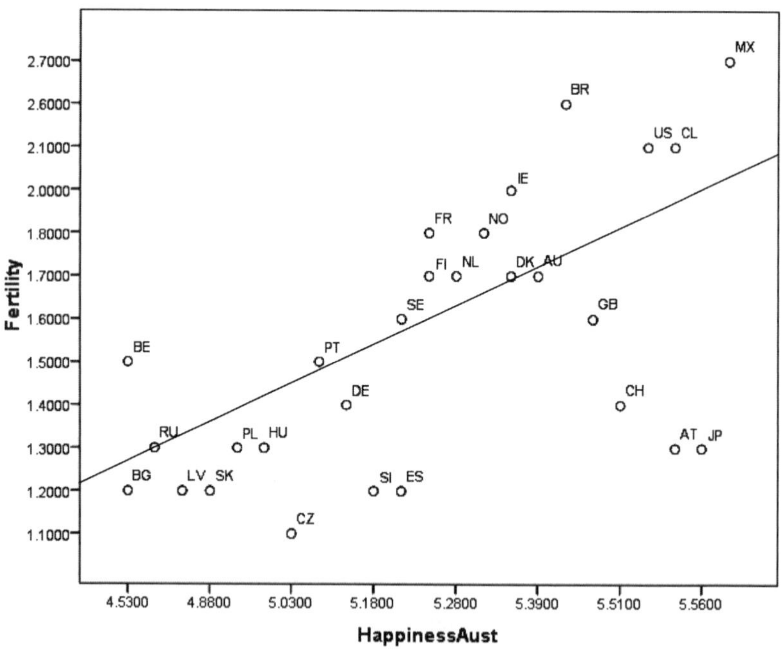

FIGURE 5.7 The relationship between fertility and happiness. (Data from World Fertility Patterns 2007, distributed through the UN Department of Economic and Social Affairs, Population Division at http://www.un.org/esa/population/publications/worldfertility2007/WorldFertilityPatterns%202007_UpdatedData.xls [accessed August 25, 2009].)

TABLE 5.4 **Effects of religiosity and optimism on number of children**

Model	Unstandardized coefficients		Standardized coefficients		
	B	Std. error	Beta	t	Sig.
(Constant)	2.672	0.112		23.870	0.000
Ever been divorced or separated	−0.372	0.043	−0.079	−8.646	0.000
Marital status	0.323	0.050	0.061	6.490	0.000
Family income in constant $	−1.814E−6	0.000	−0.026	−2.761	0.006
How often R attends religious services	0.078	0.006	0.115	12.624	0.000
Lot of the average man getting worse	−0.152	0.034	−0.041	−4.508	0.000

Source: From Margaret F. Brinig and Steven L. Nock, "Can Law Shape the Development of Unconditional Love in Children?" Notre Dame Legal Studies Paper No. 07-20, available at http://ssrn.com/abstract=973821 as "Best Love of the Child."
Note: Dependent variable = Number of children

capital is, from generation to generation. Outside communities, and in particular religious communities, seem to provide support for the growth of social capital. We turn now to ways in which the same mimetic or imitative behavior may go wrong, and what conditions may minimize the harm done by human tendencies to scapegoat on a microeconomic level.

CHAPTER SIX

What Happens When Trust Fails? Mimetics in Families Gone Wrong

The previous chapters have claimed that families benefit from the support of outside communities. Families also enhance their surrounding communities in a myriad of ways.[1] As Jeremy Bentham put it centuries ago:

> Under whatever point of view the institution of marriage is considered, the utility of this noble contract is striking. It is the bond of society, the foundation of civilization. . . . Marriage, considered as a contract, has drawn women from the hardest and most humiliating servitude; it has distributed the mass of the community into distinct families; it has created a domestic magistracy; it has trained up citizens; it has extended the views of men to the future, through their affection for the rising generation; it has multiplied the social sympathies. In order to estimate all its benefits, it is only necessary to imagine, for a moment, what would be the condition of Man without the institution.[2]

For one thing, as we have seen, families create much social and human capital. Families are themselves communities. As one Pilgrim father famously put it, each family is "a little commonwealth."[3] We can easily list ways in which this is so. Families produce goods (whether market goods,[4] children, or increased individual productivity in the labor force[5] or simply happiness). Families develop their own rules,[6] their own histories, and sometimes their own language. Family members may specialize in the ways they contribute,[7] and, to the extent they do, the family may reap the benefits of comparative advantage, much as nations do in a world market.[8] Like nations welcoming immigrants, they may take in new members through adoption, marriage, or foster parenting. In extreme cases, they may expel, or at least disinherit, members who cannot get along or fit in. Families may well be viewed by those on the outside as a single unit.[9] For their members, as governments do, families provide shelter, protection, support, and, for children, education. Historically, at any rate, families had rulers or heads, and the parent-child relationship functioned in many ways like that of master and servant.[10]

Families, like countries, may become troubled. Economists Bernheim and Stark argue that the altruism in families by its very nature entails exploitability, so that it does not necessarily contribute to marital stability.[11] For an example of how far the family/community analogy may be taken, one model of resistance to domestic violence calls it revolution in the face of tyranny.[12] The film *The War of the Roses*[13] pictured a divorcing couple as doing battle, as does Mary Ann Mason's *Custody Wars*.[14] In this chapter, I explore whether the social science and humanities literature on larger communities in trouble helps to explain troubled families and, if it does, whether similar legal or policy steps could prevent family violence. Some of the patterns others have explored for intracommunity crises might also apply to the less violent conflicts of divorce and early (involuntary) emancipation of children.

Stanford Professor Réne Girard has written a series of books explaining the connection between community formation, violence, and religion. He begins his book *I See Satan Fall Like Lightning*[15] by observing that people learn by copying, as we discussed in the last chapter. He maintains that, in fact, copying, or imitating others, is what sets humans apart from other animals.[16] We desire mimetically, or imitatively, what others, our role models, desire.[17] However, as we saw with James Coleman, Girard moves this idea about essential human motivation[18] almost at once out of the family and to the societal level. The exception is that in *Deceit, Desire, and the Novel* he does explain some "love triangles" in novels by Stendhal and Dostoyevsky using what he calls the mimetic desire theory.[19] There he traces that tendency writ large and from what is with children essentially necessary and good to something sinister. Mimetic desire always mediates: that is, something is not desired because of its intrinsic benefits, but because the other, a model turned rival, wants it.[20]

Girard puts forth masses of historical, anthropological, and literary evidence to make his case that societies use violence,[21] resolved in a particular way, to solve what economists would call the collective action problem. That is, if there is no way to measure how much effort or investment each person in a group is making, people are likely to shirk since they will get the same or a similar benefit whether or not they contribute.[22] Periodically, Girard maintains, when society is under great stress from something like an epidemic or famine, jealousies, ambition, and envy (all of which are characteristics of mimetic desire) surface within the population. The looming crisis is finally resolved by identification of a single person or small group of people[23] through what he describes as a contagious mob action. The victim or victims are vilified as the source of the problem and ultimately punished by violence—murder or expulsion from the community. If there is sufficient unanimity by the community, the scapegoats are afterward treated as mythical heroes or demigods. He uses examples ranging from Greek and other mythology through Jonah in the Bible to medieval witch hunts and Nazi Germany[24] to illustrate his point. (His scholarly disciple Gil Bailie[25] updates these to include incidents like the Rodney King police beating and various African civil wars.) Once the societal catharsis occurs, the perpetrators of the violence will feel they have done the correct thing and will be for a time united as a cohesive group, frequently using the occasion as the beginning of a new society. If there is not sufficient agreement (or unanimity minus one, who is the scapegoat), the violence will escalate. Society may descend into Thomas Hobbes's vision of "all against all":[26]

> If now to this naturall proclivity of men, to hurt each other, which they derive from their Passions, but chiefly from a vain esteeme of themselves: You adde, the right of all to all, wherewith one by right invades, the other by right resists, and whence arise perpetuall jealousies and suspicions on all hands, and how hard a thing it is to provide against an enemy invading us, with an intention to oppresse, and ruine, though he come with a small Number, and no great Provision;. it cannot be deny'd but that the naturall state of men, before they entr'd into Society, was a meer War, and that not simply, but a War of all men, against all men; for what is WAR, but that same time in which the will of contesting by force, is fully declar'd either by Words, or Deeds? The time remaining, is termed PEACE.

Girard's *I See Satan* turns from anthropology to theology when he maintains that the Judeo-Christian tradition sees through this pattern by sympathizing with the victim rather than the perpetrators of violence. He sees less contemporary success on the societal level for resolving unity problems through mimetic crisis and scapegoating because we do not mythologize what happened. That is, the mythologizing was accompanied by social unification. Now there may just be mimetic violence. However, although we are still likely to be carried away by the crowd frenzy (as I remember from my college days in the 1960s), Girard maintains that we may be able to turn away and refrain from the lynching (or mimetic cycle), especially if we can imitate God by thinking largely in trusting and loving ways. Those who do so will be rewarded, in Richard McAdams's secular social norms terminology, as "heroes."[27] Though God is imitated mimetically, Girard argues that violence will not result because of the hierarchical and transcendent distance between the desiring human and the desired mediator, God. Consequently, the desire takes the form of admiration or veneration rather than envy and rivalry.[28]

Girard describes the scapegoat, the innocent victim upon whom the crowd settles in a mimetic crisis, as most often somehow an outsider: someone foreign or distinguishable because disfigured (or beautiful) or suffering from a mental handicap, sometimes from a rival social class.[29] Though this person (or group, if a minority is targeted, as in Nazi Germany) probably has nothing to do with the outward crisis or catastrophe, the crowd believes, at least temporarily, that the scapegoat caused the problem. Or, as with Caiaphas the head priest in the Christian Bible, there is at least a utilitarian explanation: "[I]t is better that one man should die for the people, than for the whole nation to be destroyed."[30]

Although Girard's work has received tremendous attention in the humanities and criminal justice literature,[31] it makes only occasional appearances in the legal journals, and then mostly is applied directly to questions of punishment or mob violence.[32] As far as I can tell, it has never been applied to family law, nor, as far as I know, distilled out of the macrocontext in which it began and analyzed in smaller social units (other than by Girard himself in *Deceit, Desire, and the Novel*, as discussed above). Families of course face crises too—infertility, unemployment, substance abuse, illness, disabled children, death of children or parents, and so forth. Although few will claim that such obstacles are pleasant or easy, many families weather the storm. Once they have emerged, couples are likely to say that the adversity made their relationships stronger or taught them to value the other more. But a small number of families will do on a small scale precisely what Girard predicts—they will escalate into violence or fly apart. As Girard's work on the difference between externally and internally mediated mimetics points out, such dramatic results might be a relatively recent problem. When families were more hierarchical, there would have been less propensity for internally mediated mimetics, that is, occasions where the model-rival is within the household rather than outside it—complete with envy and revenge. In other words, wives are much more apt to be rivalrous with their husbands not only in terms of love affairs (hence the "lover's triangles") but also, occasionally, in the labor force. The opportunity for violence and scapegoating, therefore, has increased once in the late nineteenth–early twentieth centuries as married women's property acts and women's suffrage were enacted and once again at the end of the twentieth century as married women not only entered the labor force but also sometimes earned the same or more than did their husbands. As we will see later in this chapter, the small number of families in which domestic violence occurs often contain unemployed or underemployed spouses.

For another family illustration, Gil Bailie, the anthropologist who popularized Girard's work in the United States, uses the familiar example of children in a nursery fighting over a toy to explain what he means by mimetic desire and rivalry, which he calls "the human predilection for falling under the influence of the desires, positive or negative, adulating or accusatory—of others."[33] One child walks into a room where another child sits among many toys. The newcomer starts to pick up the toy closest to the sitting child, and a struggle begins with the sitting child (who hadn't been interested in it before now) desiring the toy because it seems to be so wanted by the newcomer. The conflict escalates to crying and hitting until stopped by an adult (or until the toy breaks). Bailie also discusses[34] the Suzanna story from the Catholic and Eastern Orthodox Book of Daniel[35] in which two lecherous elders ogle the attractive wife of a wealthy merchant, are inflamed by mimetic desire, and then attempt to blackmail her. (Daniel, a bystander who ends up judging the proceedings, cleverly catches them in their lies and has them executed.) Susanna is attractive from the start because she "belongs" to her husband, a rival, but becomes irresistibly attractive precisely because each of the elders sees that she is attractive in the other's eyes.[36]

Girard names the undesirable qualities of mimetic rivalry as envy, jealousy, resentment, and hatred.[37] Always they become inflamed because another externally validates the desire. As Richard McAdams says in his work, "The effectiveness of one's investment in satisfying relative preferences depends entirely on the amount that others invest."[38] Frequently, as in the Susanna story, the object of desire is still more valuable because it is somehow unobtainable or forbidden. This, of course, is the covetousness forbidden in the Judeo-Christian tradition by the Tenth Commandment.[39]

Applying the scapegoating paradigm to family conflicts, a clergyman recently wrote in one of his sermons:

> Similarly, even though I'm no psychologist, I have noted that families often seem to unite around a troubled child. One child becomes identified as the "problem child," and fretting over this troubled child becomes the force that unifies the other members of the family. The "troubled child," now cast in this role, is doomed to play this part, failing and struggling so that others might succeed."[40]

Similarly, a popular Web site on family therapy advises:

> In the early part of the twentieth century, the psychologist Carl Jung noted that children tend to live out the unconscious conflicts of their parents. And, as Family Systems Theory teaches, all too often a child will be marked as a "problem," the "scapegoat" or "black sheep" of the family—the *Identified Patient*, in Family Systems language—when really the entire family is locked into some dysfunctional pattern of interaction.[41]

Adolescents, in particular, are apt to perceive differences in treatment between themselves and their siblings.[42] Even more to the point, a guide to prevention of family violence notes:

> Thus, psychologists describe a situation where frustration caused by blocked goals can lead to aggressive behavior against a family member.[43] When the person or situation responsible for the frustration is not available as a target of the aggression, people sometimes direct their aggression out on an innocent person, or scapegoat.[44]

We can see scapegoating at work not only in contemporary advice literature but also in the reported legal cases to which we now turn.

Family Law Cases and Mimetic Cycles

Cases involving crises coming from outside causes

A legal example of a mimetic cycle brought about by the perpetrator's unemployment, with a scapegoat who was clearly not at fault, is the New

York case of *Havell v. Islam.*[45] Both spouses were stockbrokers, though the wife, Theresa, was significantly more successful than the husband, whose job was eventually eliminated by his large firm. After this, and for the last ten years of the marriage, he was unemployed but spent his time taking care of the couple's three children (for whom they also had a full-time nanny), reading, and gardening. Though he had been violent toward his wife and children throughout the marriage, the crisis occurred one morning after the wife told the husband she was seeking a divorce. She awoke to find he had broken into her bedroom and was holding a barbell and wearing rubber gloves. He then tried to kill her by striking her with the barbell in the face, neck, and chest and was only prevented by the intervention of the three daughters, to whom he announced he had in fact killed her. They held him down and called 911. She was hospitalized for three weeks and had to have extensive plastic surgery but survived. (He sought an equal share of the approximately $13 million in property they had accumulated during the twenty-one-year marriage after he was indicted for attempted murder and plead guilty to assault, being sentenced to eight years and three months in prison.)

Aftab Islam, the husband, fits many of the standard characteristics of an abusing spouse as well as one likely to be involved with mimetic violence. His wife was the source of his feeling inferior but had not (at least not according to the case report) done anything wrong. She was only successful, in fact more than he was. He was unemployed[46] and she had recently told him she was seeking a divorce (making her not only the object of his vocational jealousy but also unavailable to him sexually). He had apparently been abusive before, but the abuse did not change what was to him an intolerable situation. He did something that apart from mimetic crisis most of us would consider irrational as well as despicable. He attacked the source of his livelihood who was also his spouse and the mother of his children, and he did so in the children's presence—a decision on his part that would maximize the harm to them.[47] The court in *Havell* allowed the wife to retain almost all the property and to pay him no alimony.

Another well-known case, *North Carolina v. Norman*,[48] stands for a traditional opposition to the so-called battered women's syndrome but illustrates the dual stresses of unemployment and substance abuse. While he slept, Judy Norman shot and killed the husband who had abused her for years, forced her to support him by her daily prostitution, and at the same time made her sleep on the concrete floor and eat out of a dog or cat dish. J. T. Norman, like Islam, was unemployed. He was also an alcoholic who became more vicious to his wife after he drank. Judy Norman testified at her murder trial that she had left him before on several occasions and that each time he found her, took her home, and beat her. She said that she was afraid to take out a warrant on her husband because he had said that if she ever had him locked up, he would kill her when he got out.[49]

THE BRESCHEL CASE. In *Breschel v. Breschel*,[50] decided in 1979, both husband (Robert) and wife (Lurlene) had been married before and had children from their prior marriages. For the first year of their marriage, the only children living with them were the wife's teenagers from her prior marriage. Then Robert obtained custody of his son Henry and brought the seven-year-old into the household.

Henry apparently campaigned to get rid of Lurlene. He refused to obey her and did not accept her as a member of the household. According to a social worker who testified in the case and who had met with him, Henry indicated that he was misbehaving so that he would be returned to the custody of his mother and "that he was doing everything he could to drive his stepmother out of the home."[51]

Lurlene suffered from multiple sclerosis, and her condition deteriorated significantly due to her inability to take care of the house (for which the wealthy husband refused to provide a cleaning person) and her inability to cope with Henry. She warned Robert that if Henry remained in the home over the summer, she "was going to her mother's until her health got better." Robert refused to send Henry away for the summer, so Lurlene moved out, believing her "health was endangered by remaining in the home." The court found that she was without legal fault in breaking off cohabitation since she had "unsuccessfully taken whatever [other] reasonable measures might eliminate the danger." She was therefore entitled to alimony although if she had been at fault, Virginia would have disallowed it.[52]

MORE ABOUT PHILLIP B. In the section dealing with intervention by unrelated third parties, chapter 4 included a discussion of what I then described as a "poignant" case, *Guardianship of Phillip B.*[53] Phillip, you will remember, was a Down syndrome boy whose parents institutionalized him and later did not wish to have him undergo heart surgery that would prevent his death by age thirty. Another couple who had volunteered at the institution befriended Phillip and became his "psychological parents" and, after successful litigation, eventually adopted Phillip. I did not tell you two important factors in that discussion. The first was what Phillip's father, Warren Becker, said about Phillip. According to a *New York Times* article about the case[54] (which matches the brief written on behalf of the Heaths), Warren Becker referred to the newborn Phillip as "a Mongoloid, Down's child with simian characteristics" and "that simian." Mr. Becker, who had two other sons, said at the first trial in the case (when the Beckers were accused of medically neglecting Phillip because they refused to consider the heart surgery) that he thought Phillip would be better off dead than alive. Second, the Beckers' pediatrician had considered Phillip's life "devoid of those qualities which give it human dignity." At the time of the appeal, Mr. Becker said the surgery "might extend his life for a few years, but for what purpose? He's almost 17 and he's still carrying a teddy bear." He would forever be a burden on others.

These last two cases are both about what Girard would call expulsion, not active violence, perpetrated upon scapegoated family members (though physical harm to the scapegoat is indirectly involved in both). In the *Breschel* case, the husband's biological child does everything he can to force out his stepmother, and his father sides with the boy. In *Phillip B.*, the undesirable child is moved out of sight to an institution and at least the father and a physician feel he "would be better off dead." In both cases, there are biological children in whom the parents would rather invest resources (Phillip's nondisabled brothers and Henry Breschel).[55] Taking care of an adult with multiple sclerosis or a Down syndrome person would be expensive, stressful, and, particularly in the MS case, ultimately heart rending. To some extent, these victims (and all other disabled people who are mistreated) are different from the victims of mass violence (Girard's mimetic violence) chosen by lot or because they belong to a minority ethnic or religious group since, through no fault of their own, they do add stress to families and require expenditure of resources. In these cases, the very fact of the disability may provoke the crisis. This also may explain why adopted children whose adoptive parents knew the biological parents had problems are less likely to do well.[56] In the adoption situation, children whose biological parents are known to have problems will get worse grades, finish fewer grades in school (see table 6.1) earn less, and have less-stable marriages (see table 6.2). Once the children reveal some behavior the adoptive parents feel is problematic, the parents may (with some justification) blame the biological parents' contribution rather than any deficiency in their own parenting. They may also feel that they always knew the child would turn out to be a "bad actor."

TABLE 6.1 **Prediction of a Child's Years of Education Based upon Characteristics of the Parent**

	Unstandardized coefficients		Standardized coefficients		
Model	B	Std. error	Beta	t	Sig.
Constant	15.104	0.368		41.052	0.000
Parents divorced	0.387	0.514	0.051	0.754	0.452
Marital status	−8.28E−02	0.069	−0.081	−1.194	0.234
Cohabited before marriage	9.778E−03	0.071	0.010	0.138	0.890
Grades	−0.439	0.106	−0.287	−4.143	0.000
Indication of problems with biological parents	−0.766	0.256	−0.205	−2.996	0.003

Source: Data from the Iowa Adoption Study, Department of Psychiatry, University of Iowa, Iowa City. Regressions available from the author.
Note: Dependent Variable = YRSCHOOL
R^2 (adj.) = .123

TABLE 6.2 **Prediction of the Number of Child Divorces Based upon Characteristics of the Parent**

	Unstandardized coefficients		Standardized coefficients		
Model	B	Std. error	Beta	t	Sig.
Constant	−6.96E−03	0.218		−0.032	0.975
Indication of problems with biological parents	−0.148	0.126	−0.132	−1.176	0.244
Parents divorced	−0.335	0.303	−0.124	−1.103	0.274
Importance of religion	0.193	0.089	0.248	2.174	0.034
Cohabited before marriage	8.841E−02	0.033	0.310	2.713	0.009
Employed	7.317E−02	0.051	0.160	1.449	0.153
Indication of spouse abuse	−1.89E−02	0.037	−0.057	−0.514	0.609
Adoptive parents told of problems with biological parents	−0.140	0.067	−0.229	−2.099	0.040

Source: Data from the Iowa Adoption Study, Department of Psychiatry, University of Iowa, Iowa City, Iowa. Regressions available from the author.
Note: Dependent Variable = DIV#
R^2 (adj.) = .224

Several parts of this book have mentioned the role biology plays in creating family communities and even in establishing norms.[57] Thus, the presence of stepparents or adult cohabitants may confound families, and kin caregivers might be expected to do a better job with children than do unrelated foster parents.[58] Here, in addition to the mimetic violence of Girard and as an alternative to it, we will continue the biological explanation with behavior that, while explicable, is criminal: child and spousal abuse.[59] While domestic, as opposed to institutional, elder abuse can be explained by mimetics as well, I leave that for a future project.[60] In a context that is similar because of the amount of time that must be diverted to the "special" child, one article suggests that families "with premature infants endure a variety of psychosocial stresses. . . . They may be worried about long-term development, and they are often burdened with large hospital bills and ongoing medical expenses. Premature infants may require a tremendous investment of time, energy, and patience. Siblings can become jealous and should be persuaded to help care for the infant whenever possible."[61] Please keep in mind that families in which violence occurs are not the norm—they are rare. However, hopefully through understanding the mechanism by which the violence occurs and is directed against particular family members we can learn not only to prevent these rare but tragic occurrences but also how to guard against the less violent forms we see in many families.

When Might a Child Become a Scapegoat?

As Martha Minow notes, living with people who are different—who may be considered ugly or are disabled in some way—may enrich our lives.[62] But many parents will prefer their healthy to their disabled offspring.[63] For example, a premature or very ill newborn might be harmed not only because he is malformed but also because he must spend many days in intensive care apart from his parents,[64] so they do not see him as an attractive child when he is finally released to their care.[65]

On the other extreme, throughout their lives, beautiful people are revered by a society that rewards vigor and youth.[66] They are popular as dates and chosen early as mates. The most beautiful of all may grace magazine covers or feature films. Unattractive people are discriminated against in job[67] and marriage[68] markets. These tendencies are mutually reinforcing. For example, the child who seems less likely to be able to reproduce may be seen as more unattractive[69] and, therefore, be less likely to marry and rear children. As a consequence, they are less likely to be able to support their parents in old age[70] and, if disabled, may even be unable to support themselves.[71] They are therefore seen as a burden to their parents, who have even on occasion sought damages for their "wrongful birth."[72] Since they are less valuable from a genetic standpoint, they are more apt to be abused by their parents.

The child who has learning disabilities or mental handicaps, like Phillip Becker, is particularly likely to become a scapegoat.[73] Contrary to the last paragraph, he might in fact have just as many chances as the average person to reproduce (especially if somewhat careless about birth control) and, depending on the severity of the disability, may well enjoy a productive life as an adult. However, the parents of a learning-disabled child, especially a bright one, may find the school years much more frustrating, and more expensive, than they would with a normal child.[74] The parent might need to "run interference" with school authorities and continually set limits for the child. There may be special education needs or trips to a counselor or medication. All this stretches the parents' capacity and limits leisure time. Further, the child with hyperactivity or attention deficit disorder will frequently be emotionally taxing for the parent.[75] This is, of course, a cost in money, time, and psychological terms. For the parents of an eccentric genius, the problems of raising the child may be compensated by the enormous respect earned when the genius reaches adulthood.[76] For the disabled (and particularly the mentally handicapped) child, such compensations are highly unlikely. As one researcher put it, "[S]ome parents do not successfully cope with a disabled child, whose presence may be a constant reminder of disappointed aspirations, perceived punishment, or embarrassment. A disability can also create social and economic pressures that further strain family relationships and budgets, increasing the general level of stress."[77]

The child who is in the way may also become a scapegoat. For example, the child of a single mother might impede her chances on the marriage market or interfere with a new romantic interest.[78] Second marriages involving children of prior relationships stand a much greater chance of dissolving.[79] Further, this child may become a victim of scapegoating because of a biological concern. The parent or stepparent may consciously or unconsciously feel that the child competes for the other adult's affection,[80] thus threatening the mate's chances for producing offspring from the new relationship[81] or, from a psychological perspective, the ongoing adult relationship.

Social capital theory overlaps with this rapidly growing field in evolutionary biology. As genes determine a large part of one's looks, capacities, and character traits, scholars, including Francis Fukuyama,[82] consider genes the engine of evolutionary change. Behavioral biologists[83] see the gene as programmed to replicate itself, using the body in which it is from time to time lodged as a way station. The most successful genes are those best able to reproduce successfully, when an individual produces the most offspring who will be able to carry on successfully in the world. The behavioral biologists would not be able to explain spouse abuse as well as mimetic theory does, however. While a "selfish gene" might explain a spouse's desire to keep the other out of the labor force to better reproduce or care for children, the theory would not seem to account for abuse by unemployed spouses.

Evolutionary biology theories provide an explanation for the presumption of parental fitness (as opposed to third parties unrelated by blood or adoption), with a selfish parental gene seeking to ensure its survival across time in the replicated genes of offspring.[84] But biological theories also suggest that a disabled or unattractive child will be less successful at passing along a parent's genes and will, therefore, threaten the parent and be a target for direct abuse.[85] In addition, the child who interferes with the parent's new romantic relationship competes directly with the selfish gene.[86] The other adult or even the child's parent might harm or "eliminate" this threat to the relationship (and potential offspring with the new partner).

Regardless of the source of the problem—whether the competition or disaffection is financial, genetic, or psychological or stems from mimetic rivalry—there is reason to suspect that parents of disabled children who have already abused are less likely to profit from reunification services than those of nondisabled children. Likewise, if a parent or other caregiver is choosing a new mate rather than the child and therefore physically abuses the child or permits abuse, preventing escalation of the abuse or other harm to the child seems to trump the "parental rights" of chapter 4. Not all children will be treated as scapegoats, of course, and family autonomy ought to be the preferred approach in most cases. Children once treated as scapegoats by their parents will be far more likely to be repeatedly abused than other children will, however.

We turn now to empirical tests of these competing theories, the sociobiological and the mimetic. The data indicates that the biological explanations work well for many cases of child abuse but not those dealing with ADHD children and not marital violence. Mimetic rivalry explanations fit all the data and also provide an explanation for why religion seems so important in findings of healthier families. Because family violence is relatively infrequent and the data kept either secret or maintained confidentially by courts, all the data sets presented here will, of necessity, be smaller.

Empirical Tests

We begin with a specific group of disabled children for whom the sociobiology explanation seems the least appropriate: those with Attention Deficit Disorder (ADD) and/or Learning Disability (LD). These children, who are sometimes quite bright (as were Albert Einstein and Thomas A. Edison)[87] as well as physically attractive (think of Keanu Reaves, Orlando Bloom, and Tom Cruise), may well be able to successfully mate and bear children. In fact, to the extent that they are less careful and more spontaneous than others are, they may be more likely to have unplanned children.[88] Thus, if passing on of one's genes were all that was important, parents of ADHD children should not be more likely to abuse them.

Alternatively, parents of ADHD children frequently feel frustrated.[89] The children may not appear to listen, may constantly wander away from the table or homework, and may well have disappointing school performances.[90] One can easily imagine how, on the margin, understandable frustration may mutate into something much darker when the family is stressed by marital crises or money problems.[91] However, some evidence also shows that these children may at least sometimes be scapegoats without themselves provoking the violence. For example, a large proportion of child abuse comes where there is a history (in other words, prior indications) of marital violence. A perpetrator may be acting out of mimetic rivalry (that is, being rivalrous with a spouse) while targeting the more susceptible victim, who will not fight back—a child.[92]

If this alternative explanation were correct, we would expect to see a higher percentage of ADHD children in families where abuse occurs than in the general population.[93] If the family where abuse is found consists of more than one child, and at least one is not abused, we would expect the target of the abuse to be more likely than the nonabused child to have ADHD, holding everything else constant.

Further, if the mimetics-and-scapegoating idea proves out in this context, we would hypothesize a greater number of families where abuse occurs would be characterized by divorce and dissolution than in the general population. This is in fact the case.[94] Many of the families particularly stressed by the ADHD child would also have low incomes or unemployment.[95]

Finally, we would expect positive coefficients for the combination of dissolution or divorce with ADD[96] and for the combination of low income and ADD. In a study of girls at a summer camp, 60% of whom had ADHD, Allison Briscoe-Smith and Stephen Hinshaw[97] found that there were significantly higher rates of abuse for girls with ADHD (14.3%) compared to the population without it (4.5%). Similarly, in a study of boys[98] with various problems, Janet Wozniak and her coauthors found that 7% of the ADHD population of boys had suffered from child abuse of various kinds compared to 0.1% of their comparison sample. A simple frequencies count for the Linn County, Iowa, sample[99] shows that 25.2% of the children in the sample had been diagnosed with or were suspected of having ADHD.[100] This is compared to only 5.2% ADHD children reported in Iowa between 1997 and 1999.[101]

Testing whether disabilities, and particularly ADHD, will result in the scapegoating of children presents empirical challenges. The first is a legal one: the information about disability, because it involves children (and their parents), is privileged (and, if not discovered, secret). Getting access to abused children's files is therefore a nontrivial task. Further, because the population of abused children is very small (about .025% of all children), the number of families who would need to be sampled (to establish a control group) is extremely large. Most of the empirical papers dealing with abuse therefore measure whether the sample of abused children contains a significantly higher percentage of disabled children, say, than the total population contains.[102] My own work deals with families in which children were abused, but only one of a number of siblings was the target. Many of these problems were solved by Briscoe-Smith and Hinshaw in the previously mentioned study.[103] Their method was to study girls at a North Carolina summer camp, where 60% of the girls who attended had ADHD and 40% did not. They then compared various traits of the ADHD girls (the target group) against the non-ADHD children (the controls). This method means that the sample was not random (since they all attended the special camp), so care should be taken to extrapolate from it to the general population. In addition, while the children were socioeconomically and racially diverse, they all came from the Carolinas, so they might not be typical of children from the United States at large. What the authors reported was that the children with ADHD were more than three times as likely to have been abused as the non-ADHD children, even controlling for factors that normally increase the risk of abuse (socioeconomic status, single parenthood, and so forth).

TABLE 6.3 **Descriptive Statistics**

Name	Mean	Std. dev.	Variance	Minimum	Maximum
Disability of Child	0.15094	0.3588	0.12877	0.00000	1.0000
Age of Child	8.0613	4.9010	24.020	0.00000	17.000
Sex of Child	0.47170	0.50038	0.25038	0.00000	1.0000
Stepparent or Cohabitant in Home	0.28774	0.45378	0.20592	0.00000	1.0000
Likelihood that Child was Victim of Abuse	0.31604	0.46603	0.21718	0.00000	1.0000
Likelihood that Child was Victim of Neglect	0.09434	0.29299	0.085845	0.00000	1.0000
Sex * age	3.8538	5.3752	28.893	0.00000	17.000

Source: From Margaret F. Brinig and F. H. Buckley, "Parental Rights and the Ugly Duckling." *Journal of Law and Family Studies* 1, no. 1, 1999.
N = 212

Some work has focused specifically on families with ADHD children. In 1995, Baldwin, Brown, and Milan noted that parents from lower socioeconomic backgrounds are apt to be at greatest risk for increased stress.[104] In turn, the stress increased the symptoms displayed in the ADHD children. A later paper[105] argued that ADHD and impairment of daily functioning was highest among youth who live in contexts where their families' financial circumstances are advantaged or deprived in relation to their neighbors. All ADHD families exhibited some stress and tended to use more negative-reactive and fewer positive parenting strategies than did their control group of non-ADHD parents.[106] Further, marital happiness was lower and day-to-day marital problems higher for families with ADHD children.[107]

The results are similar to the results on abuse and neglect presented by Frank Buckley and me,[108] which comes from a panel set prepared by Cornell University researchers[109]drawn from a national sample of abused children and their families taken in 1991. The abuse cases were matched with 300 cases of children with disabilities (prior to any abuse) from the same counties.[110] Because all the sampled (reported) families had at least one abused child, there was no obvious "normal" group to act as a control. We therefore concentrated on families containing at least two children to see whether the disabled "ugly" child was more likely to be "picked on."[111] Table 6.3 reports on a study of a group of 212 children from seventy-five families with two or more children, who had abused one but not all of the children and where this was the first proven instance of abuse.

We believed that disabled children were more likely to be abused than other children were. We also expected that child abuse and neglect might be correlated with other factors, such as the child's age, gender, and whether she might be a threat to adult "competitors" in the home.[112] We sought to determine whether these characteristics would be similar for children who were neglected as well as those physically abused.

Results are given in table 6.4. The coefficient for the child being disabled (the first row of table 6.4) is positive and significant in all six equations in which it appears, whether on its own or with other variables held constant. A child's disability nearly doubles the chance of being neglected, as can be seen from the line reporting the weighted elasticity, which is the third row from the bottom of table 6.4.

The presence of a stepparent or other romantic interest in the home (denoted Step in table 6.4) is certainly significant in predicting mistreatment: it is negatively and significantly related to neglect and positively and significantly related to abuse. The presence of a stepparent decreased the chances that a child would be neglected by 13% to 14%, while it increased the chance that physical (or sexual) abuse would occur by more than 25%. This is as we expected: when a child competes with an unrelated adult for affection, the child may become a scapegoat. On the other hand, the formation of a "new" family, often with an additional breadwinner, eases the financial problems that are closely correlated, here as elsewhere, with neglect.[113]

Of the other variables, the coefficient for the child's gender was negative but insignificant in the neglect equation but positive and significant in the abuse equation (indicating that girls were more likely to be abused),[114] as would be consistent with their relative helplessness, a parental preference for boys, and the greater likelihood for girls to be sexually abused. The age coefficient was positive for both neglect and abuse but was significant only in the abuse equation. As the child ages, it is easier for the parent to see that she does not measure up to expectations. These findings are consistent with other studies, which report that disabled children are significantly more likely to be abused than nondisabled children.[115]

The profile of the neglected child is quite different from that of the abused child, even though both are chosen from among their siblings for abuse by their parents. Though both are likely to be disabled, the neglected child is not likely to have a stepparent (or surrogate) living in the home. The age and sex of the neglected child are not statistically relevant. In contrast, for the abused child, the presence of a stepparent is very important,

TABLE 6.4 **Selective Abuse in Families**

Variable name	(1) Probit-dependent neglect (20)	(2) Probit-dependent neglect (20)	(3) Probit-dependent neglect (20)	(4) Probit-dependent abuse (67)	(5) Probit-dependent abuse (67)	(6) Probit-dependent abuse (67)
Disabled	1.5265 (5.4183)**	1.5491 (5.2232)**	1.5475 (5.0856)**	0.47821 (1.9692)**	0.70448 (2.6852)**	0.71907 (2.7368)**
Step		−0.84276 (−2.0000)**	−0.92744 (−2.0939)**		0.85623 (4.1169)**	0.76962 (3.7296)**
Child's age			0.00089910 (0.030849)			0.053656 (2.6773)**
Child's sex			−0.48651 (−1.6362)			0.47953 (2.4460)**
Sex*age		−0.029092 (−1.0143)			0.078756 (4.4157)**	
Constant	−1.7637 (−10.309)**	−1.5212 (−7.4356)** (−9.0270)**	−1.4129 (−4.6141)**	−0.55662 (−5.6298)**	−1.1987 (−7.4458)**	−1.5257 (−6.1623)**
Elasticity disabled/step	0.94735	0.89470 /−0.13360	0.87783 /−0.14435	0.90838E−01	0.10988 /0.30416	0.11861 /0.26089
N	212	212	212	212	212	212
R^2 (Maddala)	0.1322	0.1574	0.1641	0.1804E−01	0.1595	0.1327

Source: From Margaret F. Brinig and F. H. Buckley, "Parental Rights and the Ugly Duckling." *Journal of Law and Family Studies* 1, no. 1, 1999.

** $p < 0.01$

as is disability. Abused children are significantly more likely to be girls (because, with stepparents, much of the abuse tends to be sexual) and to be among the older children in the family.

A few prior studies[116] and at least one book,[117] written for the social work community, have investigated the scapegoating phenomenon as applied to child abuse. These earlier works have found a relationship between such factors as disability and abuse, but there have often been methodological problems with the studies[118] that may have caused policy makers to pay less than strict attention to them.

Legal Recommendations Based on Biology

Although the presumption of parental autonomy—that parents, more than any others, must be trusted to act in their children's best interests—maximizes social capital for the majority of families, it may be that the pendulum has swung too far in the direction of parental rights even after parents have abused their children. It has become extremely difficult to prove permanent parental unfitness.[119] More to the point, children are often returned to their parents after quite horrifying examples of abuse. One prominent standard requires the child to be returned unless "[t]he child has been removed from the parents previously, has been returned to his/her parents, has been found to be endangered a second time, requiring removal, has been out of the home for at least six months, and there is a substantial likelihood that sufficient legal justification to keep the child from being returned home . . . will continue to exist in the foreseeable future."[120] The first impulse of the current system has been to try to "cure" the problem through the provision of social services, such as counseling, to the families.[121]

In the famous example of the Supreme Court case of *DeShaney v. Winnebago County Department of Social Services*,[122] Joshua was three times admitted to a hospital with multiple bruises and abrasions, including head injuries. Social workers investigated these incidents but always returned the child to his father. The child's stepmother and neighbors often told the police that they had seen or heard the father or the father's lover beating Joshua. A social worker visited the home nearly twenty times and later testified that "I just knew the phone would ring some day and Joshua would be dead." The father finally beat the boy into a coma, from which he suffered brain damage so severe that he is expected to spend the rest of his life in an institution for the profoundly retarded.[123]

In New York, a three-year-old boy whose father kicked him to death had been removed from his home three times in the ten months prior to his death. However, authorities returned him to the home each time despite reports from his grandmother, doctors, and day-care teachers that he was being abused.[124] Also in New York, in 1986, one-third of the 112 children who died of child abuse had families that the city had previously investigated.[125]

In the press accounts of a Maryland case,[126] a son who had been previously removed because of neglect was eventually returned to his father and his new girlfriend. The father and "stepmother" had a daughter and an infant son of their own, and various authorities began to suspect that the older son was being abused. When the infant died at home, neighbors who took care of the two older children reported that the five-year-old boy was ravenously hungry and that his younger half sister repeatedly bit him. Investigators found that he had been tied to a bedpost with a cat leash for up to twenty-two hours a day and had been intentionally burned and starved by the girlfriend who worried that he was interfering with her relationship with the boy's father. Similarly, in 2007, two separate investigations into abuse allegations following reports of suspicious injuries of a Milwaukee toddler were closed and the child remained in the home where she was allegedly murdered by her mother's crack-addicted boyfriend.[127]

The greater procedural protections required to protect the parents' constitutional rights and the increased number of reported cases of abuse have increased the social work caseload, while the resulting lack of attention to individual cases has in turn contributed to a mounting crisis in child abuse.[128] Child abuse has also increased as a consequence of an upswing in drug dependencies and related pathological behavior amongst parents. Finally, the increase in child abuse has come at a time of declining local government revenues and a reduction in the budgets of many social welfare agencies.

The federal Adoption and Safe Families Act of 1997, signed by President Clinton in November of 1997, allows states to add the protection of the child to the goal of reuniting the family.[129] In response, states have now changed some of their rules, though they have little guidance on how best to protect children.[130] Even though as it has placed new emphasis on the child's well-being, Congress has asked for more studies to show which families should be reunified and which dissolved. To this end, I suggest that evidence that a child has been scapegoated might be considered as a factor in the dependency or termination decision, but, again, only where there has already been proven abuse.

Such a change might have prevented many tragic cases of abuse that have occurred where a scapegoated child was returned to his parents after serious abuse.[131] Such cases include a disabled child who was killed despite a previous intervention by social services because he was unable to tell time,[132] a stepfather who tortured his stepdaughter after temporarily losing custody,[133] and an in-the-way child beaten into a permanent vegetative state by his father.[134] A recognition that scapegoated children might be continued targets for parental abuse might also have led to a different result in many landmark decisions, including *Santosky v. Kramer*,[135] *Lassiter v. Department of Social Services*,[136] and *M. L. B. v. S. L. J.*[137] In all of these cases, parental rights were terminated without proper procedural protections, according to the Supreme Court, and in all, the Court supported stronger procedural protections to protect the *parent* against mistakes.

By itself, the mere propensity to become a scapegoat—whether caused by disability or the problems of a "blended family"—should never alone be a reason to alter family arrangements, for then many children would be doubly harmed by losing the emotional support of their parents. The overwhelming majority, after all, will not be abused. But when the parents have put their love into question by abusing the child, when they have violated societal trust, the fact that she has served as a scapegoat should reasonably be taken into account as a factor suggesting the likelihood of continued abuse. Child protective laws might be amended to provide that, after a finding of serious abuse or neglect, a court may take into account the attributes of the child and the family structure which appear to have contributed to the mistreatment and which make continued parental abuse more likely.

The proposal should be restricted to the most serious forms of abuse. There are many different ways to raise a child, and short of serious physical abuse, one must be leery of second guessing parental decisions.[138] Likewise, standards for coercive intervention should take cultural differences into account. The fact that the vast majority of the children in the Cornell data-set who were neglected were also poor suggests that one appropriate role for government may be providing the medical and educational resources the child needs (relieving the stress the family feels or contributing to the capital with which they have to work).

According to the biological theories discussed previously, biological parents (and, after them, other relatives) are almost always to be preferred to adoptive parents. But this presumption appears weaker when the child is disabled and when he may be perceived by his parents, even on a very basic level, as a defective agent for the transmission of their genes. In such cases, a finding of serious abuse is tantamount to a finding that the parent's "selfish gene" has abandoned the child's replicated gene. In the stepparent cases, the new romantic interest may bring in children who seem "more fit" on some level even to the genetic parent because their other parent lives in the home, or it may seem important to preserve the relationship even at the cost of the child. Alternatively, the stepparent may abuse because there is no genetic connection with the child.

The problem addressed here is particularly pressing because many of the children currently awaiting adoption are disabled.[139] There is therefore a special concern for screening the fitness of parents who agree to adopt disabled children. In addition, such adoptive parents might reasonably be offered greater financial support in the form of child allowance subsidies to relieve stress.[140] As I mentioned earlier, neglect and abuse of ADHD children are very strongly correlated with lack of financial resources.

At the same time, the legal environment has grown more challenging. The Supreme Court has set high standards for interference with family autonomy,[141] which I have earlier argued is a good thing, and has required significant procedural protections for parents threatened by abuse and neglect proceedings.[142] Meanwhile, Congress has shifted the focus of child protection from preservation of families to promotion of child safety.[143] The federal government has conditioned receipt of significant funds on moving children rapidly out of foster care to return them to their families of origin or to free them for adoptive placement.[144]

What these constraints mean is that each dollar of child protective funding and each hour of a child protective service worker's time must be carefully spent. Studies like those reported here reveal which families are most in need of services and, in some cases, show that interventions are critical to meet the demand of child protection. Further, advocates for the disabled will be quick to note the connection between abuse, family disruption, and special needs such as ADHD.

One child welfare advocate, Douglas Besharov, writes that no one can know which parents will be repeat child abusers, so that the number of mistaken "false positives" (or families interrupted unjustifiably) is unacceptably high.[145] However, the scapegoating phenomenon reveals some indicia that can improve the accuracy of judgments (largely made by social workers or law enforcement officers, but sometimes by judges who decide whether or not to return children to their homes). I would advocate the use of profiles that might help identify times when the state should intervene in repeated abuse cases or should proceed with termination of parental custody after a finding of abuse.[146] The profiles which fit both the biological and mimetic scapegoating theories focus both on past behavior of the parent (since in most cases some abuse of the child will already have occurred) and characteristics of the child or family. For instance, various studies of abused children show that those with parents who abuse substances (which, like unemployment, place families into a crisis mode) are likely candidates for repeat abuse.[147] Besharov himself pushed for termination of parental rights where parents were substance addicted.[148] In those circumstances where a behavior, or combination of behaviors, elevates the risk of repeat abuse, I propose a shift in the burdens of proof as follows. I would change the burden of proof from a presumption of "best interests" for mothers who abuse illegal drugs during pregnancy to a presumption the newborns should be removed.[149] There are five indicia that create an increased need for intervention:

- Abuse + parental alcohol or drug abuse
- Abuse + boyfriend/girlfriend/stepparent (nonadoptive) in the home
- Abuse + child is disabled (widen abuse to nonprovision of medical care)
- Serious abuse of another sibling
- Abuse of the other parent

As I have already discussed, sociobiologists, including Martin Daly and Margo Wilson,[150] have found that children are at greater risk when a nonrelated adult is living in the home.[151] Special attention should be paid when children are "disciplined" in these homes.[152] Again, I would not intervene until there was actually a finding of abuse, however. I have described research indicating that children who are disabled are at much greater risk for abuse by parents.[153] For disabled children, I would intervene earlier and "second guess" parental medical care decisions like the one in *Phillip B.* if the parents are reluctant to provide routine or life-saving medical treatment.[154]

Where abuse has already occurred, the need to shift away from the presumption that parents always act in their children's best interests is reflected in federal legislation.[155] When there has already been abuse of a sibling, the federal legislation changes the presumption of reunification to one of termination.[156] The ALI has included similar language in its child custody standards when a parent has previously abused, neglected, or abandoned a child.[157] There is some evidence that a parent abused as a child is likely to repeat that pattern of abuse when he or she has children[158] as an unfortunate kind of mimetic behavior.

Most people who have thought about the problem in a pictorial way would have the area occupied by abusers and the area represented by occasions of family interventions correspond exactly. The world being what it is, we cannot do so. Curtailing definitions of abuse does not help parents or children. Parents seem infinitely inventive in abusing their children,[159] and abuse often escalates, as the mimetic cycle shows. Thus, even if it is not obvious at the first sign of abuse that the parent will be a repeat offender, steps must be taken to ensure that the child likely to become a scapegoat will not be seriously damaged by remaining in an abusive atmosphere.

The problem stems from society's inability to accurately predict behavior in combination with the conflicting rights and needs of parents and children. One view chooses to protect parental autonomy and, in so doing, hopes to benefit the majority. In contrast, under special circumstances, I choose to protect child victims. Rather than limiting the degree of intervention and placing children at risk of further abuse, the previously mentioned indicia for intervention can be used to reduce the incidence of error in intervention decisions.

With dysfunctional marriages, in contrast to child abuse, the trick seems to be early identification before the violent phase of the scapegoating mechanism begins.[160] This may be a real advantage of no-fault divorce, since it allows scapegoated spouses to exit simply by separating rather than having to prove the violence, risking escalation of the harm during separation.[161] Where a couple is unwilling to divorce, substance abuse prevention and treatment programs may be most effective. Very religious couples, like those in Louisiana covenant marriages, may be unlikely to divorce even in extreme circumstances. Whether this is a good thing is questionable.[162]

Social Capital Solutions to Mimetic Violence

As I mentioned at the beginning of this chapter, the concept of mimetic violence may prove more useful for describing family violence than the biological explanation. Not only does it account for cases of marital violence where behavioral biology does not, but, without negating the importance of biology, mimetic violence theory also explains why religion may mitigate all kinds of violence in the family. Further, evolutionary biology has been misused in the past and can raise reader's hackles unnecessarily. While mimetic violence may be controversial in some circumstances—Girard takes on Sigmund Freud in *Violence and the Sacred*, for example—mimetic desire explains the data well and offers solutions that are novel and relatively inexpensive.

Girard suggested at the end of *I See Satan Fall Like Lightning*[163] that while our desire to imitate was just part of human nature, the dangerous mimetic cycling could be stopped. He said this could be done by shifting the focus of our attention away from wanting for the sake of benefiting ourselves and increasing our esteem in the sight of others toward what he characterized as the God-like characteristics of trusting, serving others, and loving unconditionally.[164] These are all qualities that, as we have seen in chapter 5, can be created in families, the "mezzo level"[165] between individuals and society. As Rowthorn,[166] Lundberg,[167] and McAdams[168] all note, trust and unconditional love are norms that set people apart, that cause people to become heroes. If we can inculcate them in our families, perhaps the inverse of the "unraveling" of cooperative behavior characteristic of the "last period problem" in game theory will spread social capital.[169] Game theory predicts that if two contracting or negotiating partners (marital or otherwise) know when their relationship will end, they will each attempt to take advantage of the other in the "last period." Then, because they know each will do this in the last period, they will "cheat" or take advantage in the next-to-last period, and so forth. If, instead, they were to spread social capital, its good effects would be multiplied throughout the community they touch.

Social capital, you will remember, increases the ability of individuals and families to acquire and benefit from human and financial capital. The most important aspect came in the form of a "moral code, especially a code supporting trust and confidence between men: a true belief that they will not always let you down in favor of short-term gains."[170] Research shows that at least trust (or lack of it) flows through the values spread from mothers to daughters, especially in the experiences of marriage and divorce.[171] Society can reinforce these human capital values particularly through promulgation of mediating institutions, the most successful apparently being voluntary religious associations.[172]

A recent literature review by Kristin Ferguson mentions five components of social capital originated by the Coleman piece discussed in chapter 4[173] that have been featured in empirical studies[174]. These are family structure (in Coleman's piece, a two-parent family), the quality of parent-child relations (social interactions, such as the nonreligious activities we considered in chapter 5), the adult's interest in the child, parents' monitoring of the child's activities, and extended family exchange and support (considered in the discussion of help by grandmothers in chapter 1). The Ferguson review poses an optimal profile of high family and community social capital suggested by the empirical precedents: a two-parent family structure with either a father or stepparent present; frequent parent-child interactions; high interaction in daily lives; high monitoring of children's activities; and embeddedness in surrounding social networks, including immediate and extended family supports, local social institutions, and regular church attendance.[175] These are certainly consistent with what has been presented in prior chapters. After all, social capital, after lack of poverty, is the best predictor of children's welfare. However, the characteristics operate in different ways depending upon the racial or ethnic background of the family (as we have also seen). Parenting, home environment, neighborhood, and maternal depression have significant effects on internalizing and externalizing problems for white and black children, but neighborhoods do not matter significantly for Latino families.[176] On the other hand, for poor Latina women (and not Anglo women), familism (the attitude and participation of kin in social networks) does have a significant effect upon whether or not they abuse.[177]

In abuse prevention studies, social capital seems to reduce the incidence of both domestic violence and child abuse. In these studies, while the more social capital, the better, the most effective instruments measured were church attendance and having two parents. Social capital, even in the worst of circumstances, seems to increase the odds of children doing well.[178] In the studies, social capital includes church attendance, perception of personal social support, and support within the neighborhood. Two or more indices of social capital defined by these terms increased the odds of doing well by about two-thirds.[179] For adolescents, their own social capital involves their peers and their use of common spaces as well.[180] This of course returns us precisely to what Coleman and Fukuyama claimed on a societal level in the literature we reviewed in chapters 3 and 4. Even more to the point of the violence we have been discussing in this chapter, social capital reduces domestic violence and child abuse. For twenty-five years, academics have reported that social capital in the form of personal networks (neighbor-friend and kinship networks) may also reduce the stress that tends to be the outside force inflaming child abuse and setting off that particular scapegoating cycle.[181] Consistent with what was reported in chapter 1, kinship social support did not seem to matter for either inner-city boys' or girls' depression or sense of personal safety.[182]

What Girard's mimetic cycle predicts is thus consistent with the broader social capital literature. Not only is religion important for protecting children, but it seems to improve marriages. The role of religion in marriage is explored at length by psychologist Annette Mahoney and her coauthors, who studied ninety-seven couples sampled from public health records of births in a midsized Midwestern metropolitan area.[183] They find that it is shared religious activity and the integration of religion and marriage that are significantly associated with husbands' and wives' reports of greater global marital adjustment, more perceived benefit, less marital conflict (only reports by wives were always significant), and less use of verbal aggression (husbands' reports) and stalemate (wives' reports) in dealing with disagreements.[184] In other words, what they term proximal religiosity, as opposed to individual religiousness or shared denomination, matters. Mahoney and her coauthors speculate that spouses who view their marriage as having sacred, transcendent qualities may be more willing to forgive and accept their partners, more likely to minimize or dismiss minor conflicts, and more likely to make greater use of religious coping methods (seeking spiritual support).[185] Similarly, Bradford Wilcox,[186] using the NSFH, found less abuse and more fathers likely to hug and praise their children in conservative Protestant households, though the fathers did use more corporal punishment.[187] These men were significantly less likely to commit domestic violence[188] than other husbands, including mainline Protestants. In fact, Wilcox notes that religion is apt to affect family life and vice versa. Most recently, Nock and his coauthors found that for the Louisiana covenant marriage couples they studied, religiosity performed an important buffering role even in times of severe marital stress. "First, religious individuals perceive God as a benefactor and protector of marriage. Second, religious individuals perceive a duty to God to develop strong relationship management and communication skills. Third, religious individuals actively rely on their view of marriage as sacred to manage severe marital crisis, often with great success."[189]

Discussing how we avoid the Hobbesian world of "all against all" without resorting to what we here identify as mimetic cycles, Anthony Kronman wrote twenty years ago that, among other approaches, people operating outside enforceable contracts could use a strategy he called union.[190] Union was defined as the building of solidarity ("any arrangement that seeks to reduce divergence by promoting a spirit of identification or fellow-feeling between the parties") through such things as company sports leagues, and, tellingly, family rituals.[191] Of course these rituals are also building social capital.

More recently, Geoffrey Miller[192] wrote a piece that includes many themes we have discussed previously. He noted that rituals resemble social norms since both exist outside the formal legal system and join the individual to the group. Ritual, he writes, unlike law or norms, governs behavior *ex-ante* by assigning social roles and inducing the individuals and others to accept them.[193] Miller discusses three kinds of rituals, all of which we have used as examples elsewhere in this book. The first Miller calls a ritual of *reformation*, for which he lists marriage as an example.[194] To this, we should add adoption, which also reforms family roles and alliances. Miller's second type is *renewal*, for which he lists services and sacrifice. We have discussed the way formal religious participation (and sometimes, with parenting, individual faith) seems to bind families together.[195] The third category mentioned by Miller is *restoration*, for which he lists confession, purification, and cure as examples. In this book, the restoration theme can be seen most fully in the discussion in chapter 2 of the Navajo peacemaking ritual, which seems to permanently resolve intractable domestic violence situations.

Though he begins by using transaction cost analysis rather than this chapter's language of mimetic behavior, Miller notes that these ritual activities will help people to make credible commitments and follow basic cooperative norms.[196] In other words, they build social capital by shaping and changing identity and by transforming people, so they will act not only to avoid sanctions from others (Eric Posner's threats)[197] but also to "experience the pleasurable sense of felicity that comes with acting consistently with one's sense of identity."[198] As Miller notes, rituals "may channel and control negative emotions" such as jealousy, disappointment, and envy,"[199]which might otherwise "erupt in uncontrolled and dangerous ways." Miller does note that initiation rituals, in particular, are often marked by violence.[200] Miller maintains that we are likely to observe relatively more ritual in societies somewhat insulated from technological change than those in the midst of rapid development, because ritual "tends to fix social relationships" including those structuring technological production "in a fairly rigid form,"[201] and in places where the legal structure is relatively weak. He uses the example of impoverished neighborhoods, noting that "organized religion is likely to play an important role."[202] Of course, this is what was covered in chapter 1 in the discussion of the relatively poor, black, single-mother family.

I conclude, then, with the thought that while the evolutionary biology explanations for child abuse may be helpful and important, more territory can be covered by Girard's mimetic cycling theory. In addition, this better fits the social capital literature in which, in Fukuyama's work for example, biology plays a helpful, though not completely satisfying, role. The closer one gets to the problem of transmitting genes and survival, the greater the appeal of behavioral biology. But the more the family resembles wider society as opposed to the family of our earliest human ancestors, the less well the theory fits. Social capital and mimetic theory in particular seem to do a more complete job of explanation.

Conclusion

This book has featured the role of trust throughout. The way we have used trust shows how the book has progressed from the social norms literature through that on social capital to that dealing with mimetic behavior. First, in the context of social norms, trust was described as needed to insure that signals given by marital[1] or parental status[2] are credible.[3] Trust even has a role in making marriage[4] or parenting successful. Loss of trust signaled the demise of important relationships like marriage or, for noncustodial parents, a diminished societal confidence in the ability to parent in the best interest of children. Later, as we moved to the social capital portion of the book, an increase in trust became the visible sign that social capital was being created. Social capital also served as the mechanism by which social capital could function to improve what families could accomplish. Finally, trust becomes a key, if not the key, value transmitted through imitation of others. Resolution of mimetic conflict comes only as the perpetrator is restored to trust and full membership in the community. Mimetic conflict is only avoided when participants can emulate characteristics of selflessness and unconditional love, both of which, of course, involve trust.

This book has treated many topics and owes intellectual debts to many scholars in a number of fields. I will try to acknowledge them as I briefly recap the intellectual threads that bind the volume. The social norms literature in law, at any rate, has flourished under the leadership of Robert

Ellickson,[5] Eric Posner,[6] and Richard McAdams.[7] Each of these scholars, usually writing in other fields, has treated families or households in his work. Each sees the importance of signaling, self-esteem and trust—all nonlegal means of influencing important behavior. Each of these law professors uses the tools of institutional economics to explain the way sanctions and reciprocity can function in small groups like families and households and the role the wider community plays in creating and reinforcing these norms. While much of what I have written flows naturally from their analyses, Ellickson, Posner, and McAdams are more apt than I to view families under an exchange model, though Ellickson in particular writes that the paybacks may come only, with regularity, at some time in the future. The very casual model I draw here depends upon less distinct reciprocity—what I call unconditional love.

Two nonlawyers figured heavily in the first section of the book in which we dealt with trust as it features in the social norms literature. Robert Rowthorn,[8] an economist, writes not only of marriage as a signal (as does Posner) but also of the whole institution's mission as creating trust. Francis Fukuyama,[9] a political scientist, sees trust as the means of getting groups to cooperate, whether in families or through mediating institutions like religious organizations.

In the initial section of the book we have seen evidence for the centrality of trust in society's choices of which relationships to privilege[10] as well as the effect (again, through increased stability and good outcomes for children) of the community recognition.[11] We have also explored how gender and other norms sometimes operate more strongly—and less perversely—than laws do in the family context.

We moved from social norms to social capital in the next section. Here trust works like a symptom or product. The more social capital, the more trust that will be measurable. In these chapters, where we saw the creation of social capital and the critical role families and voluntary organizations play,[12] we moved away from legal academics entirely, considering the work of sociologist James Coleman,[13] political scientist Robert Putnam,[14] and, again, Francis Fukuyama.[15]

From a legal perspective, we discussed whether it makes good sense for people in family relationships to assert constitutional rights against each other (as opposed to as against the state). Typically, once the constitution is invoked, the relationship is in serious trouble. We returned to law and economics models when we considered third-party interventions through the analogy of Michael Heller's tragedy of the anticommons[16] and the corporate analogy of stakeholder interests[17] that will be inefficient if they do not ultimately serve the interests of shareholders.[18]

Finally, we turned to mimetics, a topic virtually untouched by legal academics in a family context (with the exception of Geoffrey Miller's general piece on rituals, in which families play a part).[19] We saw how children learn to trust by imitating their parents and their peers. When imitation becomes mimetic desire, drawing from the work of René Girard,[20] we examined child and spousal abuse, both extreme violations of trust, and some of the causes[21] and consequences of family violence.

This brief summary of its layout does not make it obvious, perhaps, that we have addressed most of the "hot topics" in family law in the course of this book. Among many subjects, we have moved from cohabitation and same-sex marriage to considerations of a return to fault divorce, to interracial adoptions to joint physical custody to state intervention for children's welfare, particularly in minority families. More traditional treatments would address each as discrete and separate problems.

Policymakers can learn much about families from looking at their interaction with communities. The section on trust has direct relevance for the design of child custody rules (toward a standard replicating existing parental patterns and away from equal custody preferences) and kinship care and for a preference for marriage as opposed to cohabitation, as well as perhaps an argument for civil union recognition, if not same-sex marriage. The second section suggests an alternative rationale for doctrines of parental autonomy including the 2000 *Troxel*[22] decision. With *Elk Grove v. Newdow*,[23] we can explore not only why the federal courts should not be involved in most family disputes but also how the presumption that parents act in their children's' best interests may be rebutted in divorce situations. We can also see how imitation can work for good or ill to produce outcomes for children, with some partial answers to questions about the relative role of parents and peers. The material suggests that there be special standards to prevent repeat abuse when either disability or substance abuse is involved. Social capital solutions presented throughout suggest at least a neutral position toward voluntary associations, of which the most often studied (and the one that appears most often here) is religious.[24] It admittedly is a bit unclear how these work and whether the direction is from participation to social capital or vice versa.[25]

This is a book written by a law professor, and, not surprisingly, there are a number of legal recommendations scattered through it. For the most part, these suggest maintaining the status quo. Most of the time, I have concluded, social norms lead law. There will be exceptions, however, for laws that can affect the way in which people look at themselves and others, examples of which are the laws affecting same-sex relationships. I consistently advocate laws that encourage the building of social capital.

Here are some concrete suggestions, all of which have been discussed earlier in some form. First, maintaining the distinction between cohabitation and marriage should remain a high priority. This means that states should not adopt the ALI's domestic partnership provisions and should not encourage couples who could marry to live together without marriage or civil union, where that is an alternative. The other side of this coin is that civil marriage should not be abolished in favor of a private contractual regime supplemented, on election, by religious tradition.

Second, spouses should be encouraged to work out their own arrangements for housework, child-care, and labor-force responsibilities. The division of family labor should not be defaulted to a form of contract (with payment or immediate reciprocity expected) but should legally be kept more like a gift. Instead, to facilitate gender equality, which I also favor, family friendly policies should be made more attractive in the workplace, and care should be taken to police gender discrimination in the paid labor force.

Third, parenting relationships, rather than strict equality between parents, should be stressed (as in the ALI's replication custody principle). Physical custody arrangements should not force children to be nomads, and continuity of living situations should be encouraged. If the parents themselves favor a joint physical custody arrangement and it seems to work for them, however, that pattern may enhance well-being. Every effort should be made to assure that custody allocations are not made merely to reduce child support payments and that custody is not used as a tool to advance vindictive or controlling interests of either parent.

Fourth, adoption and child safety should continue to be stressed over family reunification once parents have been found unfit. However, all groups are not the same, and in situations where kinship care is common and legal status does not seem to matter much, informal family relationships may be preferred over third-party adoption.

Fifth, in general, legal rights should be downplayed compared to relationships. By this I mean that family autonomy, and the trust built by it, should allow fit parents to exclude others who claim rights to visit or otherwise parent.

Sixth, the parental presumption reflected in the last paragraph should, however, be overcome in certain cases where mimetic violence is likely. Thus, special considerations should govern cases where parents abuse or refuse medical care to disabled children, or where there has been abuse and there are unrelated parent figures in the home and/or alcohol or drug abuse.

Seventh, law and policy should encourage procedures for reconciling family members to the community if their trust has been lost. The example in the book is the Navajo peacemakers. Similarly, premarital programs that promote healthy communication and trust should receive support. These seem to generate better results than post-separation counseling requirements.

Eighth, in general, law and policy should encourage mediating institutions that build trust, such as voluntary associations. Law and policy should not discourage the role of religion that seems to matter critically for marriage and parenting (and that sets the United States apart from much of the developed world).

Finally, family policies should be made in a context of interdisciplinary research. This suggestion undoubtedly is true for other realms of life as well. We can learn much from all kinds of scholars, and, if we are informed, we are much less likely to make suggestions (particularly those that are "path dependent") that address only one aspect of a complex problem. This suggestion recognizes that not all families in America share the same cultural background and ways of generating and maintaining trust.

Notes

Introduction

1. From Adam Smith, "Of the Accumulation of Capital, Or of Productive and Unproductive Labour." In *An Inquiry into the Nature and Causes of the Wealth of Nations*, vol. 2. New York: Oxford University Press, 1976, paragraph II.3.13. H. Hennings, "Capital as a Factor of Production." In *The New Palgrave: A Dictionary of Economics*, vol. 1, edited by John Eatwell, Murray Milgate, and Peter Newman. London: Macmillan Press, 1987, 327–33.

2. For Becker's review of this concept in his own work and that of others, see Gary S. Becker, "Nobel Lecture: The Economic Way of Looking at Behavior." *Journal of Political Economy* 101, no. 3 (1993): 385–409, especially 392–400.

3. James S. Coleman, "Social Capital in the Creation of Human Capital." *American Journal of Sociology* 94 (1988): S95–S120, especially S98. Coleman uses as examples the diamond market, where relationships functioned as extralegal and comparatively inexpensive sources of control. For two applications of precisely this concept, see Avner Greif, "Contract Enforceability and Economic Institutions in Early Trade: The Maghribi Traders' Coalition." *American Economic Review* 83, no. 3 (1993): 525–48, and Lisa Bernstein, "Opting Out of the Legal System: Extralegal Contractual Relations in the Diamond Industry." *Journal of Legal Studies* 21, no. 1 (1992): 115–57.

4. *Alons v. Iowa District Court for Woodbury Co.*, 698 N.W.2d 858, 865 (Ia. 2005). They were held not to have standing to challenge this decision.

Chapter One

1. See, e.g., David Popenoe and Barbara DaFoe Whitehead, *Should We Live Together? What Young Adults Need to Know about Cohabitation before Marriage*. New Brunswick, NJ: National Marriage Project, Rutgers University, 1999, http://marriage.rutgers.edu/Publications/swlt2.pdf (accessed August 20, 2009).

2. See, e.g., Winifred Holland, "Intimate Relationships in the New Millennium: The Assimilation of Marriage and Cohabitation." *Revue Canadienne De Droit Familial* 17 (2000): 114; *Miron v. Trudel*, [1995] 2 S.C.R. 418 (Can.); *M v. H*, [1999] 2 S.C.R. 3, 46 R.F.L. (4th) 32; Katharina Boele-Woelki, "Private International Law Aspects of Registered Partnerships and Other Forms of Non-Marital Cohabitation in Europe." *Louisiana Law Review* 60, no. 4 (2000): 1053 (discussing recent statutory enactments giving legal status to nonmarital cohabitation between same or opposite-sex partners).

3. National Centre for Social Research (UK), "New British Social Attitudes Report Published Today," January 23, 2008, http://www.natcen.ac.uk/natcen/pages/news_and_media_docs/BSA_24_report.pdf (accessed August 20, 2009).

4. The figure was 50.5%. See "Births Outside Marriage Are Now in the Majority" at http://www.insee.fr/en/themes/document.asp?ref_id=ip1170&reg_id=0#inter3 (accessed August 20, 2009).

5. American Law Institute, *Principles of the Law of Family Dissolution*. Chestnut Hill, PA: American Law Institute, 2002, chapter 6.

6. Tavia Simmons and Martin O'Connell, "Married-Couple and Unmarried-Partner Households: 2000." *Census* 2000 *Special Reports*. Washington, DC: U.S. Dept. of Commerce, Economics, and Statistics Administration, U.S. Census Bureau, 2003, table, http://www.census.gov/prod/2003pubs/censr-5.pdf (accessed August 20, 2009). The same table shows that 22.3% of gay and 34.3% of lesbian households list children under 18 living with them.

7. A. Chandra et al. *Fertility, Family Planning, and Reproductive Health of U.S. Women: Data from the* 2002 *National Survey of Family Growth*. Hyattsville, MD: U.S. Dept. of Health and Human Services Centers for Disease Control and Prevention National Center for Health Statistics, 2005, p. 10 and fig. 6, http://www.cdc.gov/nchs/data/series/sr_23/sr23_025.pdf (accessed August 20, 2009).

8. See, e.g., Ga. Code §16-6-16 (1975); Idaho Code tit. 18, §6.603; Mass. Code 272 § 18; Utah Code § 76-7-104; W.V. Code §61-8-4. It is unclear whether any of these prohibitions in notes 8-10 will constitutionally survive *Lawrence v. Texas*, 539 U.S. 558 (2003), which struck down Texas's prohibition against same-sex sodomy.

9. Sodomy remains a crime under Ala. Code § 13A-6-65A-3; Fla. Stat. § 800.02; Idaho Code § 18-6605; Mass. Code ch. 272 § 34; Miss. Code §97-29-59; S.C. Code § 16-15-60; Va. Code § 18.2-361; Ariz. Stat. § 13-1411; Kan. Code § 21-3505; Okla. Code tit. 21 § 886; R.I. Code §11-10-1. Ryan Goodman ("Beyond the Enforcement Principle: Sodomy Laws, Social Norms, and Social Panoptics." *California Law Review* 89, no. 3 (2001): 693) points out that even if not enforced, laws against sodomy inhibit relationships and character.

10. Cohabitation remains a crime in Fla. Code §798.02; Mich. Code §750.32 (if divorced), 750.335; Miss. Code § 93-5-29 (by divorced former spouse); § 97-29-1; Va. Code § 18.2-345; W.V. Code §61-8-4 (lewd and lascivious); Mass. Code ch. 208 §40 (after divorce); *Rehak v. Mathis*, 238 S.E.2d 81 (Ga. 1977); *Long v. Marino*, 441

S.E.2d 475 (Ga. Ct. App.1994); *Liles v. Still*, 335 S.E.2d 168 (Ga. Ct. App. 1985); *Hewitt v. Hewitt*, 394 N.E.2d 1204 (Ill. 1979); *Crawford v. City of Chicago*, 710 N.E.2d 91 (Ill. Ct. App. 1999); *Schwegmann v. Schwegmann*, 441 So. 2d 316 (La. Ct. App. 1984), would not even recognize agreements between cohabiting couples because of the underlying illegality of the relationship. *Zysk v. Zysk*, 404 S.E.2d 721 (Va. 1990), would not even allow a wife to sue her husband for the venereal disease she contracted from him while they were cohabiting.

11. Though parents have the duty to support children regardless of marital status, in order for the child to be able to recover under a father's will, for example, some states require affirmative action on his or the mother's part. *Levy v. Louisiana*, 393 U.S. 898 (1968). Unwed fathers have increasingly been granted at least the opportunity to "grasp the relationship" with their children, but this is their right, not the child's. *Lehr v. Robinson*, 463 U.S. 248 (1972); *Quilloin v. Walcott*, 434 U.S. 246 (1978); *Caban v. Mohammed*, 441 U.S. 380 (1979); *Stanley v. Illinois*, 405 U.S. 635 (1972). But see *Michael H. v. Gerald G.*, 491 U.S. 110 (1989) (right belonged to adults in marriage relationship, not adulterous genetic father).

12. Some domestic partner legislation, and C-23 in Canada, does this (Holland, "Intimate Relationships" [see n. 2]). It is rarer for the duty of support during the relationship to be the same as in marriage. The civil union legislation in Vermont would be an example, 2000 Vermont Laws P.A. 91, §§ 1202 et seq.

13. Aid to Families with Dependent Children (AFDC) historically worked to deny benefits to cohabiting indigent adults. *Smith v. King*, 392 U.S. 309 (1968). This was on the theory that the cohabitant could support the indigent mother and children so the government didn't need to. More recently, public assistance payments have been structured to encourage marriage. Though married couples may receive temporary assistance, the second wage earner must be unemployed or disabled if the couple cohabits.

14. Martha Ertman, "Reconstructing Marriage: An InterSEXional Approach." *Denver Law Review* 75, no. 4 (1998): 1215; Martha Fineman, *The Neutered Mother, the Sexual Family, and Other Twentieth Century Tragedies*. New York: Routledge, 1994.

15. Quoted in Adam Liptak, "A Troubled 'Marriage': Core of Massachusetts Dispute is Tied to Traditional Exclusivity of the Word." *New York Times*, February 12, 2004, A26.

16. What about same-sex cohabitation vis-à-vis marriage? As a matter of social science evidence, until more jurisdictions legalize same-sex marriage, we cannot compare the consequences of marriage versus cohabitation for same-sex couples, although there are reasons for believing that some if not all of the benefits of formal marriage would apply to these couples. The benefits of domestic partnership or civil unions (or religious commitment ceremonies) for same-sex couples compared to more informal unions have not received adequate scholarly attention. Until more jurisdictions adopt same-sex marriage and other legal recognitions and more

research is done, the case for public policies encouraging same-sex marriage and/or for ritualized public celebrations of commitment for these couples are generally made on other grounds.

17. Steven L. Nock, "A Comparison of Marriages and Cohabiting Relationships." *Journal of Family Issues* 16, no. 1 (1995): 53.

18. Marsha Garrison, "Marriage Matters: What's Wrong with the ALI's Domestic Partnership Proposal." In *Reconceiving the Family: Critique on the American Law Institute's Principles of the Law of Family Dissolution*, edited by Robin Fretwell Wilson. New York: Cambridge University Press, 2006, 305–30.

19. Nock, "A Comparison of Marriages and Cohabiting Relationships," 15 (see n. 17).

20. Robert Rowthorn, "Marriage as a Signal." In *The Law and Economics of Marriage and Divorce*, edited by Antony W. Dnes and Robert Rowthorn. Cambridge: Cambridge University Press, 2000, 132–56. This would comport with Eric Posner's theory that signaling must be costly to the one who signals to be effective in showing one is a "good type." To the extent that the marriage signal is diluted by frequent divorce, Jill Deines et al. ("Covenant Marriage as a Signal: Religion and Commitment in Modern America." Bowling Green State University, Working Paper 2005–9, 2005) argue that covenant marriage serves as a stronger signal.

21. Pamela J. Smock and Sanjiv Gupta, "Cohabitation in Contemporary North America." In *Just Living Together: Implications of Cohabitation on Families*, edited by Alan Booth and Ann C. Crouter. New York: Routledge, 2002, 53, 66, note that "evidence has recently begun to emerge from both Canada and the United States that cohabitation's central features have been changing fairly substantially over very short periods of time. The most important implication of these changes is that cohabitation has lost much ground as a precursor to marriage. The matter is complex, however. Although cohabitations appear to be increasingly unstable and less likely to lead to marriage, there may be a growing segment of cohabiting unions that do endure, with our without childbearing."

22. Surprisingly, cohabiting men do the same amount of housework as married men (on average 19 and 18 hours per week), while cohabiting women do 31 hours of housework per week compared to 37 for married women. Smock and Gupta, "Cohabitation in Contemporary North America," 68–69 (see n. 21).

23. Eric Posner, *Law and Social Norms*. Cambridge, MA: Harvard University Press, 2000. For a critique, see Richard H. McAdams, "Signaling Discount Races: Law, Norms, and Economic Methodology." *Yale Law Journal* 110, no. 4 (2001): 625.

24. Posner, *Law and Social Norms*, 18–22 (see n. 23).

25. Ibid., 71. See also Rowthorn, "Marriage as a Signal" (see n. 20).

26. Posner, *Law and Social Norms*, 76–78 (see n. 23).

27. Ibid., 72ff. The exchanges might be tit for tat, though the community will also enforce through nonlegal sanctions. Marriage is a system of blanket rather than agreed-upon rules precisely so that the community can enforce them easily. Ibid.,

78. A helpful taxonomy of gift and trade is Carol M. Rose, "Giving, Trading, Thieving, and Trusting: How and Why Gifts Become Exchanges, and (More Importantly) Vice Versa." *Florida Law Review* 44, no. 3 (1992): 295.

28. Heather Mahar, "Why are there so Few Prenuptial Agreements?" *Harvard Law School John M. Olin Center for Law, Economics and Business Discussion Paper Series*. Paper 436. Cambridge, MA: Harvard Law School, 2003. Her results may be a bit skewed since antenuptial agreements also importantly deal with asset distribution at death.

29. Twenty-seven percent (27%) of the law students and 16% of the general population and only 1.5% of the applicants for marriage licenses they studied expressed any interest in entering into a prenuptial agreement. See Lynn Baker and Robert E. Emery, "When Every Relationship is Above Average: Perceptions and Expectations of Divorce at the Time of Marriage." *Law and Human Behavior* 17 (1993): 439, for the statistic that virtually no couples thought their own marriages would end in divorce.

30. Robert C. Ellickson, "Unpacking the Household: Informal Property Rights Around the Hearth." *Yale Law Journal* 116, no. 2 (2006): 226. Ellickson's article has recently been turned into a monograph, though page references herein are to the article. Robert C. Ellickson, *The Household: Informal Order around the Hearth*. Princeton, NJ: Princeton University Press, 2008.

31. Ellickson, "Unpacking the Household," 303–4 (see n. 30).

32. Ibid., 305.

33. I will argue later that even that much "keeping track" may be dangerous to the relationship. And Ellickson also notes the "staggering amounts of altruistic gift-giving" in love-infused households. Ibid., 281, n. 206. These are truly altruistic gifts, as opposed to gift exchange. Ibid., 305, n. 302.

34. Ibid., 308.

35. Ibid., 308.

36. Ibid., 309, n. 314.

37. Ernst Fehr et al. "Neuroeconomic Foundations of Trust and Social Preferences: Initial Evidence." *American Economic Review* 95, no. 2 (2005): 346.

38. Richard H. McAdams, "The Origin, Development, and Regulation of Norms." *Michigan Law Review* 96, no. 2 (1997): 338.

39. Ibid., 398.

40. Richard H. McAdams, "A Focal Point Theory of Expressive Law." *Virginia Law Review* 86, no. 8 (2000): 1649. McAdams and Janice Nagler test and find some support for this theory using two experimental games in Richard H. McAdams and Janice Nadler, "Coordinating in the Shadow of the Law: Two Contextualized Tests of the Focal Point Theory of Legal Compliance" (May 5, 2008). *Law and Society Review*, 42 (forthcoming); *Law and Society Review*, 42 (2008): 865–98; University of Chicago Law and Economics, Olin Working Paper No. 406; University of Chicago, Public Law Working Paper No. 184; Northwestern Law and Economics Research

Paper No. 08-04. Available at SSRN, http://ssrn.com/abstract=1016488 (accessed August 20, 2009).

41. Deines et al., "Covenant Marriage as a Signal" (see n. 20).

42. McAdams, "The Origin, Development, and Regulation of Norms" (see n. 39).

43. Chandra et al. *Fertility, Family Planning, and Reproductive Health*, 86, table 23 (see n. 7).

44. Kathleen Kiernan, "Cohabitation in Western Europe: Trends, Issues, and Implications." In Booth and Crouter, 171 (see n. 21); Smock and Gupta, 59 (see n. 21): "Given the wide variation in data, samples, measures of marital instability, and independent variables, the degree of consensus about this central finding is impressive."

45. Larry Bumpass and Hsien-Hen Lu, "Trends in Cohabitation and Implications for Children's Family Contexts in the United States." *Population Studies* 54, no. 1 (2000): 29; Susan L. Brown, "Child Well-Being in Cohabiting Families." In Booth and Crouter, 173 (see n. 21); Kiernan, "Cohabitation in Western Europe" (see n. 45).

46. Susan L. Brown and Alan Booth, "Cohabitation versus Marriage: A Comparison of Relationship Quality." *Journal of Marriage and the Family* 58, no. 3 (1996): 668; Jan E. Stets, "Cohabiting and Marital Aggression: The Role of Social Isolation." *Journal of Marriage and the Family* 53, no. 3 (1991): 669; Jan Stets and Murray A. Straus, "The Marriage License as a Hitting License: A Comparison of Assaults in Dating, Cohabiting and Married Couples." In *Violence in Dating Relationships: Emerging Social Issues*, edited by Maureen Pirog and J. E. Stets. New York: Praeger, 1989.

47. Shannan Catalano ("Intimate Partner Violence in the United States." U.S. Department of Justice, Office of Justice programs, Bureau of Justice Statistics, 2006, http://www.ojp.usdoj.gov/bjs/intimate/ipv.htm#contents [accessed August 20, 2009]) examines fatal and nonfatal violence by intimates (current or former spouses, girlfriends, or boyfriends) since the redesign of the National Crime Victimization Survey (NCVS) in 1993. The study reports a similar *number* of incidents of violence perpetrated by spouses and cohabitants (http://www.ojp.usdoj.gov/bjs/intimate/victims.htm [accessed August 20, 2009]). Since many more people were married than cohabiting, the *rate* for cohabitants is higher.

48. Nock, "Comparison of Marriages and Cohabiting Relationships" (see n. 17).

49. Martha A. Fineman, "Why Marriage?" *Virginia Journal of Social Policy and the Law* 9, no. 1 (2001): 239; Judith Stacey, "Good Riddance to 'the Family': A Response to David Popenoe." *Journal of Marriage and the Family* 55, no. 3 (1993): 545–47.

50. Steven L. Nock, "Why Not Marriage?" *Virginia Journal of Social Policy and the Law* 9, no. 1 (2001): 273; David Popenoe, "American Family Decline, 1960–1990: A Review and Appraisal." *Journal of Marriage and the Family* 55, no. 3 (1993): 527.

51. Nock, "Comparison of Marriages and Cohabiting Relationships" (see n. 17).

52. See, e.g., Wendy Manning and Pamela Smock, "Measuring and Modeling Cohabitation: New Perspectives from Qualitative Data." *Journal of Marriage and Family* 67, no. 4 (2005): 989, 998; Marsha Garrison, "Marriage Matters," 305–30 (see n. 18).

53. Posner, *Law and Social Norms*, 70–72 (see n. 23), develops this signaling story and applies it to marriage. So does William Bishop, "Is He Married? Marriage as Information." *University of Toronto Law Journal* 34 (1984): 245.

54. "I love you so, I always will / And though devotion rules my heart I take no bows / But Bill you're never gonna take those wedding vows." "Wedding Bell Blues" by Laura Nyro. Published in 1973 by Sony. (Whether the couple in the song is cohabiting as opposed to just in love is unclear from the lyrics). See also the statement in *Marvin v. Marvin*, 557 P.2d 106 (Cal. 1976) (Opinion of the Trial Court on Remand, Superior Court of Los Angeles County, 1979), reprinted in Carl E. Schneider and Margaret F. Brinig. *An Invitation to Family Law: Principles, Process, and Perspectives*. American Casebook Series, 3rd ed. St. Paul, MN: West Group, 2005, 533, 537. "On cross-examination, plaintiff testified that they were "always very proud of the fact that nothing held us. We weren't—we weren't legally married." After the breakup, she declared to an interviewer: We used to laugh and feel a great warmth about the fact that either of us could walk out at any time."

55. Brown and Booth, "Cohabitation Versus Marriage" (see n. 47); Brown, "Child Well-Being in Cohabiting Families" (see n. 46).

56. Linda J. Waite and Karen Joyner, "Emotional and Physical Satisfaction with Sex in Married, Cohabiting, and Dating Sexual Unions: Do Men and Women Differ?" *Sex, Love, and Health in America*, edited by Edward Laumann and Robert T. Michael. Chicago: University of Chicago Press, 2000, 239.

57. Wendy D. Manning, "The Implications of Cohabitation for Children's Well-Being." In Booth and Crouter, 121, 143 (see n. 21). A paper by Shelly Lundberg and Elaina Rose ("The Effects of Sons and Daughters on Men's Labor Supply and Wages." *Review of Economics and Statistics* 84, no. 2 (2002): 251) suggests that although men respond with more work and higher wages at the birth of a child, they do so significantly more in response to births of sons than to the births of daughters. The authors stated, "Our results are consistent with a model in which the gender composition of a couple's offspring affects the returns to marriage," Lundberg and Rose, 252. They found no difference of an effect of child gender on the labor-market outcomes of mothers.

58. Larry L. Bumpass and James A. Sweet, "National Estimates of Cohabitation." *Demography* 26, no. 4 (1989): 615; Neil G. Bennett, Ann Klimas Blanc, and David E. Bloom, "Commitment and the Modern Union: Assessing the Link between Premarital Cohabitation and Subsequent Marital Stability." *American Sociological Review* 53, no. 1 (1988): 127; William G. Axinn and Arland Thornton, "The Relationship between Cohabitation and Divorce: Selectivity or Causal Influence?" *Demography* 29, no. 3 (1992): 357; Bumpass and Lu, "Trends in Cohabitation" (see

n. 46); Smock and Gupta, "Cohabitation in Contemporary North America," 59–60 (see n. 21) (reviewing other studies).

59. Marsha Garrison, "Marriage Matters" (see n. 18).

60. Kathryn Edin and Maria Kefalas, *Promises I Can Keep: Why Poor Women Put Motherhood Before Marriage*. Berkeley: University of California Press, 2005.

61. Ibid., 6.

62. Ibid., 211.

63. "We saw that income accounted for about half of the difference in high school dropout rates, teen birth rates, and idleness rates between children in single-parent families as compared with children in two-parent families." Sara McLanahan and Gary Sandefur, *Growing up With a Single Parent: What Hurts, What Helps?* Cambridge, MA: Harvard University Press, 1994, 111.

64. The following argument is drawn in substantial part from Margaret F. Brinig and Steven L. Nock, "Legal Status and Effects on Children." *University of St. Thomas Law Review* 5, no. 2 (2009): 548.

65. Margaret F. Brinig and Steven L. Nock, "The One-Size Fits All Family." *Santa Clara Law Review* 49, no. 1 (2008): 137. The other variables held constant in the regressions in this book can be found in table 1.3. In addition to income, they include family form, legal status (marriage, divorce, adoption), race and ethnicity, education of the mother, and age of mother and child.

66. Alfred Lord Tennyson, *In Memoriam*, 1850, line 27, stanza 4.

67. Katherine Spaht, "The Modern American Covenant Marriage Movement: Its Origins and Its Future." In *Covenant Marriage in Comparative Perspective*, edited by John Witte Jr. and Eliza Ellison. Grand Rapids, MI: Eerdman's Publishing Company, 2005, 239–40.

68. Martha L. A. Fineman, "Masking Dependency: The Political Role of Family Rhetoric." *Virginia Law Review* 81, no. 8 (1995): 2181.

69. Ibid., 2194.

70. Dorothy Roberts, "Child Welfare and Civil Rights." *University of Illinois Law Review* 2003 (2003): 171. Orlando Patterson would agree only in part, since he believes that bad gender relations, stemming from slavery, cause the problems in the African American family. Orlando Patterson, *Rituals of Blood: Consequences of Slavery in Two American Centuries* New York: Basic Books, 1998.

71. See Fineman, "Masking Dependency" (see n. 69), and the more extended argument in Martha Albertson Fineman, *The Neutered Mother: The Sexual Family and Other Twentieth Century Tragedies*. New York: Routledge, 1995.

72. Dorothy Roberts, "The Moral Exclusivity of the New Civil Society." *Chicago-Kent Law Review* 75, no. 2 (2000): 555, 558.

73. Fineman, "Masking Dependency," 2183 (see n. 69); Nancy Polikoff, "We Will Get What We Ask For: Why Legalizing Gay and Lesbian Marriage Will Not 'Dismantle the Legal Structure of Gender in Every Marriage,'" *Virginia Law Review*

79, no. 7 (1993): 1535. More recently, Linda McClain suggests that marriage be retained, but with a profound commitment to gender equality. Linda C. McClain, *The Place of Families: Fostering Capacity, Equality, and Responsibility*. Cambridge, MA: Harvard University Press, 2006.

74. Martha Ertman, "The Business of Intimacy: Bridging the Private-Private Distinction." In *Feminism Confronts Homo Economicus*, edited by Martha Albertson Fineman and Terence Dougherty. Ithaca, NY: Cornell University Press, 2005, 467–500.

75. Roberts, "Moral Exclusivity," 571 (see n. 73).

76. Ibid., 579.

77. See, e.g., Michael J. Broyde, "The Covenant-Contract Dialectic in Jewish Marriage and Divorce Law" In Witte and Ellison, 53, 68–69 (see n. 68).

78. Law Commission of Canada, *Beyond Conjugality: Recognizing and Supporting Close Personal Adult Relationships*. Ottawa: Law Commission of Canada, 2001.

79. The history of the change in the Canadian understanding of marriage as well as the conclusion that "[m]arriage will remain a fundamental social institution in Canada" can be found in Nicholas Bala, "The History and Future of the 'Legal Family' in Canada." Queen's Faculty of Law, Legal Studies Research Paper Series, Working Paper, No. 07-16, 26, http://papers.ssrn.com/sol3/papers.cfm?abstract_id=1030534 (accessed August 20, 2009).

80. Robin Fretwell Wilson, "The Overlooked Costs of Religious Deference." *Washington and Lee Law Review* 64, no. 1 (2008): 4, is concerned about abuse in religious fundamentalist families.

81. Dorothy E. Roberts, "Kinship Care and the Price of State Support for Children." *Chicago-Kent Law Review* 76 (2001): 1619, is primarily concerned about families at risk for involvement in the child welfare system.

82. We can also say nothing directly about the effects of same-sex parenting, since no couples of that type self-identified in the data set. Even if they were represented at what is assumed to be the normal rate, according to table 1.1, this would only be .7% of unmarried households (which themselves comprise 27% of the total), or around .2% of the whole. In our sample of 3,000 children, that would be 6 children.

83. Posner, *Law and Social Norms* (see n. 23).

84. McAdams, "The Origin, Development, and Regulation of Norms" (see n. 39).

85. See, e.g., Henry N. Butler, "The Contractual Theory of the Corporation." *George Mason Law Review* 11 (1989): 99; Mitu Gulati, "When Corporate Managers Fear a Good Thing is Coming to an End: The Case of Interim Nondisclosure." *University of California Los Angeles Law Review* 46 (1999): 675, 713–16; Richard A. Posner, *Aging and Old Age*. Chicago: University of Chicago Press, 1995, 58ff.

86. Andrew Cherlin, "Remarriage as an Incomplete Institution." *American Journal of Sociology* 84, no. 3 (1978): 634.

87. Ibid., 643. More recently, see Jan Bartlema, "Modeling Step-Families: Exploratory Findings." *European Journal of Population* 4, no. 3 (1988): 197, 219.

88. Bartlema, "Modeling Step-Families," 197, 219 (see n. 88).

89. Cherlin, "Remarriage as an Incomplete Institution," 636 (see n. 87).

90. Ibid., 644.

91. Matthew D. Bramlett and William D. Mosher, "Cohabitation, Marriage, Divorce, and Remarriage in the United States." *National Center for Health Statistics, Vital Health Statistics* 23, no. 22 (2002): 78 and table 37. If there were two or more children, the probability falls to .70.

92. For a lengthy description, see David Popenoe, "The Evolution of Marriage and the Problem of Stepfamilies: A Biosocial Perspective." In *Stepfamilies: Who Benefits? Who does Not?* edited by Alan Booth and Judy Dunn. Hillsdale, NJ: Lawrence Erlbaum Associates, 1994, 3–27.

93. E. Mavis Hetherington and Kathleen M. Jodl, "Stepfamilies as Settings for Child Development." In Booth and Dunn, 55, 70 (see n. 93).

94. Susan D. Stewart, "How the Birth of a Child Affects Involvement with Stepchildren." *Journal of Marriage and Family* 67 (May 2005): 461, 463.

95. Robin Fretwell Wilson, "Children at Risk: The Sexual Exploitation of Female Children after Divorce." *Cornell Law Review* 86, no. 2 (2001): 251, 255. Wilson cites Rebecca M. Bolen, "Predicting Risk to be Sexually Abused: A Comparison of Logistic Regression to Event History Analysis." *Child Maltreatment* 3, no. 1 (1998): 157, 167. Bolen reports that 38.6% of a sample of 930 random individuals in California had been sexually abused before age 18, a figure that is 100 times the reported amount. What is probably more accurate is that holding other variables constant, children living with males in the household after separation of their birth parents were 3.4 times more likely to be sexually abused than those continuing to live with both parents. Bolen at 167.

96. Popenoe and Whitehead, *Should We Live Together?* (see n. 1).

97. For physical abuse, see Martin I. Wilson and Margo Daly, "Risk of Maltreatment of Children Living with Stepparents." In *Child Abuse and Neglect: Biosocial Dimensions*, edited by Richard J. Gelles and Jane B. Lancaster. New York: Aldine De Gruyter, 1987, 215–32. Preschool children living with unrelated male were nearly fifty times more likely to be killed than those living in a home with both parents. Heather A. Turner, David Finkelhor, and Richard Ormrod, "The Effect of Lifetime Victimization on the Mental Health of Children and Adolescents." *Social Science and Medicine* 62, no. 1 (2006): 13, 15.

98. Margaret F. Brinig and F. H. Buckley, "Parental Rights and the Ugly Duckling." *Journal of Law and Family Studies* 1, no. 1 (1999): 41, 52, 65 and table 3.

99. Sarah Hrdy, *Mother Nature: Maternal Instincts and How They Shape the Human Species*. New York: Ballantine Books, 2000. I thank an anonymous reader for this suggestion.

100. Lynn K. White and Alan Booth, "The Quality and Stability of Remarriages: The Role of Stepchildren." *American Sociological Review* 50, no. 5 (1985): 689–98, quoting Jessie Bernard, *Remarriage: A Study of Marriage*. New York: Dryden Books, 1956, 14.

101. Hetherington and Jodl, "Stepfamilies as Settings," 55, 57 (see n. 94).

102. For example, see Bramlett and Mosher, "Cohabitation, Marriage, Divorce, and Remarriage," 17, 26, tables 21, 41 (see n. 92). First marriage breaks up 33% of the time after ten years; second marriage without children at virtually the same rate, but when there is at least one child, at 42% and with an "unwanted" child, 44%.

103. Baker and Emery, "When Every Relationship is Above Average" (see n. 29).

104. Norval D. Glenn, "Biology, Evolutionary Theory, and Family Social Science." In Booth and Dunn, 45, 58 (see n. 93); Hetherington and Jodl, "Stepfamilies as Settings," 62–63 (see n. 94).

105. See, e.g., Lawrence A. Kurdek, "Remarriages and Stepfamilies Are Not Inherently Problematic." In Booth and Dunn, *Stepfamilies*, 37, 38 (see n. 93).

106. Lynn K. White and Alan Booth, "The Quality and Stability of Remarriages: The Role of Stepchildren." *American Sociological Review* 50, no. 5 (1985): 689.

107. It probably does not emanate from the stepchildren, since the greatest risk of abuse is to children under two years of age. Wilson and Daly, "Risk of Maltreatment,"215–32, table 9.2 (see n. 98).

108. Gary S. Becker, Elisabeth M. Landes, and Robert T. Michael, "An Economic Analysis of Marital Instability." *Journal of Political Economy* 85, no. 6 (1977): 1141.

109. Ibid., 1155. They analogize to a worker's specific capital in one firm lowering productivity once he or she moves to another because "accustomed" to the first firm's methods and organization. Ibid., n. 20.

110. White and Booth, "The Quality and Stability of Remarriages," 693, table 2 (see n. 101). A double remarriage (both parties divorced) with stepchildren was far more likely to end in divorce.

111. R. Turner, "Half of all Women Who Remarry Bear a Child with their New Spouse." *Family Planning Perspectives* 22, no. 5 (1990): 237.

112. White and Booth, "The Quality and Stability of Remarriages," 695 (see n. 101).

113. Ibid., 695, 696, table 5.

114. Ibid., 696.

115. Lynn White, "Stepfamilies over the Life Course: Social Support." In Booth and Dunn, *Stepfamilies*, 109, 115, 121, 123, table 9.2 (see n. 93).

116. Ibid., 130.

117. Elizabeth Marquardt, *Between Two Worlds: The Inner Lives of Children of Divorce*. New York: Crown Publishers, 2005, 57–58.

118. For some examples, see N.Y. Fam. Ct. Act § 415 (2007); *Ruben v. Ruben*, 461 A.2d 733 (N.H. 1983).

119. See, e.g., *Brinkerhoff v. Brinkerhoff*, 945 P.2d 113 (Utah 1997); Wash. Rev. Stat. §§ 26.16.205, 26.19.001 et seq.; *Bryan v. Bryan*, 645 P.2d 1267 (Az. 1982), see generally, 44 A.L.R.4th 520.

120. Bartlema, "Modeling Step-Families," 218 (see n. 88).

121. Susan D. Stewart, "How the Birth of a Child Affects Involvement with Step-children." *Journal of Marriage and Family* 67 (May, 2005): 461, 462, 467, table 2.

122. Marquardt, *Between Two Worlds* (see n. 118).

123. White, "Stepfamilies over the Life Course," 112, table 9.2 (see n. 116).

124. *Crane Ice Cream v. Terminal Freezing & Heating Co.*, 128 A. 280 (Md. 1925).

125. Ibid., 283.

126. *Burger King v. Family Dining*, 426 F. Supp. 485 (E.D. Pa. 1977).

127. *Lee v. Joseph E. Seagram & Sons, Inc.*, 552 F.2d 447 (2d Cir. 1977).

128. Ibid., 452.

129. *Nanakuli Paving & Rock Co. v. Shell Oil Co.*, 664 F.2d 772 (9th Cir. 1981).

130. Ibid., 788, n.23.

131. Hetherington and Jodl, "Stepfamilies as Settings," 66, 67 (see n. 94).

132. Samuel E. Vuchinich et al., "Parent-Child Interaction and Gender Differences in Early Adolescents' Adaptation to Stepfamilies." *Developmental Psychology* 27, no. 4 (1991): 618.

133. Nan Lin, *Social Capital: A Theory of Social Structure and Action*. New York: Cambridge University Press, 2001, 155, table 9.1.

134. Ibid., 158.

135. Peter Kollock, "The Emergence of Exchange Structures: An Experimental Study of Uncertainty, Commitment, and Trust." *American Journal of Sociology* 100, no. 2 (1994): 313–45.

136. Margaret F. Brinig and Steven L. Nock, "How Much Does Legal Status Matter? Adoptions by Kin Caregivers." *Family Law Quarterly* 36, no. 3 (2002): 449.

137. National datasets I have used (including the NSFH, Add Health, the PSID, and NLSY) all include very few black parents who have adopted. This folk wisdom is that African Americans do remove more than their share of children from foster care, see, e.g., http://encyclopedia.adoption.com/entry/black-adoptive-parent-recruitment-programs/67/1.html (accessed August 20, 2009), but I wonder whether this is to adoption or to kinship care. A recent case treats kinship guardians similarly to natural parents in a dispute between them and an unmarried biological father about relocation out of state. *New Jersey Division of Youth & Fam. Servs. v. T. M.*, 945 A.2d 39 (N.J. Sup Ct. App. Div., 2008).

138. See Institute of Judicial Administration and American Bar Association's Juvenile Justice Standards Project, *Standards Relating to Abuse and Neglect* § 6.6 (D).

139. The Adoption and Safe Families Act, Pub. L. No. 105–89, 111 Stat. 2115, codified as amended, 42 U.S.C. §§ 671, 675, 473A, 1320a-9. 629a (1994 & Supp. V

1995–2000), and cases like *Welfare of J. M.*, 574 N.W.2d 717 (Minn. 1998) illustrate this point.

140. P.L. 105–89, 105th Congress, 1997 H.R. 867. Sec. 2 (a) (ii), (II).

141. See Proclamation 7048, November 3, 1997 (William J. Clinton), announcing initiatives to double the number of adoptions from foster care by 2002 and stressing department policies that would advance that goal. Congress in P.L. 105th Congress-First Session, 1997, sec. 201, provided for adoption incentive payments in 42 U.S.C. § 673b (Supp. V. 1995–2000).

142. Dorothy Roberts, "Is There Justice in Children's Rights? The Critique of Federal Family Preservation Policy." *University of Pennsylvania Journal of Constitutional Law* 2, no. 1 (1999):112.

143. Madeleine L. Kurtz, "The Purchase of Families into Foster Care: Two Case Studies and the Lessons They Teach." *Connecticut Law Review* 26, no. 4 (1994): 1453; Betty Mandell, *Where are the Children? A Class Analysis of Foster Care and Adoption*. Lexington, KY: Lexington Books, 1973; Richard Kagan and Shirley Schlosberg, *Families in Perpetual Crisis*. New York: Norton, 1989.

144. For an extensive discussion, see Margaret F. Brinig, "Moving toward a First-Best World: Minnesota's Position on Multiethnic Adoptions." *William Mitchell Law* Review 28, no. 2 (2001): 553, nn. 23–34, 104–21.

145. Leslie Doty Hollingsworth, "Symbolic Interactionism, African American Families, and the Transracial Adoption Controversy." *Social Work* 44, no. 5 (1999): 443 (quoting Position Paper: "Preserving African American Families," National Association of Black Social Workers [1994]).

146. Perry calls this transmission "survival skills." Twila Perry, "The Transracial Adoption Controversy: An Analysis of Discourse and Subordination." *New York University Review of Law and Social Change* 21, no. 1 (1994): 33, 64 (referring to "complex skills for dealing with the subtle racism in our society). See also Valerie Phillips Hermann, "Transracial Adoption: 'Child-Saving' or 'Child-Snatching'." *National Black Law Journal* 13 (Spring 1993): 147, 160 (stating, "[M]ost supporters of the NABSW viewed transracial adoption as a conspiracy to destroy the Black race."). David L. Wheeler, "Black Children, White Parents: The Difficult Issue of Transracial Adoption." *Chronicle of Higher Education* (September 15, 1993): A9.

147. See, e.g., Catherine M. Brooks, "We Belong to 'Nobody's Children'—We Are the 'They' Who Must Change." *Capital University Law Review* 28, no. 1 (1999): 91.

148. Ibid., 94.

149. Rita J. Simon, "Transracial Adoptions: Does the Law Matter?" *American Experiment Quarterly* 2, no. 3 (1999): 85, 90.

150. Judith K. McKenzie, "Adoption of Children with Special Needs." *Future of Children* 3, no. 1 (1993): 62–76; Christine A. Bachrach et al., *Adoption in the 1980s*. Advanced Data from Vital and Health Statistics Report No. 181. Hyattsville,

MD: National Center for Health Statistics, 1989 (1% interracial adoptions by white mothers, including international adoptions).

151. National Council for Adoption, *Adoption Factbook III*. Washington, DC: National Council for Adoption, 1999, 127. Such payments are made to parents adopting "special needs" children.

152. Marianne Takas, *Kinship Care and Family Preservation: Options for States in Legal and Policy Development*. Washington, DC: American Bar Association Center on Children and the Law, 1994.

153. Naomi Cahn, "Children's Interests in a Familial Context: Poverty, Foster Care, and Adoption." *Ohio State Law Journal* 60, no. 4 (1999): 1189.

154. Center for Advanced Studies in Child Welfare, School of Social Work, University of Minnesota, "Kinship Care." *Practice Notes* no. 3 (1998): 2. In 1996, California paid $345 per child per month for foster care provided to children up to age four, $375 for children aged five to eight, and $484 for youths aged 15 or more. So, for example, if siblings ages 8 and 16 were in foster care, their caregiver would receive $859 per month. In contrast, California's AFDC payment for one child was $293 per month, and only $479 for two children. Jill Duerr Berrick, "When Children Cannot Remain Home: Foster Family Care and Kinship Care." *Future of Children* 8, no. 1, Protecting Children from Abuse and Neglect (1998): 72, 75.

155. Multiethnic Placement Act, 42 U.S.C. §671(18) (A) and (B), P.L. 103-432, Title II § 203(b), 108 Stat. 4456 (1994), as amended by Pub. L. 104-188, Title I, § 108(d) (2), August 22, 1996.

156. 42 U.S.C. § 675(E) (i).

157. 42 U.S.C.A. § 671(18) (West Supp. 1998).

158. 42 U.S.C. § 1320a-9 (C).

159. Faith Johnson Bonecutter and James P. Gleeson, *Achieving Permanency for Children in Kinship Foster Care: A Training Manual*; Howard Dubowitz, Susan Feigelman, and Susan Zuravin, "A Profile of Kinship Care." *Child Welfare* 72, no. 2 (March/April 1993), 153–69; Berrick, "When Children Cannot Remain Home," 78, table 2 (see n. 155); Susan J. Wells and Jean M. Agathen, *Evaluating the Quality of Kinship Foster Care*. Urbana: Children and Family Research Center, School of Social Work, University of Illinois at Urbana-Champaign, 1999.

160. Wells and Agathen, *Evaluating the Quality of Kinship Foster Care* (see n. 159).

161. However, nonkin foster parents were twice as likely as licensed kinship foster parents to have confirmed reports of maltreatment. Berrick, "When Children Cannot Remain Home," 79 (see n. 155).

162. For citations, see Brinig, "Moving toward a First-Best World," 578–79, nn. 82–91 (see n. 145).

163. Richard Udry and Peter Bearman, National Longitudinal Study of Adolescent Health, from the Carolina Population Center, Chapel Hill: University of North Carolina, 1994–95. The URL for the study is http://www.cpc.unc.edu/projects/

addhealth (accessed August 20, 2009). To protect the privacy of the children involved and their families, strict controls are maintained over use of the data.

164. Informal kinship care—live-in, daily care provided by relatives outside of the child welfare system—is provided to about 1.8 million children in the United States today, or 2.2% of the child population. Berrick, "When Children Cannot Remain Home," 80 (see n. 155).

165. The precise questions that make up the various indices are included in Brinig and Nock, "How Much Does Legal Status Matter?" 464, nn. 453–55 (see n. 137), as is significantly more statistical information.

166. Berrick, "When Children Cannot Remain Home," 82 (see n. 155).

167. For the majority of kin foster parents (and proportionately more than for "stranger" foster parents), there are no "special needs" other than race that would suggest payment of adoption subsidies. For nonkin, adopting a child with whom the parent already has formed bonds will more often incur no financial penalty. For the disproportionately less affluent kin caretaker, most adoptions come at a very high price. The United States Department of Health and Human Services, Washington, DC, 2003, AFCARS Report noted that 88% of the children adopted received an adoption subsidy, while 16% of the children adopted had been relatives (while "[r]elatives who were also foster parents were counted as relatives.").

168. These are authorized, even in cases where a child's ethnic background makes him or her difficult to place, by 42 U.S.C. § 673(c) (2).

169. National Council for Adoption, *Adoption Factbook*, 127 (see n. 152). The three states are Minnesota, Montana, and Colorado.

170. McAdams, "Focal Point" (see n. 41).

171. *In re May's Estate*, 114 N.E.2d 4 (N.Y. Court of App. 1953).

172. Ibid., 493 (emphasis added).

173. *Loving v. Virginia*, 388 U.S. 1 (1967).

174. *Naim v. Naim*, 87 S.E.2d 749 (Va. 1955).

175. Ibid., 756.

176. Laura Sanchez et al., "Is Covenant Marriage a Policy That Preaches to the Choir? A Comparison of Covenant and Standard Married Newlywed Couples in Louisiana." Bowling Green State University, 2002–6, Working Paper 48, http://www.bgsu.edu/organizations/cfdr/page46507.html (accessed August 20, 2009).

177. Margaret F. Brinig and Steven L. Nock, "What Does Covenant Mean for Relationships?" *Notre Dame Journal of Law and Public Policy* 18, no. 1 (2004): 137, 148, table 2. On average, the covenant ceremonies had 178 people in attendance. The average number at standard ceremonies was 109 (F sig < .001). The data come from the Marriage Matters survey and are reported there. All are in email attachment from SLN of July 16, 2003.

178. Posner, *Law and Social Norms*, 74 (see n. 23).

179. Margaret F. Brinig, "In Search of Prince Charming." *Journal of Gender, Race and Justice* 4 no. 2 (2001): 321, 334–35, nn. 383, 384.

180. Rose Krieder, "Interracial Marriage and Marital Instability" (PhD diss., University of Maryland, 1999), 6, 102, 136, table 1.2 (using the NSFG).

181. Ibid., app. C, 208–9. This is precisely the number that might be expected for black marriages, which disrupt at a higher rate than white marriages do. See M. D. Bramlett and W. D. Mosher, *Cohabitation, Marriage, Divorce, and Remarriage in the United States*. National Center for Health Statistics, Vital Health Statistic Report 23, Number 22, table 21 (http://www.cdc.gov/nchs/data/series/sr_23/sr23_022.pdf [accessed August 20, 2009]). Probability of first marriage disruption by duration of marriage and selected characteristics: All races, women 15–44 years of age, 1995, .03 (whites) and .05 (blacks) after one year; .32 (whites) and .47 (blacks) after 10 years.

182. *Chambers v. Ormiston*, 935 A.2d 956 (R.I. 2007).

183. Ibid., 972–73.

184. *Beth R. v. Donna M.*, 853 N.Y.S.2d 501 (N.Y. Sup. Ct. 2008).

185. Goodman, "Beyond the Enforcement Principle," 693 (see chap. 1, n. 9).

186. There was a progression of litigation that culminated in adoption of the Civil Union Bill in 2006, which permits the "voluntary union of two persons, which is solemnized and registered by either a marriage or a civil union."

187. McAdams, "The Origin, Development and Regulation of Norms," 403 (see n. 39).

188. *Lawrence v. Texas*, 539 U.S. 558 (2003).

189. Ibid., 567. See also *In re Marriage Cases*, 815–16, 783 P.3d 384 (Cal. 2008), noting "the opportunity to become a part of one's partner's family providing a wider and often critical network of economic and emotional security." *In re Marriage Cases*, 817.

190. *Baker v. State*, 744 A.2d 864 (Vt. 1999).

191. Ibid., 889. See also *In re Marriage Cases*, 183 P.3d 384 (Cal. 2008).

192. *In re Marriage Cases*, 183 P.3d 384 (Cal. 2008).

193. Making a theoretical argument for why the differences might matter, see Douglas W. Allen, "An Economic Assessment of Same-Sex Marriage." *Harvard Journal of Law and Public Policy* 29, no. 3 (2006): 949.

194. Margaret F. Brinig, "Empirical Work in Family Law." *University of Illinois Law Review* 2002, no. 4 (2002): 1083, offers more suggestions for how such a study might be designed.

195. Brinig and Nock, "Legal Status and Effects on Children," 574, table 7 (see n. 65).

196. Ibid., 569 table 5.

197. Ibid., 577, table 9.

198. Hillary Clinton, *It Takes a Village: And Other Lessons Children Teach Us*. New York: Simon & Schuster, 1996. A much more academic version appears in Peggy Cooper Davis, *Neglected Stories: The Constitution and Family Values*. New York: Hill and Wang, 1997.

199. *Moore v. City of East Cleveland*, 431 U.S. 494, 504 (1977).

200. Ibid., 506, 509 (Justices Brennan and Marshall concurring).

201. Orlando Patterson, *Rituals of Blood*. New York: Basic Books, 1998, 142 et seq.

202. L. Brown and Wendy D. Manning, "Family Boundary Ambiguity and the Measurement of Family Structure," *Demography* 46, no. 1 (2009): 85.

203. See http://www.theblackchurchpage.com (accessed March 1, 2009). It is "the anchoring institution in the Africa American Community." Mary Pattillo-McCoy, "Church Culture as a Strategy of Action in the Black Community." *American Sociological Review* 63, no. 6 (December 1998): 767, 769.

204. Pattillo-McCoy, "Church Culture as a Strategy," 770 (see n. 204). "Churches provide social and economic support by meeting emergency needs, providing a network of friends for emotional and physical well-being, and attending to families' special needs." Andrew Billingsley and Cleopatra Howard Caldwell, "The Church, the Family, and the School in the African American Community." *Journal of Negro Education* 60, no. 3, Socialization Forces Affecting the Education of African American Youth in the 1990s (Summer 1991), 427.

205. Pew Global Attitudes Survey, 2002, http://pewglobal.org/reports/display.php?ReportID=167 (accessed August 20, 2009).

206. This data is based upon the General Social Survey, 1998. Chicago: National Opinion Research Council.

207. The help variable is V15973 is Total Known Hours of Help Received from Head's/Wife's/"Wife's" Parents Outside the FU (0–72). The religion variable is importance of religion to you (respondent parent) asked in 2002, Q22J7. "Apart from attending religious services, how important would you say religion is to you?" (1–3).

208. These figures represent changes from the y-intercept while holding constant all other variables (a total of 23). These include who lives in the child's household, the legal status of the mother and her marital history, the age of the mother and child, parental warmth, and income (total family income divided by census needs standard). In figure 1.4, the hours of help received from the grandmother are not statistically significant; while the mother's religious belief is significant at the .014 level. In figure 1.5, while both values are statistically significant at $p < .01$, the size of the coefficients is quite different.

209. This terrain was well ploughed in, for example, Andrew M. Greeley, *Catholic High Schools and Minority Students* (Edison, NJ: Transaction Press, 2001); Timothy Walsh, *Parish School: American Catholic Parochial Education from Colonial Times to the Present* (Washington, DC: National Catholic Educational Association, 2003); Patrick J. McCloskey, *The Street Stops Here: A Year at a Catholic High School in Harlem* (Berkeley: University of California Press, 2008).

210. And this may have the unintended effect of hurting church attendance and religiosity according to Anthony Gill and Erik Lundsgaarde, "State Welfare Spending and Religiosity." *Rationality and Society* 16, no. 4 (2004): 399.

211. A recent paper has found that family support, and therefore relationship stability, increased for couples entering into civil unions in Vermont rather than simply remaining in same-sex relationships without the legal status. Kimberly F. Balsam, Theodore P. Beauchaine, Esther D. Rothblum, and Sondra E. Solomon. "Three-Year Follow-Up of Same-Sex Couples Who Had Civil Unions in Vermont, Same-Sex Couples Not in Civil Unions, and Heterosexual Married Couples." *Developmental Psychology* 44, no. 1 (2008): 102–11

212. Gill and Lundsgaarde, "State Welfare Spending," 406 (see n. 211).

213. Ibid., 405. The term is explained most fully in Phillip Nelson, "Information and Consumer Behavior." *Journal of Political Economy* 78, no. 2 (1970): 311–29.

214. Gill and Lundsgaarde, "State Welfare Spending," 408–11 (see n. 211). See also Eric A. Posner, "Symbols, Signals, and Social Norms in Politics and the Law." *Journal of Legal Studies* 27, no. 2, (1998):765,794, 795, for a somewhat earlier explanation.

215. Sheran Michelle and Christopher A. Swann, "The Take-Up of Cash Assistance among Private Kinship Care Families." *Children and Youth Services Review* 29, no. 8 (2007): 973–87.

Chapter Two

1. Aristotle, *Nicomachean Ethics*, Book 2, Chapter 3, http://www.greektexts.com/library/Aristotle/Nicomachean_Ethics/eng/573.html (accessed August 20, 2009).

2. Eric Posner, *Law and Social Norms* (see chap. 1, n. 23).

3. Ellickson, "Unpacking the Household," 226 (see chap. 1, n. 30).

4. Posner, *Law and Social Norms*, 74–78 (see chap. 1, n. 23).

5. McAdams, "The Origin, Development, and Regulation of Norms." 338 (see chap. 1, n. 38).

6. Ira Mark Ellman, "'Contract Thinking' was Marvin's Fatal Flaw." *Notre Dame Law Review* 76, no. 5 (2001): 1374, citing Steven L. Nock, "Time and Gender in Marriage." *Virginia Law Review* 86, no. 8, Symposium: The Legal Construction of Norms (2000): 1981.

7. Ellickson, "Unpacking the Household," 305 (see chap. 1, n. 30).

8. Gary S. Becker, "A Theory of Marriage: Part I." *Journal of Political Economy* 81, no. 4 (1973): 813.

9. Ira Mark Ellman, "Marital Roles and Declining Marriage Rates." *Family Law Quarterly* 4, no. 3 (2007): 455.

10. Frances K. Goldschneider and Linda J. Waite, *New Families, No Families? The Transformation of the American Home*. Berkeley: University of California Press, 1991, 204–5.

11. Peter Kollock, "The Emergence of Exchange Structures: An Experimental Study of Uncertainty, Commitment, and Trust." *American Journal of Sociology* 100, no. 2 (1994): 313.

12. Steven L. Nock and Margaret F. Brinig, "Weak Men and Disorderly Women: Divorce and the Division of Labor." In Dnes and Rowthorn, *The Law and Economics of Marriage and Divorce*, 171–90 (see chap. 1, n. 20).

13. This continues to hold true for the third wave. See Lisa Belkin, "When Mom and Dad Share It All." *New York Times*, June 15, 2008, MM column O, at p. 44.

14. Margaret F. Brinig and Steven L. Nock, "Covenant and Contract." *Regent University Law Review* 12, no. 1 (2000): 16. See also Nock, "Time and Gender in Marriage," 1981 (see n. 6).

15. Yoram Ben-Porath, "The F-Connection: Families, Friends, and Firms and the Organization of Exchange." *Population and Development Review* 6, no. 1 (1980): 3.

16. Milton C. Regan, *Family Law and the Pursuit of Intimacy*. New York: New York University Press, 1992: 19, 67.

17. Helen E. Fisher, "The Four-Year Itch." *Natural History* 96 (1987): 22, 33. Fisher maintains that "[p]ermanent relationships between compatible partners, in the right ecological circumstances, must have had genetic and cultural payoffs too."

18. Ellman, "'Contract Thinking,'" 1367 (see n. 6).

19. Ibid., 1375.

20. Nock, "Time and Gender in Marriage." 1975 (see n. 6).

21. Linda C. McClain, *The Place of Families: Fostering Capacity, Equality, and Responsibility*. Cambridge, MA: Harvard University Press, 2006.

22. Nock, "Time and Gender in Marriage." 1974 (see n. 6).

23. Steven L. Nock, "Turn-taking as Rational Behavior." *Social Science Research* 27, no. 3 (1998): 235.

24. Saul Levmore, "Love It or Leave It: Property Rules, Liability Rules, and Exclusivity of Remedies in Partnership and Marriage." *Law and Contemporary Problems* 58, no. 2, (1995): 221.

25. McClain, *The Place of Families* (see n. 21).

26. Becker, "A Theory of Marriage," 813–46 (see n. 8).

27. Steven L. Nock, *Marriage in Men's Lives*. Oxford: Oxford University Press, 1999. See also Sarah Fenstermaker Berk, *The Gender Factory: The Apportionment of Work in American Households*. New York: Plenum Press, 1995.

28. Carol Gilligan, *In a Different Voice: Psychological Theory and Women's Development*. Cambridge, MA: Harvard University Press, 1993.

29. See, e.g., Nock, *Marriage in Men's Lives*, 47 (see n. 27). Obviously, this isn't true for all situations for any of us and isn't true even for gender roles for some people. See, e.g., Jeffrey Eugenides, *Middlesex*. New York: Picador, 2003.

30. See Brian Braiker, "Just Don't Call Me Mr. Mom." *Newsweek*, October 08, 2007, 52–55; Michael Winerip, "Parenting: But Can Mr. Mom Tie a Ponytail?" *New York Times*, May, 13, 2007, 4.

31. This is the position of writers like Vicki Schultz. Vicki Schultz, "Life's Work." *Columbia Law Review* 100, 7 (2000): 1881.

32. See, for example, Katharine Silbaugh, "Turning Labor into Love: Housework and the Law." *Northwestern University Law Review* 91, 1 (1996): 1; Martha Albertson Fineman, "Masking Dependency: The Political Role of Family Rhetoric." *Virginia Law Review* 81, 8 (1995): 2181; Nancy D. Polikoff, "Recognizing Partners but Not Parents/Recognizing Parents but Not Partners: Gay and Lesbian Family Law in Europe and the United States." *New York Law School Journal of Human Rights* 17, no. 2 (2000): 711.

33. One thing they do is to add more traditional ideas about gender roles, particularly for boys. See, e.g., Megan Fulcher, Erin Sutfin, and Charlotte Patterson, "Individual Differences in Gender Development: Associations with Parental Sexual Orientation, Attitudes, and Division of Labor." *Sex Roles* 58, no. 5 (2008): 330. In general, they provide role models for how to become fathers. David Blankenhorn, *Fatherless America: Confronting Our Most Urgent Social Problem*. New York: Basic Books, 1995, 66.

34. See the evidence of the last chapter, showing greater exposure to abuse when living with stepfathers (David Finkelhor et al., "Sexually Abused Children in a National Survey of Parents: Methodological Issues." *Child Abuse and Neglect* 21 (1997): 1–9) and particularly their mothers' boyfriends (Leslie Margolin, "Child Abuse Mothers' Boyfriends: Why the Overrepresentation?" *Child Abuse and Neglect* 16 (1992): 541–51). See also Robin Fretwell Wilson, "Children at Risk: The Sexual Exploitation of Female Children after Divorce." *Cornell Law Review* 86, no. 2 (2001): 251.

35. Margaret F. Brinig, "Does Parental Autonomy Require Equal Custody at Divorce?" *Louisiana Law Review* 65, no. 4 (2005): 1345, 1372–74, tables 2–4.

36. Nock, *Marriage in Men's Lives*, 50 (see n. 27) (citing many sources including David Gilmore, *Manhood in the Making: Cultural Concepts in Masculinity*. New Haven, CT: Yale University Press, 1990, 41–42; and John E. Williams and Deborah L. Best, *Measuring Sex Stereotypes: A Multi-Nation Study*. Thousand Oaks, CA: Sage Publications, 1990, 228.

37. Margaret F. Brinig and Steven L. Nock, "'I Only Want Trust': Norms, Trust, and Autonomy." *Journal of Socio-Economics* 32, no. 5 (2003): 471–87.

38. See, e.g., *Havell v. Islam*, 751 N.Y.S.2d 449 (N.Y. App. Div. 2002). See generally Laura Ann McCloskey et al., "A Comparative Study of Battered Women and Their Children in Italy and the United States." *Journal of Family Violence* 17, no. 1 (2002): 53–74.

39. Margaret F. Brinig, "The Story of Mary Sue and Junior Davis." In *Family Law Stories*, edited by Carol Sanger. New York: Foundation Press, 2008, 195–218, 199.

40. Margaret F. Brinig, "Penalty Defaults in Family Law: The Case of Child Custody." *Florida State University Law Review* 33, no. 3 (2006): 779.

41. Shelly Lundberg and Elaina Rose, "Investments in Sons and Daughters: Evidence from the Consumer Expenditure Survey." In *Family Investments in Children:*

Resources and Behaviors That Promote Success, edited by Ariel Kalil and Thomas DeLeire. Philadelphia: Lawrence Erlbaum Associates, 2004, 163–80. Shelly Lundberg and Elaina Rose, "Child Gender and the Transition to Marriage." *Demography* 40, no. 2, (2003): 333–49 (4% higher expenditures on housing by U.S. married couples with one boy than on couples with one girl and same level of income).

42. Shelly Lundberg, "Sons, Daughters, and Parental Behavior." *Oxford Review of Economic Policy* 21, no. 3 (2005): 340–56.

43. Lundberg and Rose, "Child Gender and the Transition to Marriage" (see n. 41).

44. See, e.g., Lundberg, "Sons, Daughters, and Parental Behavior" (see n. 42). S. Philip Morgan and Michael Pollard, "Do Parents of Girls Really Have a Higher Risk of Divorce? Revisiting Father Involvement and Marital Stability." Paper presented at the annual meetings of the Population Association of America, Atlanta, GA, May 9–11, 2002; (less true in CPS after 1988).

45. S. P. Morgan, D. Lye, and G. Condran, "Sons, Daughters, and the Risk of Marital Disruption." *American Journal of Sociology* 94, no. 1 (1988): 110–29.

46. See, e.g., Lundberg, *supra* n. 42; Aphra R. Katzev, Rebecca L. Warner, and Alan C. Acock, "Girls or Boys? Relationship of Child Gender to Marital Instability." *Journal of Marriage and Family* 56, no. 1 (1994): 89–100.

47. See, e.g., Lundberg, "Sons, Daughters, and Parental Behavior," 350, 352 (see n. 42).

48. In nearly 68% of the 687 cases involving noncustodial fathers, at least one boy was involved, compared to 57% where at least one girl was involved. The difference is statistically significant at $p < .001$. For noncustodial mothers, the comparable numbers for the 54 cases were 59.3% and 63% (not statistically significant). Data is available on request from the author.

49. Shelly Lundberg and Robert A. Pollak, "Do Husbands and Wives Pool Their Resources? Evidence from the United Kingdom Child Benefit." *Journal of Human Resources* 32, no. 3 (1997): 463–80. This was an empirical study based upon the authors' earlier theoretical work, Shelly Lundberg and Robert A. Pollak, "Bargaining and Distribution in Marriage." *Journal of Economic Perspectives* 10, no. 4 (1996): 139–58.

50. Bina Agarwal, "'Bargaining' and Gender Relations: Within and Beyond the Household." *Feminist Economics* 3, no. 1 (1997): 2, n. 2.

51. Steven L. Nock, "The Marriages of Equally Dependent Spouses." *Journal of Family Issues* 22, no. 6 (2001): 755–75.

52. Agarwal, "'Bargaining' and Gender Relations" (see n. 50). She cites Paula England and Barbara Kilbourne, "Markets, Marriages, and Other Mates: The Problem of Power." In *Beyond the Marketplace: Rethinking Economy and Society*, edited by R. Friedman and A. F. Robertson. New York: Aldine de Gruyter, 1990.

53. Agarwal, "Bargaining' and Gender Relations" (see n. 50).

54. Ibid., 25–27.

55. Liana C. Sayer and Suzanne M. Bianchi, "Women's Economic Independence and the Probability of Divorce: A Review and Reexamination." *Journal of Family Issues* 21, no. 7 (2000): 906–43.

56. Nock, "The Marriages of Equally Dependent Spouses," 770 (see n. 51).

57. Sayer and Bianchi, "Women's Economic Independence," 938 (see n. 55).

58. Margaret F. Brinig and Douglas W. Allen, "'These Boots Are Made for Walking': Why Most Divorce Filers are Women." *American Law and Economics Review* 2, no. 1 (2000): 126–69.

59. Nock, "The Marriages of Equally Dependent Spouses," 774 (see n. 51).

60. Ibid., 762.

61. Ibid., 765.

62. Ibid., 768.

63. Ibid., 770.

64. Sara Raley and Suzanne Bianchi, "Sons, Daughters, and Family Process: Does Gender of Children Matter?" *Annual Review of Sociology* 32, no. 1 (2006): 401; Merril Silverstein, "Stability and Change in Temporal Distance between the Elderly and their Children." *Demography* 32, no. 1 (1995): 29–46.

65. Eunju Lee, Glenna Spitz, and John Logan, "Social Support to Parents-in-Law: The Interplay of Gender and Kin Hierarchies." *Journal of Marriage and Family* 65 (2003): 396–403.

66. Raley and Bianchi, "Sons, Daughters, and Family Process," 416 (see n. 64).

67. Nora Underwood, "Mid-life panic: Thousands of Canadians are Caught between Children and Elderly Parents," *Maclean's*, August 19, 1991.

68. Gerald J. Jogerst et al., "Domestic Elder Abuse and the Law." *American Journal of Public Health* 93, no. 12 (2003): 2131–36.

69. Margaret F. Brinig et al., "The Public Choice of Elder Abuse Law." *Journal of Legal Studies* 33, no. 2 (2004): 517–49.

70. Fisher, "The Four-Year Itch" (see n. 17).

71. Posner, *Law and Social Norms*, 76 (see chap. 1, n. 23).

72. See, for example, literature on community reaction to spousal violence in Donna Coker, "Enhancing Autonomy for Battered Women: Lessons from Navajo Peacemaking." *UCLA Law Review* 47, no. 1 (1999): 1.

73. Posner, *Law and Social Norms*, 77 (see chap. 1, n. 23).

74. McAdams, "Origins of Social Norms," 413–17 (see chap. 1, n. 38) (discusses gossip in terms of "nosy" or other-regarding norms, and used in the negative example of enforcing norms against interracial dating).

75. For a lengthier discussion, see Margaret F. Brinig, "Equality and Sharing: Views of Household across the Iron Curtain." *European Journal of Law and Economics* 7, no. 1 (1999): 55–63.

76. This was the rule of the GDR Supreme Court. "Every person, and also every woman, has to put her working capacity at the service of the fulfillment of the eco-

nomic plan." Supreme Court, Decision of December 1, 1950, 1 Entscheidungen des Obersten / gerichts in Zivilsachen (OCZ) 65, 67.

77. Wilhelm Wolf, "Shall Housekeeping Tasks Become a Duty for Husbands?" *European Journal of Law and Economics* 7, no. 1 (1999): 47–53.

78. Inga Markovits, "Marriage and the State: A Comparative Look at East and West German Family Law." *Stanford Law Review* 24, no. 1 (1971): 138, n. 168; that according to the East German Institute for Market Research in Leipzig, in 1968 men were only doing 6.8% of the cooking, 12.5% of the cleaning, 2.9% of the laundry, and 11.8% of the shopping. The labor-force rates are reported in Brinig, 56, (see n. 75).

79. Brinig, "Equality and Sharing," 59 (see n. 75), notes that the East German divorce rate was 3.0 per thousand population in 1989 compared to 1.9 per thousand population in West Germany.

80. Inga Markovits, "Family Traits." *Michigan Law Review* 88, no. 6 (1990): 1734, 1751.

81. Pierre-Carl Michaud, *Employment Dynamics of Married Women in Europe*. Bonn: IZA, 2005, reports that as of 2005, the number for all married women in Germany was 65.1%, and 81% for the highly educated, http://ideas.repec.org/p/iza/izadps/dp1706.html (accessed August 20, 2009).

82. Rates for the U.S. are from Dan Black, Natalia Kolesnikova, and Lowell Taylor, *The Labor Supply of Married Women: Why Does It Differ Across U.S. Cities?* Research Division, Federal Reserve Bank of St. Louis, Working Papers 2207-43b, 2007 30, table 2 (http://ideas.repec.org/p/fip/fedlwp/2007-043.html [accessed August 20, 2009]) (50 metropolitan areas). For Europe, they come from Pierre-Carl Michaud and Konstantinos Tatsiramos, *Employment Dynamics of Married Women in Europe*. IZA Discussion Papers, 1706, Institute for the Study of Labor (IZA), 2005, http://ideas.repec.org/p/iza/izadps/dp1706.html (accessed August 20, 2009).

83. *Marvin v. Marvin*, 557 P.2d 106, 110 (Cal. 1976).

84. Margaret Brinig, "The Influence of *Marvin v. Marvin* on Housework during Marriage." *Notre Dame Law Review* 76, no. 5 (2001): 1311.

85. See, e.g., Martha L. Fineman, "Implementing Equality: Ideology, Contradiction, and Social Change." *Wisconsin Law Review* 1983, no. 4 (1983):789–886, 809–11.

86. Doris Jonas Freed and Henry H. Foster, "Family Law in the Fifty States: An Overview." *Family Law Quarterly* 17, no. 3 (1984): 365, 381, table 5.

87. See Susan Westerberg Prager, "Sharing Principles and the Future of Marital Property Law." *University of California Los Angeles Law Review* 24, no. 1 (1977): 1; Michael J. Vaughn "The Policy of Community Property and Inter-Spousal Transactions." *Baylor Law Review* 19, no. 1 (1967): 20, 21.

88. See, e.g., Isabel Marcus, "Locked In and Locked Out: Reflections on the History of Divorce Law Reform in New York State." *Buffalo Law Review* 37, no. 2

(1988–89): 375, 450, n. 255, stating that otherwise the system is fundamentally unfair.

89. See Margaret F. Brinig, "Property Distribution Physics: The Talisman of Time and Middle Class Law." *Family Law Quarterly* 31, no. 1 (1997): 93–118.

90. See June Carbone, "Economics, Feminism, and the Reinvention of Alimony: A Reply to Ira Ellman." *Vanderbilt Law Review* 43, no. 5 (1990): 146, 1487, n. 100.

91. American Law Institute, *Principles of the Law of Family Dissolution*, § 5.05 (see chap. 1, n. 5).

92. See Nock, "Turn-taking as Rational Behavior," 238–39 (see n. 23).

93. Nancy Staudt, "Taxing Housework, *Georgetown Law Journal* 84, no. 5 (1996): 1571, 1647.

94. See, e.g., "UGA President's Wife to Receive Stipend." *Florida Times-Union*, October 19, 2000, B5 (reporting that the president's wife will receive a $30,000 annual compensation). See generally Julianne Basinger, "A Paycheck for Presidents' Spouses?" *Chronicle of Higher Education*, September 22, 2000, A37.

95. See Fineman, "Masking Dependency," 2200 (see n. 32).

96. See generally Scott M. Stanley et al., "Strengthening Marriages and Preventing Divorce: New Directions in Prevention Research." *Family Relations* 44, no. 4, Helping Contemporary Families (1995): 392–401; see also William Doherty Home Page, http://www.drbilldoherty.org (accessed August 20, 2009).

97. Katharine T. Bartlett, "Feminism and Family Law." *Family Law Quarterly* 33, no. 3 (1999): 475–500. Feminists have questioned "the justice of a legal regime that has permitted, even reinforced, the subordination of some family members to others."

98. This section draws on Brinig and Nock, "I Only Want Trust" (see n. 37).

99. Elizabeth S. Scott and Robert E. Scott, "Marriage as Relational Contract." *Virginia Law Review* 84, no. 7 (1998): 1225.

100. National Conference of Commissioners on Uniform State Laws, *Uniform Premarital Agreement Act*. St. Paul, MN: West Publishing Company, 1983, vol. 9B.

101. Steven L. Nock, Laura A. Sanchez, and James D. Wright. *Covenant Marriage: The Movement to Reclaim Tradition in America*. New Brunswick, NJ: Rutgers University Press, 2008.

102. Ibid., 10.

103. Stewart Macaulay, "Non-Contractual Relations in Business: A Preliminary Study." *American Sociological Review* 28, no. 1 (1963): 55.

104. *Nanakuli Paving & Rock Co. v. Shell Oil Co.*, 664 F.2d 772 (9th Cir. 1981).

105. Judith Wallerstein and Sandra Blakeslee, *The Good Marriage*. Boston: Houghton-Mifflin, 1995.

106. Johann W. von Goethe, *Elective Affinities*. Translated by David Constatine. Oxford: Oxford University Press, 1994, 65.

107. Steven L. Nock, "A Comparison of Marriages and Cohabiting Relationships." *Journal of Family Issues* 16, no. 1 (1995): 53–76.

108. Elizabeth Marquardt, *Between Two Worlds: The Inner Lives of Children of Divorce*. New York: Crown Publishing, 2005.

109. I thank Dean Patricia O'Hara for this suggestion. See, e.g., Elaine Appleton Grant, "First, the Merger Then, the Culture Clash: How to Fix the Little Things That Can Tear a Company Apart." *Inc.*, January 2008, 38–39; Joann S. Lublin and Bridget O'Brian, "Merged Firms Often Face Culture Clash." *Wall Street Journal*, February 14, 1997, Eastern Edition, 229, A9A.

110. Iowa Code § 596.5 (2003).

111. Carl E. Schneider, "The Channeling Function in Family Law." *Hofstra Law Review* 20, no. 3 (1992): 495, 497; Regan, *Family Law and the Pursuit of Intimacy*, 269–74 (see n. 16).

112. Arlie Hochschild, *The Time Bind: When Work Becomes Home and Home Becomes Work*. New York: Holt, 1997, 123–24.

113. The NSFH was first administered in 1987–88 and included personal interviews with 13,007 respondents from a national sample. The NSFH was administered by the Center for Demography and Ecology of the University of Wisconsin-Madison.

114. John H. Johnson and Christopher J. Mazingo, "The Economic Consequences of Unilateral Divorce for Children." University of Illinois CBA Office of Research Working Paper 00-0112, July 2000, http://ssrn.com/abstract=236227 (accessed August 20, 2009).

115. Tim B. Heaton and Stan L. Albrecht, "Stable Unhappy Marriages." *Journal of Marriage and the Family* 53, no. 3 (1991): 747–58.

116. Paul R. Amato, "The Consequences of Divorce for Adults and Children." *Social Science Research* 62, no. 4 (2000): 1269–87.

117. Regan, *Family Law and the Pursuit of Intimacy* (see n. 16).

118. Elizabeth S. Scott and Robert E. Scott, "Parents as Fiduciaries." *Virginia Law Review* 81, no. 8 (1995): 2401.

119. Brinig and Nock, "I Only Want Trust" (see n. 37).

120. Barbara Bennett Woodhouse, "Hatching the Egg: A Child-Centered Perspective on Parents' Rights." *Cardozo Law Review* 14, no. 6 (1993): 1746; David D. Meyer, "Family Ties: Solving the Constitutional Dilemma of the Faultless Father." *Arizona Law Review* 41, no. 3 (1999): 753; Carol Sanger, "Separating from Children." *Columbia Law Review* 86, (1996): 375.

121. The ALI *Principles* (see chap. 1, n. 5), call this "decision making responsibility." See id. comment (e) to § 2.03, 48, which notes that it gives the parent "the authority to make significant decisions delegated to parents as a matter of law, such as those relating to health care, education, permission to marry at certain ages, or to enlist in the military."

122. Judith A. Seltzer, "Legal Custody Arrangements and Children's Economic Welfare." *American Journal of Sociology* 96, no. 4 (1991): 895–929; Catherine A. Albiston, Eleanor E. Maccoby, and Robert R. Mnookin, "Does Joint Legal Custody Matter?" *Stanford Law and Policy Review* 2 (1990): 167.

123. Judith A. Seltzer, "Father by Law: Effects of Joint Legal Custody on Nonresident Fathers' Involvement with Children." *Demography* 35, no. 1 (1998): 135–46.

124. Devon W. Carbado and G. Mitu Gulati, "Conversations at Work." *Oregon Law Review* 79 (2000): 103.

125. Robert J. Sampson, Jeffrey D. Morenoff, and Felton Earls, "Beyond Social Capital: Spatial Dynamics of Collective Efficacy for Children." *American Sociological Review* 64, no. 5 (1999): 633–60; Coleman, "Social Capital" (see intro., n. 3); James S. Coleman, *Foundations of Social Theory*. Cambridge, MA: Harvard University Press, 1990.

126. Allen W. Parkman, "Why Are Married Women Working So Hard." *International Review of Law and Economics*, 18 (1998): 41.

127. This section is drawn from Brinig and Allen, "These Boots are Made for Walking," 142, table 3 (see n. 58).

128. Scott and Scott, "Parents as Fiduciaries" (see n. 118).

129. *Troxel v. Glanville*, 530 U.S. 57, 65 (2000).

130. Marsha Garrison, "Autonomy or Community? An Evaluation of Two Models of Parental Obligation." *California Law Review*, 86, no. 1 (1998): 41, 57.

131. Robert E. Fay, "The Disenfranchised Father." *Advances in Pediatrics* 36 (1989): 415.

132. Joan Williams, "Gender Wars: Selfless Women in the Republic of Choice." *New York University Law Review* 66 (1991): 1559.

133. Mary Ann Mason, *The Custody Wars: Why Children Are Losing the Battle and What We Can Do About It*. New York: Basic Books, 1999, 7.

134. Fay, "The Disenfranchised Father," 407 (see n. 131).

135. Robert H Mnookin, "Child Custody Adjudication: Judicial Functions in the Face of Indeterminacy." *Law and Contemporary Problems* 39, Summer (1975): 226.

136. Lloyd Cohen, "Marriage, Divorce and Quasi-Rents; or 'I Gave Him the Best Years of My Life,'" *Journal of Legal Studies* 16, no. 2 (1987): 267, 300–302; Ira Mark Ellman, "Should the *Theory of Alimony* Include Nonfinancial Losses and Motivations?" *Brigham Young University Law Review* 1991, no. 1 (1991): 259.

137. Sayer and Bianchi, "Women's Economic Independence," 929–31, 938 (see n. 55).

138. Nock, *Marriage in Men's Lives*, 5 (see n. 27); Linda Waite and Maggie Gallagher, *The Case for Marriage*. New York: Doubleday, 2000.

139. American Law Institute, *Principles of the Law of Family Dissolution*, § 209(1) (a) (see chap. 1, n. 5).

140. The complete scale can be found in Nock and Brinig, "I Only Want Trust," 478–79 (see n. 37).

141. Lenore Sawyer Radloff, "The CES-D Scale: A Self-Report Depression Scale for Research in the General Population." *Applied Psychological Measure-*

ment 1, no. 3 (1977): 385–401; D. A. Santor and J. C. Coyne, "Shortening the CES-D to Improve Its Ability to Detect Cases of Depression." *Psychological Assessment* 9, no. 3 (1997): 233.

142. Steven E. Finkel, *Causal Analysis with Panel Data.* Beverley Hills, CA: Sage Publications, 1995, 4–6.

143. The equation includes two values of each variable that might change for each wave of interviews, the value at time 1 and at time 2 (or a measure of change between waves). Since factors such as race cannot change, these are entered only once. The outcome (dependent variable) is the depression scale, and its value in the first round of interviews is entered as an independent variable. This makes it possible to study how the scores on this scale change over time.

144. Dierdre D. McCloskey and Stephen H. Zillak, "The Standard Error of Regressions." *Journal of Economic Literature* 34, no. 3 (1996): 97.

145. Nock, *Marriage in Men's Lives*, 50–52, 58–59 (see n. 27).

146. Jamil S. Zainaldin. "The Emergence of a Modern American Family Law: Child Custody, Adoption, and the Courts, 1796–1851." *Northwestern University Law Review* 73, no. 6 (1979): 1038.

147. Edward Kruk, "The Disengaged Noncustodial Father: Implications for Social Work Practice with the Divorced Family." *Social Work* 39, no. 1 (1994): 15–25.

148. Marilyn Ihinger-Tallman, "Problems in Remarriage: An Exploratory Study of Intact and Terminated Remarriages." *Journal of Divorce and Remarriage* 20, no. 1 (1993): 63; Sally C. Clarke and Barbara F. Wilson, "Remarriages: A Demographic Profile." *Journal of Family Issues* 13, no. 9 (1992): 123.

149. American Law Institute, *Principles of the Law of Family Dissolution*, § 6.04 (see chap. 1, n. 5).

150. Brinig and Allen, "These Boots Are Made for Walking" (see n. 58).

151. Ibid.

152. Richard Chused, Private Acts in Public Places: A Social History of Divorce in the *Formative Era of American Family Laws*. Philadelphia: University of Pennsylvania Press, 1994; Lawrence M. Friedman and Robert Percival, "Rights of Passage: Divorce Law in Historical Perspective." *Oregon Law Review* 63, (1984): 671, 675, 681.

153. B. G. Gunter and Doyle P. Johnson, "Divorce Filing as Role Behavior: Effect of No-Fault Law on Divorce Filing Patterns." *Journal of Marriage and Family* 40, no. 3 (1978): 571, 572, table 1.

154. Barbara Stark, "Divorce Law, Feminism, and Psychoanalysis: In Dreams Begin Responsibilities." *University of California Los Angeles Law Review* 38, no. 6 (1991): 1483, 1514, n. 149.

155. Friedman and Percival, "Rights of Passage" (see n. 151).

156. Ibid.

157. For two of many studies, see Greg G. Duncan and Saul D. Hoffman, "A Reconsideration of the Economic Consequences of Marital Dissolution." *Demography*

22, no. 4 (1985): 485; Richard R. Peterson, "A Re-Evaluation of the Economic Consequences of Divorce," 61, no. 3 *American Sociological Review* (1996): 528; Pamela J. Smock, "Gender and the Short-Run Economic Consequences of Marital Disruption." *Social Forces* 73, no. 1 (1994): 243.

158. Andrew Cherlin, *Marriage, Divorce, Remarriage*. Cambridge, MA: Harvard University Press, 1992.

159. Cohen, "Marriage, Divorce, and Quasi-Rents," 267–304 (see n. 136).

160. For examples, see Judith Wallerstein and Joan B. Kelly, *Surviving the Breakup: How Children and Parents Cope with Divorce*. New York: Basic Books, 1980; Hetherington E. Mavis et al., "Effects of Divorce on Parents and Children." In *Nontraditional Families: Parenting and Child Development*, edited by Michael E. Lamb. Hillsdale, NJ: Lawrence Erlbaum Associates, 1982.

161. Allen M. Parkmen, *No-Fault Divorce: What Went Wrong?* Boulder, CO: Westview Press, 1992, 85; Cohen, "Marriage, Divorce and Quasi-Rents," 288–89 (see n. 136).

162. Gunter and Johnson, "Divorce Filing as Role Behavior," 572–73 (see n. 152).

163. Cohen, "Marriage, Divorce and Quasi-Rents" (see n. 136).

164. Sanford L. Braver, Marnie Whitley, and Christine Ng, "Who Divorced Whom? Methodological and Theoretical Issues." *Journal of Divorce and Remarriage* 20 (1993): 1–19.

165. Judith Wallerstein and Julia Lewis, "Sibling Outcomes and Disparate Parenting and Stepparenting after Divorce." *Psychoanalytic Psychology* 24, no. 3 (2007): 554–458; Suzanne Bianchi, *Family Disruption and Economic Hardship: The Short-Run Picture for Children*. Washington, DC: U.S. Dept. of Commerce Bureau of the Census, 1991 (for sale by Supt. of Docs. U.S. G.P.O.).

166. NSFH, Wave 2, Self-Enumerated Codebook Primary Respondent and Ex-Spouse, Which Spouse, SE-3, MT308 0173. Data acquired from James A. Sweet and Larry L. Bumpass, "The National Survey of Families and Households, Waves 1 and 2: Data Description and Documentation." Center for Demography and Ecology, University of Wisconsin–Madison, 1996, http://www.ssc.wisc.edu/nsfh/home.htm (accessed August 25, 2009).

167. This is not merely just what is reported; clinical studies show a lower prevalence rate of first-onset major depression for women than for men. Martha L. Bruce and Kathleen M. Kim, "Differences in the Effects of Divorce on Major Depression in Men and Women." *American Journal of Psychiatry* 149, no. 7 (1992): 914–17. For health benefits, see Charlotte A. Schoenborn and Marie Marano, *Health Characteristics of Married and Unmarried Persons, Current Estimates from the National Health Interview Survey*, Series 10, No. 166. Hyattsville, MD: U.S. Bureau of the Census, 1988. Women get some psychological benefits from marriage that they do not receive when single. However, divorced and separated women got higher marks for personal autonomy and sufficiency as well as personal growth. Nadine F.

Marks, "Flying Solo at Midlife: Gender, Marital Status, and Psychological Well-Being." *Journal of Marriage and Family* 58, no. 4 (1996): 917–32.

168. Catherine Riessman, *Divorce Talk: Women and Men Make Sense of Personal Relationships*. New Brunswick, NJ: Rutgers University Press, 1990.

169. Heaton and Albrecht, "Stable Unhappy Marriages" (see n. 115).

170. Martin Zelder, "Inefficient Dissolutions as a Consequence of Public Goods: The Case of No-Fault Divorce." *Journal of Legal Studies* 22 (1994): 503.

171. Victor Fuchs, *Women's Quest for Economic Equality*. Cambridge, MA: Harvard University Press, 1988, 72.

172. E. Mavis Hetherington et al., "What Matters? What Does Not? Five Perspectives on the Association between Marital Transitions and Children's Adjustment." *American Psychologist* 53, no. 2 (1998): 167–84.

173. Ann M. Driscoll, Comment, "In Search of a Standard: Resolving the Relocation Problem in New York." *Hofstra Law Review* 26, no. 1 (1997): 175.

174. Jordan Paul, "'You Get the House. I Get the Car. You Get the Kids. I Get Their Souls.' The Impact of Spiritual Custody Awards on the Free Exercise Rights of Custodial Parents." *University of Pennsylvania Law Review* 138, no. 2 (1989): 583; David B. Ezra, "Sticks and Stones Can Break My Bones, But Tobacco Smoke Can Kill Me." *Saint Louis University Public Law Review* 13, no. 2 (1994): 547, 574–90; Brooke A. Masters, "Child Custody's Moving Problem." *Washington Post*, September 20, 1998, B1.

175. Yoram Weiss and Robert Willis, "Transfers among Divorced Couples: Evidence and Interpretation." *Journal of Labor Economics* 11, no. 4 (1993): 629–79.

176. Herma Hill Kay, "An Appraisal of California's No-Fault Divorce Law." *California Law Review* 75, no. 1 (1987): 291; Ira Ellman, "The Theory of Alimony." *California Law Review* 77, no. 1(1989): 1.

177. Yoram Weiss and Robert Wills, "Children as Collective Goods in Divorce Settlements." *Journal of Labor Economics* 3, no. 3 (1985): 268; Margaret F. Brinig, "The Family Franchise: Elderly Parents and Adult Siblings." *Utah Law Review* 1996, no. 2 (1996): 393, 421–23.

178. June Carbone, *From Partners to Parents: The Second Revolution in Family Law*. New York: Columbia University Press, 2000, 180.

179. Mavis et al., "Effects of Divorce on Parents and Children" (see n. 159).

180. Margaret F. Brinig and F. H. Buckley, "Joint Custody: Bonding and Monitoring Theories." *Indiana Law Journal* 73, no. 2 (1998): 393, 393–427; Joan C. Williams, *Unbending Gender: Why Family and Work Conflict and What to Do About It*. Oxford: Oxford University Press, 1999.

181. Fay, "The Disenfranchised Father" (see n. 131).

182. Margaret F. Brinig, "Feminism and Child Custody under Chapter Two of the American Law Institute's Principles of the Law of Family Dissolution." *Duke Journal of Gender Law and Policy* 8, Spring/Summer (2001): 301.

183. In the NSFH, we do not know who filed for divorce, but we do know who got custody.

184. See Belkin, "When Mom and Dad Share It All" (see n. 13).

185. This does not mean that no-fault decreases the number of divorces; in fact, the evidence is to the contrary. There is some evidence that no-fault has increased the divorce rate. Margaret F. Brinig and F. H. Buckley, "No-Fault Laws and At-Fault People." *International Review of Law and Economics* 18, no. 3 (September 1998): 325; Leora Friedberg, "Did Unilateral Divorce Raise Divorce Rates? Evidence from Panel Data." *American Economic Review* 88, no. 3 (1998): 608–27; Douglas W. Allen, "Marriage and Divorce, Comment." *American Economic Review* 82, no. 3 (1992): 679–93.

186. American Law Institute, *Principles of the Law of Family Dissolution*, § 2.07 (see chap. 1, n. 5).

187. Margaret F. Brinig, "Penalty Defaults in Family Law" (see n. 40); Brinig, "Does Parental Autonomy Require Equal Custody at Divorce?" (see n. 35). Another, under review, is Douglas W. Allen and Margaret F. Brinig, "Anticipated and Unanticipated Legal Changes: The Case of Joint Parenting." Department of Economics, Simon Fraser University.

188. Again, please note that the Oregon terminology (as opposed to the way the federal government wants the status classified, and therefore the way the Department of Vital Statistics recorded the result) is "parenting arrangements."

189. This "longer view" was calculated using data from the *National Center for Health Statistics, Marriage and Divorce Data, 1989–95*, CD-ROM, issued October 1997. The data is also available on the Center's Web site, http://www.nber.org/data/marrdivo.html (accessed August 20, 2009). I extracted the Oregon divorces (a sample of the total divorces in the state—a total of 22,019 for the seven years) and eliminated those with missing custody data or those with no children. I totaled the number of children in each custody arrangement and divided the "joint custody" number by the "total number of custody children."

190. Robert H. Mnookin and Lewis A. Kornhauser, "Bargaining in the Shadow of the Law: The Case of Divorce." *Yale Law Journal* 88, (1979): 950.

191. Child support is set according to statewide guidelines mandated by Congress. Oregon's current version can be found online at http://www.dcs.state.or.us/forms/csf020809f.pdf (accessed August 20, 2009). These went into effect March 26, 2003. The prior version appears at http://www.dcs.state.or.us/oregon_admin_rules/guidelines_archive.htm (accessed August 20, 2009). Before 2003, the amount authorized for two children in a family with a combined gross income of $1,500 a month was $375. For a combined gross income of $3,000 a month, the amount was $673. According to the inflation calculator found at http://www.bls.gov (accessed August 20, 2009), $375 in 1995 had the equivalent spending power of $469.98 in 2002. Conversely, $375 in 1995 would only have purchased $299.21 in 2002. Similarly, the $673 in child support awarded in 1995 would only have purchased $536.99 worth of

goods in 2002. So despite the apparent lack of change, the recipient was worse off in 2002 than in 1995.

192. Making filing possible for pro se modification or enforcement petitioners was one of the explicit goals of the Oregon Task Force Report that proposed the 1997 legislation.

193. The new authorized amount for two children when parents have a combined income of $1,500 a month is $411, while it is $754 for a combined income of $3,000. The first change does not meet the inflation rate, while the second exceeds it (http://www.dcs.state.or.us/forms/csf020809f.pdf [accessed August 20, 2009]).

194. The spousal support amount seems to have decreased (from an average of $165.89 to $109.52 a month), though it was only awarded in about 10% of the cases and, thus, is not statistically significant.

195. These failed mediation cases take up very significant court time. If the case is resolved by some other method, the average number of incidents is 33. If the divorce comes after a trial following a failed mediation, the average incidents is 53.

196. For many years, the academic literature has suggested that cases involving domestic violence are particularly bad candidates for mediation. Lisa Lerman, "Mediation of Wife Abuse Cases: The Adverse Impact of Informal Dispute Resolution on Women." *Harvard Women's Law Journal* 7, no. 1 (1984): 57. There were 48 cases in which there was a domestic violence order and a failed mediation, and only 69 with a successful mediation. This comparison of course does not include the other costs of forcing such spouses to mediate.

Chapter Three

1. This section is drawn substantially from two prior works, Margaret Brinig, "Troxel and the Limits of Community." *Rutgers Law Journal* 32, no. 3 (2001): 733–81; Margaret F. Brinig, "Community Involvement and Its Limits in Marriage and Families." In *Revitalizing the Institution of Marriage for the Twenty-First Century*, edited by Alan J. Hawkins, Lynn D. Wardle, and David Orgon Coolidge. Westport, CT: Praeger, 2002, 15–28.

2. Margaret Brinig, *From Contract to Covenant: Beyond the Law and Economics of the Family*. Cambridge, MA: Harvard University Press, 2000; Brinig and Nock, "Covenant and Contract," 9–26 (see chap. 2, n. 14).

3. Ben-Porath, "The F-Connection," 1–30 (see chap. 2, n. 15).

4. Posner, *Law and Social Norms*, 82 (see chap. 1, n. 23).

5. Ben-Porath, "The F-Connection," 11 (see chap. 2, n. 15).

6. Ibid., 3.

7. Ibid., 4.

8. Ibid., 5.

9. Ibid., 12.

10. Brinig and Buckley, "Joint Custody," 393 (see chap. 2, n. 180); Weiss and Willis, "Children as Collective Goods," 288 (see chap. 2, n. 177); Judith A. Seltzer, "Consequences of Marital Dissolution for Children." *Annual Review of Sociology* 20, no. 1 (1994): 235.

11. Brinig and Buckley, "Joint Custody," 408 (see chap. 2, n. 180); for discussions of the principal-agent problem generally, see Robert Cooter and Bradley J. Freedman, "The Fiduciary Relationship: Its Economic Character and Legal Consequences." *New York University Law Review* 66, no. 4 (1991): 1045; Stephen A. Ross, "The Economic Theory of Agency: The Principal's Problem." *American Economic Review* 63, no. 2 (1973): 134; as applied to parents, Scott and Scott, "Parents as Fiduciaries." 2401–7 (see chap. 2, n. 118).

12. Ira C. Lupu, "The Separation of Powers and the Protection of Children." *University of Chicago Law Review* 61, no. 4 (1994): 1317–74.

13. Scott and Scott, "Marriage as Relational Contract," 1267 (see chap. 2, n. 99).

14. Ibid., 1269, 1298.

15. *Foster v. Bass*, 575 So. 2d 967 (Miss. 1990).

16. Ben-Porath, "The F-Connection" 21–22 (see chap. 2, n. 15).

17. Ibid., 22.

18. Scott and Scott, "Parents as Fiduciaries" (see chap. 2, n. 118).

19. Such shared tasks were a striking feature in the books of Laura Ingalls Wilder's Little House series. See also Glenda Riley, *The Female Frontier: A Comparative View of the Prairie and the Plains*. Lawrence: University Press of Kansas, 1988; Herb Plambeck, *Iowa's Heritage of Pioneer Family Farms*. Ames, IA: Sigler Printing and Publishing, 1996; Glenda Riley, *Prairie Voices: Iowa's Pioneering Women*. Ames: Iowa State University Press, 1996.

20. See Coleman, "Social Capital," S104 (see intro., n. 3).

21. Sampson, Morenoff, and Earls, "Beyond Social Capital," 633–60 (see chap. 2, n. 125).

22. A survey by the AFL-CIO noted that "nearly half of all women who are married or living with someone (46%) say they work a different schedule from their spouses or domestic partners. Among married women with young children, the figure rises to 51%." According to their Web site, "During 1999, the AFL-CIO Working Women's Department hosted 5,000 group discussions in kitchens, workplaces, conference rooms, and town halls around the country. In January 2000, the AFL-CIO followed up with a scientific survey of a large and nationally representative random sample of working women 18 and older." The results can be found at www.aflcio.org/mediacenter/prsptm/pr03092000.cfm, "New Findings on Working Women's Irregular Hours Help Explain Stresses in Balancing Work and Family, March 9, 2000.

23. For a fictional account, see Amy Tan, *The Joy Luck Club*. New York: Ivy Books, 1989. For a discussion of a similar institution among Hispanic immigrants,

see Charles Daum, O.P., *Parish Ministry in a Hispanic Community*. New York: Paulist Press, 2004.

24. These financial institutions, and those in many other cultures, are reviewed extensively by Eric A. Posner, "The Regulation of Groups: The Influence of Legal and Nonlegal Sanctions on Collective Action." *University of Chicago Law Review* 63, no. 1 (1996): 133. Collective action and its relationship with social norms are well discussed in Jenny Onyx and Paul Bullen, "Measuring Social Capital in Five Communities." *Journal of Applied Behavioral Science* 36, no. 1 (2000): 23–42.

25. Francis Fukuyama, *Trust: The Social Virtues and the Creation of Prosperity*. New York: Free Press Paperbacks, 1995, 300–302; Ivan Hubert Light and Edna Bonacich, *Immigrant Entrepreneurs: Koreans in Los Angeles,* 1965–1982. Berkeley: University of California Press, 1988, 272.

26. Fukuyama, *Trust*, 270 (see n. 25).

27. Clifford Geertz, "The Rotating Credit Association: A 'Middle Rung' in Development." *Economic Development and Cultural Change* 10, no. 3 (1962): 246–48; Hubert Light and Bonacich, *Immigrant Entrepreneurs*, 248 (see n. 25).

28. Anthony Kronman, "Contract Law and the State of Nature." *Journal of Law, Economics, and Organization* 1, no. 1 (1985): 1–32.

29. Chalandra M. Bryant and Rand D. Conger, "Marital Success and Domains of Social Support in Long-Term Relationships: Does the Influence of Network Members Ever End?" *Journal of Marriage and Family* 61, no. 2 (1999): 447.

30. Regan, *Family Law and the Pursuit of Intimacy* (see chap. 2, n. 16).

31. See, e.g., Catharine E. Beecher and Harriet Beecher Stowe, *The American Woman's Home*. New York: J. B. Ford and Company, 1869; *Cradle of the Middle Class: The Family in Oneida County, New York,* 1790–1865. New York: Cambridge University Press, 1981, 40.

32. Lawrence W. Sherman, "Domestic Violence and Restorative Justice." *Virginia Journal of Social Policy and the Law* 8, no. 1 (2001): 263–89.

33. Sherman was earlier a leading advocate of mandatory arrest in domestic violence cases. Lawrence W. Sherman, Douglas A. Smith, Janell D. Schmidt, and Dennis P. Rogan, "Crime, Punishment, and Stake in Conformity: Legal and Informal Control of Domestic Violence." *American Sociological Review* 57, no. 5 (1992): 680–90.

34. For a complete account, see Coker, "Enhancing Autonomy for Battered Women," 32–33, chap. 2, n. 72.

35. Robert Yazzie, "'Life Comes from It': Navajo Justice Concepts." *New Mexico Law Review* 24, no. 2 (1994): 178, n. 22.

36. James W. Zion and Elsie B. Zion, "Hozho' Sokee'—Stay Together Nicely: Domestic Violence under Navajo Common Law." *Arizona State Law Journal* 25, no. 2 (1993): 415.

37. Witherspoon, Gary. *Navajo Kinship and Marriage*. Chicago: University of Chicago Press, 1996, 37.

38. Coker, "Enhancing Autonomy for Battered Women," 45–46 (see chap. 2, n. 72), "First, the abuser or his family or both may agree to provide nalyeeh (reparations) in the form of money, goods, or personal services for the victim. Nalyeeh is a concrete recognition that the harm of battering is real and that responsibility for it extends beyond the individual batterer."

39. Sherman, Smith, Schmidt, and Rogan, "Crime, Punishment, and Stake in Conformity" (see n. 33); Lawrence W. Sherman, Janell D. Schmidt, Dennis P. Rogan, and Douglas A. Smith. "The Variable Effects of Arrest on Criminal Careers: The Milwaukee Domestic Violence Experiment." *Journal of Criminal Law and Criminology* 83, no. 1 (1992): 137.

40. See generally John Braithwaite, *Restorative Justice and Responsive Regulation*. New York: Oxford University Press, 2002; Sherman, Smith, Schmidt, and Rogan, "Crime, Punishment, and Stake in Conformity" (see n. 33).

41. Clinton, *It Takes a Village* (see chap. 1, n. 198).

42. Virginia and Tennessee have different waiting periods for those divorcing on no-fault grounds with and without children. See Va. Code § 20-91(9) (a) (six months separation for those without children; one year with minor children and a separation agreement); Tenn. Code Ann. § 36-4-103(3) ("irreconcilable differences" divorce requires a 90-day-from-filing waiting period if there are children; 60 days if not).

43. Elizabeth S. Scott, "Rational Decisionmaking about Marriage and Divorce." *Virginia Law Review* 76, no. 1 (1990): 9–94; Parkman, *No-Fault Divorce: What Went Wrong?* (see chap. 2, n. 161).

44. Mary Ann Glendon, "Family Law Reform in the1980s" *Louisiana Law Review* 44, no. 6 (1984): 1553–73; Judith T. Younger, "Light Thoughts and Night Thoughts on the American Family." *Minnesota Law Review* 76, no. 4 (1992): 891–916.

45. For two relatively recent constitutional challenges to state statutes that reach opposite conclusions, see *Curtis v. Kline*, 666 A.2d 265 (Pa. 1995) (violates equal protection to require college education support only of divorced parents) and *Crocker v. Crocker*, 971 P.2d 469 (Or. 1998) (rational basis for requiring payment for college education only from divorced parents).

46. See, e.g., Annette Baran and Reuben Pannor, "Open Adoption." In *The Psychology of Adoption*, edited by David Brodzinsky and Marshall D. Schechter. New York: Oxford University Press, 1990, 316.

47. See, e.g., *Alma Soc'y, Inc. v. Mellon*, 601 F.2d 1225 (2d Cir), cert denied, 444 U.S. 995 (1979); *In re Roger B.*, 418 N.E.2d 751 (Ill.), app. dism'd, 454 U.S. 806 (1981).

48. See, e.g., Lisa Bernstein, "Merchant Law in a Merchant Court: Rethinking the Code's Search for Immanent Business Norms." *University of Pennsylvania Law Review* 144, no. 5 (1996): 1765; Lisa Bernstein, "Opting Out of the Legal System: Extralegal Contractual Relations in the Diamond Industry." *Journal of Legal Stud-*

ies 21, no. 1 (1992): 115; Jennifer Gerarda Brown and Ian Ayres, "Economic Rationales for Mediation." *Virginia Law Review* 80, no. 2 (1994): 327.

49. Mark M. Gray, Paul M. Perl, and Tricia C. Bruce, *Marriage in the Catholic Church: A Survey of U.S. Catholics*. Washington, DC: Center for Applied Research in the Apostolate, Georgetown University, 2007, 71.

50. This of course is part of the message of Posner and McAdams, discussed in chapter 1. See also the discussion of Deines et al., "Covenant Marriage as a Signal," 11 (see chap. 1, n. 20).

51. Gary S. Becker, "The Economic Way of Thinking." *Journal of Political Economy* 205 (1993) (guilt); see also, John Locke, *Second Treatise of Government*, 1690, par. 66.

52. Donald Cox and Oded Stark, "Intergenerational Transfers and the Demonstration Effect." Boston College Working Papers in Economics, no. 329 (1998), http://ideas.repec.org/p/boc/bocoec/329.html#provider (accessed August 20, 2009).

53. See David Crary, "Interracial Adoption Debate Plagues Family." *Harrisburg Patriot*, July 3, 2000, B20; see also *In re Adoption No.* 12612 (Md. Ct. App. 1999) and comments by Arlo Wagner, "Pixley Loses Custody." *Washington Times*, January 12, 2000.

54. Jennifer Roback Morse, *Love and Economics: Why the Laissez-Faire Fam ily Doesn't Work*. New York: Spence Publishing, 2001, 25–38. See also Margaret F. Brinig and F. H. Buckley, "The Price of Virtue." *Public Choice* 98, (1–2) (January 1999): 111–29.

55. A complete list appears at http://www.wowpages.com/specialmoments/wedding.html (accessed August 20, 2009). These quandaries often form the backdrop for the good-natured banter on the sports radio talk show "Mike and Mike."

56. See, e.g., Brinig and Allen, "These Boots Are Made for Walking," 126 (see chap. 2, n. 58) (divorce rate); Brinig and Buckley, "The Price of Virtue," 119, 120, tables 3–4 (see n. 54) (unwed births).

57. Posner, *Law and Social Norms* (see chap. 1, n. 23).

58. For a recent case, see *Powell v. Lane*, 275 S.W.3d 666, 2008 WL 375969 (Ark. Ct. App.) For a statute, see, e.g., Va. Code Ann. § 20-14.2 (2000). Even in states that recognize common law marriages, the preferred and much more common ceremonial form requires a license. See, e.g., Iowa Code § 595.3 (2000).

59. See, e.g., Iowa Code Ann § 595.1 ("Marriage is a civil contract, requiring the consent of the parties capable of entering into other contracts, except as herein otherwise declared") and the fairly typical Iowa Code Ann § 595.2 (1996) (age of 18, except that minors between 16 and 18 may marry with parental consent with a judicial bypass provision of "consent has been unreasonably withheld").

60. See, e.g., Iowa Code Ann. § 595.19 (1996) (persons related by blood or who has a living husband or wife).

61. For another and particularly vivid example, consider the Moroccan (Islamic) traditions described in M. E. Combs-Schilling's *Sacred Performances* (New York:

Columbia University Press, 1989), where through a number of processions, visits to a spring, and finally gun play, the bridegroom joins the elder generation of men, symbolically reestablishing the Muslim community.

62. See generally Sheryl Scheible, "Defining 'Support' Under the Bankruptcy Law: Revitalization of the 'Necessaries' Doctrine." *Vanderbilt Law Review* 41, no. 1 (1988): 1.

63. See, e.g., *In re Higgason's Marriage*, 516 P.2d 289 (Cal. 1973); *Favrot v. Barnes*, 332 So. 2d 873 (La. Ct. App. 1976); *Matthews v. Matthews*, 162 S.E.2d 697 (N.C. Ct. App. 1968); *Cumming v. Cumming*, 102 S.E. 572, 574 (Va. 1920).

64. The legislation is collected at "Americans for Divorce Reform," http://www.divorcereform.org (accessed August 20, 2009).

65. See Brinig, "The Family Franchise," 404–5 (see chap. 2, n. 177).

66. Regan, *Family Law and the Pursuit of Intimacy*, 26–27 (see chap. 2, n. 16) (citing Steven Mintz and Susan Kellogg, *Domestic Revolutions: A Social History of American Family Life*. New York: Free Press, 1988, 48).

67. Kronman, "Contract Law and the State of Nature" (see n. 28).

68. This slogan of the Family Rosary Crusade, founded by Father Patrick Peyton, appeared on numerous bumper stickers in the 1970s.

69. For example, Catholics must obtain ecclesiastical annulments before they can remarry. Orthodox Jewish women need to obtain their husband's get, compare *Avitzur v. Avitzur*, 58 N.Y.2d 108, 459 N.Y.S.2d 572, 446 N.E.2d 136 (N.Y. 1983). See generally Joel Nichols, "Multi-Tiered Marriage: Ideas and Influences from New York and Louisiana to the International Community." *Vanderbilt Journal of Transnational Law* 40, no. 1 (2007): 135–96.

70. See Gray, Perl, and. Bruce, *Marriage in the Catholic Church*, 7 (see n. 49); see Maja Beckstrom, "Pollster's Data Tell Churches How Their Believers Behave." *Commercial Appeal (Memphis)*, August 17, 1996, 16A.

71. Margaret F. Brinig, "Unhappy Contracts: The Case of Divorce Settlements." *Review of Law and Economics* 1, no. 2 (2005): 266, table 3.

72. Vaughn R. A. Call and Tim B. Heaton, "Religious Influence on Marital Stability." *Journal for the Scientific Study of Religion* 36, no. 3 (1997): 382–92; Paul Nakonezy, Robert D. Shull, and Joseph Lee Rodgers, "The Effect of No-Fault Divorce Law on the Divorce Rates Across the 50 States and Its Relation to Income, Education, and Religiosity." *Journal of Marriage and the Family* 57, no. 2 (1995): 477–88; George Gallo and Jim Castelli, "Attitudes on Marriage Surveyed, Catholic, Protestant Divorce Rates Similar." *Washington Post*, April 8, 1989, C13; Larry L. Bumpass, Teresa Castro, and James A. Sweet, "Recent Trends in Marital Disruption." *Demography* 26, no. 1 (1990): 37–52.; Tim B. Heaton and Edith L. Pratt, "The Effects of Religious Homogamy on Marital Satisfaction and Stability." *Journal of Family Issues* 11, no. 2 (1990): 191–207.

73. Call and Heaton, "Religious Influence on Marital Stability," 386–87 (see n. 72).

74. Ibid., 383. See also Deines et al., "Covenant Marriage as a Signal," 45, table 1 (see chap. 1, n. 20), showing that 51.4% of the covenant married couples attended church every week as a couple compared to 13.4% of the standard married couples, while 54.5% of the covenant couples felt it was extremely important for spouses to feel the same way about religion.

75. Call and Heaton, "Religious Influence on Marital Stability,"391 (see n. 72), citing Walter R. Schumm, "Beyond Relationship Characteristics of Strong Families: Constructing a Model of Family Strengths." *Family Perspective* 19, no. 1 (1985): 1; Lynn K. White and Alan Booth, "Divorce over the Life Course: The Role of Marital Happiness." *Journal of Family Issues* 12, no. 1 (1991): 5.

76. Call and Heaton, "Religious Influence on Marital Stability," 391 (see n. 72).

77. Gray, Perl, and Bruce, *Marriage in the Catholic Church*, 7 (see n. 49).

78. Scott J. South and Glenna Spitze, "Determinants of Divorce over the Marital Life Course." *American Sociological Review* 51, no. 4 (1986): 589; to the same effect, but adding to parental effectiveness, see Sampson, Morenoff, and Earls, "Beyond Social Capital" (see chap. 2, n. 125). See also Marygold S. Melli and Patricia R. Brown, "Exploring a New Family Form: The Shared Time Family." *International Journal of Law, Policy and the Family* 22, no. 2 (2008): 231, showing the effect of home stability resulting from joint custody on children.

79. Brinig and Buckley, "No-Fault Laws and at-Fault People." 335, 337, table 5 (see chap. 2, n. 185) (citing other studies for the urban finding).

80. Margaret F. Brinig, "Finite Horizons: The American Family." *International Journal of Children's Rights* 2, no. 3 (1994): 293, details laws requiring support of aged parents and the relationship between treatment of children and aged parents living in the home. See also Fukuyama, *Trust*, 150 (see n. 25).

81. This is the Fourth of the Ten Commandments, Exodus 20:12.

82. Both the Old Testament books of Exodus and Leviticus and in the New Testament parables and epistles stress the need to support the elderly widow and orphan (see, e.g., Deut. 24:19–21, Job 24:21, Timothy 5:3–8,) and the duty to support one's own aged parents (Exodus 20:12, Lev. 20:9, Lev. 19:3, Eph. 6:1).

83. The facts that the Amish did not use public welfare and were exempted from Social Security because of their community's self-sufficiency were noted by the court in *Wisconsin v. Yoder*, 406 U.S. 205, 222 (1972).

84. See the example in Deines et al., "Covenant Marriage as a Signal," 33–34 (see chap. 1, n. 20). But see also W. Bradford Wilcox, "Conservative Protestant Childrearing: Authoritarian or Authoritative?" *American Sociological Review* 63, no. 6 (1998): 796–809.

85. See (for Asian marriages generally) Yasmin Alibhai-Borwn, "Marriage of Minds Not Hearts." *New Statesman and Society* 6, no. 239 (1993): 28.

86. William G. Archer, *Songs for the Bride: Wedding Rites of Rural India*. New York: Columbia University Press, 1985, 177.

87. Liao Cailian and Tim B. Heaton, "Divorce Trends and Differentials in China." *Journal of Comparative Family Studies* 23, no. 3 (1992): 422. See also Xu Xiaohe and Martin King Whyte, "Love Matches and Arranged Marriages: A Chinese Replication." *Journal of Marriage and Family* 52, no. 3 (1990): 709–23.

88. Cailian and Heaton, "Divorce Trends and Differentials in China," 417 (see n. 87).

89. Francis L. K. Hsu, *Under the Ancestors' Shadow: Kinship, Personality, and Social Mobility in China*. Stanford, CA: Stanford University Press, 1971, 95.

90. Carol M. Rose, "The Comedy of the Commons: Custom, Commerce, and Inherently Public Property." *University of Chicago Law Review* 53, no. 3 (1986): 742.

91. For a description of the ceremony, including the prayers recited by the couple, the rabbi, and the community, see www.jewishvirtuallibrary.org/jsource/Judaism/marriage.html.

92. See http://www.african-weddings.com/jumping_the_broom (accessed August 20, 2009). The history of the broom ceremony discussion comes from Harriette Cole. *Jumping the Broom: The African-American Wedding Planner*. New York: H. Holt, 1993, 17–18. For a similar ritual, the Thai Rod-Nam-Sang, see Kriengsak Niratpattanasai, "Thai Wedding Customs," http://www.apmforum.com/columns/thai15.htm (accessed August 20, 2009).

93. Diane H. Felmlee, "No Couple Is an Island: A Social Network Perspective on Dyadic Stability." *Social Forces* 79, no. 4 (2001): 1259–87.

94. Posner, *Law and Social Norms* (see chap. 1, n. 23).

95. See, e.g., Mary Ann Glendon, *The New Family and the New Property*. Boston: Butterworth, 1981; John L. Langbein, "The Twentieth-Century Revolution in Family Wealth Transmission." *Michigan Law Review* 86, no. 4 (1988): 722.

96. This is certainly a part of Catholic doctrine. See Pope John Paul II, Familiaris Consortio [On the Family] No. 21 (1981); and Pope John Paul II, Letter to Families, No. 7, 8 (1994); see generally Teresa Stanton Collett, "Marriage, Family and the Positive Law." *Notre Dame Journal of Law, Ethics, and Public Policy* 10, no. 2 (1996): 476.

97. See, e.g., Gary S. Becker, Elisabeth M. Landes, and Robert Michael, "An Economic Analysis of Marital Instability." *Journal of Political Economy* 5, no. 6 (1977): 1141–87; Andrew Cherlin, "The Effect of Children on Marital Dissolution." *Demography* 14, no. 3 (1977): 265; Joan Huber and Glenna Spitze; "Considering Divorce: An Expansion of Becker's Theory of Marital Instability." *American Journal of Sociology* 86, no. 1 (1980): 75–89; South and Spitze, "Determinants of Divorce Over the Marital Life Course" (see n. 78); Linda J. Waite, Gus W. Haggstrom, and David E. Kanouse, "The Consequences of Parenthood for the Marital Stability of Young Adults." *American Sociological Review* 50, no. 6 (1985): 850–57; compare Arland Thornton, "Changing Attitudes toward Separation and Divorce: Causes and Consequences." *American Journal of Sociology* 90, no. 4 (1985): 856 (attitudes about divorce unfavorable when preschoolers were present).

98. Nock and Brinig; "Weak Men and Disorderly Women," 171–90 (see chap. 2, n. 12); Brinig and Allen, "These Boots Are Made for Walking" (see chap. 2, n. 58).

99. Jody VanLaningham, David R. Johnson, and Paul Amato, "Marital Happiness, Marital Duration, and the U-Shaped Curve: Evidence from a Five-Wave Panel Study." *Social Forces* 79, no. 4 (2001): 1313–41.

100. See, e.g., Glendon, "Family Law Reform in the 1980s" (see n. 44); Scott, "Rational Decisionmaking about Marriage and Divorce" (see n. 43); Judith T. Younger, "Responsible Parents and Good Children." *Law and Inequality* 14, no. 2 (1986): 489–520.

101. Brinig and Buckley, "Joint Custody," 402 (see chap. 1, n. 98).

102. Cherlin, "The Effect of Children on Marital Dissolution," 288 (see n. 97).

103. See, e.g., Anthony T. Padovano, "Marriage: The Most Noble of Human Achievements." *Catholic World*, May (1995): 140.

104. For a lengthy discussion of this point, see June Carbone, *From Partners to Parents: The Second Revolution in Family Law*. New York: Columbia University Press, 2000, 287–304.

105. David Charny, "Nonlegal Sanctions in Commercial Relationships." *Harvard Law Review* 104, no. 2 (1990): 373–467.

106. Ibid., 376, 393–94.

107. Ibid., 377, 379.

108. Charny maintains, and I agree, that these divergent approaches to contract formation and interpretation reflect a basic incompleteness in autonomy-based theories of contract. Under autonomy- or rights-based formulations of contract law, the promisor is legally obligated to keep his promise because he has "intentionally invoked a convention whose function it is to give grounds—moral grounds—for another to expect the promised performance." Ibid., 381–82.

109. Ibid., 387.

110. Ibid., 428

111. Michael J. Trebilcock, "Marriage as Signal." In *The Fall and Rise of Freedom of Contract*, edited by F. H. Buckley. Durham, NC: Duke University Press, 1999, 245.

112. Charny, "Nonlegal Sanctions in Commercial Relationships," 388 (see n. 105).

113. Ibid., 388–89.

114. Ibid., 412.

115. Ibid., 408–9.

116. See Robert C. Ellickson, *Order Without Law: How Neighbors Settle Disputes*. Cambridge, MA: Harvard University Press, 1991.

117. A useful survey can be found in McAdams, "The Origin, Development, and Regulation of Norms," 339, n. 1 (see chap. 1. n. 39).

118. For citations, see Ibid., 339, n. 2.

119. Ellickson, *Order without Law* (see n. 116); Lawrence Lessig, "Social Meaning and Social Norms." *University of Pennsylvania Law Review* 144, no. 5 (1996): 2181; Cass R. Sunstein, "On the Expressive Function of Law." *University of*

Pennsylvania Law Review 144, no. 5 (1996): 2021; Anita Bernstein, "Better Living through Crime and Tort." *Boston University Law Review* 76, no. 1 (1996): 177–80; Herbert Jacob, "The Elusive Shadow of the Law." *Law and Society Review* 26, no. 3 (1992): 565; William K. Jones, "A Theory of Social Norms." *University of Illinois Law Review* 1994, no. 3 (1994): 545; Paul H. Robinson and John M. Darley, "The Utility of Desert." *Northwestern University Law Review* 91, no. 2 (1997): 453; Walter Otto Weyrauch and Maureen Anne Bell, "Autonomous Lawmaking: The Case of the 'Gypsies.'" *Yale Law Journal* 103, no. 2 (1993): 323. Perhaps the leading example of the success of this phenomenon is the use of "business norms" in the UCC. See, e.g., Uniform Commercial Code 1-102(1) (b); Bernstein, "Merchant Law in a Merchant Court" (see n. 48); Robert Scott, "Conflict and Cooperation in Long-Term Contracts." *California Law Review* 75, no. 6 (1987): 2005.

120. See, especially Robert Boyd and Peter Richardson, "Culture and Cooperation." In *Beyond Self-Interest*, edited by Jane Mansbridge. Chicago: University of Chicago Press, 1990, 111–31.

121. Posner, "The Regulation of Groups,"133 (see n. 24).

122. Ibid., 137.

123. See, e.g., Beth Bailey, *From Front Porch to Back Seat: Courtship in Twentieth Century America*. Baltimore, MD: Johns Hopkins University Press, 1988; Margaret F. Brinig, "Rings and Promises." *Journal of Law, Economics and Organization* 6, no. 1 (1990): 203–15.

124. See, e.g., Scott and Scott. "Marriage as Relational Contract," 1225–334 (see chap. 2, n. 99).

125. Ibid., refers to many of these as transactional norms.

126. A useful survey can be found in. McAdams, "The Origin, Development, and Regulation of Norms" (see chap. 1, n. 38).

127. In the family law literature, see Martha Minow, *Not Only for Myself*. New York: New Press, 1997; Regan, *Family Law and the Pursuit of Intimacy* (see chap. 2, n. 16). See also June Carbone, "Income Sharing: Redefining the Family in Terms of Community." *Houston Law Review* 31, no. 2 (1994): 359. A very powerful empirical study of this kind is Sampson, Morenoff, and Earls, "Beyond Social Capital" (see chap. 2, n. 125).

128. For a discussion of how these played out in a struggle over a couple's frozen embryos, see Margaret F. Brinig, "The Story of Mary Sue and Junior Davis." In *Family Law Stories*, edited by Carol Sanger. New York: Foundation Press, 2008, 195–218.

129. Margaret F. Brinig and Steven L. Nock, "The One-Size-Fits-All Family," *Santa Clara Law Review* 49, no. 1 (2009): 137–64.

130. Dorothy E. Roberts, "Child Welfare and Civil Rights." *University of Illinois Law Review* 2003, no. 1 (2003): 171–82; Dorothy E. Roberts, "Kinship Care and the Price of State Support for Children." *Chicago-Kent Law Review* 76, no. 3 (2001): 1619–42.

131. For two accounts, see Peggy Cooper Davis, *Neglected Stories: The Constitution and Family Values*. New York: Hill and Wang, 1997; Clinton, *It Takes a Village* (see chap. 1, n. 198).

132. Regression analysis results are available from the author (request extendedimptce.spo).

133. Pew Global Attitudes Survey Project, "Among Wealthy Nations: U.S. Stands Alone in Its Embrace of Religion," http://pewglobal.org/reports/display.php?ReportID=167.

134. For example, though this is written about all parents, not just blacks, see Wilcox, "Conservative Protestant Childrearing," 796–809 (see n. 84).

135. John Demos, *A Little Commonwealth: Family Life in Plymouth*, 2nd ed. New York: Oxford University Press, 2000. The counterplay is well described in Fukuyama, *Trust*, 308 (see n. 25).

136. John R. Sutton, "Stubborn Children: Law and Socialization of Deviance in the Puritan Colonies." *Family Law Quarterly* 15, no. 1 (1981): 31–64.

137. 1 Hening [Va. Session Laws] 434 (March 1657–8); 2 Hening [Va. Session Laws] 165–66 (December 1662, art. IV).

138. Carl Schneider and Margaret F. Brinig, *An Invitation to Family Law: Principles, Process, and Perspectives*, 3rd ed. St. Paul, MN: West Group, 2005, 230; Carl Schneider, "Religion and Child Custody." *University of Michigan Journal of Law Reform* 25, no. 3 (1992): 879–906.

139. Scott and Scott, "Parents as Fiduciaries" (see chap. 2, n. 118).

140. Bruce C. Hafen, "The Constitutional Status of Marriage, Kinship, and Sexual Privacy." *Michigan Law Review* 81, no. 3 (1983): 486.

141. See, e.g., *Maynard v. Hill*, 125 U.S. 190, 205, 211 (1888) (Marriage "is an institution, in the maintenance of which in its purity the public is deeply interested, for it is the foundation of the family and of society, without which there would be neither civilization nor progress").

142. 107 So.2d 885, 889 (1958).

143. Locke, *Second Treatise of Government* (see n. 51): "For, to speak properly of them, the first of these is rather the privilege of children, and duty of parents, than any prerogative of paternal power."

144. Ibid., chap. 4, sec. 67. Compare Jeremy Bentham, *Principles of the Civil Code*, 1789, Chapter 3, Guardian and Ward: "This power of protection and of government, over individuals thought incapable to protect and to govern themselves, constitutes wardship, a kind of domestic magistracy, founded upon the manifest need of those who are submitted to it, and which ought to include all the powers necessary to the fulfillment of its object, and nothing more."

145. The doctrine comes from *Troxel v. Glanville*, 530 U.S. 57 (2000), discussed in chapter 4. A recent Indiana Supreme Court case utilized this doctrine to support the Restatement (Second) of Torts' position on corporal punishment of children, allowing where the force was reasonable in the circumstances and was reasonably

believed to be necessary to control the child and prevent misconduct. *Willis v. State*, 888 N.E.2d 177 (Ind. 2008).

146. A particularly helpful discussion is Jana B. Singer, "The Privatization of Family Law." *Wisconsin Law Review* 1992, no. 5 (1992): 1443–1565.

147. *State v. Rhodes*, 61 N.C. 453 (1868).

148. See, e.g., Christine Jolls, Cass R. Sunstein, and Richard Thaler, "A Behavioral Approach to Law and Economics." *Stanford Law Review* 50, no. 5 (1988): 1471–1550.The endowment effect refers to people's tendency to value something more once they have it (in a sales price) than if they are seeking to purchase it (in a purchase price).

149. For a recent review of the literature, see, e.g., Dennis P. Saccuzzo, "How Should the Police Respond to Domestic Violence: A Therapeutic Jurisprudence Analysis of Mandatory Arrest." *Santa Clara Law Review* 39, no. 3 (1999): 765.

150. Sherman, Smith, Schmidt, and Rogan, "Crime, Punishment, and Stake in Conformity" (see n. 33).

151. Janell D. Schmidt and Lawrence W. Sherman, "Does Arrest Deter Domestic Violence?" In *Do Arrests and Restraining Orders Work?* edited by Eve S. Buzawa and Carl G. Buzawa. Thousand Oaks, CA: Sage Publications, 1996, 43–53; Sherman, Schmidt, Rogan, and Smith, "The Variable Effects of Arrest on Criminal Careers" (see n. 39); Lawrence W. Sherman, "The Influence of Criminology on Criminal Law: Evaluating Arrest for Misdemeanor Domestic Violence." *Journal of Criminal Law and Criminology* 83, no. 1 (1992): 1; Richard A. Berk and Lawrence W. Sherman, "Police Responses to Family Violence Incidents: An Analysis of an Experimental Design with Incomplete Randomization." *Journal of the American Statistical Association* 83, no. 401 (1988): 70.

152. Sherman, Schmidt, Rogan, and Smith, "The Variable Effects of Arrest on Criminal Careers" (see n. 39).

153. See generally Margaret F. Brinig, "The Supreme Court's Impact on Marriage, 1967–90." *Howard Law Journal* 41, no. 2 (1998): 271–87; but see Barbara Bennett Woodhouse, "Hatching the Egg: A Child-Centered Perspective on Parents' Rights." *Cardozo Law Review* 14, no. 6 (1993): 1746–1865.

154. See, e.g., some examples from Virginia: *Patrick v. Byerley*, 325 S.E.2d 99 (1985) (former stepmother awarded custody where natural mother abandoned child); *Bailes v. Sours*, 340 S.E.2d 824 (1986) (stepmother given custody over birth mother after custodial father's death) and *Watson v. Shepard*, 229 S.E.2d 897 (Va. 1976) (maternal aunt and her husband, who had served as the child's guardians, were given custody over birth mother but were not permitted to adopt the child). As we will see, the American Law Institute calls such people "de facto" parents and grants them many of the same rights as birth parents to custody and visitation. Such a finding is different from the burden-shifting that went on in the *Troxel* case, where the mother had to prove that *not* allowing the children to visit the grandparents more than they already were was in their best interests.

155. The class of people permitted custodial allocations is much broader than grandparents and would include, for example, same-sex partners of a parent. See, e.g., the ALI treatment of "de facto parents" in §§ 2.03 and 2.21.

156. For a book-length explanation of the role of trust in reducing transaction costs, see Fukuyama, *Trust* (see n. 25). Without norms, we are forced to reinvent rituals.

Chapter Four

1. See, e.g., *Kilgrow v. Kilgrow*, 107 S. 2d 885, 888 (Ala. 1958).

2. For examples, see Ann Lacquer Estin, "Federalism and Child Support." *Virginia Journal of Social Policy and Law* 5, no. 3 (1998): 558; Susan Vivian Mangold, "Protection, Privatization, and Profit in the Foster Care System." *Ohio State Law Journal* 60, no. 4 (1999): 1295.

3. *Michael H. v. Gerald D.*, 291 U.S. 110 (1989).

4. *Parham v. J. R.*, 442 U.S. 584 (1979).

5. See, e.g., John C. Duncan Jr., "The Ultimate Best Interests of the Child Emanates from Parental Reinforcement." *Nebraska Law Review* 83, no. 4 (2005): 1244–45; Margaret F. Brinig, *Teacher's Manual to Accompany an Invitation to Family Law*, 3rd ed. Eagan, MN: West Thomson, 2005, 70; Mary Ann Glendon, "Marriage and the State: The Withering Away of Marriage." *Virginia Law Review* 62, no. 4 (1976): 663–720.

6. 29 U.S.C. § 212 (2000); upheld as constitutional in *United States v. Darby*, 310 U.S. 100 (1941).

7. Gary S. Becker and Kevin M. Murphy, "The Family and the State." *Journal of Law and Economics* 31, no. 1 (1988): 1–18.

8. 393 U.S. 503 (1969) (wearing to school of black armbands protesting the Vietnam War).

9. 443 U.S. 622 (1979). This case and *Planned Parenthood v. Danforth*, 428 U.S. 52 (1976), allowed mature minors to obtain abortions without parental consent.

10. Coleman, "Social Capital" (see intro., n. 3).

11. Mark Granovetter, "Economic Action and Social Structure: The Problem of Embeddedness." *American Journal of Sociology* 91, no. 3 (1985): 504.

12. Coleman, "Social Capital," S98 (see intro. n. 3).

13. Robert D. Putnam, *Bowling Alone: The Collapse and Revival of American Community*. New York: Touchstone, 2000.

14. Partha Dasgupta, "Economics of Social Capital." *Economic Record* 81, no. 254 (2005): S2–S21 See also Fukuyama, *Trust* (see chap. 2, n. 25) (discussing social capital in the context of the family, pp. 17–18, 36–47, and 115–120, and again using trust as the central value, pp. 47–60).

15. Dasgupta, "Economics of Social Capital," S3 (see n. 14).

16. Ibid., S3–S6.

17. This is the message of Coleman, "Social Capital," S98 (see intro., n. 3).

18. Dasgupta, "Economics of Social Capital," S14 (see n. 14); and others may inhibit the flow of resources such as physical capital from one place to another. Dasgupta S17.

19. Ibid., S17–S18.

20. Sarah Fenstermaker Berk, *The Gender Factory: The Apportionment of Work in American Households*. New York: Plenum Press, 1995.

21. Dasgupta, "Economics of Social Capital," S11 (see n. 14).

22. Putnam, *Bowling Alone*, 67 (see n. 13).

23. Katharine T. Silbaugh, "Marriage Contracts and the Family Economy," Northwestern University Law Review 93, no. 1 (1998): 65.

24. Katharine T. Silbaugh, "Turning Labor into Love: Housework and the Law." *Northwestern University Law Review* 91, no. 1 (1996): 1.

25. Silbaugh, "Marriage Contracts and the Family Economy," 99, nn. 127–28.

26. Ibid., 97.

27. As this is advocated by Brian Bix, "Bargaining in the Shadow of Love: The Enforcement of Premarital Agreements and How We Think about Marriage." *William and Mary Law Review* 40, no. 1 (1998): 145.

28. Ibid., 105, 109–10.

29. Silbaugh, "Turning Labor into Love," 101, 110 (see n. 24).

30. Ibid., 110.

31. Ibid., 122–23.

32. Ira Mark Ellman, "'Contract Thinking' was Marvin's Fatal Flaw," 1365–80 (see chap. 2, n. 60).

33. Dasgupta, "Economics of Social Capital," S10 (see n. 14).

34. *Roe v. Wade*, 410 U.S. 113, 152 (1973).

35. I am not the first to make this claim. See Mary Ann Glendon, *Rights Talk*. New York: Free Press, 1993; and Mary Ann Glendon, *Abortion and Divorce in Western Law*. Cambridge, MA: Harvard University Press, 1989.

36. *Eisenstadt v. Baird*, 405 U.S. 438, 447, n. 7 (1972)

37. *Planned Parenthood of Southeastern Pennsylvania v. Casey*, 505 U.S. 833, 834 (1992).

38. Brinig, "The Story of Mary Sue and Junior Davis," 195–218 (see chap. 2, n. 39).

39. *Lehr v. Robertson*, 463 U.S. 248 (1983).

40. 405 U.S. 645 (1972).

41. *Skinner v. Oklahoma*, 316 U.S. 535 (1942).

42. 629 N.W.2d 200 (Wis. 2001). This case might not hold up under federal court scrutiny even though the majority made it very clear that it was part of a criminal punishment, so that Mr. Oakley could have been prevented (because incarcerated)

from having intercourse at all. Compare *State v. Kruzicki*, 541 N.W.2d 482 (Wis. 1995), where the same court found unconstitutional a restriction on a pregnant woman's liberty when she was abusing cocaine.

43. 505 U.S. 833 (1992).

44. Ibid., 852.

45. *Casey*, 505 U.S., 856.

46. See, e.g., *Urso v. Illinois*, #04-CV-6056 (N.D. Ill.) (dismissed for lack of subject matter jurisdiction); *Creed v. Wisconsin*, 04-00917 (E.D. Wis.) (dismissed with prejudice for lack of subject matter jurisdiction); *Ward v. Louisiana*, 04-CV-2697 (E.D. La.); *Martin v. Florida*, 04-CV-22385 (S.D. Fla.).

47. See, e.g., Me. Rev. Stat. Ann. tit. 19-A, §1653 (amended 2004 Me. Leg. Ch. 711); Iowa Code § 598.41 (Supp. 2004).

48. A "bomb" is a long pass. A "Hail Mary" would be a long pass in the last seconds of a half or a game.

49. *Stanley v. Illinois*, 405 U.S. 645 (1972); *Quilloin v. Walcott*, 434 U.S. 248 (1978); *Caban v. Mohammed*, 441 U.S. 380, 389 (1979); and *Lehr v. Robertson*, 463 U.S. 248, 261 (1983) (with the "grasp the opportunity" language).

50. 491 U.S. 110 (1989). Nancy E. Dowd, "Fathers and the Supreme Court: Founding Fathers and Nurturing Fathers." *Emory Law Journal* 54, no. 3 (2005): 1271, discusses this case at some length, beginning p. 1304, as does David Meyer, "The Constitutionality of 'Best Interests' Parentage." *William and Mary Bill of Rights Journal* 14, no. 3 (2006): 873.

51. 491 U.S. 136, 143-44 (Justices Brennan, Blackmun, and Marshall dissenting)

52. Ibid., 113–14.

53. Ibid., 114.

54. Cal. Evid. Code Ann. § 621(a) (West Supp.1989), Section 621, enacted by Stats.1965, c. 299, Repealed by Stats.1992, c. 162 (A.B.2650), § 8, operative January 1, 1994.

55. 491 U.S., 123.

56. *Moore v. East Cleveland*, supra, 431 U.S., 503. (involving an extended family threatened by an exclusionary single-family zoning ordinance). See Brinig, "The Supreme Court's Impact on Marriage," 281–82 (see chap. 3, n. 153).

57. 491 U.S., 123.

58. Ibid., 130.

59. *Parham v. J. R.*, 442 U.S. 584 (1979).

60. 512 U.S. 700, 702 (1994). For a general comment, see Avigaell N. Cymrot, "Reading, Writing, and Radicalism: The Limits on Government Control over Private Schooling in an Age of Terrorism." *St. Mary's Law Journal* 37, no. 3 (2006): 607; see also Michael W. McConnell, "Multiculturalism, Majoritarianism, and Educational Choice: What Does Our Constitutional Tradition Have to Say?" *University of Chicago Legal Forum* 1991, no. 1 (1991): 134.

61. Indeed, the commentary focuses upon secularization and the separation of church and state. See, e.g., Thomas C. Berg, "Slouching toward Secularism: A Commentary on *Kiryas Joel School Dist. v. Grumet*." *Emory Law Journal* 44, no. 2 (1995): 433–500; Abner S. Greene, "Kiryas Joel and Two Mistakes about Equality." *Columbia Law Review* 96, no. 1 (1996): 1; Ira C. Lupu, "Uncovering the Village of Kiryas Joel." *Columbia Law Review* 96, no. 1 (1996): 104.

62. While the Satmar Jewish schools originally began as private sectarian education only, which would not have been problematic after *Pierce*, they sought the right to run an independent district in order to allow disabled students to have the benefits of special educational services unavailable in the private schools.

63. 512 U.S., 702.

64. Ibid., 721 (Justice Stevens concurring, with Justices Blackmun and Ginsburg).

65. Ibid.

66. Schneider, "Religion and Child Custody," 906 (see chap. 3, n. 138).

67. See, e.g., ibid., 904: "More important, I have tried to suggest a number of reasons we might doubt that judicial attempts to mediate those conflicts will be successful and might suspect that they will be harmful."

68. 530 U.S. 57 (2000).

69. Ibid., 66. Elizabeth Scott, "Parental Autonomy and Children's Welfare." *William and Mary Bill of Rights Journal* 11, no. 3 (2003): 1071–1100, makes the point that as parents obtain more rights vis-à-vis the state and nonparents, they will better serve their children's interests. Scott, 1072.

70. 530 U.S., 75 U.S. 721 (Justice Stevens concurring with Justices Blackmun and Ginsburg, Justice Stevens dissenting).

71. Ibid., 86.

72. Ibid., 88–89.

73. Fukuyama, *Trust*, 316 (see chap. 3, n. 25).

74. Brinig, "Troxel and the Limits of Community," 733–81 (see chap. 3, n. 1).

75. For an intriguing suggestion that the family may become more powerful by doing some advance planning, see Linda C. McClain, "Family Constitutions and the (New) Constitution of the Family." *Fordham Law Review* 75, no. 2 (2006): 841–42, suggesting both family constitutions and mission statements to replace a "family-hostile" society. McClain suggests that drafting one of these documents creates a "we" or "interdependent or social will" for the family. McClain, 845, since families do carry a vital role in "the formative project of social reproduction." McClain, 869–80.

76. *Lawrence,* 539 U.S. 558 (2003).

77. The statute invalidated was the former Tex. Penal Code Ann. § 21.06(a) (2003).

78. *Lawrence,* 539 U.S. 558 (2003), 581–82.

79. *Lawrence,* 539 U.S. 558 (2003), 578.

80. *Lawrence,* 539 U.S. 558 (2003), 567.

81. *Eisenstadt v. Baird*, 405 U.S. 438 (1972).

82. "If the right of privacy means anything, it is the right of the individual, married or single, to be free from unwarranted governmental intrusion into matters so fundamentally affecting a person as the decision whether to bear or beget a child." Ibid., 453.

83. The court noted that the case "does not involve whether the government must give formal recognition to any relationship that homosexual persons seek to enter." Ibid., 578.

84. 542 U.S. 1 (2004).

85. Some do, however, see it as a family-law case. See, e.g., Meyer, "The Constitutionality of 'Best Interests' Parentage," 870 (see n. 50); Gloria Chan, "Reconceptualizing Fatherhood: The Stakes Involved in Newdow." *Harvard Journal of Law and Gender* 28, no. 2 (2006): 472; David D. Meyer, "Parenthood in a Time of Transition: Tensions between Legal, Biological and Social Conceptions of Parenthood." *American Journal of Comparative Law* 54, no. 1 (2006): 143.

86. 542 U.S., 17–18.

87. Ibid., 15. David D. Meyer, "The Constitutional Rights of Non-Custodial Parents." *Hofstra Law Review* 34, no. 4 (2006): 1479, quotes, from a Virginia court's observation that "[c]ustody and visitation disputes between two fit parents involve one parent's fundamental right pitted against the other parent's fundamental right. The discretion afforded trial courts under the best interests test . . . reflects a finely balanced judicial response to this parental deadlock." *Griffin v. Griffin*, 581 S.E.2d 899, 902 (Va. Ct. App. 2003).

88. See Margaret F. Brinig, "Book Review: The Child's Best Interests: A Neglected Perspective on Interracial Intimacies." *Harvard Law Review* 117, no. 7 (2004): 2150–58.

89. 388 U.S. 1(1967).

90. See Schneider, "Religion and Child Custody," 889 (see chap. 3, n. 138) ("[t]he now hostile relations of the parents make us doubt some of the reasons we ordinarily have for not intervening in an intact family"). Michael Newdow and Sarah Banning had never married.

91. Brinig, "Unhappy Contracts," 252, 255–56 (see chap. 3, n. 71).

92. Ibid., 259.

93. 1997 WL 731939 (Tenn. App. 1997). See also *Felton v. Felton*, 418 N.E.2d 606, 107–08 (Mass. 1981); *Lundeen v. Struminger*, 165 S.E.2d 285 (Va. 1969); *Quiner v. Quiner*, 59 Cal. Rptr. 503 (Cal. App. 1967). For a case refusing to enforce the parent's agreement to raise the child as a Catholic, see *Lynch v. Uhlenhopp*, 78 N.W.2d 491 (Iowa 1956).

94. *Brown v. Szakal*, 514 A.2d 81 (N.J. Super. Ch. Div. 1986). See also *Grayman v. Hession*, 446 N.Y.S.2d 505 (N.Y. App. Div. 1982); *Mester v. Mester*, 296 N.Y.S.2d 193 (1969).

95. *Brown v. Szakal*, 514 A.2d 84.

96. *Newman v. Phillips*, 1996 WL 480856 (Tenn. Ct. App. 1996).

97. Religion and "lifestyle" differences were also central to the dispute between the father and maternal grandparents in the famous custody case of *Painter v. Bannister*, 140 N.W.2d 152 (Iowa 1966).

98. *In re Phillip B.*, 156 Cal. Rptr. 48 (Cal. App. 1979).

99. *Guardianship of Phillip B.*, 188 Cal. Rptr. 781 (Cal. App 1983). The case and what follows are well discussed in Robert H. Mnookin, "The Guardianship of Phillip B: Jay Spears' Achievement." *Stanford Law Review* 40, no. 4 (1988): 841.

100. William Becker, "My Turn." *Newsweek*, May 30, 1983.

101. 530 U.S. 57 (2000). The following section draws extensively on Brinig, "Troxel and the Limits of Community" (see chap. 3, n. 1).

102. Dasgupta, "Economics of Social Capital" (see n. 14).

103. Michael A. Heller, "The Tragedy of the Anticommons: Property in the Transition from Marx to Markets." *Harvard Law Review* 111, no. 3 (1998): 621. These ideas are developed in Michael A. Heller, *The Gridlock Economy: How Too Much Ownership Wrecks Markets, Stops Innovation, and Costs Lives*. New York: Basic Books, 2008.

104. Heller, "The Tragedy of the Anticommons," 623–24 (see n. 103). Examples include depleted fisheries, overgrazed fields, and polluted air. As Heller notes, the literature on the subject is vast. He particularly credits Garrett Hardin, "The Tragedy of the Commons." *Science* 162, no. 3820 (1968): 1244–45 (introducing the term); Elinor Ostrom, *Governing the Commons: The Evolution of Institutions for Collective Action*. New York: Cambridge University Press, 1990, 182–84 (discussing applications of the tragedy of the commons and showing sustainable informal management of commons resources).

105. In the former Soviet Union, one owner would be given the right to sell, one to receive sale revenue, and still others to lease, receive lease revenue, occupy, and determine use. Each could block the other owners from using the space as a storefront, and no one could set up shop without collecting the consent of all the others. Heller, "The Tragedy of the Anticommons," 623 (see n. 103).

106. See Michael A. Heller and Rebecca S. Eisenberg, "Upstream Patents and Downstream Products: A Tragedy of the Anticommons?" *Science* 280, no. 5364 (1998): 698.

107. Heller, "The Tragedy of the Anticommons," 624 (see n. 103).

108. Martin Zelder, "Inefficient Dissolutions as a Consequence of Public Goods: The Case of No-Fault Divorce." *Journal of Legal Studies* 22, no. 2 (1994): 503. See also Nancy Folbre, "Children as Public Goods." *American Economic Review* 84, no. 2 (1994): 86–90.

109. To the contrary, we saw in chapter 1 that parental warmth is statistically related to many measures of well-being.

110. Rose, "The Comedy of the Commons," 711–81 (see chap. 3, n. 90).

111. Ostrom, *Governing the Commons*, 182–84 (see n. 104).

112. See Rose, "The Comedy of the Commons," 774–77 (see chap. 3, n. 90). Rose, too, points out that formal legal rules, as opposed to the "unorganized public," may not always reach happy endings. Her "comedy of the commons" occurs when the community benefits more as more members participate. Rose, 767–68 (or "the more the merrier," hence the article's title "Comedy").

113. Heller, "The Tragedy of the Anticommons," 625, n. 17 (see n. 103).

114. Note the similarity between property ownership rights and the rights claimed by parents (and grandparents) in the visitation cases. They include, according to August Honore, the characteristics of "ownership" ("Ownership." In *Oxford Essays in Jurisprudence*, edited by Anthony Gordon Guest, 107, 112–28. New York: Oxford University Press, 1961): (1) the right to exclusive possession; (2) the right to personal use and enjoyment; (3) the right to manage use by others; (4) the right to the income from use by others; (5) the right to the capital value, including alienation, consumption, waste, or destruction; (6) the right to security (that is, immunity from expropriation); (7) the power of transmissibility by gift, devise, or descent; (8) the lack of any term on these rights; (9) the duty to refrain from using the object in ways that harm others; (10) the liability to execution for repayment of debts; and (11) residual rights on the reversion of lapsed ownership rights held by others. Incidents (1), (2), (3), (6), (7), and (8) would seem to have at least some application to child custody matters.

115. Bruce C. Hafen, "The Constitutional Status of Marriage, Kinship, and Sexual Privacy." *Michigan Law Review* 81, no. 3 (1983): 463.

116. Scott and Scott, "Parents as Fiduciaries," 2401 (see chap. 2, n. 118). The Scotts are apparently writing about the informal rules couples and parents and children set up to regulate the behavior within the family—rules like bedtimes or the observance of birthdays.

117. Trebilcock, "Marriage as Signal," 245 (see chap. 3, n. 111). See, for example, Nichols, "Multi-Tiered Marriage," 135–96 (see chap. 3, n. 69).

118. Scott and Scott, "Parents as Fiduciaries," 1330 (see chap. 2, n. 118).

119. *Smith v. Van Gorkom*, 488 A.2d 858, 872 (Del. 1985); Robert Charles Clark, *Corporate Law*. Boston: Little, Brown, 1986.

120. See, e.g., *Aronson v. Lewis*, 473 A.2d 805, 812 (Del. 1984); Margaret M. Blair and Lynn A. Stout, "A Team Production Theory of Corporate Law." *Virginia Law Review* 85, no. 2 (1999): 300–304.

121. See, e.g., E. Merrick Dodd Jr., "For Whom Are Corporate Managers Trustees?" *Harvard Law Review* 45, no. 7 (1932): 1151.

122. Coleman, "Social Capital in the Creation of Human Capital," S98 (see intro., n. 3).

123. R. H. Coase, "The Nature of the Firm." *Economica* 4, no. 16 (1937): 386

124. Eugene Fama and Michael Jensen, "Agency Problems and the Theory of the Firm." *Journal of Political Economy* 88, no. 2 (1980): 302; Frank H. Easterbrook and Daniel Fischel, *The Economic Structure of Corporate Law*. Cambridge, MA: Harvard University Press, 1991; Frank H. Easterbrook and Daniel R. Fischel, "The Corporate Contract." *Columbia Law Review* 89, no. 7 (1989): 1416–18.

125. Armen A. Alchian and Harold Demsetz, "Production, Information Costs, and Economic Organization." *American Economic Review* 62, no. 5 (1972): 777.

126. The incentives of employees to hire monitors so that each gets his fair share are discussed in Steven N. S. Cheung, "The Contractual Nature of the Firm." *Journal of Law and Economics* 27, no. 1 (1983): 8. The nature of shirking is discussed in Bengt Holmstrom, "Moral Hazard in Teams." *Bell Journal of Economics* 13, no. 2 (1982): 324.

127. Henry N. Butler and Fred S. McChesney, "Why They Give at the Office: Shareholder Welfare and Corporate Philanthropy in the Contractual Theory of the Corporation." *Cornell Law Review* 84, no. 5 (1999): 1198.

128. For the idea that the only real interests that must be protected by law are those of shareholders, see Bernard Black and Reinier Kraakman, "A Self-Enforcing Model of Corporate Law." *Harvard Law Review* 109, no. 8 (1996): 1911–21; Deborah A. DeMott, "Beyond Metaphor: An Analysis of Fiduciary Obligation." *Duke Law Journal* 1988, no. 5 (1988): 917; Jonathan R. Macey, "Fiduciary Duties as Residual Claims: Obligations to Nonshareholder Constituencies from a Theory of the Firm Perspective." *Cornell Law Review* 84, no. 5 (1999): 1267–68. For those who would consider other stakeholders, see, e.g., Margaret M. Blair, *Ownership and Control: Rethinking Corporate Governance for the Twenty-First Century*. Washington, DC: Brookings Institute, 1995, 212, n. 19.

129. Alchian and Demsetz, "Production, Information Costs, and Economic Organization" (see n. 125).

130. Butler and McChesney, Why They Give at the Office," 1199 (see n. 127). See also Werner Guth et al., "An Experimental Study of a Dynamic Principal-Agent Relationship." *Managerial and Decision Economics* 19, no. 5 (1998): 327–29; Gregg A. Jarrell et al., "The Market for Corporate Control: The Empirical Evidence since 1980." *Journal of Economic Perspectives* 2, no. 1 (Winter 1988): 49–68; Henry G. Manne, "Mergers and the Market for Corporate Control." *Journal of Political Economy* 73, no. 2 (1965): 110.

131. Arguments to this effect can be found in Black and Kraakman, "A Self-Enforcing Model of Corporate Law" (see n. 128); DeMott, "Beyond Metaphor" (see n. 128); Michael P. Dooley, *Fundamentals of Corporation Law*. Westbury, NY: Foundation Press, 1995; Milton Friedman, "The Social Responsibility of Business Is to Increase Its Profits." *New York Times Magazine*, September 13, 1970, 33, 122. The classic case is *Dodge v. Ford Motor Co.*, 170 N.W. 668 (Mich. 1919), keeping all but a small dividend within the corporation so as to lower price and employ greatest

number of workers effectively made the corporation a "semi-eleemosynary institution" and not "a business institution," *Dodge*, 683. The Michigan Supreme Court affirmed the trial court's requirement that the directors declare an extra dividend.

132. Aleta G. Estreicher, "Beyond Agency Costs: Managing the Corporation for the Long Term." *Rutgers Law Review* 45, no. 3 (1993): 593–613; Steven M. H. Wallman, "Understanding the Purpose of a Corporation: An Introduction." *Journal of Corporation Law* 24, no. 4 (1999): 809; Steven M. H. Wallman, "The Proper Interpretation of Corporate Constituency Statutes and Formulation of Director Duties." *Stetson Law Review* 21, no. 1 (1991): 170–71.

133. Robert Frank, "If Homo Economicus could Choose His Own Utility Function, Would He Want One with a Conscience?" *American Economic Review* 77, no. 4 (1987): 593.

134. For a comprehensive examination of the various plans, and which ones tend to result in more productivity, see Henry Hansmann, "When Does Worker Ownership Work? ESOPS, Law Firms, Codetermination, and Economic Democracy." *Yale Law Journal* 99, no. 8 (1990): 1749. See also David I. Levine, *Reinventing the Workplace: How Business and Employees Can Both Win*. Washington, DC: Brookings Institution, 1995.

135. Masahiko Aoki. "Toward an Economic Model of the Japanese Firm." *Journal of Economic Literature* no. 1 (1990): 1.

136. Dodd Jr., "For Whom Are Corporate Managers Trustees?" 1146–48 (see n. 121).

137. Butler and McChesney, Why They Give at the Office," 1203 (see n. 127).

138. In some cases, such as when workers have invested lots of firm-specific capital, workers and local communities will care much more deeply about a decision to close a plant than will shareholders. Macey, "Fiduciary Duties as Residual Claims," 1274 (see n. 128). However, managers may be willing to bargain with other stakeholders because these will benefit shareholders in the end. Macey, 1275. Giving workers job security and better wages will allow the corporation to attract and retain better workers, and thereby increases profitability. The concept of firm-specific capital is discussed in Benjamin Klein et al., "Vertical Integration, Appropriate Rents, and the Competitive Contracting Process." *Journal of Law and Economics* 21, no. 2 (1978): 297–315.

139. Some advocates of the stakeholder voting position include Lawrence E. Mitchell, "A Theoretical and Practical Framework for Enforcing Corporate Constituency Statutes." *Texas Law Review* 70, no. 3 (1992): 630–43; Marleen A. O'Connor, "The Human Capital Era: Reconceptualizing Corporate Law to Facilitate Labor-Management Cooperation." *Cornell Law Review* 78, no. 5 (1993): 936–65; John C. Coffee Jr., "Unstable Coalitions: Corporate Governance as a Multi-Player Game." *Georgetown Law Journal* 78, no. 5 (1990): 1495; David Millon. "Theories of the Corporation." *Duke Law Journal* 1990, no. 2 (1990): 261–62.

140. "[I]t is obvious that a rule requiring the continuation of the poorly performing plant has adverse societal consequences, even if it is more compassionate in the short run to the in-place workforce of that plant (while possibly detrimental to the corporation's workers over the long-term." Wallman, "The Proper Interpretation," 181 (see n. 132).

141. Margaret M. Blair and Lynn A. Stout, "Trust, Trustworthiness, and the Behavioral Foundations of Corporate Law." *University of Pennsylvania Law Review* 149, no. 6 (2001): 1735 at n.105.

142. Butler and McChesney, Why They Give at the Office," 1218 (see n. 127).

143. James Willard Hurst, *The Legitimacy of the Business Corporation in the Law of the United States, 1790–1970*. Charlottesville: University Press of Virginia, 1980, 15–17. Thus, "requiring all constituencies to contract explicitly, or requiring all constituencies to raise their costs to the corporation for any services they provide to compensate for the risk that their good faith expectations or trust will be breached, imposes a cost on all corporations" and therefore society as a whole. Wallman, "Understanding the Purpose of a Corporation," 812 (see n. 132).

144. Brinig, *From Contract to Covenant* (see chap. 3, n. 2).

145. Margaret F. Brinig, "Finite Horizons: The American Family." *International Journal of Children's Rights* 2, no. 3 (1994): 313–15; Margaret F. Brinig, "The Family Franchise: Elderly Parents and Adult Siblings." *Utah Law Review* 1996, no. 2 (1996): 397–98.

146. *SooHoo v. Johnson*, 731 N.W.2d 815 (Minn. 2007) (former lesbian lover granted visitation rights); *Jacob v. Shultz-Jacob*, Pa. Super. Ct., Nos. 1499 and 1527 MDA 2006, 4/30/07 (man who provided sperm to lesbian couple sued for support since three-way custody order was in place).

147. Brinig, *From Contract to Covenant*, 182–83 (see chap. 3, n. 2).

148. Indeed, this is much of what Fukuyama's books are about. Fukuyama, *Trust*, 316 (see chap. 3, n. 25).

149. This is what Justice O'Connor suggests in *Troxel*, 120 S. Ct., 2062: "In an ideal world, parents might always seek to cultivate the bonds between grandparents and their grandchildren."

150. Jennifer F. Hamer, "What African-American Noncustodial Fathers Say Inhibits and Enhances Their Involvement with Children." *Western Journal of Black Studies* 22, no. 2 (1988): 117–27.

151. Kristen Harknett and Jean Knab, "More Kin, Less Support: Multipartnered Fertility and Perceived Support among Mothers." *Journal of Marriage and Family* 69, no. 1 (2007): 237–53.

152. Coleman, "Social Capital," S105 (see intro., n. 3).

153. Francis Fukuyama, *The Great Disruption*. New York: Simon & Schuster, 1999.

154. For example, there might be tax deductions for elder care, continued differentiation (through removal of the "marriage tax penalty") between marriage

and cohabitation, legislation giving benefits for counseling prior to marriage or divorce, and generally, more support given to union-building activities. Two such family-strengthening and completely extra-legal activities that I've found in Iowa City are our block's potluck millennium party, including a number of three-generation families, and one of my colleague's holiday cookie-decorating party, to which children and grandchildren are invited, though they may bring their relations. As Carol Rose ("The Comedy of the Commons," 779–80 (see chap. 3, n. 90)) writes as she advocates public access to unique recreational sites: "recreation educates and socializes us, it acts as a 'social glue' for everyone, not just those immediately engaged; and of course, the more people involved in any socializing activity, the better."

155. Carl E. Schneider, "Moral Discourse and the Transformation of American Family Law." *Michigan Law Review* 83, no. 8 (1985): 1857–58.

156. Laura T. Kessler, "Community Parenting." *Journal of Law and Policy* 24, no. 1 (2007): 47–77.

157. Agreeing with me, Katharine K. Baker, "Bargaining or Biology? The History and Future of Paternity Law and Parental Status." *Cornell Journal of Law and Public Policy* 14, no. 1 (2004): 48–49; Elizabeth Bartholet, "Guiding Principles for Picking Parents." *Harvard Women's Law Journal* 27, no. 1 (2004): 342–43; Emily Buss, "'Parental' Rights." *Virginia Law Review* 88, no. 3 (2002): 665–66; William C. Duncan. "'Don't Ever Take a Fence Down': The 'Functional' Definition of Family: Displacing Marriage in Family Law." *Journal of Law and Family Studies* 3, no. 1 (2001): 75; David M. Wagner. "Balancing 'Parents Are' and 'Parents Do' in the Supreme Court's Constitutionalized Family Law: Some Implications for the ALI Proposals on De Facto Parenthood." *Brigham Young University Law Review* 2001, no. 3 (2001): 1184.

Chapter Five

1. Fukuyama, *The Great Disruption*, 88 (see chap. 4, n. 153).

2. Ted Bergstrom, "Economics in a Family Way." *Journal of Economic Literature* 34, no. 4 (1996): 1903–34.

3. For evolutionary reasons, altruistic behavior may eventually develop even among people who were originally strangers. See, e.g., Robert Boyd and Peter J. Richersen, "The Evolution of Reciprocity in Sizable Groups." *Journal of Theoretical Biology* 132, no. 3 (1988): 337–56. It may stem from repeated interactions. Robert Axelrod, *The Evolution of Cooperation*. New York: Basic Books, 1985.

4. Locke, *Second Treatise of Government*, chap. 6 sec. 67 ("Of Paternal Power") (see chap. 3, n. 51).

5. Gary S. Becker and Nigel Tomes, "Human Capital and the Rise and Fall of Families." *Journal of Labor Economics* 4, no. 3 (1986): S1–S39; Gary S. Becker,

Human Capital: A Theoretical and Empirical Analysis, with Specific Reference to Education, 2nd ed. New York: National Bureau of Economic Research, Columbia University Press, 1985.

6. W. Andrew Collins, Eleanor E. Maccoby, Laurence Steinberg, E. Mavis Hetherington, and Marc H. Bornstein, "Contemporary Research on Parenting: The Case for Nature and Nurture." *American Psychologist* 55, no. 2 (2000): 218–32.

7. Kristin Riggins-Caspers and Remi J. Cadoret, "Family Process as Mediator of Biology X Environment Interaction." *Marriage and Family Review* 33, no. 2 (2001): 101. See also P. Tienari, L. C. Wynne, J. Moring, et al., "The Finnish Adoptive Family Study of Schizophrenia: Implications for Family Research." *British Journal of Psychiatry* 23, no. 164 (1994): 20–26.

8. Remi J. Cadoret, Leslie D. Leve, and Eric Devor, "Genetics of Aggressive and Violent Behavior." *Anger, Aggression, and Violence* 20, no. 2 (1997): 301–20.

9. Remi J. Cadoret and Robert B. Wesner, "Use of the Adoption Paradigm to Elucidate the Role of Genes and Environment and Their Interaction in the Genesis of Alcoholism." *Banbury Report* 33, no. 1 (1990): 31–41.

10. Kristin Riggins-Caspers, Remi Cadoret, Jacques Lempers, William Panak, Edward Troughton, and Mark A. Stewart, "Gene X Environment Interaction and the Moderating Effect of Adoption Agency Disclosure on Estimating Genetic Effects." *Personality and Individual Differences* 27, no. 2 (1999): 357–80. This does not necessarily signal problems with "open adoption," since most adoptions arranged beforehand are of relatively healthy parents and children and some selection on the part of the adoptive parents typically takes place.

11. Morse, *Love and Economics* (see chap. 3, n. 54).

12. These children may suffer from attachment disorder. John Bowlby, *Attachment*, 2nd ed. New York: Basic Books, 1982; William L. Cook, "Understanding Attachment Security in Family Context." *Journal of Personality and Social Psychology* 78, no. 2 (2000): 285; Kim Chisholm, "A Three Year Follow-Up of Attachment and Indiscriminate Friendliness in Children Adopted from Romanian Orphanages." *Child Development* 69, no. 4 (1998): 1092–1106.

13. Because of greater receptivity to social skills, some of what they imitate may not even be efficient. Victoria Horner and Andrew Whiten, "Causal Knowledge and Imitation/Emulation Switching in Chimpanzees (*Pan troglodytes*) and Children (*Homo sapiens*)." *Animal Cognition* 8, no. 3–07 (2005): 164–81. We may imitate the inefficient because of "path dependence": our synapses have been trained to replicate exactly the method they've seen. Derek E. Lyons, Andrew G. Young, and Frank C. Keil, "The Hidden Structure of Over-Imitation." *Proceedings of the National Academy of Sciences* 104, no. 50 (2007): 19751–6.

14. The value of trust has been seen for millennia. See, e.g., Psalm 37:21–27.

15. This section is drawn in substantial part from Margaret F. Brinig and Steven L. Nock, "Can Law Shape the Development of Unconditional Love in Children?" (presented at the Center for Law and Religion Colloquium on Best Love of the

Child, Emory University, Atlanta, GA, 2006). It currently appears as "Best Love of the Child" at http://papers.ssrn.com/sol3/papers.cfm?abstract_id=973821.

16. Michael Bond, "The Pursuit of Happiness." *New Scientist* (UK), October 4, 2003 (based upon the 65 nation World Values Survey 1999–2000 and reflecting attitudes since 1945).

17. Jonathan Power, "What Makes the Nigerians the Happiest of All People?" *Arab News*, January 3, 2003.

18. K. K. M. Sheldon, "What Is Satisfying About Satisfying Events? Testing 10 Candidate Psychological Needs." *Journal of Personality and Social Psychology* 80, no. 2 (2001): 325.

19. Morse, *Love and Economics* (see chap. 3, n. 54).

20. Gary S. Becker, *A Treatise on the Family*, 2nd ed. Cambridge, MA: Harvard University Press, 1991, 23–24.

21. G. S. Becker and N. Tomes, "Child Endowments and the Quantity and Quality of Children." *Journal of Political Economy* 84, no. 4 (1976): S143–S162.

22. Mellman and Lazarus, *Mass Mutual American Family Values Study*. Washington, DC: Mellman & Lazarus, 1989, 14.

23. "Unconditional love develops trust because as you express this kind of love towards someone—generally he or she will sense your acceptance and feel comfortable to be vulnerable and honest about their feelings. Unconditional love actually builds self-esteem in others and alleviates their fears of rejection." Lynette J. Hoy, "Rebuilding Trust." *Women Today Magazine*, February 2003, http://womentodaymagazine.com/relationships/rebuildtrust.html. See also Nathaniel M. Lambert and David C. Dollahite, "How Religiosity Helps Couples Prevent, Resolve, and Overcome Marital Conflict." *Family Relations* 55, no. 4 (2006): 443.

24. This is the term given in Nancy Eisenberg, *The Caring Child*. Cambridge, MA: Harvard University Press 1992, 3.

25. G. L. Hansen, "Moral Reasoning and the Marital Exchange Relationship." *Journal of Social Psychology* 131, no 1 (1991): 71–81; M. F. Brinig, and S. L. Nock, "How Much Does Legal Status Matter? Adoptions by Kin Caregivers." *Family Law Quarterly* 36, no. 3 (2002): 449–74; John Wilson, "Volunteering" *Annual Review of Sociology* 26, no. 1 (2000): 215–40.

26. Altruism is discussed extensively in Jane Mansbridge, ed. *Beyond Self-Interest*. Chicago: University of Chicago Press, 1990; Tit for tat is discussed in Anatol Rapoport, *Fights, Games, and Debates*. Ann Arbor: University of Michigan Press, 1960; and Robert Axelrod, *The Evolution of Cooperation*. New York: Basic Books, 1984.

27. Gary S. Becker, "Altruism in the Family and Selfishness in the Market Place." *Economica*, 48, no. 189 (1981): 1–15 (http://ideas.repec.org/a/bla/econom/v48y1981i189p1-15.html). Some years ago, I attended a talk given by Gillian Hadfield at the University of Toronto at which she explained her frustration with a male economist trying to discuss family relationships in terms of symbolic representations

of "interdependent utility functions." The idea was something like $U_A = f(c_A + U_B(Hw_A - c_A))$.

28. See the introduction to Brinig, *From Contract to Covenant* (see chap. 3, n. 2); Brinig and Nock, "Covenant and Contract," 9–26 (see chap. 2, n. 14).

29. See Jennifer Roeback Morse. "Marriage, the Family, and the State." In *The Economics of Family Law*, edited by Margaret Brinig. Northampton, MA: Edward Elgar, 2007.

30. A slightly more nuanced understanding of love appears in the film *Love, Actually* (2003)

31. See, e.g., B. Rogoff, *Apprenticeship in Thinking: Cognitive Development in Social Context*. New York: Oxford University Press, 1990; Tedra A. Walden and Tamra A. Ogan, "The Development of Social Referencing." *Child Development* 59, no. 5 (1988):1230–40.

32. D. Narvaez and D. Lapsley, "The Psychological Foundations of Everyday Morality and Moral Expertise." In *Character Psychology and Character Education*, edited by D. Lapsley and C. Power. Notre Dame, IN: University of Notre Dame Press, 2005, 140–65; Grazyna Kochanska, David R. Forman, Nazan Aksan, and Stephen B. Dunbar, "Pathways to Conscience: Early Mother-Child Mutually Responsive Orientation and Children's Moral Emotion, Conduct, and Cognition." *Journal of Child Psychology and Psychiatry* 46, no. 1 (2005): 19–34.

33. Paul L. Harris and Melissa Koenig, "Trust in Testimony: How Children Learn About Science and Religion." *Child Development*, 77, no. 3 (2006): 505–24.

34. Marvin W. Berkowitz and John H. Grych, "Fostering Goodness: Teaching Parents to Facilitate Children's Moral Development." *Journal of Moral Education* 27, no. 3 (1998): 371–391 (http://parenthood.library.wisc.edu/Berkowitz/Berkowitz.html). See John Bowlby, *Attachment and Loss*, vol. 1, *Attachment*. New York: Basic Books, 1969; Mary D. S. Ainsworth et al., "Object Relations, Dependency, and Attachment: A Theoretical Review of the Infant-Mother Relationship." *Child Development*, 40 (1968): 969–1025. Indeed, it has been argued that the attachment relationship is the template for most later relationships (Samuel Oliver and Pearl Oliver, *The Altruistic Personality: Rescuers of Jews in Nazi Europe*. New York: Free Press, 1988); L. Allen Sroufe and June A. Fleeson, "Attachment and the Construction of Relationships." In *Relationships and Development*, edited by W. W. Hartup and Z. Rubin. Hillsdale, NJ: Erlbaun, 1986, 51–71. This takes place over time.

35. Wyndol Furman, Valerie A. Simon, Laura Shaffer, and Heather A. Bouchey, "Adolescents' Working Models and Styles for Relationships with Parents, Friends, and Romantic Partners." *Child Development* 73, no. 1 (2002): 241–55.

36. For an economic look at why it might be a glimpse only, see Brinig and Buckley, "Joint Custody (see chap. 2, n. 180).

37. See, e.g., Brinig, "Does Parental Autonomy Require Equal Custody at Divorce?" 1345 (see chap. 2, n. 35).

38. J. Wallerstein and S. Blakeslee, *The Good Marriage*. Boston: Houghton-Mifflin, 1995.

39. Shelly Lundberg and Robert A. Pollak, "Separate Spheres Bargaining and the Marriage Market." *Journal of Political Economy* 101, no. 6 (1993): 988–1010.

40. G. L. Hanson, "Moral Reasoning and the Marital Exchange Relationship." *Journal of Social Psychology* 13, no. 1 (1990): 71–81.

41. Brinig, "Community Involvement" (see chap. 3, n. 1).See also Steven L. Nock et al., "Intimate Equity: The Early Years of Standard and Covenant Marriages." Bowling Green State University, Department of Sociology, Working Paper 03–04.

42. See Pope Benedict XVI, Encyclical Letter, Deus Caritas Est (On Christian Love), Rome, December 25, 2005. One Biblical source is 1 Jn. 4:9–10. See also, Nathaniel M. Lambert and David C. Dollahite, "How Religiosity Helps Couples Prevent, Resolve, and Overcome Marital Conflict." *Family Relations* 55, no. 4 (2006): 443.

43. Sociological work on religion indicates that it is religiosity, not denomination, that is important. See, e.g., V. R. A. Call and T. B. Heaton, "Religious Influence on Marital Stability." *Journal for the Scientific Study of Religion* 36, no. 3 (1997): 382–92.

44. The First Amendment prohibits Congress from establishing religion. See, e.g., *Everson v. Board of Education*, 330 U.S. 1, 15 (1947).

45. IRC § 190 allows for deductions from taxable income for contributions to charitable corporations.

46. IRC § 501(c) (3) allows these organizations to be tax exempt so long as they refrain from political lobbying activities and do not undertake profit making ventures. For a discussion of this doctrine, see E. G. Stone, "Adhering to the Old Line: Uncovering the History and Political Function of the Unrelated Business Income Tax." *Emory Law Journal* 54, no. 4 (2005): 1478–1556.

47. These were upheld in *Zelman v. Simmons-Harris*, 536 U.S. 639 (2002).

48. See Patricia Wen, "Catholic Charities Stuns State; Ends Adoption." *Boston Globe*, March 11, 2006.

49. Margaret F. Brinig, "Does Mediation Disadvantage Women?" *William and Mary Journal of Women and the Law* 2, no. 1 (1995): 1.

50. Gary S. Becker, "Altruism, Egoism, and Genetic Fitness: Economics and Sociobiology." *Journal of Economic Literature* 14, no. 3 (1976): 818.

51. Richard Posner, *Sex and Reason*. Cambridge, MA: Harvard University Press, 1992, 189.

52. Edward Wilson, *Sociobiology*. Cambridge, MA: Harvard University Press, 1975, 117.

53. John J. Seater, "Ricardian Equivalence." *Journal of Economic Literature* 31, no. 1 (1993): 147.

54. Paula England, "The Separative Self: Androcentric Bias in Neoclassical Assumptions." In *Beyond Economic Man: Feminist Theory and Economics*, edited

by Marianne Ferber and Julie Nelson. Chicago: University of Chicago Press, 1993, 45.

55. Jon Elster, "Selfishness and Altruism." In *Beyond Self-Interest*, edited by Jane Mansbridge. Chicago: University of Chicago Press, 1990, 44–45.

56. Regan, *Family Law and the Pursuit of Intimacy*, 114 (see chap. 2, n. 16).

57. Robyn Dawes, Alphons J. C. van de Kragt, and John M. Orbell, "Cooperation for the Benefit of Us—Not Me, or My Conscience." In *Beyond Self-Interest*, edited by Jane Mansbridge. Chicago: University of Chicago Press, 1990, 101–3.

58. Margaret F. Brinig, "Does Mediation Systematically Disadvantage Women?" *William and Mary Journal of Women and the Law* 2, no. 1 (1995): 1–34.

59. The chi-squared for the equation was 21.058, showing that the results in all probability did not happen by chance.

60. Steven L. Nock, Paul William Kingston, and Laura M. Holian, "The Distribution of Obligations." In *Intergenerational Caregiving*, edited by Alan Booth, Ann C. Crouter, Suzanne M. Bianchi, and Judith A. Seltzer. Washington, DC: Urban Institute, 2008.

61. Fukuyama, *The Great Disruption*, 88 (see n. 1).

62. See especially Brinig, *From Contract to Covenant* (see chap. 3, n. 2) and M. F. Brinig and S. L. Nock, "Marry Me Bill: Should Cohabitation be the (Legal) Default Option?" *Louisiana Law Review* 64, no. 3 (2004): 403–42; Brinig and Steven Nock, "Covenant and Contract" (see chap. 2, n. 14).

63. M. F. Brinig. and S. L. Nock, "'I Only Want Trust': Norms, Trust, and Autonomy." *Journal of Socio-Economics* 32, no. 5 (2003): 471–87.

64. See also Paul R. Amato and Jacob Cheadle, "The Long Reach of Divorce: Divorce and Child Well-being Across Three Generations." *Journal of Marriage and Family* 67, no 1. (2005): 191–206.

65. S. L. Nock, L. Sanchez, et al. "Covenant Marriage Turns Five Years Old." *Michigan Journal of Gender and Law* 10, no. 1 (2003): 169–88.

66. Brinig, "Book Review: The Child's Best Interests" (see chap. 4, n. 88). Interreligious marriages were less stable in the late 1970s, Gary S. Becker, Elisabeth M. Landes, and Robert Michael, "An Economic Analysis of Marital Instability." *Journal of Political Economy* 5, no. 6 (1977): 1141, but it seems to be the strength of people's religious adherence, or religiosity, that matters more than denomination. Vaughn R. A. Call and Tim B. Heaton, "Religious Influence on Marital Stability." *Journal for the Scientific Study of Religion* 36, no. 3 (1997): 382.

67. S. L. Nock, "A Comparison of Marriages and Cohabiting Relationships." *Journal of Family Issues* 16, no. 1 (1995): 53–77; Brinig and Nock, "Marry Me Bill'" (see n. 62).

68. Of course, the child's behavior could also modify the parental attitudes and parenting. See Collins et al., "Contemporary Research on Parenting," 222, 226 (see chap. 1, n. 6).

69. K. J. Zullig, R. F. Valois, et al. "Associations Among Family Structure, Demographics, and Adolescent Perceived Life Satisfaction." *Journal of Child and Family Studies* 14, no. 2 (2005): 195–206.

70. The most famous and controversial publication was Judith Rich Harris, *The Nurture Assumption*. New York: Free Press, 1998. A more scholarly version is Judith Rich Harris, "Socialization, Personality Development, and the Child's Environments: Comment on Vandell." *Developmental Psychology* 36, no. 6 (2000): 711–23. For a review of the literature, pro and con, see Collins et al., "Contemporary Research on Parenting" (see chap. 1, n. 6).

71. Bureau of Labor and Statistics, "The National Longitudinal Survey of Youth: 1997," http://www.bls.gov/nls (accessed August 20, 2009), with nearly 9,000 nationally representative observations, about 3,800 of whom are ages 12–14.

72. See also Mark Feinberg, Jenae Neiderhiser, George Howe, and E. Mavis Hetherington, "Adolescent, Parent, and Observer Perceptions of Parenting: Genetic and Environmental Influences on Shared and Distinct Perceptions." *Child Development* 72, no. 4 (2001): 1266–84.

73. The original reference is Bowlby, *Attachment and Loss* (see n. 34). The more recent work includes Mary Main and Jane Cassidy, "Categories of Response to Reunion with the Parent at Age 6: Predictable from Infant Attachment Classifications and Stable over a 1-month Period." *Developmental Psychology* 24, no. 3 (1988): 415–26.; Everett Waters, Nancy S. Weinfield, and Claire E. Hamilton, "The Stability of Attachment Security from Infancy to Adolescence and Early Adulthood: General Discussion." *Child Development* 71, no. 3 (2000): 703–6.

74. William T. Dalton III, Donna Frick-Horbury, and Katherine M. Kitzmann, "Young Adults' Retrospective Reports of Parenting by Mothers and Fathers: Associations with Current Relationship Quality." *Journal of General Psychology* 133, no. 1 (2006): 5–18.

75. Rand D. Conger, Ming Cui, Chalandra M. Bryant, and Glen H. Elder Jr., "Competence in Early Adult Romantic Relationships: A Developmental Perspective on Family Influences." *Journal of Personality and Social Psychology* 79, no. 2 (2000): 224–37.

76. Rand D. Conger, "Family Economic Stress and Adjustment of Early Adolescent Girls." *Developmental Psychology* 29, no. 2 (1993): 206.

77. M. M. Curran, "How Representations of the Parental Marriage Predict Marital Emotional Attunement During the Transition to Parenthood." *Journal of Family Psychology* 20, no. 3 (2006): 477.

78. Paul R. Amato and Alan Booth, *A Generation at Risk: Growing up in an Era of Family Upheaval*. Cambridge, MA: Harvard University Press, 1997.

79. Ibid., 123.

80. Ibid., 137.

81. See, e.g., Patrick T. Davies and E. Mark Cummings, "Marital Conflict and

Child Adjustment: An Emotional Security Hypothesis." *Psychological Bulletin*, 116, no. 3 (1994): 387–411.

82. Amato and Booth, *A Generation at Risk*, 139 (see n. 78).

83. Ibid., 144.

84. Ibid., 207.

85. Ibid., 204.

86. Paul R. Amato and Danelle D. DeBoer, "The Transmission of Marital Instability Across Generations: Relationship Skills or Commitment to Marriage?" *Journal of Marriage and the Family* 63 no. 4 (2001): 1038.

87. Paul R. Amato, "The Consequences of Divorce for Adults and Children." *Social Science Research* 62, no. 4 (2000): 1269.

88. Timothy Page and Inge Bretherton, "Representations of Attachment to Father in the Narratives of Preschool Girls in Post-Divorce Families: Implications for Family Relationships and Social Development." *Child and Adolescent Social Work Journal* 20, no. 2 (2003): 99–122.

89. Christine Falci, "Family Structure, Closeness to Residential and Nonresidential Parents, and Psychological Distress in Early and Middle Adolescence." *Sociological Quarterly* 47, no. 1 (2006): 123–46.

90. Glen R. Waddell, " Labor-Market consequences of Poor Attitude and Low Self-Esteem in Youth." *Economic Inquiry* 44, vol. 1 (2006): 69–97.

91. Rutger C. M. E. Engels, Maja Dekovic, et al. "Parenting Practices, Social Skills, and Peer Relationships in Adolescence." *Social Behavior and Personality: An International Journal* 30, no. 1 (2002): 3.

92. Brian E. Vaughn, Jeanne H. Block, et al. "Parental Agreement on Child Rearing during Early Childhood and the Psychological Characteristics of Adolescents." *Child Development* 59, no. 4 (1988): 1020.

93. Elizabeth Marquardt, *Between Two Worlds: The Inner Lives of Children of Divorce*. New York: Crown Publishing, 2005.

94. Mark T. Morman and Kory Floyd, "Good Fathering: Father and Son Perceptions of What It Means to Be a Good Father." *Fathering: A Journal of Theory, Research, and Practice about Men as Fathers* 4, no. 2 (2006): 123.

95. Ibid., 118.

96. Anne C. Fletcher and Robin A. Shaw, "Sex Differences in Associations Between Parental Behaviors and Characteristics and Adolescent Social Integration." *Social Development* 9, no. 2 (2000): 133–48.

97. Nock, Kingston, and Holian, "The Distribution of Obligations" (see n. 60).

98. Falci, "Family Structure" (see n. 89).

99. C. Carrie George, K. C. Keith Herman, et al. "The Family Environment and Developmental Psychopathology: The Unique and Interactive Effects of Depression, Attention, and Conduct Problems." *Child Psychiatry and Human Development* 37, no. 2 (2006): 163.

100. Ibid., 173.

101. Krieder, "Interracial Marriage," 6, 102, 136, table 1.2 (see chap. 1, n. 180) (using the National Survey of Family Growth).

102. Ibid., app. C, 208–9, and with precisely the number of divorces that might be expected for black marriages, which disrupt at a higher rate than white marriages do.

103. W. Bradford Wilcox and Nicholas H. Wolfinger, "Then Comes Marriage? Religion, Race, and Marriage in Urban America." *Social Science Research*, 36, no. 2 (2007): 578 and fig. 1.

104. Three-quarters of a convenience sample of divorced African American men reported differences in religious behavior as a reason for their divorce. Erma Jean Lawson, "Black Men Make Sense of Marital Distress and Divorce." *Family Relations* 44, no. 2 (1995): 213, table 2.

105. Andrew J. Cherlin, "Marriage and Marital Dissolution Among Black Americans." *Journal of Comparative Family Studies* 29, no. 1 (1998): 147–58; Jennifer Roebuck Bulanda and Susan L. Brown, "Race-ethnic Differences in Marital Quality and Divorce." *Social Science Research* 36, no. 6 (2007): 945–67. Cherlin noted that approximately 47% of African American women separate from their husbands within 10–15 years of marriage compared with 28% of white women. Terri L. Orbuch, Joseph Veroff, Halimah Hassan, and Julie Horrocks, "Who Will Divorce: A 14-year Longitudinal Study of Black Couples and White Couples." *Journal of Social and Personal Relationships* 19, no. 2 (2006): 191, suggests that in their sample, the African American couples were more than twice as likely to be at risk for divorce as whites.

106. Wilcox and. Wolfinger, "Then Comes Marriage?" 585 (see n. 103).

107. Orbuch, Veroff, Hassan, and Horrocks, "Who Will Divorce," 200 (see n. 105).

108. Liana C. Sayer and Suzanne M. Bianchi. "Women's Economic Independence and the Probability of Divorce: A Review and Reexamination." *Journal of Family Issues* 21, no. 7 (2000): 906–43.

109. Orbuch, Veroff, Hassan, and Horrocks, "Who Will Divorce," 199 (see n. 105). Frequent discussions about the relationship after the first couple of years of marriage were also predictors of unstable marriages. See also Sayer and Bianchi, "Women's Economic Independence."

110. Bulanda and Brown, "Race-ethnic Differences" (see n. 105).

111. Ibid., 956, 958, tables 1–2.

112. Ibid., 950.

113. Wilcox and Wolfinger, "Then Comes Marriage?" 584 (see n. 103).

114. Annette Mahoney, Kenneth I. Pargament, Tracey Jewell, Aaron B. Swank, Eric Scott, Erin Emey, and Mark Rye, "Marriage and the Spiritual Realm: The Role of Proximal and Distal Religious Constructs in Marital Functioning." *Journal of Family Psychology* 13, no. 3 (1999): 329 and table 3.

115. Steven L. Nock and Margaret F. Brinig, "What Does Covenant Mean for Relationships?" *Notre Dame Journal of Law and Public Policy* 18, no. 1 (2004): 182 (covenant marriages end in divorce less than half as often as standard marriages).

116. The International Social Survey Programme (ISSP) 2001, social relations and support, question 35. German Social Science Infrastructure Services, http://www.gesis.org/fileadmin/upload/dienstleistung/daten/umfragedaten/issp/excerpts/excerpt_gmr_2001.pdf (accessed August 20, 2009). A table containing this data is reported in David G. Blanchflower and Andrew J. Oswald, "Happiness and the Human Development Index: The Paradox of Australia." *Australian Economic Review* 38, no. 3–09 (2005): 310 and table 1 (happiness).

117. From Table II. United Nations, "Total Fertility Rate by Country," http://www.un.org/esa/population/publications/worldfertility/Selected_Indicators.xls (accessed August 20, 2009).

118. Kevin McQuillan, "When Does Religion Influence Fertility." *Population and Development Review* 30, no. 1 (2004): 25–56; Alicia Adsera, "Religion and Changes in Family-size Norms in Developed Countries." *Review of Religious Research*, 47, no. 3 (March 2006): 271–86.

Chapter Six

1. *Principles of the Civil Code*, 1789, part 3, chap. 3, Guardian and Ward). See also *Maynard v. Hill*, 125 U.S. 190, 205, 211 (1888).

2. Jeremy Bentham, *The Works of Jeremy Bentham*. 11 vols., published under the Superintendence of his Executor, John Bowring. Edinburgh: William Tait, 1838–43, vol. 1. part 3, chapter 5 (http://oll.libertyfund.org/title/2009/139725). First published in French in 1802.

3. The "Little Commonwealth" statement comes from Governor John Winthrop's speech, "A Modell of Christian Charity." In *Winthrop Papers*, vol. 2, Boston: Massachusetts Historical Society, 1931, 294 (sermon entitled "Christian Charity" preached aboard *The Arabella*, Massachusetts Bay, 1630).

4. Becker, *Treatise on the Family*, 31–33 (see chap. 5, n. 20); Gary Becker, "A Theory of the Allocation of Time." *Economic Journal* 75, no. 299 (1965): 493; Paula England and Gary Farkas, *Households, Employment, and Gender*. New York: Aldine Pub. Co, 1986, 73–74. Making the point that increased goods, in fact, require an "ideal worker," usually male, who can be more productive only at the expense of his spouse, is Joan C. Williams, *Unbending Gender*. New York: Oxford University Press, 2000.

5. Studies have shown that married executives are paid more than their single counterparts. Victor Fuchs, *Women's Quest for Economic Equality*. Cambridge, MA: Harvard University Press, 1988, 78. They may be freed to be the "ideal worker"

because of what their wives do. See Felice N. Schwartz, "Management Women and the New Facts of Life." *Harvard Business Review* 67, no 1 (1989): 65.

6. For an extended discussion, see Scott and Scott, "Marriage as Relational Contract," 1225 (see chap. 2, n. 99).

7. Gary Becker's theory of the family is built to a large extent on the economic doctrines of comparative advantage and specialization. Becker, *Treatise on the Family* (see chap. 5, n. 20).

8. Comparative advantage within the family is discussed in Becker, *Treatise on the Family* (see chap. 5, n. 20) The economist most famous for beginning the discussions in the market context is David Ricardo, The Principles of Trade and Taxation, 1819, http://socserv2.socsci.mcmaster.ca/~econ/ugcm/3ll3/ricardo/prin/index.html.

9. Regan, *Family Law and the Pursuit of Intimacy* (see chap. 2, n. 16). Another example is the law of necessaries, which allows merchants to extend credit for family purposes to one spouse that will affect the estate of the other. See, e.g., Note, "The Unnecessary Doctrine of Necessaries." *Michigan Law Review* 82, no. 7 (1984): 1767.

10. See, e.g., Sir William Blackstone, *Commentaries on the Laws of England*, vol. 1 (chap. 15–16, pp. 422–32, for husband and wife, then parent and child), http://avalon.law.yale.edu/18th_century/blackstone_bk1ch15.asp; Michael Grossberg, *Governing the Hearth*. Chapel Hill: University of North Carolina Press, 1985, 259.

11. B. Douglas Bernheim and Oded Stark, "Altruism Within the Family Reconsidered: Do Nice Guys Finish Last?" *American Economic Review* 78, no. 5 (1988): 1044.

12. Jane Maslow Cohen, "Regimes of Private Tyranny: What Do They Mean to Morality and for the Criminal Law." *University of Pittsburgh Law Review* 57, no. 3 (1996): 757.

13. Danny De Vito, dir. (Twentieth Century Fox 1989).

14. Mary Ann Mason, *Custody Wars: Why Children Are Losing The Legal Battle and What We Can Do About It*. New York: Basic Books, 1999.

15. Rene Girard, *I See Satan Fall Like Lightning*. Maryknoll, NY: Orbis, 2001.

16. Citing many sources, see Derek E. Lyons, Andrew G. Young, and Frank C. Keil, "The Hidden Structure of Overimitation." *Proceedings of the National Academy of Sciences of the United States of America* 104, no. 50 (2007): 19751–56. One particularly interesting one is Horner and Whiten, "Causal Knowledge" (see chap. 5, n. 130).

17. Robert H. Frank, "The Demand for Unobservable and Other Nonpositional Goods." *American Economic Review* 75, no. 1 (1985): 101. People want to see how their things compare with those owned by others.

18. Coleman is criticized for discarding the importance of family in Nan Marie Astone, Constance A. Nathanson, Robert Schoen, and Young J. Kim, "Family Demography, Social Theory, and Investment in Social Capital." *Population and Development Review* 25, no. 1 (1999): 6–8.

19. Rene Girard, *Deceit, Desire, and The Novel: Self and Other in Literary Structure*. Baltimore, MD: Johns Hopkins University Press, 1961; and Rene Girard, *Violence and the Sacred*. Baltimore, MD: Johns Hopkins University Press, 1977, 19–52.

20. Girard, *Deceit, Desire, and The Novel*, 7 (see n. 18).

21. These theories first surfaced in Girard, *Deceit, Desire, and The Novel* (see n. 18) and Girard, *Violence and the Sacred* (see n. 18).

22. See, e.g., Jenny Onyx and Paul Bullen, "Measuring Social Capital in Five Communities." *Journal of Applied Behavioral Science* 36, no. 1 (2000): 23–42; John Brehm and Wendy Rahn, "Individual-Level Evidence for the Causes and Consequences of Social Capital." *American Journal of Political Science* 41, no. 3 (1997): 999–1000, 1014.

23. According to Richard H. McAdams, "Relative Preferences." *Yale Law Journal* 102, no. 1 (1992): 17, envy requires not only that one desires or covets what another has but also that he consequently feels a threat to self-esteem and acts to preserve himself in a socially inappropriate matter.

24. Rene Girard, *The Scapegoat*. Baltimore, MD: Johns Hopkins University Press, 1986. For an application, see, e.g., Andrea Dworkin, *Scapegoat: The Jews, Israel, and Women's Liberation*. New York: Free Press, 2000.

25. Gil Bailie, *Violence Unveiled: Humanity at the Crossroads*. New York: Crossword Publishing Company, 1999.

26. Thomas Hobbes, *De Cive* (1651) "War of All against All."

27. McAdams, "The Origin, Development, and Regulation of Norms" (see chap. 1, n. 38).

28. Girard, *Deceit, Desire, and The Novel*, 9 (see n. 18).

29. Girard, *The Scapegoat*, 25–46 (see n. 23); Bailie, *Violence Unveiled*, 187 (see n. 24).

30. John 11:49.

31. For some random examples, see Wolfgang Palaver, "A Girardian Reading of Schmitt's Political Theology." *Telos* 92, no. 93 (1992): 43–69; Sharon Zukin, "Mimesis in the Origins of Bourgeois Culture." *Theory and Society* 4, no. 3 (1977): 333–58; Reinier Leushuis, "The Mimesis of Marriage: Dialogue and Intimacy in Erasmus's Matrimonial Writings." *Renaissance Quarterly* 57, no. 4(2004):1278–1307.

32. See, e.g., David LaChance, "Last Words, Last Meals, and Last Stands: Agency and Individuality in the Modern Execution Process." *Law and Social Inquiry* 32, no. 3 (2007): 701–24.

33. Bailie, *Violence Unveiled*, 51 (see n. 24).

34. Bailie, *Violence Unveiled*, 185–95 (see n. 24).

35. Daniel 13. While other Bibles, including the Hebrew Bible, contain this book, they do not include the Suzanna story.

36. Bailie, *Violence Unveiled*, 188 (see n. 24).

37. Girard, *I See Satan Fall Like Lightning*, 16–17 (see n. 14). Bailie adds covetousness, rivalry, and contempt. Bailie, *Violence Unveiled*, 112 (see n. 24).

38. McAdams, "Relative Preferences," 5 (see n. 22); Rowthorn, "Marriage as a Signal," 142 (see chap. 1, n. 20). The comparison most often will be with someone else of relatively close social standing. This was true in the Suzanna story, as Bailie notes. See also Frank, "The Demand for Unobservable and Other Nonpositional Goods," 111 (see n. 16).

39. Girard, *I See Satan Fall Like Lightning*, 7–9 (see n. 14).

40. Stephen Felder, PhD, Homily on Palm Sunday, 2004, St. Michael and All Angels Church, Carmel, CA, http://www.stmikescdm.org/homilies/Passion%20Sunday%202004.htm (accessed March 1, 2009).

41. Raymond Lloyd Richmond, "A Guide to Psychology and Its Practice: Family Therapy," http://www.guidetopsychology.com/famlytx.htm (accessed August 20, 2009). In family therapy, the "identified patient (IP) is the family member with the symptom that has brought the family into treatment. The concept of the IP is used by family therapists to keep the family from scapegoating the IP or using him or her as a way of avoiding problems in the rest of the system." For an example and a way of handling the problem, see http://www.fiu.edu/~kennym/Family%20Therapy.htm (accessed August 20, 2009).

42. Mark E. Feinberg, Jenae M. Neiderhiser, Sam Simmens, David Reiss, and E. Mavis Hetherington, "Sibling Comparison of Differential Parental Treatment in Adolescence: Gender, Self-esteem, and Emotionality as Mediators of the Parenting-adjustment Association." *Child Development* 71, no. 6 (2000): 1611. Self-esteem seems to moderate the effect. As with the perceptions that husbands and wives do not do equal shares of housework, there is some truth to this perception. Recent work indicates that parents spend more time with older children than their siblings. Joseph Price, "Parent-Child Quality Time: Does Birth Order Matter?" *Journal of Human Resources* 43, no. 1 (2008): 240–65 (a total of 2,000 hours more).

43. Alternatively and more typically, Becker and Lewis predict that we should transfer nonhuman capital to children to compensate for their lower endowments. Gary S. Becker and H. Gregg Lewis, "On the Interaction between the Quantity and Quality of Children." *Journal of Political Economy* 81 (1973): 279. Becker and Tomes argue that parents also reinforce higher "giftedness" with human capital. Becker and Tomes, "Child Endowments," S161 (see chap. 5, n. 21).

44. "Family Violence Prevention Services," http://www.serve.com/fvps/ (accessed August 20, 2009). See, e.g., John Dollard, *Frustration and Aggression*. New Haven, CT: Publication for the Institute of Human Relations by Yale University Press, 1939; Elliot Aronson et al., *Social Psychology: The Heart and Mind* New York: Harper Collins College Publishers, 1994, 523.

45. 751 N.Y.S.2d 449 (App. Div. 2002).

46. Glenda Kaufman-Kantor and Murray A. Straus, "Substance Abuse as a Precipitant of Wife Abuse Victimizations." *American Journal of Drug and Alcohol Abuse* 15, no. 2 (1989): 173–90.

47. For example, see Bambade H. Shakoor and Deborah Chalmers, "Covictimization of African-American Children Who Witness Violence: Effects on Cognitive, Emotional, and Behavioral Development." *Journal of the American Medical Association* 83 (1991): 233–39.

48. 378 S.E.2d 8 (N.C. 1989).

49. Judy Norman's defense was unsuccessful because, according to the North Carolina Supreme Court, she was not under actual attack or threat of attack at the moment she used deadly force. However, her sentence (of six years in prison) was commuted by the governor after three months.

50. 269 S.E.2d 363 (Va. 1979)

51. 269 S.E.2d, 365.

52. This would now be true only for adultery, though other fault may be taken into account in figuring the amount of alimony. Va. Code 20–107.1(E).

53. 188 Cal. Rptr. 781 (Cal. App. 1983).

54. Robert Lindsey, "Surgery Follows Pact on Custody." *New York Times*, October 10, 1983, A12.

55. As a parent, an overriding human motivation is a taste for seeing that one's children are launched in life as successfully as possible—which depends on how their skills and endowments compare with others." Frank, "The Demand for Unobservable and Other Nonpositional Goods," 102 (see n. 16). Relative standing is far more important than the absolute level of consumption in determining well-being. Frank, 106.

56. Riggins-Caspers, Cadoret, Lempers, Panak, Troughton, and Stewart, "Gene X Environment Interaction" (see chap. 5, n. 10).

57. Fukuyama, *The Great Disruption* (see chap. 4, n. 153) is grounded in biology. See, e.g., Owen D. Jones, "On the Nature of Norms: Biology, Morality, and the Disruption of Order." *Michigan Law Review* 98, no. 6 (2000): 2072–103, reviewing it. For a review of the economics literature from a behavioral biology perspective, see Ted Bergstrom, "Economics in a Family Way." *Journal of Economic Literature* 34, no. 4 (1996): 1903–34.

58. For a recent paper, see David J. Herring, "Kinship Foster Care: Implications of Behavioral Biology Research." University of Pittsburgh, Legal Studies Research Paper Series 2008–01, Pittsburgh, PA, 2008. Herring says that kinship care should be ordered the way genetics would suggest caregivers might be most apt to treat children well—first to maternal grandmothers, last among grandparent choices to paternal grandfathers.

59. Robin Wilson has a string of articles discussing the danger of child sexual abuse. The latest in the string is Robin Fretwell Wilson, "The Cradle of Abuse: Evaluating the Danger Posed by a Sexually Predatory Parent to the Victim's Sib-

lings." *Emory Law Journal* 51, no. 1 (2002): 241–308. On child abuse by genetically unrelated adults, see Owen D. Jones, "Evolutionary Analysis in Law: An Introduction and Application to Child Abuse." *North Carolina Law Review* 75, no. 4 (1997): 1117–242; as well as Brinig and Buckley, "Parental Rights and the Ugly Duckling" (see chap. 1, n. 98), from which part of this section will be drawn.

60. For studies examining the causes of elder abuse, see Mark S. Lachs, Christianna Williams, Shelley O'Brien, Leslie Hurst, and Ralph Horwitz, "Risk Factors for Reported Elder Abuse and Neglect: A Nine-Year Observational Cohort Study." *Gerontologist* 37, no. 4 (1997): 469–74; Margaret W. Baker, "Elder Mistreatment: Risk, Vulnerability, and Early Mortality." *Journal of the American Psychiatric Nurses Association* 12, no. 6 (2007): 313–21; Mark S. Lachs and Karl Pillemer, "Abuse and Neglect of Elderly Persons." *New England Journal of Medicine* 332, no. 7 (1995): 438, table 1, lists the following risk factors that parallel scapegoating characteristics: poor health and functional impairment in the elderly person, cognitive impairment in the elderly person, substance abuse or mental illness on the part of the abuser, dependence of the abuser on the victim, shared living arrangements, external factors causing stress, social isolation, and a history of violence (particularly between spouses).

61. Mary Lou Hulseman and Lee A. Norman, "Fundamentals of Outpatient Care: The Neonatal ICU Graduate." *American Family Physician* 45, no. 4 (1992): 1696.

62. Martha Minow, *Making All The Difference.* Ithaca, NY: Cornell University Press, 1991.

63. This section draws from Brinig and Buckley, "Parental Rights and the Ugly Duckling" (see chap. 1, n. 98).

64. See, e.g., Mary I. Benedict et al., "Reported Maltreatment in Children with Multiple Disabilities." *Child Abuse and Neglect* 14, no. 2 (1990): 207–17; Roger White et al., "Physical Disabilities as Risk Factors for Child Maltreatment: A Selected Review." *American Journal of Orthopsychiatry* 51, no. 1 (1987): 96.

65. Premature infants are at increased risk for physical abuse and neglect. K. K. Minde, "The Impact of Prematurity on the Later Behavior of Children and on their Families." *Clinics in Perinatology* 11, no. 1 (1984): 227–33.

66. See, e.g., Matt Ridley, *The Red Queen: Sex and the Evolution of Human Nature.* New York: Macmillan, 1993; Lloyd Cohen, "Marriage, Divorce and Quasi-Rents; or, I Gave Him the Best Years of My Life." *Journal Legal Studies* 16, no. 2 (1987): 267.

67. See, e.g., *Bd. of Curators of Univ. of Missouri v. Horowitz*, 435 U.S. 78 (1978); Daniel S. Hamermesh and Jeff E. Biddle, "Beauty and the Labor Market." *American Economic Review* 84, no. 5 (1994): 1174–94; Peter Passell, "An Ugly Subject: The Prejudice Against Hiring Homely People." *New York Times*, January 27, 1994, 2.

68. Paula England and Gary Farkas, *Households, Employment, and Gender*. New York: Aldine Publishing Company, 1986, talk about a "D" or desirability quotient.

69. Ridley, *The Red Queen*, 146–49 (see n. 65).

70. Richard A. Posner, *Aging and Old Age*. Chicago: University of Chicago Press, 1995, 220–22.

71. The birth of a child with a physical or mental disability begins a mourning process with specific stages of resolution, characterized by "chronic, relentless stress." White et al., "Physical Disabilities" (see n. 63).

72. *Berman v. Allen*, 80 N.J. 421, 404 A.2d 8 (1979).

73. For example, an eleven-year-old boy was recently killed by his father for being unable to tell time. The child's great-grandmother said that he was a slow learner and was attending special education classes. Sari Horwitz, "Father Is Charged in Beating Death of District Boy." *Washington Post*, May 1, 1997, A1.

74. For examples, see Lawrence E. Frisch and Frances A. Rhoads, "Child Abuse and Neglect in Children Referred for Learning Evaluation." *Journal of Learning Disabilities* 15, no. 10 (1982): 585.

75. See, e.g., Stanley R. Friedman, "The Need for Intensive Follow-Up of Abused Children." In *Helping the Battered Child and His Family*, edited by C. Henry Kempe and Ray E. Helfer. Philadelphia: Lippincott, 1972.

76. Becker and Tomes, "Child Endowments" (see chap. 5, n. 21).

77. Elisabeth Krents, Valerie Schulman, and Sheila Brenner, "Child Abuse and the Disabled Child: Perspectives for Parents." *Volta Review* 89, no. 5 (1987): 83.

78. Martin Daly and Margo Wilson, "Child Abuse and Other Risks of Not Living with Both Parents." *Ethology and Sociobiology* 6, no. 4 (1985): 197; Joy L. Lightcap, Jeffrey A. Kurland, and Robert L. Burgess, "Child Abuse: A Test of Some Predictions from Evolutionary Theory." *Ethology and Sociobiology* 3, no. 2 (1982): 61.

79. Forty-seven percent (47%) of couples divorcing where the wife had a previous marriage had children. Sally C. Clarke, "Advance Report of Final Divorce Statistics, 1989 and 1990.", *Monthly Vital Statistics Report* 43, no. 9, Supplement (1995). Hyattsville, MD: National Center for Health Statistics.

80. See generally Sigmund Freud, *Basic Writings of Sigmund Freud*. New York: Modern Library, 1995; Gary S. Anderson and Robert Tollison, "A Theory of Rational Childhood." *European Journal of Political Economy* 7, no. 2 (1991): 199.

81. Judith Seltzer reports that men in particular are far more attached to the children of a new relationship than children of a prior one with whom the man no longer lives. Judith A. Seltzer, "Consequences of Marital Dissolution for Children." *Annual Review of Sociology* 20, no. 1 (1994): 235.

82. Fukuyama, *The Great Disruption* (see chap. 4, n. 153); reviewed in Jones, "On the Nature of Norms" (see n. 56).

83. Edmund Wilson, *Sociobiology*. Cambridge, MA: Harvard University Press, 1975; Ridley, *The Red Queen* (see n. 65); Robert Wright, *The Moral Animal*. New York: Pantheon, 1994; Robert Trivers, "Evolution of Reciprocal Altruism." *Quarterly Review of Biology* 46, no. 1 (1971): 35. Sociobiological discussions are beginning to appear in mainstream social science journals. See, e.g., Lisa Laumann-

Billings and Robert E. Emery, "Distress Among Young Adults from Divorced Families." *Journal of Family Psychology* 14, no. 4 (2000): 677; Steven L. Nock, "The Consequences of Premarital Fatherhood." *American Sociological Review* 63, no. 2 (1998): 251.

84. Richard Epstein, "Justice Across the Generations." In *The Dialogue of Justice, Toward a Self-Reflective Society*, edited by Peter Laslett and James S. Fishkin. New Haven, CT: Yale University Press, 1992, 84–89.

85. William N. Friedrich and Allison J. Einbender, "The Abused Child: A Psychological Review." *Journal of Clinical Child Psychology* 12, no. 3 (1983): 244–56.

86. Daly and Wilson, "Child Abuse and Other Risks" (see n. 77); Lightcap, Kurland, and Burgess, "Child Abuse" (see n. 77). Evolutionary psychologists have pointed to risks of jealousy and "mate guarding" as well as the protective function for genetics as factors in abuse. See, e.g., Robert L. Burgess et al., "Violence to the Family." In *Life Span Developmental Psychology: Nonnormative Events*, edited by Edward J. Callahan and Kathleen A. McCluskey-Fawcett. New York: Academic Press, 1983; Martin Daly and Margo Wilson, "Violence Against Stepchildren." *Current Directions in Psychological Science* 5, no. 3 (1996): 77.

87. See, e.g., One ADD Place, "Famous People With Attention Deficit and Learning Disorders," http://www.oneaddplace.com/famous.htm (accessed August 20, 2009).

88. See, e.g., David Lyman, "Possible Link Between Attention-Deficit/Hyperactivity Disorder and Reproductive Complications." *Journal of Clinical Psychiatry: Primary Care Companion* 4, no. 1 (2002): 104; Miriam H. Mulsow, Keri K. O'Neal, and Velma McBride Murry, "Adult Attention Deficit Hyperactivity Disorder, the Family, and Child Maltreatment." *Trauma, Violence, and Abuse* 2, no. 1 (2001): 36–50.

89. Cheryl-Lynn Podolski and Joel T. Nigg, "Parent Stress and Coping in Relation to Child ADHD Severity and Associated Child Disruptive Behavior Problems." *Journal of Clinical Child Psychology* 30, no. 4 (2001): 503.

90. Allison M. Briscoe-Smith and Stephen P. Hinshaw, "Linkages Between Child Abuse and Attention-Deficit/Hyperactivity Disorder in Girls: Behavioral and Social Correlates." *Child Abuse and Neglect* 30, no. 11 (2006): 1241. See also Joseph C. Crozier and Richard P. Barth, "Cognitive and Academic Functioning in Maltreated Children." *Children and Schools* 27 no. 4 (2005): 197–206.

91. M. J. Breen and R. A. Barkley, "Child Psychopathology and Parenting Stress in Girls and Boys with Attention-Deficit Disorder." *Journal of Pediatric Psychiatry* 13, no. 2 (1988): 265. This stress leads to more divorce among these parents. See Charlotte Johnston, "Parent Characteristics and Parent-Child Interactions in Families of Nonproblem Children and ADHD Children with Higher and Lower Levels of Oppositional-Defiant Disorder." *Journal of Abnormal Child Psychology* 24, no. 1 (1996): 85.

92. Andrea L. Hazen, Cynthia D. Connelly, Kelly Kelleher, John Landsverk, and Richard Barth, "Intimate Partner Violence Among Female Caregivers of

Children Reported for Child Maltreatment." *Child Abuse and Neglect*, 28, no. 3 (2004): 301–19, reports that 44.7% of female caregivers of abused children reported that they experienced physical violence at the hands of a partner, with 29% reporting it in the last year (nationally representative sample of families referred to child protective services).

93. See also Mulsow, O'Neal, and McBride Murry, "Adult Attention Deficit Hyperactivity Disorder" (see n. 87).

94. See, e.g., Alicia M. Weissman, Gerald D. Jogerst, and Jeffrey G. Dawson, "Community Characteristics Associated with Child Abuse in Iowa." *Child Abuse and Neglect* 27, no. 10 (2003): 1151, 1153, table 2.

95. See, e.g., Rachel A. Gordon et al., "Family and Neighborhood Income: Additive and Multiplicative Associations with Youths' Well-Being." *Social Science Research* 32, no. 2 (2003): 210.

96. Briscoe-Smith and Hinshaw, "Linkages Between Child Abuse and Attention-Deficit/Hyperactivity Disorder in Girls" (see n. 89) (citing Mariellen Fischer, "Parenting Stress and the Child with Attention Deficit Hyperactivity Disorder." *Journal of Clinical Child Psychology* 19, no. 4 (1990): 337–346.

97. Briscoe-Smith and Hinshaw, "Linkages Between Child Abuse and Attention-Deficit/Hyperactivity Disorder in Girls" (see n. 89).

98. Janet Wozniak et al., "Antecedents and Complications of Trauma in Boys With ADHD: Findings From a Longitudinal Study." *Journal of the American Academy of Child and Adolescent Psychiatry* 38, no. 1 (1999): 48–55.

99. See Carolyn Copps Hartley, "The Co-occurrence of Child Maltreatment and Domestic Violence: Examining Both Neglect and Child Physical Abuse." *Child Maltreatment* 7, no. 4 (2002): 349; and Carol Coohey and Patrick O'Leary, "Mothers' Protection of Their Children After Discovering They Have Been Sexually Abused: An Information-Processing Perspective." *Child Abuse and Neglect* 32, no. 2 (2008): 245.

100. Briscoe-Smith and Hinshaw, "Linkages Between Child Abuse and Attention-Deficit/Hyperactivity Disorder in Girls" (see n. 89).

101. Center for Disease Control and Prevention, Attention-Deficit / Hyperactivity Disorder (ADHD), http://www.cdc.gov/ncbddd/adhd/medicated.html (accessed August 20, 2009). This estimate may be high according to the NIMH (3–5% nationally). These children are also more likely to be injured without intervention by their parents. C. DiScala et al., "Injuries to Children With Attention Deficit Hyperactivity Disorder." *Pediatrics* 102, no. 6 (1998):1415–21.

102. See, e.g., Friedrich and Einbender, "The Abused Child" (see n. 83). Frisch and Rhoads, "Child Abuse and Neglect" (see n. 72); Krents, Schulman, and Brenner, "Child Abuse and the Disabled Child." 78, 83 (see n. 75); William A. Friedrich and Jerry A. Boriskin, "The Role of the Child in Abuse: A Review of the Literature." *American Journal of Orthopsychiatry* 46, no. 4 (1987): 583–84; White et al., "Physical Disabilities," 96 (see n. 63).

103. Briscoe-Smith and Hinshaw, "Linkages Between Child Abuse and Attention-Deficit/Hyperactivity Disorder in Girls" (see n. 89).

104. Kevin Baldwin, Ronald T. Brown, and Michael A. Milan, "Predictors of Stress in Caregivers of Attention Deficit Hyperactivity Disordered Children." *American Journal of Family Therapy* 23, no. 2 (1995): 149 (30 children with confirmed diagnosis of ADHD).

105. Gordon et al., "Family and Neighborhood Income." 213 (see n. 94).

106. Charlotte Johnston, "Parent Characteristics and Parent-Child Interactions in Families of Nonproblem Children and ADHD Children with Higher and Lower Levels of Oppositional-Defiant Behavior." *Journal of Abnormal Child Psychology* 24, no. 1 (1996): 95, table 2.

107. Ibid., 98, table 3.

108. Brinig and Buckley, "Parental Rights and the Ugly Duckling" (see chap. 1, n. 98).

109. National Data Archive on Child Abuse and Neglect, *The Maltreatment of Children with Disabilities and Child Maltreatment in Substance Abusing Families, 1991: NDACAN Dataset Number* 68, *User's Guide and Codebook*. Ithaca, NY: National Data Archive on Child Abuse and Neglect, Family Life Development Center, Cornell University, 1991 (http://www.ndacan.cornell.edu/NDACAN/Datasets/UserGuidePDFs/068user.pdf [accessed August 20, 2009]).

110. Of the 300 children with disabilities, 81 were abused, for an average of 0.269103 (see AH05.dif). Corresponding overall national figures for 1991 indicate that an average of 4.2 children per thousand were abused, for an average of .024, less than one-tenth as high.

111. There were 512 such families that had full information, including the ages and physical conditions of all the children and where parents or other relatives, as opposed to outsiders, abused the child. Abuse was identified as physical assault, sexual abuse, emotional abuse, physical neglect, medical neglect, abandonment, expulsion, inadequate supervision, inattention to special education need, other specified educational neglect, inadequate nurturing or affection, refusal or delay of psychological care, other specified emotional neglect, other specified maltreatment, and drug/alcohol toxicology, addiction, or abuse in the child. See National Data Archive on Child Abuse and Neglect, *The Maltreatment of Children with Disabilities and Child Maltreatment in Substance Abusing Families* (see n. 108, Appendix A: Codebook Information for AHNRCD3). We classified physical assault, sexual abuse, and emotional abuse as abuse cases and the rest as neglect cases.

112. In the analysis reported here, we could not run the usual ordinary least squares regression but needed to look at the probability that a particular child would be abused based upon the various factors. This type of multivariate analysis is called probit.

113. Notably, all but three of the neglect cases in our data set involved parents with less than the median income (approximately $13,000 for rural areas and

$17,000 for urban areas) of those in the study. See also Laumann-Billings and Emery, "Distress Among Young Adults," 127 (see n. 82).

114. Owen D. Jones, "Sex Selection: Regulating Technology Enabling the Predetermination of a Child's Gender." *Harvard Journal of Law and Technology* 6, no. 1 (1992): 10; Lucinda Richards, "Controlling China's Baby Boom." *Contemporary Review* 268, no. 1 (1996): 5, reporting that the Chinese gender gap represents 1.7 million fewer female babies appearing on Chinese birth records every year than worldwide rates would lead us to expect.

115. See, e.g., Shirley Cohen and Rachel D. Warren, "The Intersection of Disability and Child Abuse in England and the United States." *Child Welfare* 69, no. 3 (1990): 253; Linda J. Diamond and Paula K. Jaudes, "The Handicapped Child and Child Abuse." *Child Abuse and Neglect* 9, no. 3 (1985): 341; Shirley Cohen and Rachel D. Warren, "Preliminary Survey of Family Abuse of Children Served by United Cerebral Palsy Centers." *Developmental Medicine and Child Neurology* 29, no. 1 (1987): 12; Astrid James, "Abuse of Disabled Children." *Lancet* 341, no. 8844 (1993): 553.

116. Cohen and Warren, "The Intersection of Disability and Child Abuse," 254 (see n. 114); Diamond and Jaudes, "The Handicapped Child and Child Abuse" (see n. 114); Cohen and Warren, "Preliminary Survey of Family Abuse" (see n. 114); James, "Abuse of Disabled Children" (see n. 114).

117. Vimala Pillari, *Scapegoating in Families: Intergenerational Patterns of Physical and Emotional Abuse.* New York: Brunner/Maze1, 1991.

118. For example, the total number of children observed may be very small, see Sarah H. Ramsey and Robert F. Kelly, "Using Social Science Research in Family Law Analysis and Formation: Problems and Prospects." *Southern California Interdisciplinary Law Journal* 3, no. 2 (1994): 631, or they may all have come from a particular population that suggests they aren't representative of all abused children, Cohen and Warren, "The Intersection of Disability and Child Abuse," 254 (see n. 114) or even of the group in question.

119. Regardless of substantive standards, the parent has impressive due process protections. See, e.g., *M. L. B. v. S. L. J.* 136 L. Ed. 2d 473 (1996) (parent's right to free transcript); *Santosky v. Kramer*, 455 U.S. 745 (1982) (enunciating a "clear and convincing" evidence standard before making the finding of abuse); *Lassiter v. Dept. of Soc. Servs.*, 452 U.S. 18 (1981) (parent's right to court-appointed counsel in termination proceedings on a case by case basis).

120. Institute of Judicial Administration–American Bar Association Joint Commission on Juvenile Justice Standards. *Standards Relating to Abuse and Neglect.* Cambridge, MA: Ballinger Publishing, 1981, Standard 8-3(C)(2) (excerpted in Schneider and Brinig, *An Invitation to Family Law* [see chap. 1, n. 54]). Obviously, this requires at least two proven instances of abuse plus a substantial time in foster care.

121. See, e.g., Douglas Besharov, *Combating Child Abuse: Guidelines For Co-operation Between Law Enforcement and Child Protective Services*. Washington, DC: American Enterprise Institute for Public Policy Research, 1990, 2–6.

122. 489 U.S. 189 (1989).

123. Ibid., 209.

124. See Timothy Egan, "Child Abuse Cases Draw New Attention." *New York Times*, January 1, 1988, A5.

125. Gary Langer, "Saddest Tragedies of Child Abuse: Preventable Cases." *Los Angeles Times*, December 13, 1987, 2. See generally Lorene Fuerbach Schaefer, "Abused Children and State-Created Protection Agencies: A Proposed Section 1983 Standard." *University of Cincinnati Law Review* 57, no. 4 (1989): 1419; see also Child Fatality Review Panel, *Child Fatality Review Panel: Annual Report for 1993*. New York: New York City Human Resources Administration, 1995.

126. See, e.g., Steve Vogel, "Woman Convicted of Abusing Boy, 5, Montgomery Judge Calls Imprisonment, Other Treatment 'Bizarre' and 'Malicious.'" *Washington Post*, November 15, 1997, B1; Steve Vogel, "'Mommy Put a Leash on Them,' Social Worker Recalls Boy's Explanation for Marks on Feet, Other Injuries." *Washington Post*, November 7, 1997, B7.

127. Mary Zahn and Sarah Carr, "Abuse Fears Got No Action: Two Doctors Warned of Suspicious Injuries Months Before Toddler was Killed." *Milwaukee Journal-Sentinel*, May 16, 2007.

128. Douglas L. Besharov and Lisa Lauman-Billings, "Don't Call it Child Abuse if It's Really Poverty." *Journal Children and Poverty* 3, no. 1 (1997): 5; Laumann-Billings and Emery. "Distress Among Young Adults," 125 (see n. 82). One of the classic articles on the subject is Robert H. Mnookin, "Foster Care: In Whose Best Interest?" *Harvard Education Review* 43, no. 4 (1973): 599; see also John E. B. Myers, "The Legal Response to Child Abuse: In the Best Interest of Children?" *Journal of Family Law* 24, no. 2 (1985–86): 149; Marsha Garrison, "Child Welfare Decisionmaking: In Search of the Least Drastic Alternative." *Georgetown Law Journal* 75, no. 6 (1987): 1745.

129. P.L. 105–89,105th Congress, 1997 H.R. 867.

130. See, e.g., Va. Code Ann. §§16.1–248, 1 et seq.

131. See Laumann-Billings and Emery, "Distress Among Young Adults," 131 (see n. 82) citing Ching-Tung Lung and Deborah Darro, *Current Trends in Child Abuse Reporting and Fatalities: The Results of the* 1995 *Annual Fifty State Survey*. Chicago: National Committee to Prevent Child Abuse, 1996 (between 35 and 50% had already been brought to law enforcement or child protective agencies' attention).

132. See, e.g., Horwitz, "Father Is Charged in Beating Death of District Boy" (see n. 72).

133. See, e.g., Brian Mooar, "Florida Jury Convicts Man in Stepdaughter's Death." *Washington Post*, November 19, 1996, B1.

134. *DeShaney v. Winnebago Co. Dept. of Soc. Servs.*, 489 U.S. 189 (1989).

135. *Santosky v. Kramer*, 455 U.S. 745 (1982).

136. *Lassiter v. Department of Soc. Servs.*, 452 U.S. 18 (1981).

137. 519 U.S. 102 (1996).

138. Juvenile Justice Standards Project, § 1.4 (see n. 119).

139. One study reported that 82% of the children awaiting adoption have special needs. Child Welfare League of America, "The State of Adoption in America." *Children Today*, May-June 1989, 3.

140. James A. Rosenthal, "Outcomes of Adoption of Children with Special Needs." *Future of Children* 3, no. 1 (1993): 77. Rosenthal notes that adoptions of disabled children are as successful as those of "normal" children when the children are adopted before age three.

141. *Troxel v. Glanville*, 530 U.S. 57 (2000)

142. *M. L. B. v. S. L. J.*, 519 U.S. 102 (1996); *Santosky v. Kramer*, 455 U.S. 745 (1982); *Lassiter v. Dept. of Soc. Servs.*, 452 U.S. 18 (1981).

143. 42 U.S.C.A. § 671(a) (15) (Supp. 2000).

144. Adoption Assistance and Child Welfare Act, 42 U.S.C. §§ 670 et seq. (1980) (current version at 42 U.S.C.A. §§ 670 et seq. (Supp. 2000)).

145. Douglas J. Besharov, "Child Abuse Realities: Over-Reporting and Poverty." *Virginia Journal of Social Policy and the Law* 8, no. 1 (2000): 165–203.

146. See also Carol Coohey, "Physically Abusive Fathers and Risk Assessment." *Child Abuse and Neglect* 30, no. 5–05 (2006): 467–80 (using Linn County Iowa families, found that unemployment and having unrelated children in the family were among the factors indicating likely reabuse).

147. For data demonstrating these results, see National Data Archive on Child Abuse and Neglect, *The Maltreatment of Children with Disabilities and Child Maltreatment in Substance Abusing Families* (see n. 108). Analysts have estimated that between 24–90% of all child maltreatment reports involve substance abuse. See, e.g., Elizabeth M. Tracy, "Maternal Substance Abuse: Protecting the Child, Preserving the Family. *Social Work* 39, no. 5 (1993): 534; Bridgett A. Besinger, Ann F. Garland, Alan J. Litrownik, and John A. Landsverk, "Caregiver Substance Abuse Among Maltreated Children Placed in Out-of-Home Care." *Child Welfare* 78, no. 2 (1999): 221–39 (79% of caregivers met criteria for caregiver substance abuse in a sample of 639 children removed from their homes for maltreatment).

148. See, e.g., Douglas J. Besharov, "Children Deserve Chance to Live; The System Won't Accept the Uncomfortable Truth: Some Parents Are Beyond the Help of Treatment Programs." *Orlando Sentinel*, December 22, 1996, G1; Douglas J. Besharov, "The Children of Crack: Will We Protect Them?" *Public Welfare* 46, no. 1 (1989): 7–11.

149. Cf. *Angela M. W. v. Kruzicki*, 209 Wis. 2d 112, 561 N.W.2d 729 (1997), a troubling case in which a postviability pregnant cocaine-addicted mother was hospitalized involuntarily for the duration of her pregnancy, causing the amendment

of Wis. Stat. § 48.02 to include in its definition of abuse "[w]hen used in referring to an unborn child, serious physical harm inflicted on the unborn child, and the risk of serious physical harm to the child when born, caused by the habitual lack of self-control of the expectant mother of the unborn child in the use of alcohol beverages, controlled substances or controlled substance analogs, exhibited to a severe degree" and providing in § 17m for special treatment or care including professional services of drug treatment for such unborn children. 1997 Act 292.

150. Martin Daly and Margo Wilson, "Family Violence: An Evolutionary Psychological Perspective." *Virginia Journal of Social Policy and the Law* 8, no. 1 (2000): 77.

151. See, e.g., Daly and Wilson, "Child Abuse" (see n. 77); Jones, "Evolutionary Analysis in Law" (see n. 58).

152. See, e.g., Vogel, "Woman Convicted of Abusing Boy" (see n. 125); Vogel, "Mommy Put a Leash on Them" (see n. 125).

153. The exception is Brinig and Buckley, "Parental Rights and the Ugly Duckling" (see chap. 1, n. 98).

154. *In re Phillip B.*, 92 Cal. App. 3d 796,156 Cal. Rptr. 38 (1979) (parents decided not to perform heart surgery on child with Down syndrome); *In re K. I., B. I., and D. M.*, 735 A.2d 448 (D.C. App. 1999) (premature baby with serious medical problems was seriously neglected by his mother).

155. 42 USCA 671, § 15.

156. 42 USCA 671(15) (D) (2). This was the case in *Santosky v. Kramer*, and *In re Adoption No. 12612*, 1999 Md. LEXIS 51.

157. American Law Institute, "Principles of the Law of Family Dissolution." §2.11(1) (a) (2002), limiting allocation of custodial responsibility to parents who have not abused according to state law.

158. Murray A. Strauss, Richard A. Gelles, and Suzanne K. Steinmetz, *Behind Closed Doors: Violence in the American Family*. Garden City, NY: Anchor Press/Doubleday, 1980, 409.

159. *In re Alyne E.*, 113 Misc. 2d 307, 448 N.Y.S.2d 984 (1982) (failure to aid a psychologically disturbed adolescent found abuse); *In re Shane T.*, 115 Misc.2d 161, 453 N.Y.S.2d 590 (1982) (verbal abuse by father who repeatedly called his son derogatory terms indicating that the boy was gay); *State v. Payne*, 240 Conn. 766, 695 A.2d 525 (1997) (emotional abuse case, not by parent, where accused forced young boys to urinate into cup); *Cheseborough v. State*, 255 So. 2d 675 (Fla. 1971) (parents demonstrated "how babies were made" to their young son).

160. Robert Ellickson depicts the process in "Unpacking the Household," 226, 300–305 (see chap. 1, n. 30).

161. See Michael B. First et al., "Personality Disorders and Relational Disorders: A Research Agenda for Addressing Crucial Gaps in DSM." In *A Research Agenda for DSM-V*, edited by David J. Kupfer, Michael B. First, and Darrel A. Regier. Washington, DC: American Psychiatric Association, 2002, 166; Martha R. Mahoney,

"Legal Images of Battered Women: Redefining the Issue of Separation." *Michigan Law Review* 90, no. 1 (1991): 8.

162. Nock, Sanchez, and Wright, *Covenant Marriage*, 133–39 (see chap. 1, n. 100).

163. Girard, *I See Satan Fall Like Lightning* (see n. 14).

164. See also Nathaniel M. Lambert and David C. Dollahite, "How Religiosity Helps Couples Prevent, Resolve, and Overcome Marital Conflict." *Family Relations* 55, no. 4 (2006): 443: "Aside from unifying couples by providing a shared vision, religiosity seemed to help prevent marital conflict by fostering what we call relational virtues. . . . Selflessness and unconditional love were especially emphasized."

165. Kristin M. Ferguson, "Social Capital and Children's Wellbeing: A Critical Synthesis of the International Social Capital Literature." *International Journal of Social Welfare* 15, no. 1–01 (2006): 2–18.

166. Robert Rowthorn, "Marriage and Trust: Some Lessons from Economics." *Cambridge Journal of Economics*, 23, no. 5 (1999): 661–91.

167. Shelly Lundberg, "Sons, Daughters, and Parental Behavior." *Oxford Review of Economic Policy* 21, no. 3 (2005): 340–56.

168. McAdams, "Relative Preferences," 2 (see n. 22) ("rational actors seek not an absolute end, but relative position among peers").

169. See, e.g., David Kreps, Paul Milgrom, John Roberts, and Robert Wilson, "Rational Cooperation in Finitely Repeated Prisoners' Dilemma." *Journal of Economic Theory* 27, no. 2 (1982): 245–52.

170. Astone, Nathanson, Schoen, and Kim, "Family Demography," 11 (see n. 17) (quoting from George Caspar Homans, *Social Behavior: Its Elementary Forms*. New York: Harcourt, Brace, and World, 1961, 38).

171. Daniel J. Weigel, "Parental Divorce and the Types of Commitment-Related Messages People Gain from Their Families of Origin." *Journal of Divorce and Remarriage* 47, no. 1/2 (2007): 15–32, relies on a number of studies showing that trust (or lack of it) flows through girls' experiences of parental divorce. Lack of trust and fidelity in the message they gained from families of origin was the single largest difference between children of divorce and those who come from intact families (significant at $p < .001$), Weigel, 19, citing Susan E. Jacquet and Catherine A. Surra, "Parental Divorce and Premarital Couples: Commitment and Other Relationship Characteristics." *Journal of Marriage and the Family* 63, no. 3 (2001): 627–38; and also his own experiment (Weigel, 22, table 1).

172. Annette Mahoney, Kenneth I. Pargament, Tracey Jewell, Aaron B. Swank, Eric Scott, Erin Emey, and Mark Rye, "Marriage and the Spiritual Realm: The Role of Proximal and Distal Religious Constructs in Marital Functioning." *Journal of Family Psychology* 13, no. 3 (1999): 321–38. Adam J. Zolotor and Desmond K. Runyan, "Social Capital, Family Violence, and Neglect." *Pediatrics* 117, no. 6 (2006): 1124–31; Li-Ching Lee, Jonathan B. Kotch, and Christine E. Cox, "Child Maltreat-

ment in Families Experiencing Domestic Violence." *Violence and Victims* 19, no. 5 (2004): 575.

173. Coleman, "Social Capital" (see intro., n. 3).

174. Ferguson, "Social Capital," 5 (see n. 164).

175. Ibid., 9. See also Lee, Kotch, and Cox, "Child Maltreatment," 587 (see n. 171) "social supports such as the availability of a helpful grandparent and church attendance may mitigate the effect of violence on children in homes experiencing domestic violence."

176. Lee M. Pachter, Peggy Auinger, Ray Palmer, and Michael Weitzman, "Do Parenting and the Home Environment, Maternal Depression, Neighborhood, and Chronic Poverty Affect Child Behavioral Problems Differently in Different Racial-Ethnic Groups?" *Pediatrics* 117, no. 4 (2006): 1329–38 (using the NSFH).

177. Carol Coohey, "The Relationship Between Familism and Child Maltreatment in Latino and Anglo Families." *Child Maltreatment* 6, no 2–05 (2001): 130–41.

178. Desmond K. Runyan, Wanda M. Hunter, Rebecca R. S. Socolar, Lisa Amaya-Jackson, Diana English, John Landsverk, Howard Dubowitz, Dorothy H. Browne, Shrikant I. Bangdiwala, and Ravi M. Mathew, "Children Who Prosper in Unfavorable Environments: The Relationship to Social Capital." *Pediatrics* 101, no. 1–1 (1998): 12–18. Though income mattered, too, maternal education (maternal human capital) was not significantly related to child well-being.

179. Jonathan B. Kotch, Dorothy C. Browne, Christopher L. Ringwalt, Vincent Dufort, Ellen Ruina, Paul W. Stewart, and Jin-Whan Jung, "Stress, Social Support, and Substantiated Maltreatment in the Second and Third Years of Life." *Child Abuse and Neglect* 21, no. 11 (1997): 1031, figure 1.

180. Virginia M. Morrow, "'Dirty Looks' and 'Trampy Places' in Young People's Accounts of Community and Neighbourhood: Implications for Health Inequalities." *Critical Public Health* 10, no. 2–06 (2000): 141–52 (using qualitative data on British children ages 12–15).

181. James M. Gaudin and Leonard Pollane, "Social Networks, Stress, and Child Abuse." *Children and Youth Services Review* 5, no. 1 (1983): 91–102.

182. Howard C. Tvenson, "Raising Safe Villages: Cultural-Ecological Factors that Influence the Emotional Adjustment of Adolescents." *Journal of Black Psychology* 24, no. 1 (1998): 44–59 at page 52. Neighborhood social capital did matter significantly in this study.

183. Mahoney et al., "Marriage and the Spiritual Realm" (see n. 114).

184. Mahoney, "Legal Images of Battered Women," 329, table 3 (see n. 160). The adjusted R^2 changes (or explanatory power) of the various variables ranged from about .05 to .19 for the variables where both husbands' and wives' measures were statistically significant, controlling for individual religiosity.

185. Ibid., 334.

186. W. Bradford Wilcox, *Soft Patriarchs, New Men: How Christianity Shapes Fathers and Husbands*. Chicago: University of Chicago Press, 2004, 121, figure 4.4.

187. Ibid., 129, figure 4.3.

188. Ibid., 182, figure 6.34.

189. Nock, Sanchez, and Wright. *Covenant Marriage*, 126 (see chap. 1, n. 100).

190. Anthony Kronman, "Contract Law and the State of Nature." *Journal of Law, Economics, and Organization* 1, no. 1 (1985): 20–23.

191. See also Regan, *Family Law and the Pursuit of Intimacy*, 26–27 (see chap. 2, n. 16).

192. Geoffrey P. Miller, "The Legal Function of Ritual." *Chicago-Kent Law Review* 80, no. 3 (2005): 1181–1233.

193. Ibid., 1183.

194. Ibid., 1184.

195. Sometimes sacrifices are precisely what Girard discusses as the climax of mimetic violence, if they are directed at another rather than the person seeking unity with the group.

196. Miller, "The Legal Function of Ritual," 1184 (see n. 191).

197. Posner, *Law and Social Norms*, 25–26 (see chap. 1, n. 23).

198. Miller, "The Legal Function of Ritual," 1188 (see n. 191).

199. Ibid., 1193.

200. Ibid., 1199.

201. Ibid., 1231.

202. Ibid., 1231.

Conclusion

1. Rowthorn, "Marriage and Trust," 666–68 (see chap. 6, n. 166) (both signal and guarantee).

2. For an account of what happens if the parental relationship is never legally recognized, see Katherine R. Allen, "Ambiguous Loss after Lesbian Couples with Children Break Up: A Case for Same-Gender Divorce." *Family Relations* 56, no. 2 (2007): 175–83.

3. William Bishop, "Is He Married? Marriage as Information." *University of Toronto Law Journal* 34, no. 3 (1984): 245–62.

4. Rowthorn, "Marriage and Trust," 697 (see chap. 6, n. 166).

5. Ellickson, "Unpacking the Household" (see chap. 1, n. 30).

6. Posner, *Law and Social Norms* (see chap. 1., n. 23).

7. McAdams, "The Origin, Development, and Regulation of Norms," 338 (see chap. 1, n. 38).

8. Ibid.

9. Fukuyama, *Trust* (see chap. 3, n. 25).

10. Garrison, "Marriage Matters" (see chap. 1, n. 18).

11. See, e.g., Allen, "Ambiguous Loss (see n. 2).

12. For example Rowthorn, "Marriage and Trust," 665 (see chap. 6, n. 166).

13. Coleman, "Social Capital" (see intro., n. 3).

14. Putnam, "Bowling Alone" (see chap. 4, n. 13)

15. Fukuyama, *The Great Disruption* (see chap. 4, n. 153).

16. Heller, "The Tragedy of the Anticommons," 621 (see chap. 4, n. 103).

17. For the idea that the only real interests that must be protected by law are those of shareholders, see Bernard Black and Reinier Kraakman, "A Self-Enforcing Model of Corporate Law." *Harvard Law Review* 109, no. 8 (1996): 1921; Deborah A. DeMott, "Beyond Metaphor: An Analysis of Fiduciary Obligation." *Duke Law Journal* 1988, no. 5 (1988): 917; Jonathan R. Macey, "Fiduciary Duties as Residual Claims: Obligations to Nonshareholder Constituencies from a Theory of the Firm Perspective." *Cornell Law Review* 84, no. 5 (1999): 1266. For one who would consider other stakeholders, see, e.g., Margaret M. Blair, *Ownership and Control: Rethinking Corporate Governance for the Twenty-First Century*. Washington, DC: Brookings Institute, 1995, 212 n. 19.

18. Black and Kraakman, "A Self-Enforcing Model of Corporate Law," 1921 (see n. 17) and Butler and McChesney, "Why They Give at the Office," 1195 (see chap. 4, n. 127); contra, Coffee Jr., "Unstable Coalitions," 1495 (see chap. 4, n. 139).

19. Miller, "The Legal Function of Ritual" (see chap. 6, n. 192).

20. Girard, *I See Satan Fall Like Lightning* (see chap. 6, n. 15).

21. Bailie, *Violence Unveiled* (see chap. 6, n. 25).

22. 530 U.S. 57 (2000).

23. 542 U.S. 451 (2004).

24. Lambert and Dollahite, "How Religiosity Helps Couples" (see chap. 5, n. 23).

25. Brehm and Rahn, "Individual-Level Evidence" (see chap. 6, n. 22).

Index